ENTREPRENEURSHIP
Ideas in Action 5e

Cynthia L. Greene

SOUTH-WESTERN
CENGAGE Learning™

Australia • Brazil • Japan • Korea • Mexico • Singapore • Spain • United Kingdom • United States

SOUTH-WESTERN
CENGAGE Learning™

Entrepreneurship, 5e
Cynthia L. Greene

Vice President of Editorial, Business:
Jack W. Calhoun

Vice President/Editor-in-Chief: Karen Schmohe

Executive Editor: Eve Lewis

Sr. Developmental Editor: Enid Nagel

Editorial Assistant: Anne Kelly

Marketing Manager: Linda Kuper

Content Project Manager: Lindsay Bethoney

Media Editor: Lysa Kosins

Sr. Buyer: Kevin Kluck

Production Service: PreMediaGlobal

Sr. Art Director: Tippy McIntosh

Internal Designer: PreMediaGlobal

Cover Designer: Kim Torbeck, Imbue Design

Cover Image: ©Terry Morris, iStock

Rights Acquisitions Specialist: Deanna Ettinger

For product information and technology assistance, contact us at
Cengage Learning Customer & Sales Support, 1-800-354-9706

For permission to use material from this text or product,
submit all requests online at **www.cengage.com/permissions**
Further permissions questions can be emailed to
permissionrequest@cengage.com

ExamView® is a registered trademark of eInstruction Corp. Windows is a registered trademark of the Microsoft Corporation used herein under license. Macintosh and Power Macintosh are registered trademarks of Apple Computer, Inc. used herein under license.

The Career Clusters icons are being used with permission of the:

States' Career Clusters Initiative, 2007, www.careerclusters.org

© 2008 Cengage Learning. All Rights Reserved.

Cengage Learning WebTutor™ is a trademark of Cengage Learning.

Student Edition ISBN-13: 978-0-538-49689-6

Student Edition ISBN-10: 0-538-49689-4

Annotated Instructor's Edition ISBN 13: 978-0-8400-6524-7

Annotated Instructor's Edition ISBN 10: 0-840-06524-8

South-Western Cengage Learning
5191 Natorp Boulevard
Mason, OH 45040
USA

Cengage Learning products are represented in Canada by Nelson Education, Ltd.

For your course and learning solutions, visit **www.cengage.com**

Purchase any of our products at your local college store or at our preferred online store **www.cengagebrain.com**

Printed in the United States of America
5 6 7 15

Amber C. Benson
Business Teacher
Shades Valley High School
Birmingham, Alabama

Jackie J. Crowley
Business Teacher
Marble Falls High School
Central Texas College
Marble Falls, Texas

Christopher Fama
Business Instructor
Cayuga Community College
Auburn, New York

Deborah Garcia
Business Teacher
Will C. Wood High School
Vacaville, California

Michael Hackman
Business Teacher
Columbus North High School
Columbus, Indiana

Neil Jacoby
Business Teacher
Walnut High School
Walnut, California

LaDonna Leazer
Business and Economics Coordinator
Business and Economics Academy of
    Milwaukee
Milwaukee, Wisconsin

Rita Martin
Business and Computer Applications
    Teacher
Desert Pines High School
Las Vegas, Nevada

Steven Michaud
Business Teacher
Plainville High School
Plainville, Connecticut

Virginia Muller
CTE Department Chair
Fairfax County Public Schools
Chantilly, Virginia

Antoinette Phillips
Management Professor
Southeastern Louisiana University
Hammond, Louisiana

Cindy M. Quaid
Business Teacher
Santa Maria High School
Santa Maria, California

Stephen J. Rocco
Academy of Finance Director
Smithfield High School
Smithfield, Rhode Island

Clifton F. Seigworth
Career-Technical Education Teacher
West Creek High School
Clarksville, Tennessee

Lisa Krayer Smith
Business Teacher
Academy of Finance
Hoover High School
Hoover, Alabama

Lori Townsend
Entrepreneurship Teacher
Murray County High School
Chatsworth, Georgia

Paola Trottier
Business Education Department Chair
Rugby High School
Rugby, North Dakota

Rebecca S. Tyson
Educational Specialist
T. W. Josey High School
Augusta, Georgia

Contents

About the Author

Cynthia L. Greene is an educational consultant and teacher educator. Currently she is the business manager for the Georgia Association for Career and Technical Education and she is developing the Small Business Incubator for the Newton College and Career Academy in Covington, Georgia.

Ms. Greene taught business education at the high school level for 25 years in the Fulton County School System in Atlanta. She was the program specialist for Business and Information Technology for the Georgia Department of Education for six years. An active member of the National Business Education Association, Ms. Greene served as president and is the chair of the Entrepreneurship Standards Committee.

Photo courtesy of Cynthia L. Greene

Transforming Innovations!

Have You Ever Wanted to Start Your Own Business?

An entrepreneur is someone who organizes, manages, and assumes the risks of a business or enterprise. *Entrepreneurship: Ideas in Action, 5e* helps you prepare to become an entrepreneur, provides you with the skills needed to realistically evaluate your potential as a business owner, and guides you in building a business plan.

Each lesson begins with a list of terms and goals to help you focus your reading.

Goals outline the main objectives of the lesson.

Vocabulary is the new terms defined in the lesson.

Focus on Small Business introduces concepts and provides a thought-provoking introduction to each lesson.

One key competency employers value is the ability to think creatively and logically in order to solve problems.

Sharpen Your 21st Century Entrepreneurial Skills

offers 21st Century learning skill-building information and poses critical-thinking questions.

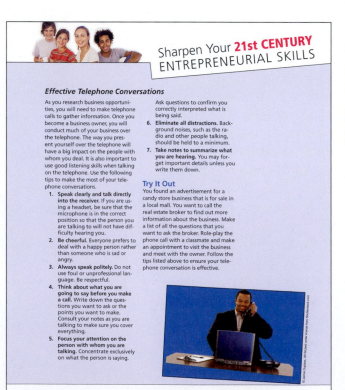

Abundant Real-Life Examples!

entrepreneur

famous

SERGEY BRIN AND LARRY PAGE What would the Internet be like if there was no Google? Just what is a Google? Thanks to Sergey Brin and Larry Page, we have Google and an explanation of the name. "Googol" is the mathematical term for a 1 followed by 100 zeros. The term was coined by the nephew of Edward Kasner, an American mathematician. Brin and Page chose a variation of this term for their company. When they started their business, Brin and Page's mission was "to organize the world's information and make it universally accessible and useful!"

Brin and Page developed a new approach to online searching while they were students at Stanford University. Using that approach, they launched Google in September of 1998 as a privately held company. Today, Google is one of the world's best-known brands. Most people have learned about Google by word of mouth from satisfied users.

How has the Internet provided new opportunities for entrepreneurs?

Google generates revenue by selling advertising space. Ads are displayed on search results pages that are relevant to the content on the page. Google tracks customer traffic to measure the cost-effectiveness of the online advertising.

Today, Brin and Page share a net worth of over $16 billion. Google handles over 2.5 billion search inquiries daily. That's not bad for a data center that started in a dorm room!

THINK CRITICALLY
Have you ever used Google? Why do you think people choose Google over other search engines?

What Went Wrong? highlights the pitfalls of real entrepreneurs and includes critical thinking questions to help students analyze the situations.

Famous Entrepreneurs profiles contributions of successful entrepreneurs throughout history.

what went wrong?

TOO BIG, TOO FAST

Webvan was founded in the late 1990s by Louis Borders. Webvan was an online grocery ordering and delivery service. Initially, customers were excited about this service that was offered in nine U.S. markets. The company's long-range plans included expansion into 26 cities. The company started with hundreds of millions of dollars from private investors and then raised $375 million in its initial public offering of stock. At one time, Webvan was worth $1.2 billion, but all was not well in the Webvan world. Customers did not sign up as founders hoped they would. But the biggest problem Webvan faced was rapidly disappearing cash reserves. It placed a $1-billion order to build high-tech warehouses, bought a fleet of delivery trucks, and purchased state-of-the-art computer systems. The management team of Webvan did not have anyone with any experience in the grocery market, and it tried to get too big, too fast. Even though customers were not happy with long lines and the quality of products in traditional supermarkets, they did not flock to the online grocery store. In less than two years after its successful initial public offering, Webvan announced it was closing.

Too many cash disbursements can lead to business failure.

THINK CRITICALLY
1. What are some of the problems Webvan faced during its short-lived operation?
2. Webvan started with a large amount of cash reserves. What caused Webvan to end up with cash flow problems?
3. What changes in operations do you think Webvan could have made that might have helped it be successful?

Business Plan and Career Coverage!

Build Your Business Plan Project concludes each chapter and is designed to help you prepare a complete business plan by the end of the course.

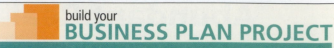

build your BUSINESS PLAN PROJECT

This activity will help you plan the operations management of your business.

1. Describe the management style you will use for managing your business. Will you always use the same style? How will you determine when to use a different style?
2. Locate and contact two professionals in your area who specialize in strategic planning. What are their credentials? What are their fees? Do you think it would be helpful to utilize the services of a strategic planner? Why or why not?
3. Develop an operating procedures manual for your business. Include the rules, policies, and procedures that your business will follow to run effectively.
4. If your business has an inventory, list all of the items you will have in inventory and your cost for each. Create a purchasing plan for your inventory.
5. Set up inventory records for your business using either a paper system or an electronic system. Be sure to list all of the items discussed in Lesson 10.2. How did you determine your reorder point? What inventory carrying costs are relevant to your business? How can you reduce your carrying costs?
6. Analyze your sales by creating a table that lists each of your products and the total sales (or estimated sales) for each. What is the percentage of total sales for each product? Based on this information, will you make any changes to your inventory?
7. Develop internal controls for your business. Explain why you chose the controls you did.

Planning a Career in E-MARKETING

"My boss gave me one hour to surf the Web to research a potential business he might develop. The time limit was to encourage me to stay focused. Each website had multiple links to other sites. Some sites were informational with pages of text, while other sites were more visually appealing by using color and graphics. Some sites had movie-quality commercials, while other sites offered free products. When the hour was up, my summary report included the assigned topic and additional information about related topics."

Why do websites contain links to other sites? Why are some websites easier to navigate than others?

E-marketing is an expanding field that helps companies reach consumers via the Internet. Website designers help companies and organizations develop websites that inform potential customers about products and services offered.

Employment Outlook
- Faster than average growth is anticipated.
- As businesses increase their dependence on the Internet for the efficient distribution of product and marketing information, demand for these jobs will continue to grow.

Job Titles
- Online Marketing and Outreach Coordinator
- Website Template Designer
- Web Page Developer
- Portal Designer
- Website Marketer

Needed Education/Skills
- A Bachelor's degree is recommended.
- Strong problem-solving and analytical skills are required.

- Computer science and business courses are helpful.
- Experience in content management, HTML, and assorted web-related software is required.

What's it like to work in E-marketing? This morning Lev, a freelance website designer, is meeting with a small group of investors who want to build a dozen windmills on property bordering a huge lake. As part of a public relations campaign to encourage community support for the project, the investors want to develop a website about the project. Lev has been contracted to develop a website that will list all of the benefits of the windmill farm. The website needs to include photos of the windmill farm's proposed design, statistics on the number of homes that can be powered from wind energy, and data reflecting flight patterns of local birds. The site also needs to provide links to similar small-scale projects that have been successful.

In the afternoon, Lev will meet with a farmer's association that wants to provide support via a website for independent farmers who want to convert corn to ethanol. This meeting will focus on the site's content and possible links to other informational sites. In addition, the group will be making design decisions related to color, icon graphics, and editorial style. To help make the project more appealing to farmers, Lev must ensure that the website is easy to navigate.

What about you? Would you like to design websites that are informative, easy to navigate, and profitable for their sponsors?

Planning a Career in... incorporates Career Clusters for a variety of careers as an Entrepreneur.

Special Features Enhance Learning!

Winning Edge helps you prepare for competitive events.

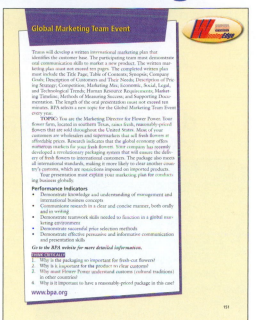

 CHECKPOINT

> What kinds of assessments should you make to determine if entrepreneurship is right for you?

Checkpoint enables you to test your understanding at key points in each lesson.

Photo Caption Questions help you connect to the content covered in each chapter.

How do small business owners aid in the economic recovery process?

Why is it important for business owners to stay up to date on the latest technology?

Special Features Enhance Learning!

Develop Your Reading Skills provides exercises to reinforce reading skills.

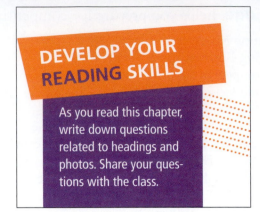

DEVELOP YOUR READING SKILLS

As you read this chapter, write down questions related to headings and photos. Share your questions with the class.

did you KNOW?

According to the National Federation of Independent Businesses (NFIB), five of the top ten concerns of small-business owners relate to costs. Leading the list is the cost of health insurance, followed by the cost and availability of liability insurance, workers' compensation costs, energy costs (natural gas, gasoline, propane, diesel, and fuel oil), and electricity rates.

Did You Know? offers additional information that relates to chapter topics.

Net Bookmark incorporates Internet activities into every chapter.

NETBookmark

Plenty of teenagers have started their own businesses, and the most successful teen entrepreneurs have prepared business plans. Access www.cengage.com/school/entrepreneurship/ideas and click on the link for Chapter 3. Read the article, "New Recording Studio at Neutral Zone Is Run by Teens but Open to All." Then answer: How did their business plan help these teens start their business? Who helped the teens prepare their business plan? What do you think would be the most difficult part of a business plan to develop? Why?

www.cengage.com/school/entrepreneurship/ideas

BE YOUR OWN BOSS

You are interested in starting your own business, but you are not sure what kind of business it should be. To help you get started, think about something you do that you really enjoy. Now think about ways that you might be able to turn this activity into a business. Make a list of businesses in your area that offer a related product or service. Write a paragraph explaining your business idea. How will your business be different from the existing businesses you listed?

Be Your Own Boss gives you the opportunity to complete the same types of activities that a real entrepreneur might do.

Abundant Review and Assessment!

An abundance of ongoing lesson and chapter assessments ensure you understand and can apply what you've learned.

Think About It contains activities to help you apply what you have learned in the lesson.

Make Academic Connections provides the integrated curriculum activities that show you how entrepreneurial concepts relate to other courses of study.

Teamwork provides you with opportunities to work with classmates on cooperative learning projects.

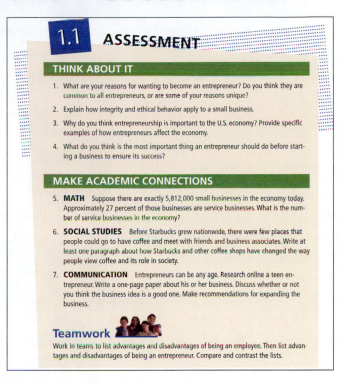

Chapter Assessment provides a summary of the main points and contains questions and activities to test your knowledge.

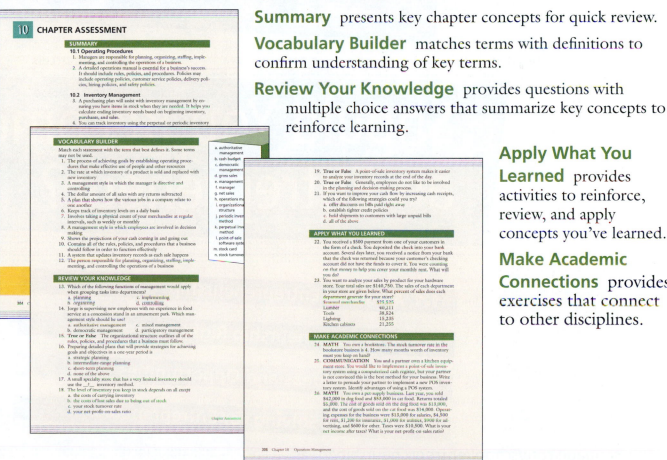

Summary presents key chapter concepts for quick review.

Vocabulary Builder matches terms with definitions to confirm understanding of key terms.

Review Your Knowledge provides questions with multiple choice answers that summarize key concepts to reinforce learning.

Apply What You Learned provides activities to reinforce, review, and apply concepts you've learned.

Make Academic Connections provides exercises that connect to other disciplines.

CHAPTER 1

© Monkey Business Images, 2010/ Used under license from Shutterstock.com

Should You Become an Entrepreneur?

 www.cengage.com/school/entrepreneurship/ideas

Going "Green" With White Rooftops

Photo courtesy of Jill Miller

Many of today's most successful businesses start with a simple idea. That idea could be a new invention or a solution to improve a current product. An entrepreneur is the person who transforms this idea into action. Entrepreneurs can be any age. They can start a business in a strong or weak economy. Being an entrepreneur takes an endless amount of hard work, but if you are willing to take the risk, you could be tomorrow's big business owner.

Jill Miller, founder, White Caps, Green Collars

Environmental enthusiast Jill Miller used a recent downturn in the economy to explore the risk of starting a business. When Jill lost her day job, she had the newfound freedom to research her idea to paint flat, black roofs with a solar-reflective, white paint. Jill's idea for her company, White Caps, Green Collars, was sparked after learning about energy-wasting black tar roofs during a local Sierra Club meeting. Jill noticed the abundance of flat, black roofs in her hometown of St. Louis and realized the city had an untapped market. While researching her idea by talking to roofing companies and contractors, Jill had a chance meeting with a small business consultant. The consultant gave her sound business and financial advice and the motivation to run with her idea. Since banks are generally reluctant to give loans during an economic downturn, Jill used her own money to get the business off the ground. And for the first summer, she and a friend did all of the hard labor of painting the roofs white. Jill's "green" idea enables businesses and homeowners to save 20 to 40 percent on energy bills and also improves air quality by cooling the areas surrounding the roofs.

Knowing the ins and outs of her business from the beginning has allowed Jill to effectively manage any day-to-day problems that occur. She said, "It is tough to troubleshoot problems if you don't know the work your employees are doing." Jill is also the sole bookkeeper of her business, which allows her to keep a watchful eye on costs.

Although the company is only in its second year of operation, Jill has big hopes for the future. She plans to expand the company locally first, which would add more "green collar" jobs to the area. Because there is a movement toward more environmentally friendly companies, Jill feels like she was in the right place at the right time.

1. What are some positive aspects about being an entrepreneur?
2. Do you know anyone that could serve as a business mentor like Jill's business consultant? Why are mentors important?
3. What is the advantage to White Caps, Green Collars of being a "green" company?

1.1

ALL ABOUT ENTREPRENEURSHIP

Goals
- Define entrepreneurship.
- Recognize the role entrepreneurs play in the U.S. economy.
- Determine the reasons that businesses succeed or fail.

Vocabulary
- entrepreneurs
- entrepreneurship
- employees

focus
on small business

Should you be your own boss?

"I'm so tired of someone telling me what to do all the time," Delia said to her friend Gloria. "I know what you mean," Gloria answered, "because I get the same thing." "It seems like there should be some way we could be in charge," Delia said. "I've got an idea," Gloria responded, "let's be entrepreneurs. Mr. Rivera talked about them in my business class last week. They are people who start and run their own businesses. We could do that!"

"What would we have to do? Would we make a lot of money? Would it be fun? Would we get to do whatever we wanted?" Delia's mind was overflowing with questions. Gloria was getting very excited as she replied, "We could be our own bosses! If we were the owners, we would be in charge! We'd get to make all the decisions!" "This is starting to sound pretty good," Delia replied as she began to share Gloria's excitement." We could decide when we work, what we do, and how we do it. And we can make lots of money! I can't wait. When do we start?"

Work as a Team   Many people go into business just so they can be in charge and make lots of money. Do you think this is the most important reason to start your own business?

Entrepreneurs can be of any age.

Entrepreneurship

The U.S. economy includes thousands of small businesses. Many of these small businesses are owned and operated by men and women who created their own companies. Some of these individuals have become legends as you hear stories about their path to success. But what makes someone an entrepreneur? What impact have entrepreneurs had in history? What impact do they have today?

DEVELOP YOUR READING SKILLS

As you read this chapter, write down questions related to headings and photos. Share your questions with the class.

Would you like to own your own business? Why or why not?

What Is an Entrepreneur?

People who own, operate, and take the risk of a business venture are called **entrepreneurs**. They are engaged in **entrepreneurship**, the process of running a business of one's own. Entrepreneurs come from all types of backgrounds and create all kinds of businesses. People of all ages choose to become entrepreneurs. Some own tiny craft shops, while others own huge construction companies. Entrepreneurs try to identify unmet needs in the marketplace. Then they provide a service or product to meet those needs. When they succeed, their businesses flourish, and profits are earned. But if their business idea is unsuccessful, they may lose the money they invested.

EMPLOYEES VS. ENTREPRENEURS Entrepreneurs assume risk. This makes them different from **employees**, who are people who work for someone else. Both may make decisions, but only the entrepreneur is directly affected by the consequences of those decisions.

Sam Jones manages a record store owned by Felipe Santiago. Sam decides to keep the store open until midnight during the week. If the additional hours bring in customers and increase profits, Sam may be praised by Felipe. He may even get a raise. However, Sam won't directly receive any of the profits because he is an employee. The additional earnings will flow to Felipe, the owner.

WHY DO PEOPLE BECOME ENTREPRENEURS? People go into business for themselves for many reasons. Some want to leave the fast-paced corporate environment and set their own schedules. Others want to be at home but still earn an income. Still others want to pursue a personal dream. You might choose to become an entrepreneur for completely different reasons.

INTEGRITY AND ETHICAL BEHAVIOR An important part of being an entrepreneur involves operating with integrity and exhibiting ethical behavior in all areas of business. Ethical business practices by entrepreneurs ensure that the highest standards of conduct are observed in their relationships with everyone affected by the business's activities.

When operating with integrity, entrepreneurs behave consistently in actions, values, methods, measures, principles, expectations, and outcomes. When considering whether or not behavior is ethical, both the actions taken by the entrepreneur and the results of those actions should be considered.

Types of Entrepreneurial Businesses

There are generally four types of businesses, and there are many opportunities for entrepreneurs in each type. See the chart below. *Manufacturing businesses* actually produce the products they sell. Using resources and supplies, they create everything from automobiles to paper. *Wholesaling businesses* sell products to other businesses rather than the final consumer. For example, a wholesaler supplies your local greeting card store with items such as cards and wrapping paper. *Retailing businesses*, such as the greeting card store, sell products directly to the people who use or consume them. *Service businesses* sell services rather than products. They include hotels, hairdressers, and repair shops, to name a few.

OTHER BUSINESS AREAS   Two other categories of businesses are (1) agricultural and (2) mining and extracting businesses. *Agricultural businesses* generate fresh produce and other farm products, such as wheat. *Mining and extracting businesses* take resources like coal out of the ground so that they can be consumed.

TYPES OF BUSINESSES			
Manufacturing	**Wholesaling**	**Retailing**	**Service**
Apparel and other textile products	Apparel	Auto and home supply stores	Appliance repair
Chemicals and related products	Electrical goods	Building materials and supply stores	Automotive repair
Electronics and other electrical equipment	Groceries and related products	Clothing stores	Babysitting
Fabricated metal products	Hardware, plumbing, heating equipment	Florists	Bookkeeping
Food products	Lumber, construction materials	Furniture stores	Consulting
Industrial machinery and equipment	Machinery, equipment, supplies	Gift, novelty, and souvenir stores	Dance instruction
Printing and publishing	Motor vehicles, automotive equipment	Grocery stores	Electrical services
Rubber and miscellaneous plastic products	Paper, paper products	Hardware stores	Exterminators
Stone, clay, and glass products	Petroleum, petroleum products	Jewelry stores	Flower decorating
		Retail bakeries	House cleaning
		Shoe stores	Lawn care
		Sporting goods and bicycle stores	Painting
			Plumbing
			Translating
			Travel agency
			Tutoring
			Web design and maintenance

Source: Small Business Administration

GREEN ENTREPRENEURSHIP Many types of businesses may focus on being organic or "green." Because of the growing movement toward environmentally friendly products, entrepreneurs who have a passion toward being green have an advantage when introducing their product or service on the market. It is important for green entrepreneurs to educate their customers about how their products or services benefit the earth or conserve resources. In addition to offering green products, entrepreneurs who use green business practices, such as recycling and working with other green-minded companies, are often favored by customers.

© dslaven, 2010/ Used under license from Shutterstock.com

Why are many businesses going "green"?

CHECKPOINT

Describe different types of entrepreneurial businesses.

Recognizing Opportunity

Many of America's most successful companies started with one person who recognized an opportunity and came up with an idea for a business in response to that opportunity. Entrepreneurs have played an important role in the history of America's economy and will continue to shape our economy in the future.

According to estimates from the U.S. Small Business Administration's Office of Advocacy, there were approximately 29.6 million businesses in the United States in 2008. Small firms with fewer than 500 employees represent 99.9 percent of these 29.6 million businesses in the United States. Only 18,000 U.S. businesses are considered large. Small businesses contribute billions of dollars to the U.S. economy every year and generate jobs that drive economic growth. According to the National Small Business Association, small businesses created 21.9 million jobs in the last 15 years compared with 1.8 million jobs created by large businesses. These small businesses are found in virtually every sector of the economy.

Entrepreneurs Who Changed America

Entrepreneurs change American business decade after decade. They establish new companies and fill unmet needs. They continuously change how things are done and contribute to the overall good of the nation. There are many businesses today that started small and have grown into large companies that are making a major impact in our economic system.

STARBUCKS COFFEE COMPANY Starbucks Coffee Company was founded in 1971, opening its first location in Seattle's Pike Place Market. Starbucks is named after the first mate in Herman Melville's novel *Moby Dick*. It is the world's leading brand of specialty coffee. Its stores receive more than 40 million customer visits per week at coffeehouses in North America, Europe, the Middle East, Latin America, and the Pacific Rim. When Howard Schultz first joined the company in the early 1980s, Starbucks was already a highly respected local roaster and retailer of whole bean and ground coffees. A business trip to Italy, where he was impressed with the popularity of espresso bars in Milan, helped Schultz recognize an opportunity to develop a similar coffee-house culture in Seattle. Espresso drinks became an essential element of Schultz's vision. He purchased Starbucks with the support of local investors in 1987. In addition to its well-situated coffeehouses, Starbucks markets its coffee and tea products through its website and through many national retail supermarkets.

THE HOME DEPOT   In 1979, Bernie Marcus and Arthur Blank opened the first two The Home Depot stores in Atlanta, Georgia, forever changing the home improvement industry. They envisioned a home improvement store that offered one-stop shopping for the do-it-yourselfer. The original stores stocked around 25,000 products. An average store today offers 40,000 products in approximately 105,000 square feet. Marcus and Blank's vision was of warehouse stores filled from floor to ceiling with a wide assortment of home improvement products at the lowest prices and with the best possible service.

famous entrepreneur

MADAM C. J. WALKER You may have heard it said that "necessity is the mother of invention." Many entrepreneurs got their start by creating something that they themselves needed and then sharing their product with others. That's exactly what made Madam C. J. Walker a millionaire. Walker, originally known as Sarah Breedlove, suffered from a scalp ailment during the 1890s and began experimenting with homemade remedies. Her remedies worked well, so she began offering them to other African-American women. In 1905, she moved to Denver, married newspaperman Charles Joseph Walker, and started her own company. She sold her products door to door and bought ad space in newspapers. Walker later opened Lelia College, where she and her daughter trained other women to use and sell the product line, which had expanded to include items such as complexion soap and dental cream. At least

Why do you think Madam C. J. Walker became such a successful entrepreneur?

20 women completed the program every six weeks. Besides becoming a millionaire from the sales of her products, Walker made a huge contribution to the African-American community by empowering women to make their own mark in the business world.

THINK CRITICALLY

Why is it important for entrepreneurs to make contributions to their community in addition to offering a product or service?

Within five years, The Home Depot expanded from Georgia to Florida, Louisiana, Texas, and Alabama. Today, it has more than 2,100 stores in the United States, Canada, and Mexico.

HARPO PRODUCTIONS, INC.   Oprah Winfrey's love of acting and her desire to bring quality entertainment projects into production prompted her to form her own production company, HARPO Productions, Inc., in 1986. Today, HARPO is a formidable force in film and television production. Based in Chicago, HARPO Entertainment Group includes HARPO Productions, Inc., HARPO Films, and HARPO Video, Inc. In October 1988, HARPO Productions, Inc., acquired ownership and all production responsibilities for *The Oprah Winfrey Show* from Capitol Cities/ABC, making Oprah Winfrey the first woman in history to own and produce her own talk show. The following year, HARPO produced its first television miniseries, *The Women of Brewster Place*, with Oprah Winfrey as star and executive producer. Oprah also produced and appeared in several television miniseries and movies.

Entrepreneurial Opportunities in Economic Recovery

Even during downturns in the economy, entrepreneurial opportunities still exist. While big businesses tend to be more conservative in their approach to economic slowdowns by scaling back production, conserving cash, and laying off workers, small businesses that have less to lose are more willing and able to make changes quickly. They can be more creative and take more risks than large companies. Their experimentation and innovation lead to technological change and increased productivity. This makes small businesses a significant part of the economic recovery process.

The American Recovery and Reinvestment Act of 2009 was passed to stimulate the American economy after the 2008 economic slowdown. It supported a number of provisions to help small businesses, including $30 billion in tax relief for small businesses and $13 billion in loans, lines of credit, and equity capital. Other provisions included:

- Increasing the Small Business Administration (SBA) guarantee on loans up to 95 percent of loan value
- Improving the liquidity of small business lending markets
- Allowing the SBA to refinance existing loans, including those with both the SBA and other lenders
- Increasing equity capital for high-growth businesses
- Providing lending assistance for borrowers locked out of traditional financing markets
- Offering tax relief in several forms

How do small business owners aid in the economic recovery process?

This stimulus package also contained significant new support to increase green businesses, including incentives to drive the growth of renewable energy, stimulate energy efficiency efforts, and update the nation's electrical grid.

 CHECKPOINT

Describe how one of the entrepreneurs discussed above recognized an opportunity to develop a successful business.

Business Success or Failure

Although there are many opportunities for entrepreneurial success, there is also a risk of failure. According to a recent study by the Small Business Administration's Office of Advocacy, 67 percent of new businesses survive at least two years, and 44 percent survive at least four years. This means that more than half of all new businesses do not survive beyond four years. These results are similar for different industries. Many people think that there is a higher failure rate for restaurants than for other types of businesses. However, leisure and hospitality establishments, which include restaurants, survive at rates only slightly below the average. Major factors in a firm's success include having adequate capital and being large enough to have employees. The owner's education level and reason for starting the firm in the first place, such as freedom for family life or wanting to be one's own boss, are also important factors. The reason must sufficiently motivate the entrepreneur to have the perseverance to succeed.

The owner's business experience is a factor that contributes to the likelihood of success. Experienced businesspeople have an understanding of how to purchase products and services. They know how to plan, negotiate with suppliers, raise money, negotiate leases, sell and market their product or service, and manage finances. Many

What makes some entrepreneurs more likely to succeed than others?

businesses fail because the owner lacks business knowledge. Someone may have an idea for a product or service but may lack the necessary business skills he or she needs to run a successful business. There is a major difference between having expertise regarding a product or service and running a business with that product or service. So when opportunity presents itself, entrepreneurs must have what it takes to succeed.

 CHECKPOINT

> What factors contribute to helping a business succeed?

1.1 ASSESSMENT

THINK ABOUT IT

1. What are your reasons for wanting to become an entrepreneur? Do you think they are common to all entrepreneurs, or are some of your reasons unique?

2. Explain how integrity and ethical behavior apply to a small business.

3. Why do you think entrepreneurship is important to the U.S. economy? Provide specific examples of how entrepreneurs affect the economy.

4. What do you think is the most important thing an entrepreneur should do before starting a business to ensure its success?

MAKE ACADEMIC CONNECTIONS

5. **MATH**   Suppose there are exactly 5,812,000 small businesses in the economy today. Approximately 27 percent of those businesses are service businesses. What is the number of service businesses in the economy?

6. **SOCIAL STUDIES**   Before Starbucks grew nationwide, there were few places that people could go to have coffee and meet with friends and business associates. Write at least one paragraph about how Starbucks and other coffee shops have changed the way people view coffee and its role in society.

7. **COMMUNICATION**   Entrepreneurs can be any age. Research online a teen entrepreneur. Write a one-page paper about his or her business. Discuss whether or not you think the business idea is a good one. Make recommendations for expanding the business.

Teamwork

Work in teams to list advantages and disadvantages of being an employee. Then list advantages and disadvantages of being an entrepreneur. Compare and contrast the lists.

1.2

IS ENTREPRENEURSHIP RIGHT FOR YOU?

Goals
- Identify the characteristics of successful entrepreneurs.
- Identify the characteristics of good team members.
- Assess whether you have what it takes to succeed in your own business.

Vocabulary
- self-assessment
- aptitude

focus on small business

Think it through!

Gloria and Delia were excited about starting their own business, but as they continued their discussions, Gloria realized they needed to slow down and think through the process carefully. "You know, Delia, it's not really easy to start our own business. When we talked about this in class, Mr. Rivera said that there are a lot of things to consider before starting a business. First, we need to decide what we like to do and what we are good at. Then we have to do a lot of research and planning if we want to be successful."

Thinking about what Mr. Rivera told her in class, Delia sighed. "This entrepreneur thing sounds like a lot of work. What do you think we should do?"

Work as a Team Many people go into business without first taking time to examine their strengths and weaknesses and what they really like to do. Do you think it's a good idea for Gloria and Delia to slow down and really examine their interests before starting the business?

© Edyta Pawlowska, 2010/ Used under license from Shutterstock.com

Examine your strengths and weaknesses before starting a business.

Characteristics of Successful Entrepreneurs

Many people dream of running their own businesses. They would like to become entrepreneurs. Entrepreneurship can be exciting, but many go into it not realizing how difficult it is to run their own business. In fact, statistics show that most new businesses will fail within a few years. These startup businesses fail because of the owner's poor planning, lack of business knowledge, lack of entrepreneurial characteristics, inability to work with others, or failure to choose the right business.

Researchers have identified several characteristics that distinguish successful entrepreneurs from those that fail.

1. **Successful entrepreneurs are independent.** They want to make their own decisions and do something they enjoy.
2. **Successful entrepreneurs are self-confident.** Entrepreneurs make all the decisions. They must have the confidence to make choices alone and bounce back from a poorly made decision.
3. **Successful entrepreneurs have determination and perseverance.** Entrepreneurs persist through hard times until goals are met.
4. **Successful entrepreneurs are goal-oriented.** They know what they want, and they are able to focus on achieving it.
5. **Successful entrepreneurs have a need to achieve and to set high standards for themselves.** They are motivated by setting and achieving challenging goals.
6. **Successful entrepreneurs are creative.** They think of new ways to market their businesses and are always looking for new solutions to problems.
7. **Successful entrepreneurs are able to act quickly.** They are not afraid to make quick decisions when necessary, which helps them beat their competitors.
8. **Successful entrepreneurs keep up to date with technology.** New technologies emerge that can help with many business activities. In order to run their business efficiently, entrepreneurs should always be on the lookout for new technology they can apply to their business.

Ryan Nelson has many entrepreneurial characteristics. Since he was 14, Ryan played for his high school basketball team. Other boys his height—just 5′8″—would not have enjoyed competing with much taller boys. Ryan accepted that he would have to work harder to win.

Why is it important for business owners to stay up to date on the latest technology?

He needed to be creative in handling the ball. Most of all, he had to believe in himself. He did, and he became one of the top players on his team. If Ryan opened his own business, the characteristics he displayed as a ball player might help him succeed.

CHECKPOINT

Name three important characteristics of entrepreneurs.

Characteristics of Good Team Members

Entrepreneurs realize that there are other stakeholders in their businesses—partners, investors, employees, suppliers, customers, creditors, and so forth. They must work with others to get their business up and running. They must have good team-building skills as well as be effective team members. Good team members display the following traits:

© Patrick Hermans, 2010/ Used under license from Shutterstock.com

1. **Commitment** They are committed to team goals and are willing to work hard to achieve the goals.
2. **Competency** They have the right set of skills needed to get the job done and to help accomplish the team's goals.
3. **Communication** They have good communication skills and can share ideas with others in both oral and written form.
4. **Cooperation** They work well with others and know that they will not always get their way. They are willing to accept the decision of the group for the good of the group.
5. **Creativity** They are able to look at things from different perspectives and suggest new ways of doing things.

Ryan Nelson displayed these traits as a member of his basketball team. He competed as a team player, recognizing that every member of the team contributed to its success. His experience will help him work effectively as part of a team in the business world. If Ryan becomes an entrepreneur, he could apply these skills when working with other people who will be important to his success.

How can participation on a sports team help prepare you to become an entrepreneur?

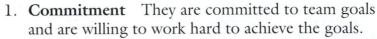

CHECKPOINT

Why is it important for entrepreneurs to be good team members?

Are You Right for Entrepreneurship?

Entrepreneurship is not for everyone. Some people lack the qualities needed to become successful entrepreneurs. Others lack the aptitude needed to run a business. For others, the advantages of entrepreneurship do not outweigh the disadvantages.

To determine if entrepreneurship is right for you, you first need to perform a self-assessment. A **self-assessment** is an evaluation of your strengths and weaknesses. You can do this in a number of ways. You can list what you believe to be your strengths and weaknesses on a sheet of paper. You can ask others what they believe your strengths are and where your weaknesses lie. There are also professional tests you can take to assess your abilities.

Assess Your Interests

Success as an entrepreneur requires a strong commitment to a business and a lot of energy. To be able to commit yourself fully to a

what went **wrong?**

EXPERIENCE NEEDED

Louise was a theater performer who sang and danced in Broadway-style musicals. The work was not always steady, so she earned additional money working part time at a print and copy shop for several years. The elderly couple who owned the shop allowed Louise to work flexible hours so that she could pursue a music career. Sadly, the husband died, and the wife decided to sell the business and move away. Louise was excited about the opportunity to purchase the business.

The former owner helped Louise gather financial information and put together a business plan. Louise's uncle cosigned a bank loan, and she

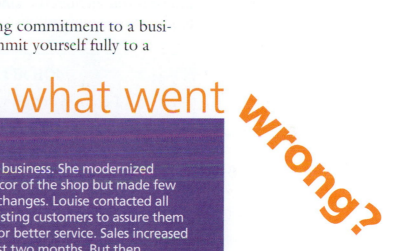

© Digital Vision/Getty Images

Get some business training before starting a business.

was in business. She modernized the décor of the shop but made few other changes. Louise contacted all the existing customers to assure them equal or better service. Sales increased the first two months. But then…

The former owner left town earlier than planned. Then Louise's chief printer quit. Using part-time employees, Louise was frantically trying to get large orders out on time. With no formal business training and no management experience, Louise couldn't begin to deal with all these problems—problems that even an experienced businessperson would find difficult. She ended up selling the business at a $50,000 loss.

THINK CRITICALLY

1. What characteristics did Louise possess that led her to become an entrepreneur?

2. What circumstances out of Louise's control led to the failure of this business?

3. Are there steps Louise could have taken to try to save her business?

business, you should choose a field that interests you and that will provide you with an experience you will enjoy. Many entrepreneurs center a business on an interest or hobby. Analyzing past experiences and jobs can also help. Have you had any jobs or experiences that you found fulfilling? Perhaps building a business around that activity could lead to success.

Assess Your Aptitude

Different jobs require different job aptitudes. **Aptitude** is the ability to learn a particular kind of job. Auto mechanics must possess an aptitude for solving mechanical problems. They must also be good with their hands. People who sell insurance must have good interpersonal skills. Answering questions like those in the Job Attributes Checklist can help you identify the kinds of entrepreneurial opportunities that might match your aptitudes and interests.

JOB ATTRIBUTES CHECKLIST

❑ 1. I enjoy working with numbers.

❑ 2. I enjoy working outdoors.

❑ 3. I enjoy working with my hands.

❑ 4. I enjoy selling.

❑ 5. I like working with people.

❑ 6. I prefer to work alone.

❑ 7. I like supervising other people.

❑ 8. I like knowing exactly what I am supposed to do.

Assess the Advantages of Entrepreneurship

Many people see significant advantages in owning their own businesses. Some of the biggest advantages include the following:

1. **Entrepreneurs are their own bosses.** Nobody tells an entrepreneur what to do. Entrepreneurs control their own destinies.
2. **Entrepreneurs can choose a business that interests them.** Entrepreneurs work in fields that interest them. Many combine hobbies and interests with business.
3. **Entrepreneurs can be creative.** Entrepreneurs are always implementing creative ideas they think of themselves.
4. **Entrepreneurs can make large sums of money.** Entrepreneurship involves risk, but if the business is successful, the business owner will reap the profits.

Assess the Disadvantages of Entrepreneurship

As the disadvantages show, entrepreneurship is not for the faint of heart. All prospective entrepreneurs must weigh the advantages and disadvantages before making the decision to start a business. Disadvantages include the following:

1. **Entrepreneurship is risky.** Just as there is the chance to earn large sums of money, there is the possibility of losing money and going out of business.
2. **Entrepreneurs face uncertain and irregular incomes.** Entrepreneurs may make money one month and lose money the next.
3. **Entrepreneurs work long hours.** Entrepreneurs are never really finished with their jobs. They can work long, irregular hours. They receive no paid days off and often work evenings and weekends.
4. **Entrepreneurs must make all decisions by themselves.** Unless they have partners, entrepreneurs have the final responsibility for all decisions that are made regarding the business.

✔ CHECKPOINT

What kinds of assessments should you make to determine if entrepreneurship is right for you?

ASSESSMENT

THINK ABOUT IT

1. Entrepreneurs can fail even if they are committed and have the characteristics needed to be successful. How can this happen?

2. What traits do good team members have? Select one trait and explain why it is important.

3. Do you think the advantages of entrepreneurship outweigh the disadvantages? Why or why not?

MAKE ACADEMIC CONNECTIONS

4. **TECHNOLOGY** In today's business environment, it is important that entrepreneurs keep up to date with technology. Research different types of technology products and services that would be useful to the owner of a business. Describe one product or service and explain how it can help business owners run their companies more efficiently.

5. **CAREER SUCCESS** Choose a business idea that interests you. Access www.cengage.com/school/entrepreneurship/ideas. Click on *Activities* and open the file *Job Attributes Checklist*. Print a copy and complete the activity. Compare your interests to your business idea. Is this a good choice for you? Why or why not?

Teamwork

Work in teams to choose a successful entrepreneur. List the traits and aptitudes this person has that have contributed to his or her success. Develop a presentation about the entrepreneur to share with the class.

EXPLORE IDEAS AND OPPORTUNITIES

Goals

- Identify sources for new business ideas.
- Recognize different business opportunities.
- Identify your own personal goals.

Vocabulary

- opportunities
- ideas
- trade shows

focus on small business

Find an idea.

Gloria and Delia realized that although there are many advantages to owning their own business, there are many responsibilities and challenges that a business owner has to face. Gloria knew that she and Delia had their work cut out for them, but she had confidence they could do it if they put their minds to it. She also knew that before they started, they needed to have a really good idea and be certain that there were people who would be willing to pay them for the product or service they wanted to sell.

"How do we decide what kind of business we should have?" Delia asked Gloria.

"There are so many businesses in our community," Gloria responded. "We have to come up with just the right idea!"

Work as a Team How do people come up with ideas for new businesses? How do you think they decide if the idea is worth pursuing?

© Benis Arapovic, 2010/ Used under license from Shutterstock.com

Spend time determining a good idea for your business.

Look for Ideas

Millions of entrepreneurs in the United States start their own businesses. You may wonder how they decided what businesses to operate. They may have acted on a new idea or an opportunity. An idea is different from an opportunity. **Opportunities** are possibilities that arise from existing conditions. **Ideas** are thoughts or concepts that come from creative thinking. Ideas can come from many different sources.

Hobbies and Interests

Many people get business ideas from their hobbies or interests. Making a list of hobbies and interests can help you decide what business is right for you.

Bill had always enjoyed working with his grandfather on the farm and had helped to build and maintain many farm structures. He built a garage and added a sunroom to his own home. He also was able to make plumbing, electrical, and carpentry repairs around the house. He started doing this for others in his spare time. Soon he had so many people calling on him for these services that he decided to start a general contracting business.

Past Experiences

Analyzing past experiences and jobs can help you come up with ideas for a business you would enjoy owning. People who excel at their jobs have generally learned much about their profession and how to satisfy customer needs. They also see how successful marketing is conducted. Through their work, they can build a network of potential customers, suppliers, employees, and distributors. When they feel confident that they can offer a product or service to this market more effectively than their current employer, they can start a new business. The experience and training they received on the job will increase their chances of success in running a new business.

Samantha Rodriguez worked as a computer network administrator for a large company. Recognizing that she could use her experience to perform the same computer services for other companies, Samantha started her own computer consulting service. She currently earns less money than she did working for a large company, but she enjoys working flexible hours and meeting new people.

Discovery or Invention

Sometimes a business opportunity arises from a discovery or invention. Someone may invent a new tool that works better than tools that are currently available. The next step would be to research and find out if the idea can be patented, who the competition is, what the manufacturing process would be, and who the target market is.

Chandra enjoyed working in her garden, but she did not like any of the tools she had for removing weeds from around the plants. She took one of her tools and made modifications to it and found that it worked perfectly. After several friends tried out the tool and liked it, Chandra decided to investigate how to market and sell her invention.

Do you have a hobby you are passionate about? Do you wish you could turn that hobby into a career? David and Wendi Kast turned their hobby into a profitable business doing what they love. Access www.cengage.com/school/entrepreneurship/ideas and click on the link for Chapter 1. Read about the Kasts' experiences and then answer these questions: What is the name of David and Wendi's business? What convinced them to turn their hobby into a business? What was the biggest challenge they faced as they started their business?

www.cengage.com/school/entrepreneurship/ideas

Where do new ideas for businesses come from?

Investigate Opportunities

People often conduct research to determine what is missing in a particular market—what needs exist that are not being met. By doing this research, they hope to find the perfect business opportunity.

Sources of Information

The Internet and the library have resources that can help you conduct research for different opportunities. These include books on entrepreneurship, magazines for entrepreneurs, trade magazines for certain businesses, and government publications. *County Business Patterns* is an annual series of publications providing economic profiles of counties, states, and the country as a whole. Data include employment, payroll, and the number of establishments by industry.

The Internet and the library are not the only places to investigate opportunities. The Small Business Administration (SBA) is an organization that exists to help small businesses and their owners. It publishes helpful information. Talking to entrepreneurs and attending trade shows, which are special meetings where companies of the same industry or related industries display their products, can also be beneficial.

Luanda Williams wanted to use her love of sports and dancing to create her own company. She found books and magazine articles at the library that gave her information on various kinds of businesses. She also talked to owners of gymnastic centers, health clubs, and dance studios. She discovered that there were not enough children's fitness programs to meet the demand in her area. Her research revealed the many opportunities available in the children's fitness industry.

Compare Different Opportunities

Once you find appealing business opportunities, you need to identify which ones have the best chance for success. Now is the time to assess each business opportunity by asking yourself the following questions:

1. Is there a market in my community for this kind of business? Will people buy my product or service?
2. How much money would it take to start this business? Will I be able to borrow that much money?
3. How many hours a week is it likely to take to run this business? Am I willing to commit that much time?
4. What are the risks associated with this business? What is the rate of business failure?
5. Does my background prepare me to run this kind of business? Do most people who own this kind of business have more experience?
6. How much money could I make running this business?

BE YOUR OWN BOSS

You are interested in starting your own business, but you are not sure what kind of business it should be. To help you get started, think about something you do that you really enjoy. Now think about ways that you might be able to turn this activity into a business. Make a list of businesses in your area that offer a related product or service. Write a paragraph explaining your business idea. How will your business be different from the existing businesses you listed?

Set Goals

For everything you do in life, you set goals. Goals help you stay on track and follow through with your plans. The best goals are SMART. SMART goals provide more direction, as shown below.

SMART GOALS	
Specific	Goals should be specific and answer "What?" "Why?" and "How?"
Measurable	Goals should establish ways to measure your progress.
Attainable	Goals should not be too far out of reach.
Realistic	Goals should represent things to which you are willing to commit.
Timely	Goals should have a timeframe for achievement.
Goal	I will learn more about starting my own business.
SMART Goal	I will learn more about starting my own catering business by obtaining information from the Small Business Administration and talking with the owners of three local catering businesses by the end of the month.

As an entrepreneur, you will need to set many goals. Goals can be categorized as financial and nonfinancial.

Financial Goals

Set specific financial goals before starting a business. Financial goals can include how much money you will earn and how quickly you will pay off debts. Make sure your goals are realistic. If one of your goals is to make large sums of money early on, you almost certainly will be disappointed. It usually takes time for businesses to become well established and profitable. Setting SMART financial goals will help you develop a realistic plan for earning a profit.

Goals should be measurable and easily attainable in the time allotted. Mo Yang wants to start a mail-order business for model trains, planes, and cars. His income goal is to earn $27,000 by the end of the first year. He estimates that after expenses he will earn $9 for each item he sells. At this rate of profit, he would have to sell 3,000 models to meet his income goal. Mo realizes that this is not realistic. He would have to lower his income goal or find another business idea.

Nonfinancial Goals

Most people who own their own businesses do so for more than just monetary gain. They are looking for personal satisfaction. They may serve a community need, do something they like, or enjoy the personal independence. You will want to specify what nonfinancial goals you want to achieve by being an entrepreneur. For example, as a business owner, you may want to offer support to a charity organization, either by making monetary donations or by offering your business's services. Setting and meeting nonfinancial goals can help an entrepreneur live a more satisfying and fulfilling life.

 CHECKPOINT

Why are financial goals important? Name some nonfinancial goals an entrepreneur may have.

1.3 ASSESSMENT

THINK ABOUT IT

1. Think about a business opportunity that appeals to you. For this business, answer the six assessment questions listed on page 20 on a sheet of paper. Is this a realistic choice for you? Why or why not?

2. In terms of annual income, what financial goals have you set for yourself for five years after you graduate? What nonfinancial goals have you set that you could fulfill by becoming an entrepreneur? Are financial or nonfinancial goals more important to you? Why?

3. Your friend has set the following goal: I plan to eat healthier. Is this a SMART goal? Explain why or why not. What suggestions would you make for improving it?

MAKE ACADEMIC CONNECTIONS

4. **MATH** You live near the beach and have a passion for snorkeling. Your dream is to give snorkeling lessons. You estimate that after expenses, you can earn an average of $10 per lesson. Each lesson will be one hour long, and you plan to offer lessons five days a week. Your income goal is $15,000 per year. How many lessons do you need to give to achieve this goal? Is this goal realistic?

5. **COMMUNICATION** Write a letter to the Small Business Administration. In your letter, indicate your interest in starting a small business. Be specific about the type of business you wish to start. Ask what specific services the SBA provides to people who wish to start this type of business. Give your letter to your teacher.

6. **SOCIAL STUDIES** Write a personal nonfinancial goal involving your local community that you would like to achieve through entrepreneurship. Be sure the goal is SMART. Write an outline for a detailed plan you can follow to achieve this goal and explain how it would benefit your community.

Teamwork

Working with classmates who have similar interests, come up with an idea for a business. Brainstorm a list of resources for finding information about similar businesses.

PROBLEM SOLVING FOR ENTREPRENEURS

Goals
- List the six steps of the problem-solving model.
- Describe ways to improve your problem-solving skills.

Vocabulary
- problem-solving model
- brainstorming

Research your ideas.

Gloria and Delia spent time on the Internet and in the local library researching ideas for their new business. As a result, they had come up with several ideas. Now they had to decide what to do with these ideas.

As they discussed their options, Gloria said, "You know, Delia, we can talk about these ideas, but we really need a system that we can use for solving problems. We want to be sure that we make the very best decisions for our business."

"Yes," Delia responded, "You are right. I remember reading about a problem-solving model in one of the books we found at the library. Let's go back and find it and see if we can adapt it for our use!"

Work as a Team How important do you think it is to use a system for solving problems and making decisions?

© Helder Almeida, 2010/ Used under license from Shutterstock.com

Research will help you examine opportunities.

Use the Problem-Solving Model

As an entrepreneur, you will be faced with making decisions and solving problems every day. Whether or not to become an entrepreneur is a big decision. Many entrepreneurs make decisions casually or base them on intuition. As a result, their decisions are based on faulty assumptions or illogical thinking. The best entrepreneurs use formal problem-solving models to gather information and evaluate different options.

A formal **problem-solving model** helps people solve problems in a logical manner. The model consists of six steps: define the problem, gather information, identify various solutions, evaluate alternatives and select the best option, take action, and evaluate the action.

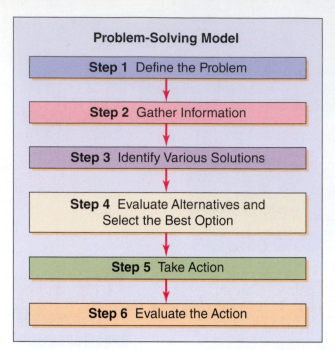

Problem-Solving Model

Step 1 Define the Problem

Step 2 Gather Information

Step 3 Identify Various Solutions

Step 4 Evaluate Alternatives and Select the Best Option

Step 5 Take Action

Step 6 Evaluate the Action

Step 1   Define the Problem

Before you can solve a problem, you need to diagnose it. Write down what the problem is and why it is a problem. Try to quantify it too. For example, you may be trying to decide whether to start your own business or accept a job offer from another company. If you accept the job offer, your income would be $30,000 a year. If you reject the job offer, you would lose that income. Quantifying the problem helps you figure out how much it is worth to you to solve it.

Dan Parker knows what his problem is: Should he start a website design company? He took many computer courses throughout high school, and he is now attending college. He has worked in the food industry throughout high school and college to earn money to help pay for his college expenses. Dan enjoys working at restaurants and has gained valuable customer service and management experience. In addition, he also volunteers his web design skills on projects for his university and local community programs. He will be graduating in the next few months with a degree in Computer Science. Dan is considering starting his own website design business, but he is not sure whether that is the right choice for him.

Step 2   Gather Information

Once the problem has been defined, you need to gather information that could help solve it. Relevant information may be obtained from many sources, including company records, industry data, and trade magazines. It is also a good idea to interview other people in the industry to find out what their experiences have been and to learn how they have solved similar problems.

In Dan's case, it would be helpful for him to take a closer look at himself. He should do a self-assessment to determine his strengths and weaknesses. He also needs to consider his skills, experience, and interests. Does he have the characteristics of a successful entrepreneur? He also needs to examine the advantages and disadvantages of running a website design company. He should talk to other professionals in the business and read trade magazines to gather information about running a website design business. Dan needs to thoroughly explore every aspect of starting and running a website design company.

Step 3   Identify Various Solutions

Most problems can be solved in various ways. Identify all possibilities before you settle on a particular solution. Dan comes up with several possible solutions to his problem.

1. Work as an employee in a position that utilizes his customer service skills and management experience

2. Work as a website designer for another company to gain more experience and then start his own business in 3 to 5 years
3. Pursue his interests in the food industry and open his own restaurant
4. Start his own website design company upon graduation

Why is it important to evaluate the decisions you make?

Step 4 Evaluate Alternatives and Select the Best Option

The decision maker next needs to evaluate the alternatives to determine the best solution. In some cases, it may be possible to quantify the costs and benefits of each alternative. In other cases, quantifying each alternative may not be possible, and the decision maker may simply have to rank each alternative.

Dan ranks option 1 the lowest because of his strong desire to be his own boss. All of the information that Dan gathered indicates that he has a strong chance of succeeding as an entrepreneur. He ranks option 3 next to lowest. Dan has considerable experience in the food industry and enjoys that type of work, but he decides he would rather pursue his interests in website design. He ranks option 2 second because he is already confident in his level of computer knowledge and experience. After evaluating all of his alternatives, Dan decides option 4 is the best solution.

Step 5 Take Action

Once you have selected the best solution to the problem, you need to take action to implement it. Dan begins putting together a business plan and spreading the word about his new venture.

Step 6 Evaluate the Action

The problem-solving process is not complete until you evaluate your action because even a well-thought-out solution may not work. After being in business for six months, Dan evaluates whether he is achieving his financial and nonfinancial goals. It seems that Dan made the right decision because his business is profitable and he is enjoying his work. He has been able to fulfill his dream of working for himself while providing a valuable service to others. Dan will continue to use the problem-solving model to make the most effective decisions for him and his new business.

What are the six steps in the problem-solving model?

Problem-Solving Skills

The more often you use the problem-solving model, the better skilled at decision making you will become. It will become a valuable tool to you throughout your career. There are a few other things you can do to improve your problem-solving skills.

How can good communication skills help you succeed in business?

Communicate

Good communication is important in the problem-solving process. When trying to resolve problems and make decisions, you most likely will have to interact with others. You may have to ask questions, request information, and express your ideas and opinions. On such occasions, it is important that you communicate clearly and confidently. You must also be a good listener. You must carefully listen to information, opinions, and suggestions from others. Listening to others' input can help you make informed decisions.

Kris is the owner of a small boutique and is looking for ways to increase sales. She decides to conduct a meeting with her employees to communicate her sales objectives. During the meeting, she listens to her employees' thoughts and ideas for boosting sales. Through this communication process, Kris is able to gather lots of good information to help her solve her sales problem.

Brainstorm

Brainstorming is a creative problem-solving technique that involves generating a large number of fresh ideas. Brainstorming is often done in a group setting, but it is a very useful activity for an individual as well. Think about the problem you are trying to solve. Brainstorm by writing down as many possible solutions to the problem as you can think of. Do not be afraid to write down any idea you have. The point of brainstorming is not to judge your ideas as good or bad but to come up with as many ideas as possible. Once you have made a list of ideas, you can use the problem-solving model to determine the best alternatives.

Learn from Mistakes

If you want to become an entrepreneur, you cannot be afraid to make mistakes. Mistakes are likely to happen, but a negative can be turned into a positive. You should view your mistakes as a learning experience. Mistakes can help you learn what to do or what not to do, which proves to be valuable in the problem-solving process.

When you read about some of the nation's most famous entrepreneurs, you will find that many of them failed before they came up with a winning idea. Colonel Sanders of KFC fame is a good example. He held many jobs and owned a motel chain, service stations, and other restaurants that were unsuccessful. While running his restaurant, he developed his secret recipe chicken. In 1952, at the age of 62, he began traveling across the country selling his chicken recipe. By 1964, there were 600 KFC restaurants in the United States and Canada, and Colonel Sanders sold KFC for $2 million.

 CHECKPOINT

How can you improve your problem-solving skills?

1.4 ASSESSMENT

THINK ABOUT IT

1. Must the six steps in the problem-solving model be performed in the order described? Why or why not?

2. How do you think strong communication skills can improve the problem-solving process? Provide specific examples of how a business owner might use communication skills to resolve a problem.

MAKE ACADEMIC CONNECTIONS

3. **MATH** In Step 3 of the problem-solving model (Identify Various Solutions), you list a variety of possible solutions to a problem. For the four options Dan Parker came up with on pages 24–25, assign a percentage weight to each based on Dan's reasoning. Give the decimal equivalent for each percentage. What must the decimal value of the four options total?

4. **PROBLEM SOLVING** You own a successful shop that buys, sells, and services bicycles. In January, the owner of the building you now lease tells you that she has found a buyer for the property and plans to sell it in six months, meaning you may have to move your business. Using the six-step problem-solving model, develop a plan for how to proceed.

Teamwork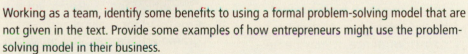

Working as a team, identify some benefits to using a formal problem-solving model that are not given in the text. Provide some examples of how entrepreneurs might use the problem-solving model in their business.

Effective Business Letters

As an entrepreneur, you might write letters to communicate your business ideas, solicit business, respond to customer questions, negotiate purchases, or deal with suppliers. To do so effectively, you need to develop your business writing skills. Writing a business letter is different from writing a letter to a friend. A certain level of formality is necessary, and certain standards must be followed. That doesn't mean business writing should be difficult to understand. Good business writing communicates ideas clearly. It also gets results by being positive and persuasive and by convincing readers that they should accept what the writer is communicating.

Certain basic rules should be followed in writing business letters, as outlined below and as shown in the letter on the next page.

1. **Key all formal correspondence.** Send handwritten letters only when they are intended as personal letters.

2. **Spell all names correctly and have the correct address.** No matter how well written your letter is, its effect will be dramatically reduced if you misspell the name of the person to whom you are writing or refer to his or her company by the wrong name. Addressing a letter incorrectly may cause it to arrive late or to be returned.

3. **Always date your business correspondence.** It may be necessary to refer to this date at a later time.

4. **Use names and titles appropriately.** Use the person's first name if you know him or her well. If you do not know the person or the letter is very formal, use the person's last name, along with the appropriate title (Dr., Mr., Mrs., Ms., or Miss).

5. **Be direct and positive.** Always maintain a positive tone and portray your message in an optimistic light, even if your letter contains bad news.

6. **Be persuasive and specific.** Make sure the action or result you want from the reader is clear. Use nonthreatening language that will persuade the reader that this action or result is the most desirable.

7. **Avoid using fancy language.** Use straightforward language that says exactly what you mean.

8. **Be polite.** Deal with complaints in a businesslike fashion. Don't whine or express outrage, and never become abusive or insulting. Be especially polite in writing rejection or bad news letters.

9. **Use an appropriate closing.** Make sure your closing corresponds with the content of the letter you have written. If you have written a letter to a supplier to complain about poor service, do not use "With warmest regards." Common closings are "Sincerely" and "Sincerely yours."

10. **Proofread for spelling and grammatical errors.** The most persuasive and positive letter can be ruined by a single mistake.

Creative Web Designs

10 E. 34th Street • Baltimore, MD 21218
(410) 555-4321 CWD@internet.com

April 11, 20—

Ms. Chelsey Wright
Advantage Marketers
692 Kemper Road
Baltimore, MD 21209

Dear Ms. Wright

Are you looking for new ways to energize your website? If so, I would like to introduce myself and talk with you about my company, Creative Web Designs.

As a recent graduate of Piedmont State University with an Associate degree in Computer Science, I am ready to put my skills to work for you. After providing web development services for the local university and for other local community programs for the past several years, I have decided to offer my services to other local businesses such as yours. Services provided include the following:

Creation of visibly appealing and compelling web pages

Revitalization of existing websites

Hyperlink development

Technical support

Please call for a free consultation to discuss how you can have a website that works effectively for your company. Samples of my website creations are available for you to review. References can be provided upon request. I look forward to hearing from you.

Sincerely

Dan Parker

Dan Parker
Owner

Try It Out

You own a shop that sells comic books. Write a business letter to your main supplier, a comic book wholesaler. Tell the supplier that you have not received the shipment you ordered of the most recent edition of a popular comic. Be sure to follow the basic rules for writing business letters. Create names for your business and your supplier's business.

SUMMARY

1.1 All About Entrepreneurship

1. Entrepreneurship is the process of running a business of one's own. The owner is called an entrepreneur.
2. Small businesses contribute more to the U.S. economy than all large businesses combined and contribute to the economic recovery of the country during economic downturns.
3. Factors that contribute to a new business's success or failure include having adequate capital and being large enough to have employees. The owner's education level and business experience are also important factors.

1.2 Is Entrepreneurship Right for You?

4. Successful entrepreneurs tend to be independent, self-confident, goal-oriented, and creative.
5. Entrepreneurs must have good team-building skills and be able to work well with others.
6. To determine whether entrepreneurship is right for you, you will need to assess your strengths, weaknesses, interests, and aptitudes.

1.3 Explore Ideas and Opportunities

7. Ideas for new businesses can come from many different sources, including your hobbies and interests, your past experiences, and a discovery or invention.
8. You may research business opportunities online and at the library and the Small Business Administration. Other sources of information include trade shows and other entrepreneurs.
9. Entrepreneurs should set SMART goals, which are specific, measurable, attainable, realistic, and timely. Goals can be categorized as financial and nonfinancial.

1.4 Problem Solving for Entrepreneurs

10. A problem-solving model consists of six steps: define the problem, gather information, identify various solutions, evaluate alternatives and select the best option, take action, and evaluate the action.
11. There are several ways to improve problem-solving skills, including communicating, brainstorming, and learning from mistakes.

what do you know now?

Read *Ideas in Action* on page 3 again. Then answer the questions a second time. Have your responses changed? If so, how have they changed?

VOCABULARY BUILDER

Match each statement with the term that best defines it. Some terms may not be used.

1. People who work for someone else
2. An evaluation of your strengths and weaknesses
3. A creative problem-solving technique that involves generating a large number of fresh ideas
4. Special meetings at which companies of the same industry or related industries display their products
5. People who own, operate, and take the risk of a business venture
6. Thoughts or concepts that come from creative thinking
7. The ability to learn a particular kind of job
8. The process of running a business of one's own

a. aptitude
b. brainstorming
c. employees
d. entrepreneurs
e. entrepreneurship
f. ideas
g. opportunities
h. problem-solving model
i. self-assessment
j. trade shows

REVIEW YOUR KNOWLEDGE

9. Barbara Wall had a great recipe for sweet bell pepper sauce. Her friend Lynne Wilson convinced her that they should go into business together and sell the sauce. They now ship J.T.'s Red Sauce to stores in 35 states. Wall and Wilson are examples of
   a. intrapreneurs
   b. entrepreneurs
   c. employees
   d. managers
10. Which of the following is *not* an example of an entrepreneur?
    a. Diane Molberg started By Request, a successful home bakery business.
    b. Donna Cook started a cleaning service 10 years ago.
    c. Gwen Morgan manages The Secret Garden, a business owned by her sister.
    d. Elmer Olsen created Bayfield Apple Jam and distributes the jam nationally.
11. Team members who have the right set of skills needed to get the job done are demonstrating __?__.
12. H&R Block tax service is an example of which type of business?
    a. manufacturing business
    b. wholesaling business
    c. retailing business
    d. service business
13. The plant where Goodyear tires are made is an example of which type of business?
    a. manufacturing business
    b. wholesaling business
    c. retailing business
    d. service business
14. According to the Small Business Administration's Office of Advocacy, how many new businesses survive for at least two years?
    a. 67 percent
    b. 44 percent
    c. 25 percent
    d. 10 percent
15. Possibilities that arise from existing conditions are called __?__.
16. Which of the following is *not* an advantage of entrepreneurship?
    a. Entrepreneurs are their own bosses.
    b. Entrepreneurs can be creative.
    c. Entrepreneurs take all the risks.
    d. Entrepreneurs can make large sums of money.

17. Which step of the problem-solving model involves performing research and interviewing customers, suppliers, and employees?
    a. define the problem
    b. gather information
    c. identify various solutions
    d. evaluate alternatives

APPLY WHAT YOU LEARNED

18. The six categories of privately owned businesses include manufacturing, wholesaling, retailing, service, agricultural, and mining and extracting. In small groups, compile a list of specific industries and companies that belong to each category of business. Share your results with the class.

19. Is your personality suited for becoming an entrepreneur? Access www.cengage.com/school/entrepreneurship/ideas. Click on *Activities* and open the file *Aptitude Test*. Print a copy and complete the activity. What does the test indicate?

MAKE ACADEMIC CONNECTIONS

20. **MATH**   Ellen Greenberg loves to make and fly kites. Ellen is planning to open a shop that sells custom-made kites. She asks for your advice to help her set financial goals. Ellen estimates that after expenses, she can make a $15 profit on each kite she sells. If her annual income goal is $15,450, how many kites will she have to sell? Assuming she can make only three kites per day and will work five days a week year round, is this goal realistic?

21. **HISTORY**   Research online the life and career of a famous historical entrepreneur. Find out information such as birthplace, type of business started, and what effect the person had on the economy and history. Is the business still operating? Write a short report about your findings.

22. **COMMUNICATION**   For the above History question, find a creative way to present your findings to the class. Use visual aids, skits, costumes, games, and so on.

What Would YOU Do?

Nancy and Gary had been friends since elementary school. During their senior year, Nancy told Gary about an idea she had for a business in the local community. She had done some research and thought that her idea could be turned into a profitable business. After high school graduation, Nancy went off to college, and Gary stayed home and went to the local community college. Since Nancy had not acted on her business idea before leaving for college, Gary decided that he would try to open a business using Nancy's idea. What do you think about Gary's actions? Is he doing the right thing?

build your
BUSINESS PLAN PROJECT

This activity will help you identify a business opportunity that may be right for you. You will use this business idea throughout the book.

1. Divide a sheet of paper into two columns. In the first column list all your interests. In the second column, list business opportunities that relate to each interest.

2. Do a self-assessment by listing your strengths and weaknesses. Compare this list with your list of business opportunities. For which business opportunities would your strengths most apply? For which business opportunities would your weaknesses hurt the most? Based on your strengths and weaknesses, cross out those business opportunities that no longer seem suitable for you.

3. Assess your aptitude, using the Job Attributes checklist in Lesson 1.2. Put a checkmark next to the business opportunities that relate to your aptitudes.

4. For the business opportunities remaining on your list, assess the advantages and disadvantages of each. Cross out any where the disadvantages outweigh the advantages.

5. Conduct research online to find and list sources of information that relate to the business opportunities that remain on your list. Locate at least one of these sources for each business opportunity and write a sentence stating the type of information it contains. On your list, cross out business opportunities for which you could not find any information.

6. Choose one of the business opportunities remaining on your list. Based on this business opportunity, answer the six questions listed in the Compare Different Opportunities section in Lesson 1.3.

7. Set personal financial goals for a five-year period based on the business opportunity you chose. Demonstrate that your goals are SMART (Specific, Measurable, Attainable, Realistic, and Timely). Assume you will need to borrow money to get started. How much profit do you hope to make in one year? Three years? Five years? Next, set nonfinancial goals you hope to achieve with this business. Be sure to include specific activities you can perform to help achieve each goal.

8. Write a letter to potential customers about the goods or services your business will provide. On paper, plan a telephone conversation you will use as a follow-up to the letter. Work with a classmate and do a mock phone conversation based on your plan.

9. Plan ahead to prevent any problems that may arise in your business. Think of a problem that could occur and use the six-step problem-solving model to deal with it now. Brainstorm solutions on your own or with family members or friends.

10. Save all of your materials from this project in a folder. You will continue to add to this folder as you build your business plan at the end of each chapter.

Planning a Career in

HUMAN SERVICES

"A new health club opened near my Grandma's house, and she absolutely loves going there. The club is open 24/7. As Grandma was a bit intimidated by the high-tech exercise equipment at the club, she's hired a personal trainer to help her learn how to use the equipment and to hold her accountable for her efforts. She says she feels much more energetic and relaxed than she used to. She's even considering joining the volleyball team that's been established for seniors."

In a high-tech, convenience-oriented society that often results in inactive lifestyles, how do individuals maintain physical fitness? When the weather prohibits outdoor activities, where can people go to exercise?

Fitness facilities provide the location, equipment, and instruction necessary for club members to exercise. Personal trainers help individual clients customize a workout plan that will help them achieve their personal fitness goals.

Employment Outlook
- Faster than average growth is anticipated.
- Aging baby boomers, who hope to maintain fitness in later life, are fueling the demand for fitness workers.
- Parents' desire to keep children fit as well as employers who encourage employees to stay in shape will contribute to the ongoing need for fitness workers.

Job Titles
- Corporate Personal Trainer
- Fitness Advisor
- Certified Personal Trainer
- Fitness Consultant
- Personal Fitness Coach

Needed Education/Skills
- A high school diploma and CPR certification are usually needed.
- Fitness certification from a reputable certification organization is required.
- Continuing education is often mandatory.
- Being physically fit and extroverted and having strong interpersonal skills is necessary.

What's it like to work in Human Services? Nhu, a certified personal trainer, spent the weekend at a training seminar. The session was part of her ongoing training to stay current on developments in the personal training field.

This morning Nhu taught a group exercise class at a large fitness center. She enjoyed leading a large group of people and helping them improve their fitness level. The class also gave her the opportunity to meet a large number of health club members. Some of the class attendees signed up for her personal training services at the club.

Upon signing up for personal training, club members can work with Nhu on their individual fitness goals for an hourly fee. If they elect to buy a ten-session pass, then the hourly fee is reduced.

Over the years, Nhu has also established a private personal training service. When she attends a client's home for a training session, she charges a higher hourly rate for the training. Many clients with busy schedules are more than happy to pay the higher rate to save the time of going to a gym.

What about you? Would you find it gratifying to help individuals improve their physical fitness levels?

Presentation Management Team

Participants in this event will use current desktop technologies and software to prepare and deliver an effective multimedia presentation. A team will consist of two to four members. The team shall design a computer-generated multimedia presentation on the assigned topic. A new topic is selected by BPA every year. A word processed copy, including cited works, must be submitted at the time of the presentation. The team is to make effective use of current multimedia technology in the presentation (examples: sound, movement, digital video, and so forth). Space, color, and text should also be used effectively in the presentation.

TOPIC: Business Professionals of America is a forward-thinking organization. Your team has been asked to research three growing entrepreneurship opportunities for the next decade. You will develop a presentation on these trends for the BPA Board of Trustees.

Participating teams will have from seven to ten minutes for oral presentations. Judges have an additional five minutes to ask questions about the presentation.

Performance Indicators

- Evaluate and delegate responsibilities needed to perform required tasks
- Demonstrate effective teamwork skills needed to function in a business setting
- Demonstrate knowledge of multimedia software and components
- Demonstrate effective oral communication skills
- Apply technical skills to create a multimedia presentation which enhances the oral presentation

Go to the BPA website for more detailed information.

THINK CRITICALLY

1. Why must entrepreneurs look at future trends when making business decisions?
2. Why should entrepreneurs look beyond current technology trends when making business decisions?
3. Why should statistics be used for this presentation?
4. How are entrepreneurs affected by a global economy?

www.bpa.org

©iofoto, 2010/ Used under license from Shutterstock.com

Entrepreneurs in a Market Economy

2.1 Entrepreneurs Satisfy Needs and Wants

2.2 How Economic Decisions Are Made

2.3 What Affects Price?

www.cengage.com/school/entrepreneurship/ideas

Website Marketing

Have you ever wondered why certain websites come up when you use a web search engine such as Google or Yahoo? The results you get may be due to the work of Exclusive Concepts, Inc.

© www.ExclusiveConcepts.com/
Photographer:David Fox

Scott Smigler, Exclusive Concepts founder and president

Scott Smigler, Exclusive Concepts founder and president, balanced dual roles as a student and an entrepreneur through high school and college. His company provides online marketing solutions by helping businesses stand out when someone uses a web search engine. Scott ran the company by himself in the beginning. Eventually, Scott moved from his home to his college dorm room to offices in Burlington, Massachusetts, and he now has a staff of 30. The company's estimated sales for a recent year were $3 million.

Scott's ability to develop keyword strategies, write attention-getting keyword ad copy, create and optimize bidding strategies, and analyze results for continuous improvement helped him become a leader in the field. In addition to running the company, he maintained a 3.7 GPA as a finance major at Bentley University in Burlington, Massachusetts.

Some important lessons Scott has learned include these:

- **Perseverance**   You must be organized and focused. Implementing dreams is not easy.
- **Mentorship**   You need to have a network of mentors to help you with problems.
- **Communication**   You need excellent communication skills; written agreements between your company and clients are essential.
- **Capitalization**   You should be prepared for everything to be more expensive than you think and plan for unanticipated expenses.
- **Marketing**   You must work to acquire new relationships while continuing to build existing ones. Everyone is a potential customer or client.

Scott also stresses the importance of finding the correct balance between work and play. Starting and running a business require focus, dedication, and time, but it is important to remember that there is life outside the business.

1. What type of interests do you think Scott had that helped him find success in this business?
2. Which of the lessons that Scott has learned do you think is most important?
3. Why do you think it is important to find a balance between work and play?

2.1

ENTREPRENEURS SATISFY NEEDS AND WANTS

Goals
- Distinguish between needs and wants.
- Describe the types of economic resources.
- Explain the role of entrepreneurs in the U.S. economy.

Vocabulary
- needs
- wants
- economic resources

focus on Economics

Do you *want* it or *need* it?

"Dad, I really need a new pair of shoes to wear to the Winter Dance," said Stephanie. "Do you *need* a new pair of shoes, or do you *want* a new pair of shoes?" her father responded. "Want or need—what's the difference?" Stephanie asked. "That's a good question, Stephanie. Let's look at it this way. Do you really need the shoes in order to survive, or will having the new shoes make you feel better?" asked her father.

Stephanie thought about it and then responded, "Well, Dad, it won't keep me from going to the dance if I don't have the new shoes, but I'd sure like to have them. So, I guess I'd have to answer you by saying they would make me feel better." "Then you *want* the shoes, but you don't *need* them!" her father responded. "That's what economics is all about!"

It is often difficult to distinguish between a want and a need.

Work as a Team Do you sometimes have a difficult time telling the difference between a need and a want? Do you think peer pressure makes it more difficult to distinguish between a need and a want?

Is It a Need or a Want?

Think about your favorite piece of clothing, such as a pair of jeans. First, you thought about what type of clothing you wanted, and then you went out and found it. Maybe you looked at several articles of clothing and compared prices before you decided to spend your money. If someone else gave you clothing as a gift, then that person had to think about what you might like and then make a choice. Economics is all about making choices and satisfying the wants and needs of consumers.

Do you know the difference between your needs and wants? Your **needs** are things that you must have in order to survive. Needs include food, basic clothing, and a place to live. Your **wants** are those things that you think you must have in order to be satisfied. Wants add comfort and pleasure to your life. Wants would include things like CDs, computers, and jewelry. The role of businesses is to produce and distribute goods and services that people need and want.

DEVELOP YOUR READING SKILLS

As you read this chapter, develop an outline of the main topics. Write a short summary for each topic after you read it.

Needs

People have many needs. Some are basic needs while others are higher-level needs. Abraham Maslow was a psychologist who developed a theory on the *hierarchy of needs*. It identifies five areas of needs—physiological, security, social, esteem, and self-actualization needs. The theory suggests that people's basic physiological needs, such as food, clothing, and shelter, must be satisfied first before they can focus on higher-level needs. Once basic needs are met, people will try to satisfy their security needs. When these needs are filled, individuals turn their attention to social needs, such as friendship. Esteem needs can be satisfied by gaining the respect and recognition of others. Self-actualization needs usually involve something that provides a sense of accomplishment, such as earning a college degree.

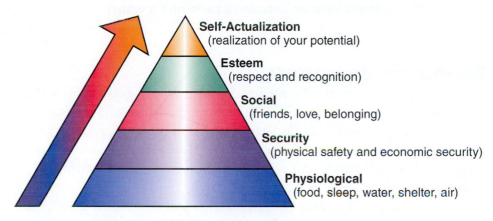

Maslow's Hierarchy of Needs Pyramid

Beyond basic needs, not all people have the same needs. Needs depend on a person's situation. You may live in a nice house in a gated community, so your security needs are met. Someone who lives in a high-crime area still may be trying to meet security needs.

Wants

Individuals have two different types of wants—economic wants and noneconomic wants. *Economic wants* involve a desire for material goods and services. They are the basis of an economy. People want material goods, such as clothing, housing, and cars. They also want services, such as hair styling and medical care. No economy has the resources necessary to satisfy all of the wants of all people for all material goods and services. The goods and services that people want must be produced and supplied.

People also have *noneconomic wants*, or the desire for nonmaterial things. These wants would include such things as sunshine, fresh air, exercise, friendship, and happiness.

Needs and Wants Are Unlimited

Your needs and wants never end. You are limited only by what your mind can think of and what businesses make available for sale. If you are going camping, you might need to buy a tent for shelter. One purchase often leads to another. After buying a tent, you might also want to buy other camping supplies. Then you might want a bigger backpack to carry your new supplies.

CHECKPOINT

What is the difference between a need and a want?

Economic Resources

Economic resources are the means through which goods and services are produced. *Goods* are products you can see and touch. *Services* are activities that are consumed as they are produced. Entrepreneurs use economic resources to create the goods and services consumers use. Consumers satisfy needs and wants by purchasing and consuming goods and services.

Goods are products you can purchase. A pair of shoes, a jacket, food, and cars are all examples of goods. Services must be provided to you at the time you need them—they cannot be stored. A haircut, a manicure, lawn mowing, and car detailing are all examples of services.

Factors of Production

In order to create useful goods and services, an entrepreneur may use three types of economic resources. These resources are called the *factors of production* and include natural resources, human resources, and capital resources.

What kind of resources are used for farming?

©Valio, 2010/ Used under license from Shutterstock.com

NATURAL RESOURCES   Raw materials supplied by nature are *natural resources*. The earth contains oil, minerals, and the nutrients needed to grow crops and timber. Rivers, lakes, and oceans are the sources of both food and water. All products you use begin with one or more natural resources. The supply of many natural resources is limited. Increased use of natural resources and damage to the environment threatens the continued availability of natural resources in many regions of the world. Conservation practices and the production of more efficient products help to preserve and renew resources. Compact fluorescent light bulbs (CFLs) cost more than old-style incandescent bulbs, but they last longer, use far less electricity, save consumers' money in the long run, and reduce greenhouse gases. One CFL keeps a half-ton of greenhouse gases (CO_2) out of the atmosphere. When consumers switch to CFLs, they help preserve energy resources and the environment for future generations.

HUMAN RESOURCES   The people who create goods and services are called *human resources*. They may work in agriculture, manufacturing, distribution, or retail businesses. As an entrepreneur, you would also be a human resource. Entrepreneurs have creative ideas and use these ideas to create new goods and services.

To increase the productivity of human resources, business owners may use specialization and division of labor. *Specialization* occurs when individual workers focus on single tasks, enabling each worker to become more efficient and productive. Even though a worker may be talented at many things, when he or she specializes in performing one task, generally, more can be produced. *Division of labor* divides the production process into separate tasks carried out by workers who specialize in those specific tasks. This division of labor allows the group as a whole to be more productive.

CAPITAL RESOURCES   The assets used in the production of goods and services are called *capital resources*. Capital resources include buildings, equipment, and supplies. They also include the money needed to build a factory, buy a delivery truck, and pay the employees who manufacture and distribute goods and services.

Limited Resources

All economic resources have a limited supply. Most resources can be used to produce several different products and services. If resources are used to produce one type of product, they may not be available for the production of another product. Individuals, businesses, and countries compete for access to and ownership of economic resources. Those resources that are in very high demand or that have a limited supply will command high prices. Control of oil fields in the Middle East has been an ongoing issue for many years. The United States has a large demand for oil but a limited supply of oil, so it is important to the United States to have access to oil from the Middle East. This high demand contributes to high gasoline prices.

Law of Diminishing Returns

To make the most efficient use of their resources, businesses should consider the law of diminishing returns. The *law of diminishing returns* states that if one factor of production is increased while others stay the same, the resulting increase in output (product produced) will level off after some time and then will decline. This means that extra workers, extra capital, extra machinery, or extra land may not necessarily raise output as much as expected. For example, increasing the number of workers (human resources) may allow additional output to be produced by using any spare capacity workers have, such as unused workspace or machinery (capital resources). Once this capacity is fully used, however, continually increasing the number of workers without increasing the workspace or number of machines will not result in an increase of output.

CHECKPOINT

List the three types of economic resources and give an example of each.

Role of Entrepreneurs in the U.S. Economy

Entrepreneurs play an important role in the U.S. economy. Because all businesses that exist in the United States today began as an entrepreneurial idea, you could say that entrepreneurs are the backbone of the U.S. economy. The development and growth of small businesses help to ensure a strong economic future.

How do entrepreneurs help meet the demands of consumers?

Digital Vision/Getty Images

Supply and Demand

As business owners, entrepreneurs play an important role in supplying goods and services to meet the demands of consumers. They continually look for unmet needs or better ways to satisfy consumers' needs and wants. They use resources and their knowledge of markets and business to produce goods and services efficiently that meet consumers' needs and wants.

Capital Investment and Job Creation

Entrepreneurs need money to finance their businesses. Sometimes they use their own money. Other times, they look to investors and lenders to supply the money they need. They may use the money to lease a building, buy equipment, or hire employees. By doing so, entrepreneurs are investing in their communities by contributing to the local economy and providing jobs.

Change Agents

Many entrepreneurs create products that change the way people live and conduct business. When you learn about American history, you see that many entrepreneurs have shaped the U.S. economy.

 CHECKPOINT

> What are some things entrepreneurs contribute to the U.S. economy?

 **ASSESSMENT**

THINK ABOUT IT

1. What role do needs and wants play in determining what is produced in an economy?

2. How does the availability of economic resources affect an entrepreneur's decisions?

3. Which of the contributions to the U.S. economy that entrepreneurs make do you think is most important? Why?

MAKE ACADEMIC CONNECTIONS

4. **SOCIAL STUDIES** Think of a business in your area. Make a list of the resources that the business uses for each factor of production.

5. **RESEARCH** Investigate and analyze the specialization and division of labor used by a business in your area. Write a paragraph explaining the impact of specialization and division of labor on the company's productivity.

6. **HISTORY** The needs of people in today's society vary greatly from the needs of people living a century ago. Conduct online research to learn about the life of the typical person living during that time period. Compare that person's needs with the needs of someone living today. Write a short report describing the differences and similarities.

Teamwork

Working in a team, make a list of the natural resources in your area. Using the Internet, almanacs, and other sources of information about your community, find out the impact these resources have on your local economy. Which businesses use these natural resources?

HOW ECONOMIC DECISIONS ARE MADE

Goals

- Compare and contrast different types of economic systems.
- Describe the characteristics of the U.S. economy.
- Explain how scarcity affects economic decisions.
- Explain how business functions are used to satisfy consumers.

Vocabulary

- capitalism
- profit
- economic decision making
- scarcity
- opportunity cost

focus on Economics

Choose between alternatives.

"Stephanie, weren't you thinking about buying a new MP3 player last week?" her dad asked. "Yes, Dad, I was," Stephanie replied, "but if I buy the new shoes I want for the Winter Dance, I won't have enough money to buy the MP3 player now." "You've just learned a lesson about opportunity cost. When you choose one item over another, the opportunity cost is the value of the item you give up—in this case, the MP3 player," her dad explained. "I understand, Dad. But if you took this opportunity to buy the shoes for me, then I wouldn't have any opportunity cost, would I?"

Work as a Team Discuss choices that you have made. Did you realize that in choosing one item over another there was an opportunity cost?

©Elliot Westacott, 2010/ Used under license from Shutterstock.com

You often have to choose one option over another.

Economic Systems

Different economic systems exist throughout the world. However, all economies must answer three basic questions.

1. What goods and services will be produced?
2. How will the goods and services be produced?
3. For whom will the goods and services be produced (in other words, whose needs and wants will be satisfied)?

If all economies struggle with the same basic questions, what is it that makes economies different? The type of economic system will determine how these three economic questions are answered. Economies must choose a way to allocate the goods and services that are available to the people who need or want them. These different allocation processes are what create different economies.

Command Economy

In a *command economy*, the government determines what, how, and for whom products and services are produced. Because the government is making the decisions, there is very little choice for consumers in what is available. The government may see no reason to have more than one type of the same item. This means individuals may not always be able to obtain exactly what they want. There will be shirts and pants, but there will not be many styles and colors from which to choose.

Market Economy

Market economies are about personal choice. In a *market economy*, individuals and businesses decide what, how, and for whom goods and services are produced. Entrepreneurship thrives in a market economy. Decisions about production and consumption are made by millions of people, each acting alone. Individual choice creates the market, so there are many items available that are very similar. If a product sells, it will remain on the market. If not, the manufacturer will not continue to produce it.

How does a country's economic system affect consumers' product choices?

Individual choice also exists in how items are produced. A furniture maker will make choices regarding the style, fabric, and durability of products made. In addition, products and services are always available to everyone who has the means to pay for them.

Traditional Economy

Before complex economic systems developed, simple economies operated according to tradition or custom. In a *traditional economy*, goods and services are produced the way they have always been produced. The traditional economy is used in countries that are less developed and are not yet participating in the global economy. Most of what is produced is consumed, and what is left over is sold or traded with people who live in nearby communities. Traditional economies lack the formal structure found in more advanced economic systems and usually have limited capital resources available to improve their conditions.

Mixed Economy

When elements of the command and market economies are combined, it is called a *mixed economy*. A mixed economy often results when a country shifts away from a command economy toward a market economy but still has government involvement in the marketplace. Many countries are making this shift.

For over 70 years, the Soviet Union operated under a command economic system called *communism*. Government control resulted in limited choices and a shortage in supply of many consumer goods.

The Soviet Union disbanded and became 15 independent states in the early 1990s, resulting in a move toward market economies.

China operates under a different type of communist government that controls most of the resources and decisions. The economy of China is adopting elements of a market system for a growing number of economic decisions. Entire regions of the country are enjoying a market economy based on greater individual freedom of choice. China is fast becoming a world leader in goods and services produced.

As countries with traditional economies develop, they often adopt mixed economies. The government makes many of the decisions about how the country's resources will be used to develop schools, hospitals, roads, and utilities. As people become educated, they are able to obtain jobs and earn money to purchase more goods and services. Often businesses from other countries will open a business in the developing country and offer jobs and locally produced products to the citizens.

✓ CHECKPOINT

How does the type of economy affect the way the basic economic questions are answered?

famous entrepreneur

Why do you think Paul Revere was a successful entrepreneur?

PAUL REVERE is best remembered as an American patriot who made a famous midnight ride, warning people that the British were coming. However, Paul Revere was also a successful entrepreneur. Trained as a silversmith, he used his engraving skills to create political cartoons to contribute to the movement for independence. He manufactured gunpowder, bullets, and cannons during the Revolutionary War. Afterward, he developed new methods for his trade and founded the Revere Copper Company in 1801. The original company evolved into Revere Copper Products, Inc., which today manufactures a wide variety of products, from industrial equipment to cookware, that bears his name, a sure sign that his business lives on!

THINK CRITICALLY
Paul Revere was able to use his silversmith skills when starting his business. How important do you think it is to have a skill that you can use when starting a business?

Photodisc/Getty Images

The U.S. Economic System

What type of economic system do you think the United States has? To answer this question, you must look at who makes most of the decisions about what is produced and consumed. Since individual businesses and consumers make most of these decisions, the U.S. system is best described as a market economy. **Capitalism**, which is the private ownership of resources by individuals rather than by the government, is another name for the economic system in the United States. Another term often associated with the U.S. economy is *free enterprise*, due to the freedom of businesses and individuals to make production and consumption decisions. This individual freedom is vital to the success of the U.S. economy.

The U.S. economic system is based on four basic principles: private property, freedom of choice, profit, and competition.

Private Property

As a U.S. citizen, you can own, use, or dispose of things of value. You are free to own anything you want, and you can decide what to do with it as long as you operate within the law.

Freedom of Choice

You can make decisions independently and must accept the consequences of those decisions. Business owners are free to choose where to open a business, what to sell, and how to operate the company. Consumers are free to choose where to shop, what to buy, and how much they want to spend. Only when individual decisions will bring harm to others does the government regulate freedom of choice.

Profit

The difference between the revenues earned by a business and the costs of operating the business is called **profit**. The opportunity to earn a profit is at the heart of the free-enterprise system. One of the main reasons entrepreneurs invest resources and take risks is to make a profit. No business is guaranteed to make a profit, so entrepreneurs are challenged to work hard, invest wisely, and produce goods and services that consumers are willing to buy.

Competition

The rivalry among businesses to sell their goods and services is called *competition*. Consumers choose products and services based on the value they think they will receive. Competition forces a business to improve products, keep costs low, provide good customer service, and search for new ideas so that consumers will choose its products or services.

 CHECKPOINT

> **Describe the four basic principles of the U.S. economic system.**

Economic Choices

Individuals and businesses are faced with economic choices every day. Decisions about needs and wants must be made. **Economic decision making** is the process of choosing which needs and wants, among several, you will satisfy using the resources you have. Two factors commonly enter into economic decision making—scarcity and opportunity cost.

Scarcity

In every economy, there are limited resources to produce goods and services. However, individuals have unlimited needs and wants. This produces the basic economic problem of scarcity. **Scarcity** occurs when people's needs and wants are unlimited and the resources to produce the goods and services to meet those needs and wants are limited. For example, land is a scarce resource. Land is used for many purposes, such as for growing crops or as a site for a business or house. The same parcel of land cannot be used to meet all of these needs. A decision on how to use it must be made.

Decisions based on scarcity affect everyone. Individuals and families have many wants and needs. They must decide how to spread their income among all these wants and needs. National, state, and city governments collect taxes from their citizens. They must decide how to use the tax collections to provide all the services that citizens expect. In both cases, someone must make difficult choices.

Scarcity forces you to make choices or decisions. Suppose you earn $150 a week. If you decide to purchase a $75 concert ticket and you owe $75 for your monthly car insurance payment, you will not have any money left over to go out for pizza. Because you have only $150, you have limited resources. With limited resources, you cannot afford to buy everything you want. You may have to make a *tradeoff* by giving up something so that you can have something else.

Opportunity Cost

When trying to satisfy your wants and needs, you most likely will have many alternatives from which to choose. Economic decision making will force you to explore all of your alternatives. When examining all of your alternatives, you should consider the opportunity cost of each one. **Opportunity cost** is the value of the next-best alternative—the one you pass up. If your grandparents give you $300 for graduation, you have to decide what to do with it. If you decide to save the money for college, the opportunity cost would be the new iPod that you really wanted and could have purchased with the money.

Diane Mayfield has $2,500 in extra cash that she wants to invest in her cake decorating business. Diane could use the money for advertising or she could purchase new equipment. If she decides to use the money for advertising, she will not be able to purchase new equipment. The opportunity cost of advertising will be the value of the new equipment—the next best alternative. Like all entrepreneurs, Diane will have to choose between various investment options.

Functions of Business

In a market economy, an entrepreneur is free to produce and offer to consumers any legal product or service. Knowledge of business activities will help entrepreneurs satisfy customers and make a profit. These activities or *functions of business* include the following:

- production
- marketing
- management
- finance

Each of these functions is dependent on the others in order for the business to be effective. Products can be produced, but if management is not functioning properly, if adequate financial records are not maintained, or if marketing is not getting the word out to consumers, the products probably will not be sold at a profit.

Production

The primary reason a business exists in a market economy is to provide products or services to consumers and to earn a profit. The production function creates or obtains products or services for sale.

Marketing

All businesses in a market economy need to complete marketing activities in order to make their products and services available to consumers. These activities make up the *marketing mix*, which includes the following:

- product
- distribution
- price
- promotion

The goal is to attract as many customers as possible so that the product succeeds in the marketplace.

Management

It is necessary for all businesses in a market economy to spend a great deal of time developing, implementing, and evaluating plans and activities. Setting goals, determining how goals can be met, and deciding how to respond to the actions of competitors is the role of management. Management also solves problems, oversees the work of employees, and evaluates the activities of the business.

Finance

One of the first responsibilities of finance is determining the amount of capital needed for the business and how the capital will be obtained.

BE YOUR OWN BOSS

You are planning to open a sandwich shop. You begin to think about the four functions of business—production, marketing, management, and finance. Describe how each function will apply to your business. Explain how the functions will work together to ensure you run a successful sandwich shop. Be prepared to share your ideas with your classmates.

The finance function also involves planning and managing the financial records of the business.

CHECKPOINT

What are the functions of business?

2.2 ASSESSMENT

THINK ABOUT IT

1. Prepare a chart showing how the three basic economic questions are answered by a command, a market, and a traditional economy.

2. Explain how each of the four basic principles of the U.S. economy contributes to the success of our economy.

3. Opportunity cost can affect you personally. Name an item you have wanted to purchase but have not bought because you wanted another item more.

4. Why is it important for all functions of business to work together?

MAKE ACADEMIC CONNECTIONS

5. **MATH**   David Kalb started a pet-walking business in New York City. He charges $20 to walk one dog twice a day. He walks six dogs five days a week for four customers. He walks three dogs seven days a week for three other customers. How much money does David get from his customers each week? If his expenses each week total $350, how much profit is he making weekly?

6. **ECONOMICS**   Research the economic system of another country. Explain the type of economic system the country has and the effect it has on the lives of the people in the country. Describe how the economic system would affect entrepreneurs in the country.

7. **PROBLEM SOLVING**   You worked for your grandmother doing odd jobs around her house. She paid you $75 for the work you did. You need $25 to fill your car with gasoline for the upcoming week, $10 for school lunch, $40 for prom tickets, and $30 for a deposit on your tuxedo/dress for the prom. How much money do you still need to cover all your expenses? Since your resources are limited, use the problem-solving model to decide how to spend the $75. Explain your choices.

Teamwork

Working in a team, choose a business with which you are familiar. For the business you choose, make a list of the activities that would take place involving each of the four functions of business.

WHAT AFFECTS PRICE?

Goals

- Recognize how supply and demand interact to determine price.
- Describe how costs of doing business affect the price of a good or service.
- Explain the effect of different market structures on price.

Vocabulary

- supply
- demand
- equilibrium price and quantity
- fixed costs
- variable costs
- marginal benefit
- marginal cost
- economies of scale

focus on Economics

Does supply match demand?

"Well, Dad, I went to the mall today to buy my new shoes and nobody had the ones I wanted," Stephanie told her father. "Every store I went to said it had sold out of the shoes because they were on sale. The manufacturer is supposed to send another shipment of the shoes next week." "Oh," her father said, "so more people want the shoes because the price is lower. And the manufacturer is willing to make more shoes even at the lower price because it is still making a profit. This is the law of supply and demand at work."

©Bestshortstop, 2010/Used under license from Shutterstock.com

Manufacturers must try to keep up with product demand.

Work as a Team In the U.S. economy, you have many choices, but sometimes you might not be able to find exactly what you want. Think of products that you have wanted to buy but could not find. Why do you think you could not find them?

How Much Is Enough?

If a market economy is based on personal choice, why does there always seem to be just enough of everything? In a market economy, individual consumers make decisions about what to buy, and businesses make decisions about what to produce. Consumers are motivated to buy goods and services that they need or want. Business owners are driven by the desire to earn profits. These two groups, consumers and producers, together determine the quantities and prices of goods and services produced.

Supply and Demand

To understand how this works, you need to understand two important forces: supply and demand. **Supply** is the quantity of a good

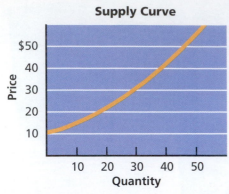

Supply Curve

Suppliers are willing to supply more of a product or service at a higher price.

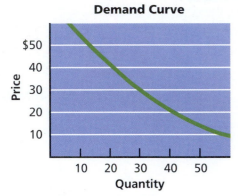

Demand Curve

Individuals are willing to consume more of a product or service at a lower price.

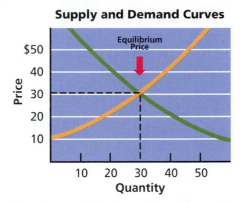

Supply and Demand Curves

The point at which the supply and demand curves intersect indicates the equilibrium price and quantity. The equilibrium price is $30 a unit, and 30 units will be produced.

or service a producer is willing to produce at different prices. Imagine that you supply car detailing services. Suppose that at a rate of $40, you are willing to spend eight hours a week providing car detailing services. If your customers are willing to pay just $20 for a car detail, you might decide not to bother detailing cars at all. If, however, the rate for car detailing rose to $60, you would probably increase the number of cars you would detail. You might even try to get some friends to help you detail even more cars.

As the price of car detailing services rises, suppliers are willing to provide more services. The quantity of car detailing services supplied rises as the price for car detailing services increases, as shown on the supply curve graph.

Now consider the demand side of the market economy. **Demand** is the quantity of a good or service that consumers are willing to buy at a given price. Suppose that you are interested in having your car detailed. At a rate of $40, you figure it is worth having your car detailed once a month. If, however, the rate fell to just $20, you might be willing to have your car detailed twice a month.

As the price of the service or product decreases, consumers are willing to purchase more of the product or service. Demand rises as the price falls, as shown on the demand curve graph.

When the demand for a product is affected by its price, this is referred to as *demand elasticity*. When a change in price creates a change in demand, you have *elastic demand*. When a change in price creates very little change in demand, you have *inelastic demand*. Demand is usually inelastic when

- There are no acceptable substitutes for a product that consumers need
- The change in price is small in relation to the income of the consumer, so consumers will continue to buy the product if they want it
- The product is a basic need for consumers, rather than just a want

When Supply and Demand Meet

How do the forces of supply and demand work together to determine price in a market economy? The point at which the supply and demand curves meet is known as the **equilibrium price and quantity**. This is the price at which supply equals demand. Above the equilibrium price, fewer people are interested in buying goods and services because they are priced too high. Below the equilibrium price, consumers are willing to purchase more of the goods or services at the lower prices, but suppliers are not willing to produce enough to meet their demand. Only at the equilibrium price does the amount that consumers want to buy exactly equal the amount producers want to supply.

Costs of Doing Business

To determine how much profit they are earning, entrepreneurs need to know how much it costs to produce their goods or services. To do so, they must consider all the resources that go into producing the good or service to determine a price to charge. Resources may include office space, materials, labor, and equipment. A company that prices its product based only on the cost of materials involved in producing it will lose money and go out of business very quickly.

Fixed and Variable Costs

Every business has fixed costs and variable costs. **Fixed costs** are costs that must be paid regardless of how much of a good or service is produced. Fixed costs are also called sunk costs. **Variable costs** are costs that go up and down depending on the quantity of the good or service produced.

The Bread and Bagel Shop is a small business owned by Michael Miller. Whether or not Michael makes any sales, he must pay the same monthly rent, the same insurance fees, and the same interest on the loans taken out to finance his business. These are Michael's fixed costs. The store also has variable costs, including the expense of buying flour, sugar, and coffee. These expenses rise directly with the number of items sold. The more bagels, donuts, and cups of coffee the company sells, the more resources it must buy to make more goods. In contrast, when customers purchase fewer loaves of bread, Michael uses less flour and other ingredients.

Understanding the difference between fixed and variable costs is important. A business with many fixed costs is a higher risk than a business with mostly variable costs because fixed costs will be incurred regardless of the level of sales. If sales are lower than expected, the business will have less revenue to pay the bills.

Marginal Benefit and Marginal Cost

Entrepreneurs make business decisions based on the concepts of marginal benefit and marginal cost. **Marginal benefit** measures the advantages of producing one additional unit of a good or service. **Marginal cost** measures the disadvantages of producing one additional unit of a good or service.

Michael Miller of The Bread and Bagel Shop wants to increase his sales. Michael is considering keeping the store open two extra hours every day. He estimates that during the last two hours of every day, he will sell an additional 50 baked goods and 20 cups of coffee, bringing in additional daily revenues of $100. This $100 represents the marginal benefit of keeping the store open an extra two hours a day.

To determine if staying open later makes economic sense, Michael needs to calculate the marginal cost of staying open later. He will need to purchase additional ingredients to produce another 50 baked goods and 20 cups of coffee. He will have to pay overtime wages to at least two employees. He will also use more electricity. After adding up these costs, Michael estimates that staying open two extra hours will cost him $125 per day. Because the marginal cost of staying open ($125) exceeds the marginal benefit ($100), Michael decides not to change the store's hours.

Economies of Scale

When a business owner decides to grow the business, he or she needs to consider the **economies of scale**, which are the cost advantages obtained due to expansion. Businesses can expand their scale of operations in many ways, such as expanding the size of their facility, obtaining specialized machinery, and using a greater specialization of labor. Economies of scale represent an increase in efficiency of production as the number of units of goods produced increases. A business that achieves economies of scale lowers the average cost per unit through increased production because costs can be spread over an increased number of units. Lower costs per unit allow businesses to lower the prices of their product or service, which may attract more customers.

what went wrong?

AVOID PERSONAL DEBT

Dave McClure took on a great amount of debt when he founded a Web and database services company, Aslan Computing. He used his own personal savings and took out a second mortgage on his home to get the money he needed to get his business off the ground. At first, it appeared that Dave's venture was successful. He made $1.8 million in sales within two years. Upon closer examination of his financial records, however, things did not look as good. Although Dave's business generated a large amount of revenue, it did not generate much profit. Aslan Computing's costs exceeded its revenues, and it incurred a net loss of $50,000 the second year. On the brink of collapse, no bank would lend Dave additional funds. He managed to sell the business for enough money to pay off his debts.

THINK CRITICALLY

1. Do you think it is wise for a business owner to take on a large amount of personal debt when starting a business?

2. What other options does an entrepreneur have if no bank is willing to loan money to help finance the business?

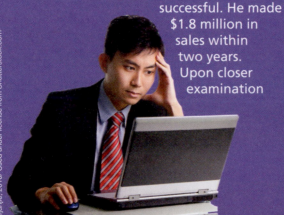

©junjie, 2010/ Used under license from Shutterstock.com

When starting your business, be sure to avoid personal debt.

Market Structure and Prices

Market structure is determined by the nature and degree of competition among businesses that operate in the same industry. The main criteria used to distinguish between different market structures are the number and size of sellers and buyers in the market, the type of goods and services being traded, and the barriers to entry into the market for sellers. There are four major market structures: perfect competition, monopolistic competition, oligopoly, and monopoly.

Perfect Competition

A market with *perfect competition* consists of a very large number of businesses producing nearly identical products and has many buyers. Buyers are well-informed about the price, quality, and availability of products. Because consumers have so many choices of similar products, price is often the deciding factor, making it difficult for a single business to raise prices. This gives consumers more control of the market. Businesses can easily enter or leave this type of market. Examples of industries in perfect competition include gasoline suppliers and producers of agricultural products such as wheat and corn.

What kind of competition do you think a TV manufacturer faces? Why?

Monopolistic Competition

A market with *monopolistic competition* has a large number of independent businesses that produce goods and services that are somewhat different. Each business has a very small portion of the market share. This is also called a competitive market. In a competitive market, many suppliers compete for business, and buyers shop around for the best deal they can find. In this kind of market, prices are said to be determined competitively. Products offered are not identical but very similar, so differentiating products is important. Businesses can easily enter or leave a market that has monopolistic competition. Businesses in this market include retail stores and restaurants.

Oligopoly

When a market is dominated by a small number of businesses that gain the majority of total sales revenue, it is called an *oligopoly*. Businesses in this market sell similar goods and services that are close substitutes, and they have influence over the price charged. With the dominance of a few businesses, it is not easy for new ones to enter the industry. Examples include the automobile and airline industries.

Monopoly

Where there is only one provider of a product or service, a monopoly exists. A company that has a *monopoly* is able to charge whatever price it wants because consumers have nowhere else to go to find a better price. This is the opposite of a competitive market where consumers can simply switch to a lower-priced good or service offered by a competitor. Monopolies usually exist because of barriers that make it difficult for new businesses to enter the market. Examples include local water and electric utility companies.

 CHECKPOINT

How does the market structure affect the price of a good or service?

2.3 ASSESSMENT

THINK ABOUT IT

1. Have you ever wanted to buy something, but you couldn't find it? What role do you think supply and demand might have played?

2. Name three fixed costs in your life. How do you plan to pay them? Name three variable costs that you have. How can variable costs be like opportunity costs?

3. Think of an item you purchase often. If the price is similar at several stores, do you always buy at the same store? Why or why not?

4. Describe the important features of each of the market structures.

MAKE ACADEMIC CONNECTIONS

5. **MARKETING**   Find advertisements for two competing products. Analyze the ads to see how the products are differentiated. Make a poster of the two ads and label the items that are different.

6. **ECONOMICS**   Create a table with two columns. In the first column, list the four market structures. In the second column, list 5 to 10 goods or services that would be available in each of the different market structures.

Teamwork

Working in a team, brainstorm a list of businesses in your state and your local area. Discuss with your teammates the type of market structure in which you think each business operates. Give reasons for your choices. Share your list with your classmates.

Effective Presentation Skills

Much of your communication as a business owner will be conducted verbally. You may have to make a presentation to sell your business idea to potential investors, or you may have to make a presentation to convince potential customers to purchase your product or service. How you present yourself will have a big impact on the people with whom you deal.

When preparing a presentation, you should be concise, but give adequate information to cover the topic being presented. An effective presentation has three parts.

1. **Introduction** You should begin your presentation with an attention-getting opener that introduces your topic. Asking a question or using a famous quote is a good way to get your audience focused on the topic.

2. **Body of Presentation** Try to limit your presentation to three main points. It is often helpful to provide a visual aid that lists your key points. Do not overwhelm your audience with too much detail. Use facts and other supporting information to reinforce your main points. Keep the presentation simple and avoid using complicated language.

3. **Conclusion** After presenting your main points, summarize what you have told your audience in a brief conclusion.

Try It Out

To practice your presentation skills, research an entrepreneur who you believe has been a change agent. Prepare an effective presentation for the class explaining the impact this entrepreneur has had on other people's lives.

©Media Bakery13, 2010/ Used under license from Shutterstock.com

SUMMARY

2.1 Entrepreneurs Satisfy Needs and Wants

1. Economics is about making choices and satisfying the needs and wants of consumers. Needs are things you must have to survive. Wants are things you think you must have to be satisfied.
2. Three kinds of economic resources are used by entrepreneurs to produce goods and services—natural resources, human resources, and capital resources.
3. Entrepreneurs play an important role in the U.S. economy. They supply goods and services, provide capital investment and job creation, and serve as agents for change.

2.2 How Economic Decisions Are Made

4. In a command economy, the government determines what, how, and for whom products and services are produced. In a market economy, individuals decide what, how, and for whom products and services are produced. A mixed economy combines elements of the command and market economies. Traditional economies are simple economies operated according to tradition or custom.
5. The U.S. economic system is based on the principles of private property, freedom of choice, profit, and competition.
6. Economic choices are necessary because of our unlimited desires and the scarcity of resources available to satisfy them. Every economic decision incurs an opportunity cost.
7. The functions of business are production, marketing, management, and finance. Each function is dependent on the others.

2.3 What Affects Price?

8. Supply is the quantity of a good or service a producer is willing to produce at different prices. Demand is the quantity of a good or service that consumers are willing to buy at a given price.
9. Fixed costs remain the same regardless of how much of a good or service is produced while variable costs go up and down depending on the level of production.
10. Market structure is determined by the nature and degree of competition among businesses that operate in the same industry. The four major market structures are perfect competition, monopolistic competition, oligopoly, and monopoly.

what do you know now?

Read *Ideas in Action* on page 37 again. Then answer the questions a second time. Have your responses changed? If so, how have they changed?

VOCABULARY BUILDER

Match each statement with the term that best defines it. Some terms may not be used.

1. Things that you think you must have in order to be satisfied
2. The means through which goods and services are produced
3. Occurs when people's needs and wants are unlimited and resources are limited
4. The process of choosing which wants you will satisfy using the resources you have
5. The value of the next-best alternative—the one you must pass up
6. The point at which supply and demand meet
7. Measures the advantages of producing one additional unit of a good or service
8. Private ownership of resources by individuals
9. The quantity of a good or service consumers will buy at a given price
10. Costs that go up and down depending on the quantity of the good or service produced

a. capitalism
b. demand
c. economic decision making
d. economic resources
e. economies of scale
f. equilibrium price and quantity
g. fixed costs
h. marginal benefit
i. marginal cost
j. needs
k. opportunity cost
l. profit
m. scarcity
n. supply
o. variable costs
p. wants

REVIEW YOUR KNOWLEDGE

11. An example of a noneconomic want is
    a. clothing
    b. housing
    c. friendship
    d. cars
12. Which of the following is *not* an example of a service?
    a. lawn care
    b. car wash
    c. bicycle
    d. cable TV installation
13. If a product has inelastic demand, a price increase will cause
    a. consumers to buy more
    b. competitors to enter the market
    c. consumers to buy less
    d. little or no change in the demand for the item
14. What are the three basic economic questions countries must answer?
15. What determines the type of economic system a country has?
    a. the political beliefs of the country's ruler
    b. the way the basic economic questions are answered
    c. the resources of the country
    d. the demands of the people
16. Which of the following is *not* a role of entrepreneurs in the U.S. economy?
    a. supply goods and services to meet consumer needs and wants
    b. provide capital investment and job creation
    c. determine how to allocate natural resources
    d. serve as agents for change
17. Another name for economic resources is
    a. factors of production
    b. goods and services
    c. supply and demand
    d. command economy

18. The four basic principles of the U.S. economic system are
    a. private property, freedom of choice, loss, competition
    b. taxed property, freedom of choice, profit, competition
    c. private property, freedom of choice, profit, competition
    d. private property, limited choice, profit, competition
19. Which of the following is *not* a function of business?
    a. production
    b. marketing
    c. job creation
    d. finance
20. If you were going to start a small cake decorating business, which type of market structure would you most likely be entering?
    a. perfect competition
    b. monopolistic competition
    c. oligopoly
    d. monopoly
21. The Ford Motor Company operates in which type of market structure?
    a. perfect competition
    b. monopolistic competition
    c. oligopoly
    d. monopoly

APPLY WHAT YOU LEARNED

22. You plan to start a grocery delivery service. Analyze the possible demand for such a service by brainstorming answers to the following questions: Who is likely to use this service? Besides delivering groceries, what other services could such a business offer? What other questions should you consider?

23. Susan Tran of Nails by Susan wants to increase her sales. Susan considers keeping the nail salon open two extra hours every day. She estimates that during the last two hours of every day, she and her staff could provide nail services to five more customers, bringing in additional revenues averaging $125 a night. Susan estimates that providing the services to five more customers each night would cost approximately $25 in supplies. Her operating expenses for electricity and water will increase by approximately $20 per night. She would also have to pay two employees to work the extra two hours at a cost of $30 each. What is the marginal benefit of staying open an extra two hours a day? What is the marginal cost? Do you think Nails by Susan should stay open two extra hours each day?

MAKE ACADEMIC CONNECTIONS

24. **MATH** You have a business baking and selling chocolate chip cookies. Access www.cengage.com/school/entrepreneurship/ideas. Click on *Activities* and open the file *Business Costs*. Print a copy and complete the activity. What are the costs of doing business? Are these fixed costs or variable costs?

25. **COMMUNICATION**   Marketing plays an important role as one of the functions of business. Research and write a report explaining how each of the other functions—production, management, and finance—depends on the marketing function. Present your report to the class.

26. **ECONOMICS**   Identify and research economies in the process of converting from a command to a market economy. What events led to this change? What involvement, if any, do U.S. companies have in these countries' economies? Discuss your findings with the class.

What Would YOU Do?

You and a partner own a home security business, which sells a variety of home security devices, such as surveillance systems, alarms, and motion detector lighting systems, among others. A senior citizen comes to your store to get some information about the types of security systems your company offers. Your partner asks the elderly customer for some basic information, such as where she lives. Using this information, your partner tries to falsely convince the customer that she lives in a crime-ridden neighborhood and, thus, needs several different security devices to ensure her safety. The customer is ready to sign a contract for the purchase of a very expensive home security package. Suddenly, your partner is called away to take a phone call and asks you to finish helping the customer. You overheard the entire discussion between your partner and the customer, and you don't believe she needs such an extensive home security system. Business is slow due to a downturn in the economy, and you need all the sales you can get. What will you do?

build your BUSINESS PLAN PROJECT

Based on the business idea you identified in Chapter 1, complete the following activities.

1. Access www.cengage.com/school/entrepreneurship/ideas. Click on *Activities* and open the file *Supply and Demand*. Print a copy and complete the activity for at least one good or service your business will provide. Then use the graph to determine the price to charge for that good or service.

2. Determine the fixed and variable costs for your business. Estimate how much money you will need to cover these costs. Make a chart showing these expenses. Do you need to adjust your pricing for your business to make a profit?

3. Consider adding another product or service to your business. What are the marginal costs and benefits of adding this new product or service? Is it a good or bad idea to add the item?

Planning a Career in PROPERTY MANAGEMENT

Business Management & Administration

"Our softball coach threw an end-of-season party for team members and their families at the pool in his neighborhood. A pool, playground, tennis courts, and clubhouse are shared and maintained by the community. He said that although the community elected a board of residents to plan for the community, the day-to-day maintenance of the community was handled by a property management company."

Who changes the light bulbs in the common areas of private communities? How is the landscaping of common areas managed in private communities? Who takes care of routine maintenance at retail sites?

Property management companies assist a variety of businesses by managing their daily operations. Retail locations, office parks, and residential communities use their services.

Employment Outlook
- Average job growth is expected.
- Almost half of property managers are self-employed.
- As new home developments form neighborhood associations to manage common areas, the need for property managers should increase.

Job Titles
- Assistant Facility Manager
- Commercial Property Assistant
- Occupancy Specialist
- Homeowners Association Field Manager
- Community Association Manager
- Portfolio Manager—Property Management

Needed Education/Skills
- A Bachelor's degree is recommended.
- Strong financial, problem-solving, and multitasking skills are required.
- A background in real estate or facilities management is helpful.

What's it like to work in Property Management? Ari, the owner of a property management company, is posting the minutes of a neighborhood's annual meeting on the neighborhood's website. Website maintenance is just one of the many services provided by Ari's company.

Ari's next task is to analyze landscaping bids for a condominium community he is managing. He will prepare a report on the three most competitive bids and present them to the condominium's board at the monthly meeting. In addition to providing a financial summary of the bids, Ari will also provide information regarding the reliability of the various landscaping companies. Because he manages several communities, Ari is able to obtain feedback on the effectiveness of a variety of landscaping companies.

After lunch, Ari reviews the time cards for the lifeguards at a neighborhood community pool. Because the neighborhood lacks the resources to manage employees, it pays Ari's firm to handle the contract for the community's lifeguards.

What about you? Would you like to manage the daily operations of communities to help them run smoothly?

Emerging Business Issues Event

The Emerging Business Issues Event provides FBLA members with an opportunity to develop and demonstrate skills in researching and presenting an emerging business issue. The event is based on team rather than individual participation. In addition to learning research skills, team participants develop speaking ability and poise through oral presentations.

Each year a national topic is selected by FBLA-PBL Inc. You can find the current topic on the FBLA website. Teams must research the topic and present an affirmative or negative argument, based upon random selection. Facts and working data should be secured from reliable sources.

Performance Competencies

- An understanding of the topic must be evident
- The topic should be presented in a logical manner
- All team members must contribute to the presentation
- Arguments should be persuasive and relevant to the topic
- Questions must be answered effectively

Go to the FBLA website for more detailed information.

GIVE IT A TRY

Using the current national topic for the Emerging Business Issues event, complete the following activities:

- Working with team members, research the topic and prepare to present either an affirmative or negative argument.
- Draw to determine whether you will present an affirmative or negative argument.
- Finalize your preparations in five minutes.
- You may use prepared notes during the preparation and presentation. In addition, each team member will be given two blank note cards for recording notes that can be used during the preparation and performance of the presentation. Information may be written on both sides of the note cards.
- No reference materials, visual aids, or electronic devices may be brought to or used during the preparation or presentation.
- Make the presentation to your class. The presentation should last no longer than five minutes.
- Be prepared to answer questions after your presentation.

www.fbla-pbl.org

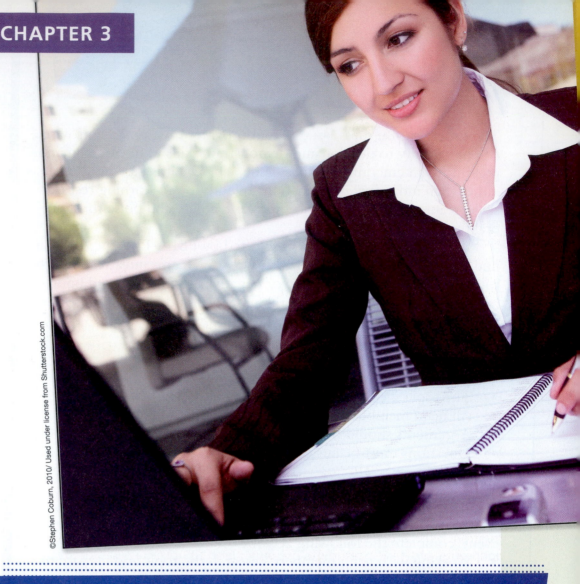

CHAPTER 3

©Stephen Coburn, 2010/ Used under license from Shutterstock.com

Develop a Business Plan

www.cengage.com/school/entrepreneurship/ideas

Turning a Summer Job into a Career

Matt Warren, owner of Warren's Landscaping

Photo courtesy of Matt Warren

A successful entrepreneur starts with a solid business plan. By age 16, Matt Warren secured a bank loan, acquired a steady stream of customers, and managed several employees. Matt quickly learned that writing a business plan was the key step that enabled him to grow Warren's Landscaping to where it is today.

His business started with humble beginnings. Looking to make some extra summer cash, twin brothers Matt and Justin Warren loaded up their dad's Jeep with equipment and mowed neighbors' lawns and washed windows. The brothers learned the valuable lessons of working hard and managing cash flow. After Justin left the business to pursue a different career path, Matt, a high school marketing and entrepreneurship student, crafted a business plan to turn his entrepreneurial dream into a reality. His local Milford, Ohio, DECA chapter taught Matt that gaining and retaining customers involves many factors, such as creating a good image by having clean trucks and well-dressed employees and giving back to the community. With his experience and strong ideals, Matt was able to prove to the bank that he could easily pay back a loan.

Matt keeps his DECA-instilled values of community involvement at the forefront of his business plan. He volunteers his company's services to area nonprofits, and he also returns to his former high school DECA chapter to advise young entrepreneurs. Matt says his community involvement helps Warren's Landscaping attract new customers. Warren's Landscaping has since expanded to larger, commercial projects and stonework. "The most rewarding part of the job is building and creating outdoor spaces for a customer's family gatherings. It's in my hands to make people happy, which makes me happy," says Matt. Matt's ethics and ideals helped him earn the Entrepreneur of the Year Award from the Milford-Miami Chamber of Commerce.

"Anyone interested in becoming an entrepreneur should get their feet wet in all areas of business and ask a lot of good questions," Matt advises. "Although working for yourself has its ups and downs, if you do the proper research, the rewards outnumber the challenges."

Writing and executing a business plan is an essential activity for the most successful companies. This first step helped Matt focus his vision and turn his money-making ideas into a profitable business.

1. How can you improve your chances of securing a bank loan?
2. What does Matt do to create a good public image?
3. Why is it important for business owners to give back to the community?

WHY A BUSINESS PLAN IS IMPORTANT

Goals
- Explain the purpose of writing a good business plan.
- Describe the importance of a business plan.

Vocabulary
- business plan

focus on small business

Look before you leap.

Tony worked for a local automobile dealership as a technician for over 20 years. He always received very high customer service ratings. One day, Tony decided that because he was such a good technician, he could make more money working on his own. At a local print and signage shop, he had business cards printed and a sign made that read "Tony the Technician." He quit his job at the dealership on Friday, put his sign up on Sunday, and was open for business on Monday.

Work as a Team What do you think are Tony's chances for success? Discuss what advice you would have given Tony if he had talked to you about his idea first.

Photodisc/Getty Images

Planning is the key when starting a business.

The Business Plan

Once you have settled on a business idea, it is time to start making plans for the business. A **business plan** is a written document that describes all the steps necessary for opening and operating a successful business. A business plan does the following:

- Describes what your business will produce, how you will produce it, and who will buy your product or service
- Explains who will run your business and who will supply it with goods
- States how your business will win over customers from competitors and what your business will do to keep customers
- Provides detailed financial information that shows how your business will succeed in earning a profit
- Describes plans for the future growth of your business

Writing a business plan is one of the most difficult and important things you will do as an entrepreneur. Writing a solid

Why would potential investors want to see your business plan?

business plan is critical because the plan can make or break your business. Some people may tell you that you do not really need a business plan, but potential investors or lenders will want to see evidence of a well-thought-out plan. The business plan will also serve as a guide for you as you get your business started.

Purposes of a Business Plan

If you think preparing a business plan is unnecessary, you should think about the many purposes it serves. The business plan serves three important purposes.

1. **A business plan explains the idea behind your business and spells out how your product or service will be produced and sold**. To convince banks or investors that your business idea is solid, you will need a completely new product or service or one that is better or less expensive than products or services that already exist. You will need to identify your target customer and show how your company will be able to obtain and keep customers.

2. **A business plan sets specific objectives and describes how your business expects to achieve them**. A good business plan includes sales projections for the short term (the first year), the medium term (two to five years after startup), and the long term (five years in the future). It describes what products and services will be introduced over the next five years and sets forth future business plans.

3. **A business plan describes the backgrounds and experience of the leadership team of the business**. Banks and investors make financing decisions based on how well they think a company can meet its objectives. If you provide good information on the background and experience of the leadership team of your company, the bank or investor will be more likely to provide funding for your business.

Importance of a Business Plan

Every new business must have a business plan. When comparing businesses that succeed to those that fail, there is often one important difference. Business owners that develop and follow a business plan are more likely to succeed. The business plan is important for several reasons.

1. **A business plan makes you think about all aspects of your business**. It will help you during the development and startup phases of the business. Stan Meyer began a graphic design business from his home. He spent many hours thinking about the business and thought he was ready to start it until he sat down to write his business plan. He had not made sales and profit projections. He had also not thought about the possibility that he might need to hire staff if the business grew too large for him to handle alone. Drafting a business plan helped Stan gain even more confidence in his business idea. It showed him that building a successful business based on his concept would be possible. Working on his business plan also helped Stan think through business strategies, recognize limits, and identify problems he might encounter.

2. **A business plan may help you secure financing for your business**. You may have a great idea, but very little capital to invest in your business. You may need to go to a bank to obtain a loan or find other investors to get startup money. Lenders and investors require a business plan before they will consider financing a business. A well-written business plan shows lenders and investors that you are serious about your business idea and have spent sufficient time in the planning process. The loan officer at Stan Meyer's bank was very impressed with the work that Stan had put into his business plan. The plan showed the loan officer that Stan thoroughly understood all that was involved in starting his own graphic design business. She recommended that he be approved for a loan.

How does creating a business plan help you see the "big picture"?

©Andresr, 2010/ Used under license from Shutterstock.com

3. **A business plan helps you communicate your ideas to others.** By the time you write your business plan, you will have given much thought to the business you want to establish. You will proceed believing that your business can succeed. If you communicate your ideas well on paper, you will also convince the readers that your business can succeed. It will give suppliers confidence in extending credit to your company. Stan presented his business plan to the owner of the local office supply company to help convince her to sell him a computer system on credit.

famous entrepreneur

Why do you think Walt Disney was a successful entrepreneur?

WALTER ELIAS DISNEY No one has entertained families more than The Walt Disney Company. Who has not experienced the Disney brand by seeing a movie, visiting a theme park, staying at a resort, buying merchandise, watching TV, or cheering on the Mighty Ducks of ice hockey? We have all been touched by the magic of Disney, the preeminent name in family entertainment.

As a young child, Walt Disney had an interest in art. To improve his drawing skills, he took art courses in high school, and at night, he attended the Academy of Fine Arts. The humble beginnings of his colossal corporation date back to 1923 when Walt arrived in California to peddle one of the cartoons he had made. Although the cartoon was not an initial success, Walt did not give up. He started working with his brother, Roy, in his uncle's garage. Success did not come quickly to the Disney brothers, but Walt's faith in himself and others helped him to succeed.

Mickey Mouse was created in 1928. Mickey made his screen debut in the world's first fully synchronized sound cartoon, *Steamboat Willie*. In the midst of the Great Depression of the 1930s, Disney took great risk and invested a then-unheard-of amount of $1.5 million to produce the first full-length animated musical feature, *Snow White and the Seven Dwarfs*. The film is still considered one of the great feats and imperishable monuments of the motion picture industry. The string of successful films that followed allowed Disney to begin construction on Disney's Burbank studio, and the staff grew to more than 1,000 artists, animators, story men, and technicians.

Disney began television production in 1954 and was among the first to present full-color programming with his *Wonderful World of Color* in 1961. Disney opened the first of many theme parks in 1955. The Disney Corporation continues with innovation and success today. Through perseverance and an entrepreneurial spirit, Walt's dreams and the dreams of millions of others have come true!

THINK CRITICALLY

Do you think success comes quickly for most entrepreneurs? What do you think Walt Disney's first business plan included as his vision for the company?

4. **A business plan can serve as a tool for managing your business.** Once your business is up and running, you can use the business plan in your decision making. Stan Meyer regularly uses his business plan to help him manage his company. Stan's plan laid out his vision of how the company would grow over time. By following the strategies in his plan, he has increased sales by offering innovative designs and reaching new clients.

 **CHECKPOINT**

Why is a business plan important to an entrepreneur?

3.1 ASSESSMENT

THINK ABOUT IT

1. Why do you think the quality of the business plan is so critical to an entrepreneur's success?

2. Melinda Rosati wants to purchase her uncle's barber shop. Because it is an ongoing business, Melinda doesn't think she needs to write a business plan. Do you agree or disagree with Melinda's opinion? Why or why not?

3. Putting your business plan in writing helps you communicate your ideas to others. Do you think discussing your business plan aloud with others can also help get your ideas across to them? Why or why not?

MAKE ACADEMIC CONNECTIONS

4. **MANAGEMENT**   André Kitaevich uses the business plan he wrote to help him run the day-to-day operations of his jewelry store. On what specific issues might André consult his plan?

5. **COMMUNICATION**   You want to start a business in the home healthcare field. Conduct online research to learn more about this field. Based on your research, write a paragraph explaining your business idea. Be sure to spell out how you plan to market your services.

Teamwork

Working in a team, choose a well-known business in operation today. Research the history of the business. Find out who started the business, why the person had the idea to start the business, and when the business was started. Prepare a presentation for your class about the history of the business.

WHAT GOES INTO A BUSINESS PLAN?

Goals

- List and describe the basic elements of a business plan.
- Describe how to pull a business plan together.

Vocabulary

- pro forma financial statement
- harvest strategy
- cover letter
- statement of purpose
- executive summary

focus on small business

Create interest in your business plan.

Having always had a strong interest in electronics and computers, Andy wanted to start a business building customized computers for business and personal use. He knew that he would need about $5,000 to get his business started. He had $2,000 in savings that he could use, but he was going to have to get a loan from family, friends, or the bank for the remaining $3,000. He sat down one night and threw together a few facts about his business and handwrote a list of items that he needed to purchase. The cost of the items on the list totaled $1,950. He showed the information he had compiled to his parents, his grandparents, his aunt and uncle, and his friend. No one was interested in making an investment in his business.

©Image Team, 2010/Used under license from Shutterstock.com

A formal business plan is the best way to share your business idea.

Work as a Team   Discuss why you think Andy could not interest anyone in making an investment in his business. How do you think a formal business plan would improve his chances of finding lenders?

Basic Elements of a Business Plan

Every new business should have a business plan, but not all business plans are alike. The content of a business plan for a small, home-based, single-owner business will differ from a business plan for a large corporation with offices in many cities. But regardless of the business, all business plans serve the same basic purposes. They should also contain the same three basic components—introductory materials, the main body, and the appendix.

The main body of the business plan will contain the bulk of the information about the business idea. It provides details on how

What kinds of information do you think investors would want to know about a new day care center?

the business will succeed. A lot of time and effort will go into writing the main body of the plan, and it should be compiled before the other components in the business plan. It should be organized into the following sections, or elements.

1. Introduction
2. Marketing
3. Financial Management
4. Operations
5. Concluding Statement

Nora Ellis and Samantha Richards are qualified child-care providers who have worked together at a day care center for many years. The center frequently has to turn away children because it does not have the room or the staff to care for more toddlers. Because of the high demand for quality day care services, Nora and Samantha know they are well positioned to meet this need. They decide to work together to create a business plan.

Introduction

The introduction section of a business plan contains many important details about the proposed business idea. The following information should be included in the introduction section.

- A detailed description of the business and its goals
- The ownership of the business and the legal structure
- The skills and experience you bring to the business
- The advantages you and your business have over your competitors

DETAILED DESCRIPTION   Something inspired the idea for your business. Describing how you came up with your idea can help lenders, investors, and others understand what your business is about. Your business plan should also outline your short-term (three months to one year), medium-term (two to five years), and long-term (more than five years) goals. Stating goals will help provide you with direction and focus for your business activities.

Nora and Samantha know their short- and medium-term goals. In the first year of business, they want to get financing that will allow them to lease or buy a facility, equip it, and staff it with eight employees. In their second and third years of business, they want to invest in more equipment and possibly expand their facility to accommodate more children. They have not yet thought through what their objectives are for the long term. Writing a business plan will force them to think about these goals, such as whether they want to remain a single day care center or expand into a regional chain of centers.

OWNERSHIP AND LEGAL STRUCTURE   In your business, you should have a section detailing your form of ownership. Will it be a sole proprietorship (one owner), a partnership (two or more owners), or a corporation (many owners that hold shares of stock in the business)? Provide information relevant to your form of business, such as who will make up your leadership team and how many shareholders you have. This section of the business plan is important because each legal form of business has an effect on how the business works and makes profits. If you use your business plan to obtain financing, the lender will be interested in this information.

SKILLS AND EXPERIENCE OF THE LEADERSHIP TEAM As the owner of the business, a written summary of your experience is an essential part of your business plan. This summary should emphasize all experience you have that relates to the business, including paid work experience, volunteer experience, and any hobbies you have that relate to your proposed business. Along with you, any other individuals that you hire to serve as managers will make up the leadership team of your business. The skills and experience of the members of your leadership team will also be relevant.

Nora and Samantha have master's degrees in early childhood education. Together, they have more than 35 years of experience in day care, including 15 years in management. To show that they are well qualified to run a center, they include copies of their resumes and letters of reference from satisfied parents.

ADVANTAGES You should list your company's advantages over the competition. These advantages may include the following:

- Performance
- Quality
- Reliability
- Distribution
- Price
- Promotion
- Public image or reputation

Marketing

The marketing section of your business plan should describe the products and/or services you will offer, the market, the industry, and your location. Developing a marketing plan will be examined in more detail in Chapter 5.

PRODUCTS/SERVICES You should describe your products and services and explain how they differ from those already on the market. Highlight any unique features, and explain the benefits customers will receive by purchasing from your business.

Nora and Samantha describe their vast experience in the day care industry. They also promote their plan for four large outdoor play structures and a state-of-the-art day care facility.

MARKET You will explain who your prospective customers are, how large the market is for your product or service, how you plan to enter that market, and how you plan to deal with competition.

Nora and Samantha's prospective customers are the parents of the 1,000 to 1,500 children between the ages of two and five who live in their area. Nora and Samantha determine that 90 percent of the families would be able to afford their center. They will advertise in local newspapers and send out fliers to their target market. They will also offer two months of care at a discounted rate for new customers.

INDUSTRY You should describe the industry in which you will operate. To find this information, you will need to perform research. Things you should include in this section are as follows:

- External factors affecting your business, such as high competition or a lack of certain suppliers
- Growth potential of the industry, including growth forecasts
- Economic trends of the industry
- Technology trends that may affect the industry

When providing information on the industry in which they will operate, Nora and Samantha include population data for their area. This information shows that demand for their service could grow over time. They also cite government sources reporting that the demand for day care services is expected to grow steadily.

LOCATION You should describe the location of your business. Lenders and investors want to know exactly where your business will be because the location of a business is often a critical factor to its success.

Nora and Samantha describe their plan to start the business in a prime location, in the heart of a suburb where most families have young children and both parents work outside the home.

Financial Management

The financial section of your business plan will help determine your financial needs. It consists of three elements.

1. **Identification of Risks** Prospective lenders and investors will want to know what risks your business faces and how you plan to deal with them. Do not be afraid to list potential problems. Lenders know that every business faces risks. They will be reassured to see that you have clearly thought through the potential problems and have a plan for dealing with them. Risks typically faced by new businesses include competitors cutting prices, costs exceeding projections, and demand for your product or service declining over time.
2. **Financial Statements** A new business must include projected financial statements in its business plan. An existing business must include current as well as projected statements. A financial statement based on projected revenues and expenses is called a **pro forma financial statement**. Each of the statements that you will need to prepare is described in Chapter 9.
3. **Funding Request and Return on Investment** You must indicate how much you need to borrow and how you plan to use the money. You should give investors an idea of how much money they can expect to earn on their investment in your business. You should state how much money you are personally investing and provide a personal financial statement. Investors will want to know who will maintain your accounting records and how they will be kept.

Nora and Samantha believe the biggest risk they face is safety. They must show concerned parents that they have addressed all safety issues that could arise on a daily basis as well as during emergencies.

Nora and Samantha have prepared a pamphlet entitled "Safety and Your Child" to use as part of their marketing package. They include a copy of this pamphlet with the business plan.

Nora and Samantha have also included pro forma financial statements for their business, which show how much money and profit they expect to earn. They require $140,000 to start their business. Together they are contributing $85,000 of their own money. This means they need a bank to loan them $55,000. They include this information in their business plan as well.

Operations

The operation of your company is critical to its success. In this section of your business plan, you should explain how the business will be

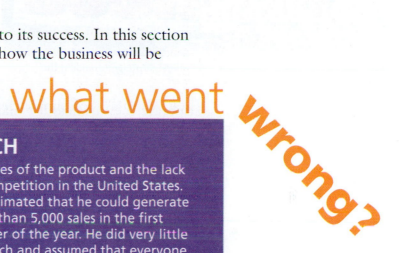

what went wrong?

CONDUCT MARKET RESEARCH

While working as a salesperson for a custom exhibit display company, Leo Hunt found a unique product not currently being marketed in the United States. It was a lightweight, portable, full-color display that could be set up and dismantled quickly. A company in Sweden was the manufacturer of this display. Leo thought it was ideal for trade shows and conventions. Leo decided to become a distributor of the special displays. He quickly prepared a business plan focusing on the unique features of the product and the lack of competition in the United States. He estimated that he could generate more than 5,000 sales in the first quarter of the year. He did very little research and assumed that everyone who exhibited at a trade show would be part of his target market. He hired 10 salespeople, placed a large order with the manufacturer, and was ready to go! Within three months, Leo had taken only 250 orders for the product, had spent 95 percent of his startup capital, and had found that many exhibitors had no need for his product. After six months, Leo had bills piling up, fewer than 500 orders, an overdrawn checking account, and some very unhappy employees. Leo decided it was best for him to close his business.

©Kutlayev Dmitry, 2010/Used under license from Shutterstock.com

Market research is critical to the success of a business.

THINK CRITICALLY

1. What mistakes did Leo make when preparing his business plan?
2. Do you think Leo should have ordered displays from the manufacturer before he had orders from customers?
3. Are there steps Leo could have taken to try to save his business?

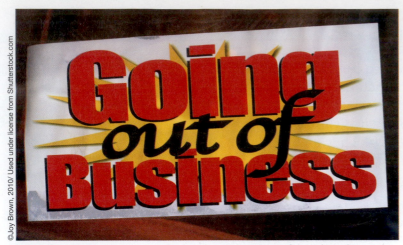

©Joy Brown, 2010/ Used under license from Shutterstock.com

Why should a business owner have a harvest strategy for ending the business?

managed on a day-to-day basis and discuss hiring and personnel procedures. You should also include information on insurance and lease or rental agreements. Describe the equipment that will be necessary for production of your products or services and how the products or services will be produced and delivered.

While planning the operations of your business, you must also think ahead and plan for ending the operations of your business. It is important to plan for this in the early stages of your business. You may plan to operate the business for many years until you retire. Or you may have a short-term plan in which you operate and grow a successful business and then sell it. In any case, you need to have a harvest strategy.

A **harvest strategy**, or exit strategy, is the way an entrepreneur intends to extract, or harvest, his or her money from a business after it is operating successfully. It details what strategy the entrepreneur has chosen and how much money he or she expects to gain. Plans for harvest could include selling the business to someone else or to another company, passing the business onto other family members, merging with another company, going public by selling shares of stock in the company to new investors, or closing the business and selling the assets such as the building and equipment. Having a harvest strategy in place gives you control over how you will end the operation of your business.

As part of the operations section of their business plan, Nora and Samantha describe hiring plans to ensure their day care center is well staffed. They also devote a section to health and safety issues. They describe procedures for dealing with allergies, illnesses, and injuries because these are common occurrences among preschool children. Currently, Nora and Samantha plan to run their business for the long term and then sell it upon retirement.

Concluding Statement

In this section, you should summarize the goals and objectives you have for your business. You should also emphasize your commitment to the success of the business.

CHECKPOINT

List the elements of the main body of a business plan and explain why each one is important.

Complete the Business Plan

After you have completed the main body of your business plan, you will need to focus your efforts on the other components—the introductory elements and the appendix. Then you must pull all the components together into a well-organized, attractive document.

Introductory Elements

Every business plan should begin with a cover letter, a title page, a table of contents, a statement of purpose, and an executive summary. These elements help set the tone for the body of your business plan.

COVER LETTER   A letter that introduces and explains an accompanying document or set of documents is called a cover letter. The cover letter for your business plan should include your name, the name of your business, and your address and telephone number. It should briefly describe your business, its potential for success, and the amount of capital you need. Nora and Samantha prepare the cover letter shown below.

THE MT. WASHINGTON

Children's

C E N T E R

5813 NORTH AVENUE, BALTIMORE, MARYLAND 21205

(410) 555-4445

April 11, 20—

Ms. Jane Stewart
Vice President
First National Bank
E. 35th Street
Baltimore, Maryland 21212

Dear Ms. Stewart

Enclosed please find a copy of the business plan for the Mt. Washington Children's Center, a proposed new day care center in northwest Baltimore that will serve approximately 50 young children. We believe that the acute shortage of high-quality day care in this part of the city will allow us to generate significant revenues for the center and that we will be earning a profit within a year of opening.

To establish the kind of center we envision, we plan to put up $85,000 of our own capital. We will need additional financing of $55,000. As you will note from our pro forma financial statements, we plan to repay the loan within five years.

Please let us know if there is any additional information you would like to receive. We look forward to hearing from you.

Sincerely yours

Nora Ellis
Nora Ellis

Samantha Richards
Samantha Richards

TITLE PAGE Your business plan should have a title page that indicates the name of your company, the date, the owner of the company, the title of the owner, and the address and phone number of the company.

TABLE OF CONTENTS A table of contents is a listing of the material included in a publication. It shows the reader what each page covers. It is similar to a table of contents in a textbook. It is important that your table of contents is accurate, so make sure the sections are listed in the proper order and the given page numbers are correct.

STATEMENT OF PURPOSE A brief explanation of why you are asking for a loan and what you plan to do with the money is called a **statement of purpose**. It should be no more than one or two paragraphs. Nora and Samantha write the statement of purpose shown here.

EXECUTIVE SUMMARY Before getting into the detail of the main body of the business plan, readers will want to read an **executive summary**, which is a short restatement of the report. It should capture the interest of its readers. If the executive summary is unconvincing, a lender may decide not to read your entire business plan. This makes a strong executive summary critical to the success of your business.

The executive summary should be no longer than one or two pages, and it should be written in a clear, simple style. Your executive summary should do all of the following:

- Describe your business concept and communicate what is unique about your idea
- Include your projections for sales, costs, and profits
- Identify your needs (inventory, land, building, equipment, etc.)
- State how much you want to borrow

Although the executive summary appears before the body of the business plan, it should be written *after* the

---

STATEMENT OF PURPOSE

The Mt. Washington Children's Center will operate as a private day care center serving approximately 50 children in northwest Baltimore. The Center will offer excellent supervision in a clean, safe, and intellectually stimulating environment.

The project is requesting $55,000 in financing. This money will be used to:

- rent and remodel 4,000 square feet of indoor space
- prepare 18,000 square feet of outdoor space for use as a playground
- purchase equipment such as swings, jungle gyms, sandboxes, and supplies
- pay salaries of eight employees until sufficient cash flow is generated to allow operating expenses to be covered

---

EXECUTIVE SUMMARY

The Mt. Washington Children's Center (MWCC) will be established as a partnership in Baltimore, Maryland. It will be owned and operated by Nora Ellis and Samantha Richards, highly respected child-care professionals with more than 35 years of experience in the field. Three experienced teachers and three teacher aides will supervise approximately 50 boys and girls between the ages of 2 and 5. In addition, a receptionist/bookkeeper and a cleaning/maintenance person will be hired.

MWCC is being established in response to the shortage of high-quality child care in northwest Baltimore. Only two small day care centers now serve a population of 45,000 upper-middle-class professionals. In 75 percent of these households, both parents work outside the home. The accessible location of the Center will make it an extremely attractive day care option for parents in the area. When completed, its facilities, which will include four large outdoor play structures and eight personal computers, will represent state-of-the-art day care. Its staff will comprise the finest day-care professionals in Baltimore, led by a management team that is recognized throughout the region.

Market research indicates that the MWCC could expect to fill 90 to 100 percent of its student positions immediately upon opening and that the center would be profitable as early as the third year of operation. Expansion could begin in the third year. To finance the startup of the company, its owners are seeking $55,000 in financing, which they would expect to repay within five years.

business plan has been completed. To write the executive summary, go through the business plan and find the most important and persuasive points you have made. Then draft an outline of an executive summary based on these points.

Once you have created a draft of your executive summary, ask people who do and do not understand your business to read the summary. If readers do not come away with a clear sense of what you plan to do and why you will succeed in doing it, your executive summary needs more work. Nora and Samantha's executive summary is shown on the previous page.

Appendix

The appendix to the business plan includes supporting documents that provide additional information and back up statements made in the body of the report. To help you determine what supporting documents to include, you should ask yourself what you would want to know about a business before you would lend it money. Documents that might be contained in the appendix include the following:

- Tax returns of the business owner for the past three years
- Personal financial statement of the owner
- Copy of proposed lease or purchase agreement for the building space
- Copy of licenses and other legal documents
- Copy of resume of the owner
- Letters of recommendation
- Copies of letters of intent from suppliers
- Copies of any large sales contracts you have already negotiated

Put It All Together

Your business plan is your best opportunity to let other people know what you want to do with your company. It gives you the chance to convince them that your idea is sound and that you have the talent and resources to make your idea a successful business venture. To make the best of this opportunity, you will want to create an attractive document that is neat, well organized, and inviting to read. Handwritten business plans are not acceptable. All business plans must be word processed and printed on standard-sized white paper. In addition, your business plan should follow a standard format and be organized as shown here.

> **OUTLINE OF BUSINESS PLAN**
> **Introductory Elements**
> - Cover Letter
> - Title Page
> - Table of Contents
> - Statement of Purpose
> - Executive Summary
>
> **Main Body**
> - Introduction
> - Marketing
> - Financial Management
> - Operations
> - Concluding Statement
>
> **Appendix of Supporting Documents**

 CHECKPOINT

> Why should you include supporting documents in your business plan?

Why are the appearance and organization of a business plan important?

3.2 ASSESSMENT

THINK ABOUT IT

1. Why is it possible to write an executive summary only after you have written the main body of your business plan? Why might the executive summary be more important than the body of the plan?

2. Why do you think it is important to include management and staffing issues in the operations section of your business plan?

3. A group of investors is planning to open a new amusement park. What supporting documents will need to be included in their business plan?

MAKE ACADEMIC CONNECTIONS

4. **MATH**   You plan to start a company. You have $67,500 in savings, but need $165,000 total to begin your business. How much money will you need from investors? What will be your percentage of ownership? If you have four outside investors, how much will each investor need to invest equally? What percentage will each investor own?

5. **COMMUNICATION**   Write short-, medium-, and long-term goals for an entrepreneur starting a new ice cream parlor.

Teamwork

Working with team members, choose a business in your local community. Make a list of the items you think this business would include in each component of its business plan—introductory elements, main body, and appendix.

HOW TO CREATE AN EFFECTIVE BUSINESS PLAN

Goals

- Describe resources available for researching your business plan.
- Name common mistakes to avoid in business planning.

Vocabulary

- Small Business Administration (SBA)
- Small Business Development Centers (SBDC)
- Service Corps of Retired Executives (SCORE)
- trade associations

focus on small business

Where do I start?

Michelle loved working with children. All of the parents in her neighborhood wanted her to babysit for them. She was always thinking up fun games to play and creative activities for the children to do. She wondered if she could do even more with these activities to earn money for college. She talked with her mother and some of the parents and came up with an idea. She would run an ice cream parlor where she could host parties and let the children make their own ice cream sundaes, play games, and watch movies. Once Michelle came up with a business idea, she knew it was time to make a detailed plan. However, she did not really know how to get started on a plan.

Photodisc/Getty Images

Your interests and hobbies can lead to a new business.

Work as a Team What kind of information do you think Michelle needs to gather? Where might Michelle find this information and whom might she talk with to learn more about starting a business?

Research the Business Plan

Your business plan needs to convince readers that you have come up with a practical business idea. To do this, you must include information and data from objective sources to show that your idea is founded on solid evidence. Researching and writing a business plan takes time. In fact, most entrepreneurs spend 50 to 100 hours developing their business plans. The process requires patience, research, thought, and a great deal of writing and editing.

Pulling together the information you will need to write your business plan involves researching all aspects of your business, from leasing space or equipment to determining what you will charge for your product or service to dealing with competitors. Researching all the parts of your business will teach you a great deal about running a business and may provide you with specific ideas for starting a company.

Community, Government, and Professional Resources

When writing a business plan, you will likely need to seek out advice from others. People from many organizations can help you with your business plan. Available resources include the SBA, the SBDC, SCORE, your local chamber of commerce, trade associations, and professional business consultants.

THE SBA The U.S. **Small Business Administration (SBA)** is an independent agency of the federal government that was created to help Americans start, build, and grow businesses. The SBA also provides aid, counsel, and assistance to protect the interests of small business concerns, to preserve free competitive enterprise, and to maintain and strengthen the overall economy of our nation.

THE SBDC The Office of **Small Business Development Centers (SBDC)** provides management assistance to current and prospective small business owners. Counselors from the SBDC provide free one-on-one assistance in developing a business plan. They also provide inexpensive workshops on topics that may help you develop your plan. SBDCs have many resources in one place to assist individuals and small businesses. SBDCs were formed as a cooperative effort of the private sector; the educational community; and federal, state, and local governments. They enhance economic development by providing small businesses with training and technical assistance. Assistance from an SBDC is available to anyone who cannot afford the services of a private consultant and who is interested in beginning a small business for the first time or improving or expanding an existing small business.

SCORE Another source of valuable assistance is SCORE. The **Service Corps of Retired Executives (SCORE)** is made up of more than 12,400 retired executives who volunteer their time to provide entrepreneurs with real-world advice and know-how. They provide free confidential advice that could be helpful to you as you prepare your business plan. You can set up a meeting with a SCORE volunteer, or you can work with a SCORE volunteer over the Internet. SCORE also offers workshops that are a valuable way to learn more about running a business and to network with other business professionals who can help you succeed. The topics of the workshops focus on important small business issues, ranging from business planning and marketing to web-based retailing. The SCORE counselors represent every business area. Some have worked as executives at Fortune 500 companies while others were small business owners themselves. SCORE can provide assistance to you for just a few sessions or for a number of years, based on your needs.

©Rob Marmion, 2010/ Used under license from Shutterstock.com

Why is it a good idea to seek the help and advice of others when writing a business plan?

CHAMBER OF COMMERCE In many communities, the local chamber of commerce offers assistance and information to entrepreneurs. It can provide information on trends affecting local businesses, local resources, and zoning and licensing information.

TRADE ASSOCIATIONS Organizations made up of professionals in a specific industry are called **trade associations**. They exist to provide information, education, and networking opportunities to individuals in their industry. These associations can be valuable sources of information to entrepreneurs.

PROFESSIONAL CONSULTANTS Some entrepreneurs hire experts to help them. Professional business consultants can be found in directories available in your library or on the Internet.

FINANCIAL INSTITUTIONS Many entrepreneurs are not familiar with the financial aspect of starting and running a business. When writing the financial section of your business plan, it may be beneficial to talk with a banker and an accountant. They can help answer your questions about loans and financial statements.

BE YOUR OWN BOSS

You want to start a plant nursery. You have taken horticulture classes in school and want to find a way to turn your acquired knowledge and love of plants into a profitable business. You start working on your business plan and realize that you need help. You decide to contact the Service Corps of Retired Executives (SCORE) for assistance.

Prepare for your first meeting with the SCORE volunteer. Write a brief summary explaining your business idea, why you want to start the business, and what you hope to accomplish by starting the business. Compile a list of questions you want to ask the SCORE volunteer.

Print Resources

Information for your business plan can come from many print resources. Your public library will have many books on entrepreneurship. In addition, books on marketing, financing, hiring and managing a staff, purchasing a business, and operating a franchise can be helpful. The library will also have books devoted specifically to writing a business plan that include sample business plans.

Magazines may also prove to be helpful—especially magazines devoted to small business ownership and to the industry in which you will be competing. Ask your librarian to help you find magazines that contain information that may be relevant to your business plan.

Government documents, including publications issued by the Small Business Administration (SBA) and other federal agencies, may provide you with useful information. The SBA district office nearest you will have many publications that can help you complete your business plan.

Online Resources

Much of the information you find in print resources is also available on the Internet. The SBA, SBDC, and SCORE websites contain much of the same information that is provided in print. Many magazine articles that deal with entrepreneurial topics can be found online. In addition, there are many sites specifically for entrepreneurs and small businesses that may give you detailed information. Web search engines can help you locate resources.

The Internet is also a good resource for finding programs that can help you prepare a business plan. A recent web search showed more than 69 million matches for "business plan software." Many entrepreneurs use these programs because they provide an easy-to-use template. By plugging your specific information into the template, you get a professional-looking finished report. If you decide to use a program to create your business plan, be sure it includes all of the essential elements. The style of the business plan you choose should be a good match for the information you want to include. And, of course, it should be one that you can use without difficulty.

Nora and Samantha found many samples of business plans on the Internet that they were able to adapt to meet their needs. Once they had an outline prepared for their business plan, they met with a counselor from their local Small Business Development Center (SBDC) to get feedback and advice for improving their business plan. The number of hours spent on research helped Nora and Samantha prepare an effective business plan.

 CHECKPOINT

What are some of the resources that are available to help you develop your business plan?

Mistakes in Business Planning

Many entrepreneurs will not take the necessary time to carefully plan their business and prepare their business plan. This can contribute to difficulties in getting their business started and may lead to business failure.

To create an effective business plan, avoid making the following common mistakes:

1. **Unrealistic Financial Projections** Many investors will go straight to the financial section of the business plan, so it is very important for the projections in this section to be realistic. Projections should be based on solid evidence for the potential growth of the company.

2. **An Undefined Target Market** You must clearly define your market and give an accurate picture of your potential customers. Explain why these customers will buy your product.

3. **Poor Research** Many potential business owners do not spend the time necessary to do good research. Use up-to-date research information and verify the facts and figures in your business plan.

Plenty of teenagers have started their own businesses, and the most successful teen entrepreneurs have prepared business plans. Access www.cengage.com/school/entrepreneurship/ideas and click on the link for Chapter 3. Read the article, "New Recording Studio at Neutral Zone Is Run by Teens but Open to All." Then answer: How did their business plan help these teens start their business? Who helped the teens prepare their business plan? What do you think would be the most difficult part of a business plan to develop? Why?

www.cengage.com/school/entrepreneurship/ideas

4. **Ignored Competition**   Do not overlook the competition and do not focus only on what the competition has done wrong. Investors want to know who your competition is and how you plan to compete in the market. Outline how you will differentiate yourself from the competition.

5. **Inconsistencies in the Business Plan**   You should review your final business plan to be sure it is well written and formatted in an attractive style. Be sure that information provided is consistent from section to section. It is a good idea to have an objective person review your final plan before you show it to investors.

✓ CHECKPOINT

List some common mistakes that are made in business planning.

ASSESSMENT

THINK ABOUT IT

1. When writing a business plan, it is important to consider all of the resources available to help you. Access www.cengage.com/school/entrepreneurship/ideas. Click on *Activities* and open the file *Business Plan Resources*. Print a copy and complete the activity.

2. Some elements of the business plan require outside source information. If your business manufactures clothing, what specific sources might you need to consult?

3. Why is it important for financial projections to be as realistic and as accurate as possible when writing your business plan?

MAKE ACADEMIC CONNECTIONS

4. **TECHNOLOGY**   Using web search engines or advertisements from magazines and newspapers, research business plan outlines, resources, and templates. Choose three of these and make a list of their features and costs. Evaluate your selections and decide which one you would choose to prepare your business plan. Justify your decision.

5. **MATH**   If you intend to borrow 20 percent of the $174,500 you need to start a business, how much of your own funds are you investing?

Teamwork

Working in a team, review a business plan that you obtained from the Internet or from a company in your community. Access www.cengage.com/school/entrepreneurship/ideas. Click on *Activities* and open the file *Business Plan Review*. Print a copy and complete the activity by listing the features that you think are effective and the features that need improvement. Make suggestions for improving the business plan.

Prepare a Resume

A resume should be part of your business plan's appendix of supporting documents. Potential lenders and investors will want to know about you, the entrepreneur. Knowing about your skills, experience, and character will help them decide whether or not investing in your business is a good idea. A personal resume describes your skills and experience to help prove you have the ability to own and manage a business. Your resume should demonstrate that your background is suitable for the business you wish to start and should convey to readers your career goal, self-image, communication skills, ability to achieve results, and personal character.

A well-written resume, as shown on the next page, includes the following information:

1. Name, address, telephone number, and e-mail address
2. A statement describing your career objective
3. A list of your work experience, arranged by date with the most recent work experience listed first, and a brief description of responsibilities and accomplishments for each position
4. A description of your education and any other training programs in which you have participated

©dragon_fang, 2010/ Used under license from Shutterstock.com

5. A list of personal activities that demonstrate that you are reliable and ambitious, including community service activities, any hobbies you have that relate to your business, and any awards or honors you have received
6. The names and contact information of three references who can verify the information on your resume

When preparing your resume, try to keep it to one page in length. Be sure that it is well organized and includes only significant information that gives evidence of your abilities. Proofread your resume carefully to ensure that your spelling and grammar are 100 percent correct.

Try It Out

Review the sample resume on the next page. Access www.cengage.com/school/entrepreneurship/ideas. Click on *Activities* and open the file *Prepare a Resume*. Complete the questionnaire to help you compile your own resume for the business idea you have been working on in the *Build Your Business Plan Project*. Your resume should communicate your ability to start, run, and manage the business. Include your resume in the appendix of your business plan.

Brian Johnson

1650 Sweetwater Boulevard
Sugar Land, TX 77479
(555) 980-7117
bjohnson@Internet.com

OBJECTIVE	To start a business selling sports-related memorabilia and other sporting goods products
WORK EXPERIENCE	Sports and More, Sugar Land, TX, 20— to present Sales Clerk: Duties include assisting customers, taking inventory, placing orders, stocking shelves, and balancing cash register
EDUCATION	Sugar Land High School Will Graduate May 20— Business Preparation • Introduction to Business • Entrepreneurship • Accounting • Business Law • Sports and Entertainment Marketing
PROFESSIONAL SKILLS	Public Speaking (DECA) Microsoft Office Certification Accounting/Bookkeeping Filing Proper Telephone Etiquette
RELATED ACTIVITIES	DECA President Habitat for Humanity Volunteer Foreign Missions Project, Local Church Regular Community Service at Assisted Care Center
HONORS AND AWARDS	First Place in Texas DECA Financial Services Team Decision Making Event Honor Roll Every Year at Sugar Land High School Character Award, September, Sugar Land High School
REFERENCES	Mrs. Donna Cecil, Marketing Coordinator (555) 999-2189 Ms. Barbara Roberts, Sports and More Store Manager (555) 304-7657 Mr. Mike Murphy, Principal (555) 999-2171

SUMMARY

3.1 Why a Business Plan Is Important

1. A business plan is a written document that describes all the steps necessary for opening and operating a successful business. It explains the idea behind your business and spells out how your product or service will be produced and sold. It sets specific objectives and describes how your business will achieve them. It describes the backgrounds and experiences of the people who will be running the business.

2. Writing a business plan is important because it makes you think about all aspects of your business, helps you secure financing for your business, enables you to communicate your ideas to others, and serves as a tool for managing your business.

3.2 What Goes into a Business Plan?

3. The main body of the business plan should include the following sections: Introduction, Marketing, Financial Management, Operations, and Concluding Statement.

4. To complete the business plan, you need to prepare introductory elements consisting of the cover letter, title page, table of contents, statement of purpose, and executive summary. The executive summary is the most important element. It should not be written until the main body of the plan is complete. You also need to compile an appendix, which includes supporting documents that provide more information to the readers of the plan.

3.3 How to Create an Effective Business Plan

5. To show you have a practical business idea, you must include information and data from objective sources. People from many organizations—including the SBA, the SBDC, SCORE, your local chamber of commerce, trade associations, business consultant agencies, and financial institutions—can help you with your business plan. Print resources can be obtained at the public library and through government agencies. An extensive amount of information is also available on the Internet.

6. Common mistakes made in business planning include unrealistic financial projections, an undefined target market, poor research, ignored competition, and inconsistencies in the business plan.

what do you know now?

Read *Ideas in Action* on page 65 again. Then answer the questions a second time. Have your responses changed? If so, how have they changed?

Match each statement with the term that best defines it. Some terms may not be used.

1. A written document that describes all the steps necessary for opening and operating a successful business
2. A financial statement based on projected revenues and expenses
3. A letter that introduces and explains an accompanying document or set of documents
4. A short restatement of a report
5. A brief explanation of why you are asking for a loan and what you plan to do with the money
6. An independent agency of the federal government created to help Americans start, build, and grow businesses
7. An entrepreneur's plan for extracting his or her money out of the business after it has become successful
8. Organization made up of retired executives who volunteer their time to provide entrepreneurs with real-world advice and know-how

a. business plan
b. cover letter
c. executive summary
d. harvest strategy
e. pro forma financial statement
f. Service Corps of Retired Executives (SCORE)
g. Small Business Administration (SBA)
h. Small Business Development Centers (SBDC)
i. statement of purpose
j. trade associations

REVIEW YOUR KNOWLEDGE

9. A business plan is *not* intended for
   a. your competition
   b. potential investors
   c. your bank
   d. any of the above
10. Purposes of a business plan include which of the following?
    a. it explains your idea for a product or service
    b. it sets specific objectives and describes how they will be achieved
    c. it describes the backgrounds and experiences of the people who will run the business
    d. all of the above
11. A business plan is important for a new business for all of the following reasons *except*
    a. it makes you think about all aspects of your business
    b. it can help you communicate your ideas to others
    c. it guarantees you will get financing for your business
    d. it can serve as a tool for managing your business
12. The main body of a business plan includes which of the following?
    a. executive summary
    b. statement of purpose
    c. financial management
    d. supporting documents
13. Which of the following is *not* a true statement regarding risks?
    a. Identifying the possible risks your business faces will alarm lenders and investors and cause them to withhold funds.
    b. Potential investors and lenders want to know the risks your business faces and how you plan to deal with them.
    c. Lenders will appreciate the fact that you know the risks you face and have a plan for dealing with them.
    d. Lenders know that every business faces risks.

14. The purpose of including supporting documents in a business plan is to
    a. make the plan lengthy
    b. provide additional information
    c. give the readers more information than they might need
    d. explain your business idea
15. Writing a business plan
    a. is a quick and easy process
    b. is quick but difficult
    c. requires patience, research, thought, and time
    d. none of the above
16. Which of the following organizations can provide assistance when writing your business plan?
    a. bank
    b. chamber of commerce
    c. Small Business Development Center
    d. all of the above
17. Organizations made up of professionals in a specific industry are called
    a. entrepreneurs   c. trade shows
    b. trade associations   d. SBDCs
18. Mistakes to avoid when preparing a business plan include all *except*
    a. providing unrealistic financial projections
    b. wasting time on research
    c. ignoring the competition
    d. failing to define the target market

APPLY WHAT YOU LEARNED

19. Obtain a sample business plan. Review the business plan and discuss whether or not the five common mistakes in writing a business plan were avoided. Provide reasons to support your decisions.
20. You plan to open a skateboarding park. What kind of research should you do? What sources will you consult for your research?

MAKE ACADEMIC CONNECTIONS

21. **COMMUNICATION**   You are preparing a business plan for a self-storage facility (U-Store-It). You are requesting a $75,000 loan to buy the property and storage lockers. Write the cover letter to the bank loan officer and a statement of purpose.

22. **RESEARCH**   Choose a business with which you are familiar. Access www.cengage.com/school/entrepreneurship/ideas. Click on *Activities* and open the file *Trade Association Research*. Print a copy and complete the activity by using the Internet to research trade associations that could provide useful information to the business.
23. **COMMUNICATION**   Think about a business you would like to start. Assume you will need a startup loan. With a partner, role-play a meeting between you and the loan officer. Based on your role-play experience, write a short report describing the do's and don'ts of requesting a loan.

What Would YOU Do?

You have a great idea for a business you want to start. Because you are going to school full time and work nights and weekends, you really do not have the necessary time to spend preparing a business plan. However, you know you need a business plan to help you secure a loan to get the business started.

While searching the Internet, you find a business plan for a company that is very similar to the one you want to start. It would save you time if you copied this plan, changed the business name, and added your personal information. What would you do? What problems might this cause?

build your
BUSINESS PLAN PROJECT

This activity will help you get started on the development of a business plan for your business idea.

1. Describe how you came up with the idea for your business project. Explain why there is a market/need for your product or service. Interview five or more people about your product or service. How many of them would buy it? Did any of them make suggestions? Prepare a one-page report that fully describes your product or service and how it differs from what is currently available.

2. List your short-, medium-, and long-term goals. What steps do you need to take to achieve each of these goals? Do you foresee any obstacles in attaining them? If so, describe them and explain how you will overcome them?

3. Contact the SBA, the SBDC, or SCORE and ask for information about your type of business. Use this information to write a paragraph about the industry in which you will be competing. What are the economic, technological, or growth trends in this industry? Is the location of your business a critical factor in its success? Why or why not?

4. Begin the financial section of your business plan by writing a report that identifies the risks your business faces. Explain how you will overcome each risk. Provide examples from magazine articles about businesspeople in your field who have succeeded when faced with similar problems.

5. Present all of the information you have compiled to your teacher or representatives from your local business community. Explain why you made the choices you did. Be prepared to defend your choices.

"We got a great deal on our house. Not only was the lawn in chaos, but there was also a problem with storm water run-off. My stepdad hired a landscape architect to re-route the storm water to comply with local regulations. Now our yard looks healthy and inviting. The city and our downhill neighbors are all quite pleased with the improved storm water routing."

Who balances the environmental, regulatory, and aesthetic outdoor needs of new developments? Who figures out how to make the external part of commercial properties look more welcoming?

Landscape architects help cities, businesses, and residential locations meet ecological, land use, regulatory, and aesthetic needs of outdoor areas.

Employment Outlook
- Faster than average job growth is anticipated.
- About one-quarter of landscape architects are self-employed.
- New construction and an increasing need to meet environmental regulations will increase demand for qualified employees.

Job Titles
- Landscape Consultant
- Open Space Planner
- Residential Landscape Architect
- Project Designer
- Historical Landscape Architect

Needed Education/Skills
- A Bachelor's degree is recommended; some positions require a Master's degree.
- Most states require licensing based on the Landscape Architect Registration Examination.
- An appreciation of nature, a creative vision, and strong analytical and communication skills are needed.

What's it like to work in Landscape Architecture? Givon, a self-employed landscape architecture consultant, has just gotten off the phone with a client. The 300-home community planned by the client requires a community park, beautified entrances, attractive boulevards, and compliance with city zoning regulations.

To develop a bid for this project, Givon needs to meet with the developer's architects, visit the site, and meet with city officials regarding legal requirements. The final bid will include a completion timeline and sketches reflecting the appearance of the neighborhood.

After lunch, Givon meets with his city's urban renewal team. The city is renovating a blighted residential area. Givon's input is needed to develop a landscaping plan that will optimize the use of a small amount of land set aside for landscaping.

After dinner, Givon prepares for his meeting tomorrow morning with a retail developer. Givon's recommendations for the retail parking lot design include planting many trees and shrubs throughout the parking lot. This greenery not only improves the aesthetics of the parking lot, but it also helps lessen "heat buildup," which is a common problem during hot summer weather.

What about you? Would you like to help develop landscaping plans that have a long-term beautifying effect on communities and businesses?

Prepared Speech

Effective speaking skills are essential to success for entrepreneurs. As an entrepreneur you will be speaking to investors, customers, and suppliers. The Prepared Speech event lets you demonstrate your communication skills in securing, arranging, organizing, and presenting information orally.

Contestants should select a topic related to business, entrepreneurship, or Business Professionals of America and develop an oral presentation of no less than five and no more than seven minutes. This event emphasizes a scholarly approach to securing information and places emphasis on content and research. Facts and working data may be secured from any source. State and federal copyright laws must be followed in the preparation of the speech.

Each contestant must do his or her own work in researching and preparing the speech. The contestant should consider the purpose of the speech, such as to inform, to educate, to motivate, or to persuade. Contestants should also keep in mind the three basic elements of an effective speech and presentation. These three basic elements include the introduction, the body, and the conclusion. Refer to the *Sharpen Your 21st Century Entrepreneurial Skills* feature in Chapter 2 for more detailed information about each of these three elements. During the speech, the contestant should be enthusiastic and use proper grammar.

The speech will be given in front of a panel of judges and a timekeeper. Contestants will be given one minute to set up for their speech. A flip chart, posters, and/or props may be used during the speech.

Performance Indicators

- Demonstrate effective communication skills
- Demonstrate skills in developing a speech using the three basic elements
- Utilize nonverbal gestures as needed
- Apply speaking techniques using appropriate tempo and pitch
- Secure facts and data from multiple sources, emphasizing research skills

Go to the BPA website for more detailed information.

THINK CRITICALLY

1. How can good speaking skills benefit an entrepreneur?
2. Why is research important when preparing a speech?
3. Why should you follow copyright laws when preparing a speech?
4. How do the three elements of a speech contribute to its effectiveness?

www.bpa.org

CHAPTER 4

Identify and Meet a Market Need

4.1 Identify Your Market

4.2 Research the Market

4.3 Know Your Competition

www.cengage.com/school/entrepreneurship/ideas

Find Your Target Market

Ben Cathers started his first business, an online advertising and marketing firm, when he was 12 years old. Seven years and two business ventures later, Ben secured a book deal. To what does the now 25-year-old owe his early success? Researching and fully understanding his target market—teenagers.

Ben Cathers, author of Conversations with Teen Entrepreneurs

Like many teens, Ben passed downtime playing video games and spending time on the computer. His interest in computers led to his first money-making plan of building and hosting websites. Ben spoke to business owners and did ample research to learn how to make money through web advertising. This first business taught Ben many lessons of entrepreneurship, much of which he shared in his book.

Ben's book, *Conversations with Teen Entrepreneurs*, came about after years of speaking with fellow teens while doing research for his startups. The book covers many topics but focuses on teens starting businesses and the hardships and successes that go along with entrepreneurship. He urges teen entrepreneurs to get out and talk to as many people as possible. Ben also recommends new entrepreneurs target their own age market. "It is easier to recognize needs when you are living in that market, and if you don't have an understanding of the market, how can you convince a client you know what you are doing?" Ben said.

After Ben graduated from Boston University School of Management, he moved to New York City to be a social media consultant and to create his fourth startup business. Ben also writes a blog covering entrepreneurship, social media, and a multitude of other topics. He said blogging is a cheap forum for teens wanting to start a business or land a new job. When meeting with potential clients or a future employer, teens can reference blog posts that could give them a leg up.

Ben writes his blog because he has a passion for business and entrepreneurship. Ben encourages teens to start businesses early because even small failures can be beneficial. He believes these failures are great learning experiences for teens because it is easier to bounce back and start over when there are fewer financial obligations to worry about. Ben also advises that while entrepreneurship offers many freedoms, it often means working long hours. Passion and drive are necessary to succeed.

1. Why is it important to research your target market before starting a business?
2. How can teen entrepreneurs use social media and networking to their advantage?
3. Why is passion such an important trait for successful entrepreneurs to have?

what do you know?

IDENTIFY YOUR MARKET

Goals

- Identify a target market by analyzing the needs of customers.
- Explain how market segmentation can help an entrepreneur analyze a target market.

Vocabulary

- target market
- market segments
- customer profile
- demographics
- psychographics
- use-based data
- geographic data

focus
on small business

Who is your customer?

Roseanne and John had their own restaurant in Los Angeles, California, when their daughter was born. Deciding that they wanted a different lifestyle for their family, they began to think about relocating and starting a new restaurant in a small-town setting. They talked about the kind of restaurant they wanted to open. They decided that they would target middle- to upper-middle-class families who had a love for good food, were willing to drive up to 30 miles to get it, and were willing to pay $10 to $15 per meal.

Work as a Team Roseanne and John put a great amount of thought into the type of customer they wanted to attract before they began to look for a location. Why is this important?

Photodisc/Getty Images

Think about the type of customer you want to attract.

Target Market

Entrepreneurs with exciting new ideas are sometimes so focused on their products or services that they forget about the customer. Coming up with a good idea for a business is not enough to guarantee success. Customers are the people or organizations who buy the products and services companies offer. Before establishing your new enterprise, you will have to determine who your primary customers are and whether these customers will be willing to buy your product or service. Market research is the key to finding out this information. Understanding people's wants and needs will allow you to identify business opportunities. The more you know about your customers, the better you will be at giving them what they need and want.

As an entrepreneur, you will need to estimate demand for your products or services by identifying your target customers. The **target market** includes the individuals or companies that are interested in a particular product or service and are willing and able to pay for it. Identifying your target market helps you reach the people who desire your products and services. Target customers are the customers you would most like to attract. A car dealer selling moderately priced minivans would target middle-class families with children. A car dealer offering expensive sports cars might target single people with higher incomes.

DEVELOP YOUR READING SKILLS

As you read this chapter, develop questions for each section that you can use as a study guide for the chapter.

Identify Your Target Market

To identify the target market for your product or service, you will need to answer the following questions:

1. Who is my potential market? Are my customers individuals or companies?
2. If my customers are individuals, how old are they? How much money do they earn? Where do they live? How do they spend their time and money?
3. If my customers are companies, what industries are they in? Where are those industries located?
4. What needs or wants will my product or service satisfy?
5. How many potential customers live in the area in which I want to operate?
6. What is the demand for my products or services?
7. Where do these potential customers currently buy the products or services I want to sell them?
8. What price are they willing to pay for my products or services?
9. What can I do for my customers that other companies are not already doing for them?

Why should a clothing store identify its target customers?

As an entrepreneur, you should put yourself in your customers' shoes before you start your business. Afterwards, you should think about your customers' needs and viewpoints every day. By continually evaluating your market, you will be ready to respond to changes in communities, consumer tastes and buying habits, and competitors' offerings.

 CHECKPOINT

What questions should you ask when identifying your target market?

Market Segments

Groups of customers within a large market who share common characteristics are known as <u>market segments</u>. Market research can be used by a business to identify market segments. Segmenting, or dividing your target market into several small groups, can help you develop a product or service that will meet specific customer needs and wants.

The process of market segmentation is important because most products and services appeal to only a small portion of the population. The leisure services market is a large market that includes many segments, such as outdoor adventurers, people who vacation frequently, couples who eat at restaurants, and more. Targeting the entire leisure market would not make sense. You would never be able to meet the needs of the entire market. Even the restaurant segment of the leisure services market has sub-segments. Some people eat fast food on a regular basis while others like a sit-down meal at a nice restaurant. Some people like Italian food while others prefer seafood or Chinese food.

Businesses can make decisions based on the information gathered about market segments. However, if the data are not analyzed correctly, the product may not meet the needs of the customers, or the business might ignore a segment of the market that would be very interested in the product.

SAMPLE CUSTOMER PROFILE FOR A SPORTING GOODS STORE

- Individual 23 to 52 years of age
- Participates in sports
- Wants good-quality sports equipment
- Looks for good prices
- Lives in city of Blanchester
- Average household income: $42,000 per year

Customer Profile

A market segment is made up of people with common characteristics. The more you learn about them, the better strategy you can develop for reaching them. A very useful part of analyzing your data is the creation of a customer profile. A <u>customer profile</u> is a description of the characteristics of the person or company that is likely to purchase a product or service. A customer profile can help you understand what you need to do to meet customer demand. Customers may be profiled based on many types of data, including demographics, psychographics, use-based data, and geographic data.

By analyzing these types of data, you will be able to develop a marketing strategy that identifies those customers you can serve more effectively than your competitors can. The data can help you determine the size of your market and how many people would be willing and able to purchase your product or service. You can design your products and services, set prices, and direct promotional efforts toward those customers.

DEMOGRAPHICS Data that describe a group of people in terms of age, marital status, family size, ethnicity, gender, profession, education, and income are called <u>demographics</u>. Women business owners between the ages of 25 and 40 who earn at least $50,000 per year would be an example of a market segment based on demographic data.

PSYCHOGRAPHICS   Data that describe a group of people in terms of their tastes, opinions, personality traits, and lifestyle habits are called **psychographics**. People who prefer to live in a downtown setting and whose musical preference is jazz would be an example of a market segment based on psychographic data.

USE-BASED DATA   Data that help you determine how often potential customers use a particular service are called **use-based data**. If you were starting a travel agency, you would want to know how often your potential customers travel.

GEOGRAPHIC DATA   Data that help you determine where your potential customers live and how far they will travel to do business with you are called **geographic data**. If you were thinking of opening a coffee shop, it would be important for you to know that people are not willing to drive more than one mile for coffee.

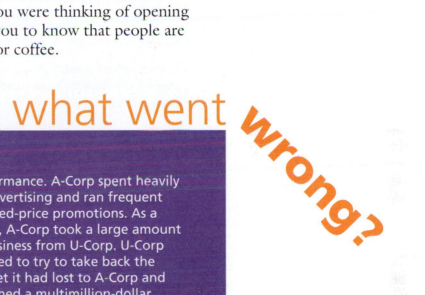

what went wrong?

PRICE WAR

U-Corp was the first company in the computer industry to offer removable hard disk drives for personal computers. For years, U-Corp had a unique position in the industry and had little direct competition. Eventually, the company was making $300 million in annual revenue.

U-Corp's first competition came from A-Corp, which offered a product similar in price and performance. A-Corp spent heavily on advertising and ran frequent reduced-price promotions. As a result, A-Corp took a large amount of business from U-Corp. U-Corp decided to try to take back the market it had lost to A-Corp and launched a multimillion-dollar marketing campaign aimed at its target market.

The two companies went head to head, selling disk drives at lower and lower prices. However, consumers do not generally need to buy multiple hard drives because of their large storage capacity. Only one company could win, and it was A-Corp. In less than two years, U-Corp suffered losses, and A-Corp bought it out.

Consider other strategies before engaging in a price war.

Photodisc/Getty Images

THINK CRITICALLY

1. What was U-Corp's major disadvantage in competing with A-Corp?
2. What did each company fail to realize about its customers?
3. How might the price war for removable hard drives have been avoided?

 **CHECKPOINT**

Name four types of customer data that may be analyzed in developing a customer profile.

 4.1 ASSESSMENT

THINK ABOUT IT

1. Why is it so important to identify your target market?

2. How are market segments useful to an entrepreneur?

3. You are thinking about offering golf lessons in your town. What types of data (demographics, psychographics, use-based, or geographic) would you collect to create a customer profile?

MAKE ACADEMIC CONNECTIONS

4. **MATH** Marcel wants to open a car wash after graduating from high school. For several days, he observed the cars being washed at a local car wash and recorded the information below.

Day 1	Day 2	Day 3	Day 4	Day 5	Day 6
50 cars	45 cars	48 cars	26 cars	47 cars	55 cars

What is the average number of cars washed each day? If the car wash were open only five days a week, how many cars might be washed per year? (Hint: There are 52 weeks in a year.)

5. **GEOGRAPHY** Think of a business you would like to open. Obtain a map of the area where you would like to locate the business. Mark the areas on the map that represent the farthest distance you believe customers would be willing to travel to do business with you. Draw a circle that encompasses the points where your customers live.

6. **COMMUNICATION** Interview a business owner. Ask the owner the nine questions listed in the lesson about identifying a business's target market. Write a report based on what you find out about the owner's target market.

7. **MARKETING** Think about a television station or network that has a particular focus (example: the Food Network or the History Channel). Identify several characteristics of a market segment that enjoys the shows broadcast on the station or network. Use the characteristics to create a customer profile for the television network.

Teamwork

Working with team members, look through magazines and newspapers for an advertisement of a new product. Based on the type of publication and the material contained in the advertisement, answer the nine questions listed in the lesson about identifying a target market. Can you determine who the target market is for the product?

RESEARCH THE MARKET

Goals

- Explain the role of market research.
- Identify the six steps involved in market research.
- Explain the role technology plays in marketing research.

Vocabulary

- market research
- primary data
- survey
- focus group
- secondary data
- customer relationship management

focus on small business

Get to know your market.

Roseanne and John decided that they would like to locate their business in South Carolina close to the areas where they grew up. They knew that it would be important for them to research the market in that area to be sure that there was a market for the type of restaurant they wanted to open. They decided to interview groups of potential customers to gather their thoughts and opinions. They also developed a survey and hired some local high school students to call residents in the community to collect more data. Finally, they explored how they could utilize technology to conduct market research.

©konstantynov, 2010/Used under license from Shutterstock.com

Interviews are just one way to gather market research.

Work as a Team Do you think that Roseanne and John are using good methods to gather data? Can you suggest any other ways they can find out what their potential customers think about the business idea?

Role of Market Research

For your business to succeed, you need to identify potential markets, analyze demand, and determine how much customers are willing to pay for your products or services. To collect this information, you will perform market research. **Market research** is a system for collecting, recording, and analyzing information about customers, competitors, products, and services. Based on the findings of market research, a business will be able to determine which marketing strategies will be most effective and most profitable. Spreadsheets and databases are used for collecting and analyzing market research data. Market research has its limits because it can be very expensive and time-consuming, but it is worthwhile when major decisions must be made. You will draw on primary data and secondary data to help you identify ways in which you can meet customer needs. Market research can also help you forecast sales and make other business decisions.

Primary Data

Most market researchers collect primary data. Information collected for the very first time to fit a specific purpose is **primary data**. A researcher collects primary data to help identify and understand the target market. There are a few different ways to collect primary data.

SURVEY The most common type of primary market research is a questionnaire, or survey. A **survey** is a list of questions you would like to ask your customers to find out demographic and psychographic information. A survey can be conducted by mail, over the phone, on the Internet, or in person.

Creating a good survey is important. Surveys should be kept to a page in length when read over the phone or mailed to respondents. Longer surveys can be used if an interview is face to face. Questions should be clear and easy to answer, and only the most important questions should be asked.

famous entrepreneur

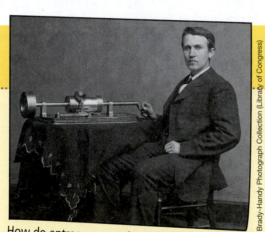
How do entrepreneurs change the way we live?

Brady-Handy Photograph Collection (Library of Congress)

THOMAS A. EDISON Could you do your homework at night if there was no light? Thanks to Thomas Edison, you can do your homework late at night! Thomas Edison is considered to be the greatest inventor in American history.

Edison showed entrepreneurial characteristics at an early age. At the age of 12, he talked his parents into letting him go to work selling newspapers, snacks, and candy on the local railroad. Then he started an entirely separate business selling fruits and vegetables.

When Edison was 14, the pre-Civil War debates between Lincoln and Douglas were taking place. He used his access to the associated news releases that were being teletyped into the railroad station each day and published them in his own newspaper. Focusing on newsworthy "scoops," he quickly had more than 300 commuters subscribing to his paper, *The Weekly Herald*.

Edison turned on the lights for all of us with his invention of the electric light bulb in 1879. As a young inventor with a curiosity about everything, he learned to invent only those things that people wanted. As one of the original founders of the General Electric Company, he tried to develop products that would work under ordinary conditions, would not easily malfunction, and could be repaired easily. Known as "The Wizard of Menlo Park," which was the home of Edison's research laboratory, Thomas Edison truly changed the world we live in!

THINK CRITICALLY
Why do you think it was important for Thomas Edison to invent items that people wanted? Do you think all inventors can become successful entrepreneurs?

OBSERVATION   Market research can also involve observation. If you are considering opening a juice bar in a shopping mall, you might want to see how many customers you could attract. You could go to the mall and count the number of people purchasing drinks at various food outlets. An entrepreneur interested in starting a motorcycle repair shop might count the number of motorcycles at a busy intersection.

FOCUS GROUPS   Another way to find out about the market is by conducting interviews with small groups of people. A **focus group** is an in-depth interview with a group of target customers who provide valuable ideas on products or services. You can ask the same kinds of questions in a focus group that you would ask in a survey, but the group setting allows for more discussion and interaction. Focus groups usually are led by a moderator, who asks questions about buying habits, likes and dislikes, and interest in particular products and services. The focus group session is recorded so that the comments can be reviewed carefully after the session.

DISADVANTAGES OF PRIMARY DATA   While primary data can provide the most up-to-date and useful information, collecting it can be time-consuming and more expensive than gathering secondary data. As an entrepreneur, you will need to determine how much primary and secondary market research data you need to collect.

Secondary Data

Entrepreneurs also research their target markets by using secondary data. **Secondary data** are found in already-published sources. Data on population, family size, household income, economic trends, industry forecasts, and other information can be found in secondary data resources. Places to find secondary data include the following:

Why is secondary data an important part of market research?

1. Publications issued by government and community organizations, such as the U.S. Census Bureau, the Small Business Administration, and the Chamber of Commerce
2. Books about specific industries
3. Information on websites for government and businesses
4. Books about other entrepreneurs who set up similar businesses
5. Trade magazines and journals
6. Newspaper articles and statistics

Kisha Nichols wanted to expand her family-owned chain of retail shoe stores. She decided to perform some secondary data research. She visited the local Chamber of Commerce website, which provided

Many retail stores collect primary data through the use of scanners. The salesperson scans the universal product code (UPC) on each item purchased. The storeowner can then determine the best- and worst-selling items and adjust inventory accordingly.

her with population demographics for her city and county and industry forecasts for local communities. This information allowed Kisha to identify the largest markets as well as any growing markets. Magazines provided information on the average income of retail shoe store owners in her state. Newspaper articles gave Kisha psychographic data on the lifestyles of people in her area. Most of them worked in professional office settings, which meant they had a need for comfortable dress shoes. The secondary data gave Kisha a good idea of which community might provide the best prospects.

CHECKPOINT

What types of data can be collected through market research?

Six Steps of Market Research

Collecting primary data can be time-consuming and expensive, but it is extremely valuable. It will tell you exactly what you want to know and uncover information you may not find through secondary sources. Conducting primary market research involves six steps.

1. Define the Question

In the first step in the market research process, you need to define exactly what you need to know. Entrepreneurs have many concerns and questions about the businesses they are planning. By determining what they need to know, they are defining the question that will be the focus of their research.

Maggie Blandin is thinking about starting a dog-walking service. Before she invests in her business, Maggie needs to determine who would be most likely to use her service (her target customers).

2. Determine the Data Needed

Once you have defined the market research question, you are ready to determine what data you need to collect to provide the answer to your question. Entrepreneurs need to be sure that the data they collect will be helpful.

It would not be helpful for Maggie to know how many families live in the area where she wants to open her business. She needs to know how many people living in the area are dog owners who lack the time to walk their dogs.

3. Collect the Data

Before you begin collecting data, you need to decide how you will go about gathering the data. Should you use a survey? Should you use an

Market Research

Step 1 Define the Question

Step 2 Determine the Data Needed

Step 3 Collect the Data

Step 4 Analyze the Data

Step 5 Take Action

Step 6 Evaluate the Results

observation method? Is a focus group appropriate? The method you use will depend on what type of information you want to gather. For example, you can find out people's opinions in a survey or focus group but not by observation. You should perform some secondary market research first to familiarize yourself with your market. Demographic and psychographic data, as well as information on economic trends and industry forecasts, will help you determine what kind of primary data research to perform. You can then choose the best research method for the information you want to gather.

If you use observation to do your research, you need to determine where and when to get the best information. If a focus group is needed, you should think about what kinds of individuals to include and what questions to ask them. If you choose a survey, think carefully about how long it should be, what questions it should include, how it should be administered, and how many people you should survey.

Maggie decides that a survey is the best way for her to find answers about customer preferences for a dog-walking service. Through her secondary data research, Maggie learned that 60 percent of the households in her area own one or more dogs and that the average annual household income is $75,000. Most households have one or more adults working in a professional field. She also found that dog ownership is on the rise in her area. Using this information, Maggie put together the survey shown on the next page, asking about the lifestyles, opinions, and choices of dog owners.

Groups of customers within a large market who share common characteristics are known as market segments. Access www.cengage.com/school/entrepreneurship/ideas and click on the link for Chapter 4. The *You Are Where You Live* feature describes every U.S. neighborhood in terms of lifestyle types. Click on the ZIP Code Look-Up tab and choose the PRIZM NE system. Enter your own ZIP code. What results did you find? In which lifestyle type (if any) do you think you and your family fit? Now choose the ConneXions system. Do the results differ from those found under the PRIZM NE system? Explain. Which system do you think more accurately describes your neighborhood?

www.cengage.com/school/entrepreneurship/ideas

4. Analyze the Data

Once you have collected all your primary and secondary data, you will need to analyze and interpret the information thoroughly. The data may be used not only to find out about your potential customers but also to forecast sales. The analysis should be in a written format so you can refer to it later.

Through her secondary data research, Maggie found that 2,500 dogs live in her area. From her primary data research, she found that 30 percent of dog owners in her area would pay $20 to have their dogs walked for 30 minutes. Many would pay to have them walked two or three times a week. Maggie determines that she could easily have 750 dogs to walk each week.

5. Take Action

Once you have analyzed and interpreted your data, you will need to determine how to use the data to make a decision. You will develop a plan of action based on the information you found in your market research.

MARKET RESEARCH SURVEY

Thank you for participating in this market research survey. We appreciate your assistance in helping us identify the needs of pet owners in our community.

PLEASE CHECK THE BOX THAT BEST DESCRIBES YOUR SITUATION.

Age: UNDER 18 ❑   19–30 ❑   31–40 ❑   41–50 ❑   51–65 ❑   OVER 65 ❑

Gender: MALE ❑   FEMALE ❑

Number of pets: 0 ❑   1 ❑   2 ❑   3 ❑   4 OR MORE ❑

Kinds of pets: DOG ❑   CAT ❑   FISH ❑   BIRD ❑   OTHER ❑ (PLEASE SPECIFY)

IF YOU OWN A DOG, PLEASE ANSWER ALL OF THE FOLLOWING QUESTIONS.

How often do you walk your dog?

EVERY DAY ❑   A FEW TIMES A WEEK ❑   ONLY ON THE WEEKENDS ❑   NEVER ❑

Would you be willing to pay someone you trusted to take your dog for walks?

YES ❑   POSSIBLY ❑   NO ❑

If you would be willing to pay someone to walk your dog, how many times a week would you utilize this service?

EVERY DAY ❑   2–3 TIMES A WEEK ❑   ONLY ON THE WEEKENDS ❑

How much would you be willing to pay to have your dog(s) walked for 30 minutes?

$10 ❑ $15 ❑ $20 ❑ $25 ❑   I WOULD NOT PAY TO HAVE MY DOG WALKED ❑

How often do you travel out of town?

ONCE A YEAR ❑   2–3 TIMES A YEAR ❑   SEVERAL TIMES A YEAR ❑   NEVER ❑

Who takes care of your dog when you are out of town?

KENNEL ❑   FRIEND ❑   NEIGHBOR ❑   OTHER ❑

Would you be interested in having someone you trust take care of your pets while you are away?

YES ❑   POSSIBLY ❑   NO ❑

Why should entrepreneurs evaluate the actions they take?

Maggie Blandin's market research has helped her conclude that her idea for a dog-walking service is profitable. From her market research, she has created a target customer profile of people aged 31 to 50 who travel often, work long hours, and earn $50,000 to $100,000 a year. She also knows the amount of money her target customers are willing to pay for her service and how much income she can expect to make.

In her first effort to get customers, Maggie plans to create a flyer aimed at her target market, which she will distribute in neighborhoods and veterinarian offices. She also plans to distribute the flyer downtown and in other business areas where many of her target customers work.

6. Evaluate the Results

Evaluation is the last step in the market research process. It is not enough just to develop a plan of action. Entrepreneurs must regularly evaluate the actions they take as a result of the plan.

Once Maggie has developed and distributed the flyer, she will need to evaluate the results. If she feels that she is getting a good response from her target market, she can assume that her plan of action is effective. However, if she is not getting a good response, then she will need to revise her plan of action.

 CHECKPOINT

What are the six steps of market research?

Technology-Driven Marketing

Customer relationship management (CRM) is the goal of a new marketing trend that focuses on understanding customers as individuals instead of as part of a group. It is a business strategy designed to increase profitability and customer satisfaction. CRM uses technology to track customer interactions and to organize business processes in a way that will produce customer-satisfying behaviors.

Interactions with Customers

In a CRM system, companies identify customer relationships, including information on who customers are, where they are located, and what products and services they buy. This is done by collecting data on all types of interactions a customer has with the company. These can include phone, web-based, or salesperson contacts. Other *touch points* where a customer might have contact with the company include a product or service registration, a request for product information, the return of a completed warranty card, or a customer talking with delivery personnel and product installers.

Many companies are now using websites as a touch point for customers to communicate with them. On the Web, companies provide forms that customers can complete to purchase products, make reservations, enter product and service preferences, and provide customer feedback. This information is transmitted through *electronic data interchange (EDI)*, which is the movement of data between locations in a structured, computer-retrievable format. The information is then used to define market segments, adjust marketing strategies, develop new products, and improve customer relationships.

Customer Database

Large amounts of data can be obtained from the interactions between a company and its customers. A business must decide what types of data it wants to acquire and how it can use the data to enhance customer relationships. Data collected can include customer contact information and data pertaining to the customer's current relationship with the company—past purchase history, quantity and frequency of purchases, average amount spent on purchases, and reactions to promotional activities.

The data are stored in a *data warehouse*, which is a large computerized database containing all of the information collected in the CRM process. Data stored in the data warehouse by one department within the company are available to other departments or to anyone else who has access to the database.

©Dean Mitchell, 2010/Used under license from Shutterstock.com

How can technology be used in the market research process?

Data mining is used to find hidden patterns and relationships in the customer data stored in the data warehouse. The value of data mining is the ability of a company to transform individual bits of data into usable information that marketers need to develop successful marketing strategies. Using data mining, marketers can search the data warehouse to find relevant data, categorize significant characteristics, and develop customer profiles. Once the most profitable customers and prospects are identified, marketing strategies that will appeal to them are created.

 CHECKPOINT

What is the goal of CRM?

4.2 ASSESSMENT

THINK ABOUT IT

1. Why do entrepreneurs need to conduct market research?

2. What are the limitations of market research?

3. What is the difference between primary and secondary data?

4. Why is it important to define the question you want your market research to answer?

5. How is data mining used?

MAKE ACADEMIC CONNECTIONS

6. **MANAGEMENT** Your family-owned business processes and sells orange juice to food distributors. In order to grow, the business needs to expand its product line. Describe how you would apply the six market research steps to help determine an additional product your business could offer.

7. **PROBLEM SOLVING** It is important to evaluate the effectiveness of a survey. Access www.cengage.com/school/entrepreneurship/ideas. Click on *Activities* and open the file *Market Research Evaluation*. Print a copy and complete the activity.

8. **TECHNOLOGY** Choose a company that you are familiar with. On the Internet, research the company's website and make a list of the different ways the company collects customer data through its website.

Teamwork

Working with team members, come up with a new product that you think will be very useful for students in your school. Develop a survey for potential consumers of this product to gauge their interest. Have students from your school complete the survey. Tabulate the results and determine if the product is a good idea.

KNOW YOUR COMPETITION

Goals

- Explain the importance of knowing and understanding your competition.
- Prepare a competitive analysis.
- Describe strategies for maintaining customer loyalty.

Vocabulary

- direct competition
- indirect competition
- competitive analysis

focus on small business

Who is your competition?

Roseanne and John needed to find out who their competition would be for their new restaurant. They drove 30 minutes in all directions from the location they chose for their restaurant and made a list of all the restaurants they saw on their trips. They also obtained menus of the restaurants to see what type of food they offered. They even ate at several of the restaurants and observed the restaurants' strengths and weaknesses. Roseanne and John determined that their restaurant would offer a different type of food from any of their competition and that the customers in their target market would be willing to try a new restaurant.

It is beneficial to check out the competition in person.

Work as a Team Roseanne and John have determined that there is a market for their restaurant. How can they differentiate their restaurant from competing restaurants? How can they keep customers coming back?

Impact of Competition

The U.S. economic system is based on private property, freedom of choice, profit, and competition. Because consumers are free to buy whatever they want from whomever they want, companies compete for their business. Most new businesses face *competitors*—companies offering similar or identical products and services to the same group of target customers. As the owner of a new business, you will have to persuade customers to buy from you instead of from your competitors. You must always watch the competition and be sure that you are offering products that are of equal or better quality at the same or lower prices.

When personal computers first came on the market, Apple computers were the biggest sellers. Then IBM developed a personal computer, and soon there were many other manufacturers of personal computers. Today, customers have many choices for personal computers. All of the computer manufacturers work hard to persuade customers to buy their product.

How can similar businesses compete for customers?

Understand the Competition

Knowing about your competition will also help you define your target market. Businesses typically enter into areas where there is competition. To survive, they have to identify some special customer need or want that is not being met. Customers may be happy with the products or services, but they may be unhappy with the prices. Customers might be dissatisfied with the quality of a product or service and would be willing to pay more for better quality. In either case, a customer need is going unmet by a competitor, indicating a possible opportunity for an entrepreneur.

Know the Types of Competition

Competitors may be categorized as either direct or indirect competition. You will need to find ways to identify and differentiate yourself from both types of competition.

DIRECT COMPETITION   A business that makes most of its money selling the same or similar products or services to the same market as other businesses is **direct competition**. Secondary data resources can give you information on your direct competition. Your direct competitors may be in the same geographic area as your business. The telephone directory or an Internet search will help you find the number and locations of competing businesses. Your local Chamber of Commerce will also have information on competitors in your business field. Observation methods can help you learn more about your direct competitors. If you start a retail business, you can visit all of the malls, shopping centers, and retail outlets in your area.

For some businesses, direct competitors may be located far away. Carmen Quinterro publishes a travel newsletter about Ireland. Carmen's target customers live all over the United States. Her competitors include five other newsletters about Ireland as well as several travel websites. Although Carmen's competitors are located far from her, they compete for the same target customers.

Why do businesses need to be concerned about indirect competition?

Photodisc/Getty Images

INDIRECT COMPETITION   A business that makes only a small amount of money selling the same or similar products and services to the same market as other businesses is <u>indirect competition</u>. Locating your indirect competition is more difficult than finding direct competitors. You should first think of all of the possible businesses that can compete with you indirectly. A large department store may stock some of the most popular products carried by a privately owned specialty shop. The department store offers many other lines of merchandise as well. It makes only a small amount of money on the same items that the specialty shop offers. This makes the department store an indirect competitor to the specialty shop.

LARGE RETAILERS   When a large retailer enters a community, it can be a source of direct and indirect competition for many other businesses. Large retailers like Walmart bring lower prices and jobs to a community, but many small businesses find it difficult to compete with them. Some of the smaller, locally owned retailers often are forced out of business. Some of the reasons that it is difficult for entrepreneurs to compete with large retailers include the following:

1. **Large retailers usually are able to keep larger quantities of products in stock.** They can purchase inventory in bigger quantities because they have more revenue and larger storage areas. Bigger orders result in volume discounts, and the savings can be passed to consumers in the form of lower prices.
2. **Large retail chains do not rely on a single product line.** If one product line does poorly, a large retail store does not go out of business because it has other successful product lines. Small businesses have risks associated with having only one product line. If its product falls out of favor with consumers, it has no other product lines to make up the difference.
3. **Large companies usually have more resources to devote to advertising**. A larger company makes more revenue and can hire advertising professionals to create effective advertising to attract more customers.

CHECKPOINT

Why is it important to understand the competition your business faces?

Competitive Analysis

Identifying and examining the characteristics of a competing firm is called a **competitive analysis**. Analyzing the strengths and weaknesses of your competition will help you identify opportunities and threats against your business. Follow these steps to begin your competitive analysis:

1. **Make a list of your competitors.** Using the Internet and *The Yellow Pages* and driving through the area in which you plan to locate your business are good ways to identify your competition. You can also talk to potential customers to find out with whom they are currently doing business. Review trade magazines and newspapers to see who is advertising the product or service you plan to offer.

2. **Summarize the products and prices offered by your competitors.** Investigate the products or services your competition offers for sale. How are they different from yours? Examine the price ranges of your competitors and determine how they compare to what you plan to charge. Are your prices higher or lower?

3. **List each competitor's strengths and weaknesses.** What does the competitor do that no one else does, or what does it do better than everyone else? Where are your competitors located? Determine if their location is better, worse, or about the same as the planned location for your business. Compare your competitors' facilities to the planned facility for your business. Are their facilities better, worse, or about the same as yours? What attracts customers to your competitors' facilities?

4. **Find out the strategies and objectives of your competitors.** A copy of each competitor's annual report would have this information. In addition, looking at competitors' websites or advertising can give you clues about their strategies and objectives.

5. **Determine the opportunities in the market.** Look at your competitors' weaknesses. How can you use these weaknesses to your advantage? Also, determine if there is an increase in demand for the product or service you plan to offer. What are the industry forecasts? If demand is predicted to increase, more opportunities exist for those wanting to enter the market.

6. **Identify threats to your business from the competition.** What would make a customer choose the competition over you? Examine your competitors' strengths. How will you compete with these strengths?

Interjit Singh wants to start a premier car wash in an expensive suburb of Washington, D.C. He does a competitive analysis as shown on the next page. He researches his direct and indirect competition. He finds that Royal Hand Wash is able to charge twice the price of the other competitors even though its location is not the best. Royal Hand Wash guarantees nonscratch car washes and waxes done by hand, not machines. Because Interjit's business will also offer car washes, waxes, and detailing done by hand, Royal Hand Wash is the

ANALYSIS OF COMPETITORS

Competitor	Price	Location	Facility	Strength	Weakness	Strategy
Standard Gas	$6.00	Excellent	Good	Excellent location	Car wash not easily accessible	Target a different market
Lakeland Car Wash	$5.50	Fair	Good	Low price	Location	Target a different market
Ray's Car Wash	$5.00	Good	Fair	Low price	Facility	Target a different market
Royal Hand Wash	$11.50	Fair	Excellent	Excellent facility	Location, high price	Offer lower prices, better service, more convenient location

direct competition. All other car wash businesses, including gas stations with automatic car wash machines, are his indirect competition. Interjit considers Royal Hand Wash's location and prices to be two of its biggest weaknesses, which open up opportunities for Interjit. He plans to capitalize on these opportunities by choosing a prime location for his car wash and charging lower prices. The biggest threat posed by Royal Hand Wash is its excellent facility. Interjit believes that having a convenient location and offering better service will stamp out this threat.

 CHECKPOINT

What is the purpose of a competitive analysis?

Maintain Customer Loyalty

Getting customers to buy your products and services instead of your competitors' is only one step in running a successful business. Once you get the customers, you must make sure they remain loyal to you and keep coming back.

How can a business use surveys to help maintain customer loyalty?

Listen and Respond to Feedback

To retain customers, you will need to continually ask customers for their opinions about your business and respond to their feedback. Businesses that ignore customer concerns will not stay in business long. Businesses stay in touch with their customers' needs in different ways. Some businesses may call customers after sales are made to ensure they are satisfied with their purchase. Many companies have a customer feedback box where customers can put complaints or positive comments about the business. You can also design a survey for your customers to complete.

Jason Rose's business, the Metropolitan Athletic Club, closed because of his failure to respond to customer feedback. Club members had repeatedly complained about the lack of cleanliness in the locker rooms and the lack of available weight machines during peak hours. Jason ignored his customers' complaints, believing that the excellent location and low monthly membership fee would ensure his success. Jason learned from his mistake. When he opened his next athletic club, he immediately tried to find out what customers wanted by conducting a market research study. His study revealed, among other things, that he should offer more aerobics classes and put high-speed hair dryers in the locker rooms. Due to his focus on customer satisfaction, Jason's club is doing very well and attracting new members all the time.

Other Strategies for Maintaining Loyalty

To maintain customer loyalty, businesses use many strategies. The main purpose of these strategies is to keep customers happy so that they will return to the business. The strategies also give the business a means for gathering data about their customers and their shopping and spending habits that can help in future decision making. Some of the most basic customer loyalty strategies businesses use include the following:

- Superior service
- More convenient hours than other businesses
- Easy return policies
- Store-specific credit cards
- Personal notes or cards for birthdays or as a way to say thanks for the business
- Frequent-buyer programs

Frequent-buyer programs have become popular among businesses. Customers must join by filling out a registration form that asks for personal information, such as your name, address, phone number, and e-mail address. Customers are then given a card, which they can use each time they make a purchase. The cashier scans the magnetic strip or barcode on the card to keep a running total of the purchases made by the customer. Rewards are given to the customer based on the frequency of purchases. The rewards help attract customers to the business. In addition, the business can collect information electronically about the buying habits of its customers, helping it know what items to stock.

BE YOUR OWN BOSS

You opened The Sweet Shop, a candy and ice cream store, on the grounds of a beach resort hotel. You get a steady stream of new customers because guests from the hotel visit your shop. However, you want to attract local residents from the community to your business to help grow a customer base year round. You decide that a frequent-buyer program is one way to get customers to visit and return to your business. What type of frequent-buyer program would be good for The Sweet Shop? Design a flyer that would introduce the program to customers. Also, design a card that you would give customers to identify them as frequent buyers.

Kathleen McGuire, the owner of Flower Markets, encourages shoppers to buy all of their flowers from her garden store by issuing them a frequent-buyer card with a magnetic strip that stores customers' information on it. Every time a customer makes a purchase, she scans the card to record the purchase. When customers have made purchases totaling $200, she offers them a 25 percent discount on their next order. Kathleen also uses the purchasing data she collects from the cards to notify customers about sales on items they frequently purchase.

 **CHECKPOINT**

What are some strategies for maintaining customer loyalty?

4.3 ASSESSMENT

THINK ABOUT IT

1. Why should entrepreneurs analyze both direct and indirect competitors?

2. Why is a competitive analysis important to an entrepreneur?

3. Why is customer feedback considered a type of market research? Is this type of market research more or less valuable than other types of research you collect? Explain your answer.

MAKE ACADEMIC CONNECTIONS

4. **MARKETING** Devise a plan to maintain customer loyalty for a hair salon. Create an advertisement to let your customers know about this plan.

5. **COMMUNICATION** Shontel Washington just started a website design company. She would like feedback from the people who have used her services. Develop a short survey that would help Shontel learn more about her customers' feelings toward her business. How can she use the data collected to beat her competition?

6. **TECHNOLOGY** Using the car wash data shown on page 114, enter the prices into a spreadsheet. Use the spreadsheet to create a bar graph that will help Interjit Singh analyze the data.

Teamwork

Working with team members, choose a successful business in your area. Then choose three competing businesses. Access www.cengage.com/school/entrepreneurship/ideas. Click on *Activities* and open the file *Competitive Analysis*. Print a copy and complete the activity by analyzing each business using the six steps listed in this lesson.

Use Spreadsheets to Analyze Data

Spreadsheets are a powerful tool for analyzing, sharing, and managing numerical data. Entrepreneurs can use spreadsheets to analyze market research, prepare budgets, measure performance, and create financial statements. One of the most valuable uses of spreadsheets is creating charts and graphs. Charts and graphs can improve decision making by presenting data in an easy-to-read, understandable format. Line graphs, bar charts, and pie charts are among the most commonly used visual aids.

Spreadsheets are especially useful in analyzing market research results. Gena has decided that she wants to open a coffee shop in her community. She wants to determine the age of her target market. She surveys 25 people in each of the following age groups: 18–25, 26–30, 31–35, and 36–40. She enters her survey results into a spreadsheet and creates the pie chart shown below. The pie chart clearly shows that consumers in the 18–25 age group are more likely to buy coffee on their way to work.

Try It Out

Maggie Blandin conducted research for her dog-walking business by surveying 2,500 dog owners. She asked what price owners would be willing to pay for a dog-walking service. She collected the following data:

Number of People	Price
500	$10
250	$15
750	$20
500	$25
500	$ 0 (not interested)

Enter the data into a spreadsheet and create a pie chart to help Maggie determine the price she should charge for her dog-walking service. Experiment with the different kinds of charts and graphs you can create.

**Consumers Who Buy Coffee
on the Way to Work**

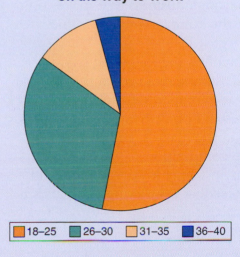

■ 18–25   ■ 26–30   ■ 31–35   ■ 36–40

SUMMARY

4.1 Identify Your Market

1. Before starting a new business, you must determine who your target market is and whether your target customers will be willing to buy your product or service. Market research is key to finding out this information.

2. You should develop a customer profile and decide which segment(s) of the market to target. Markets may be segmented based on many factors, including demographics, psychographics, use-based data, and geographic data.

4.2 Research the Market

3. Market research is important because it helps you learn about your customers and your competition. Primary data are collected for the very first time to fit a specific purpose. Secondary data are found in already-published sources.

4. The six steps of market research are: (1) define the question, (2) determine the data needed, (3) collect the data, (4) analyze the data, (5) take action, and (6) evaluate results.

5. Customer relationship management (CRM) focuses on understanding customers as individuals instead of as a group. CRM uses technology to track customer interactions.

4.3 Know Your Competition

6. All businesses have both direct and indirect competition. Direct competition comes from a business that makes most of its money selling the same or similar products and services to the same market. Indirect competition comes from a business that makes only a small amount of money selling the same or similar products to the same market.

7. Creating a competitive analysis involves the following steps: (1) make a list of competitors, (2) summarize products and prices offered by competitors, (3) list each competitor's strengths and weaknesses, (4) find out strategies and objectives of competitors, (5) determine the opportunities in the market, and (6) identify threats to your business from the competition.

8. There are many ways to maintain customer loyalty. You should ask for and respond to customer feedback. Offering superior service and frequent-buyer programs also promotes customer loyalty.

what do you know now?

Read *Ideas in Action* on page 95 again. Then answer the questions a second time. Have your responses changed? If so, how have they changed?

VOCABULARY BUILDER

Match each statement with the term that best defines it. Some terms may not be used.

1. A description of the characteristics of the person or company that is likely to purchase a product or service
2. Data that describe a group of people in terms of their age, marital status, family size, ethnicity, gender, profession, education, and income
3. An in-depth interview with a group of target customers who provide valuable ideas on products or services
4. Information collected for the first time to fit a specific purpose
5. Marketing trend that focuses on understanding customers as individuals instead of as part of a group
6. Data that describe a group of people in terms of their tastes, opinions, personality traits, and lifestyle habits
7. Data found in already-published sources
8. A business that makes most of its money selling the same or similar products or services to the same market as other businesses

a. competitive analysis
b. customer profile
c. customer relationship management
d. demographics
e. direct competition
f. focus group
g. geographic data
h. indirect competition
i. market research
j. market segments
k. primary data
l. psychographics
m. secondary data
n. survey
o. target market
p. use-based data

REVIEW YOUR KNOWLEDGE

9. Which of the following is *not* a reason that entrepreneurs need to know who their customers are?
   a. customers are a business's most important asset
   b. companies cannot remain in business without customers
   c. customers have no influence on products or services offered
   d. knowing who your customers are can help you estimate demand for products and services
10. To identify your target market, you need to know
    a. who your customers are
    b. how old your customers are
    c. where your potential customers currently shop
    d. all of the above
11. Data that help you determine where your potential customers live and how far they will travel to do business with you are
    a. demographics   c. use-based data
    b. psychographics   d. geographic data
12. Which of the following is *not* an example of primary data?
    a. a survey
    b. statistics from a government website
    c. observation of customer behavior
    d. all of the above are examples of primary data
13. Sources of secondary data include all of the following *except*
    a. customer feedback from a survey
    b. publications issued by government and community organizations
    c. trade magazines and websites
    d. newspaper articles
14. **True or False** Two disadvantages of collecting primary data are the costs and time involved.

15. It is difficult for small businesses to compete with large retailers because
    a. large retailers are able to order and stock products in larger quantities
    b. large retail chains don't rely on a single product line
    c. large companies have more resources to devote to advertising
    d. all of the above
16. Which of the following is *not* a step involved when preparing a competitive analysis?
    a. make a list of all competitors
    b. create a customer profile
    c. list your competitors' strengths and weaknesses
    d. summarize products and prices offered by competitors
17. **True or False**   Businesses do not need to identify their target market in order to succeed.
18. Which of the following is *not* a good way to get customer feedback?
    a. check with your competition
    b. call customers the day after they make a purchase
    c. use a customer feedback box
    d. have customers complete a survey after shopping with you
19. Which of the following is a strategy for maintaining customer loyalty?
    a. keeping standard business hours
    b. adhering to strict return policies
    c. offering superior service
    d. none of the above
20. **True or False**   Longer surveys are always better because you can collect more information.

APPLY WHAT YOU LEARNED

21. Set up an interview with a local entrepreneur to find out how he or she identified the target market, what kind of market research was conducted and whether any of it was technology-driven, what kind of competition the business faces, and how customer loyalty is maintained. Before conducting the interview, compile a list of questions to ask. Present your findings to the class.
22. You want to start a computer service company that keys and prints professional-looking term papers and resumes for students in your school. Design a survey to help you determine if there is a market for your company. Determine the best way to administer the survey.

MAKE ACADEMIC CONNECTIONS

23. **MATH**   You have collected primary data that indicates three-quarters of the people in your town would switch dry cleaners if they could save 50 percent on their dry cleaning. If the average resident in your town spends $7 a week on dry cleaning and the town has 5,000 residents, how much revenue could you expect to earn per year by opening a discount dry cleaner?

24. **MANAGEMENT** Maggie Blandin, who wants to open a dog-walking business in your town or city, has asked for your help in collecting data. Call your local Chamber of Commerce to gather demographics and psychographics for your community. Also ask for statistics on dog ownership in your area.

25. **RESEARCH** Use the Internet to find the names of four companies that might be able to help you conduct market research. Record information such as how long the company has been in business and what kinds of market research the business does. Summarize your findings and compare them with the findings of other students.

What Would YOU Do?

You are having a luncheon meeting with one of your suppliers at a local restaurant. Across the restaurant, you see the owner of a business that is your main competitor having lunch with someone you do not recognize. They finish eating, pay their check, and leave while you are still at your table. After they leave, you notice that a portfolio was left in one of the chairs at their table. You go to the table, pick up the portfolio, and see that it is your competitor's marketing strategy for the upcoming year. What would you do? Would you consider it your lucky day and read the business's strategy, or would you turn it in to someone at the restaurant? Why did you choose the action you did?

build your
BUSINESS PLAN PROJECT

This activity will help you develop the business plan for your business idea.

1. Identify the target market for your business. Use secondary data sources to help you assess demand for your product or service.

2. Using the secondary data, develop a customer profile for your business. Which market segment of your industry are you targeting? Be specific.

3. Conduct primary data research for your business using the steps outlined in Lesson 4.2. Develop a survey that will give you the information you need. Ask at least 30 people in your target market to complete the survey. Analyze your results and determine what course of action you will take.

4. Determine who your competitors are, both direct and indirect. Access www.cengage.com/school/entrepreneurship/ideas. Click on *Activities* and open the file *Competitive Analysis*. Use the chart to prepare a competitive analysis for your business. Be sure to address strengths, weaknesses, opportunities, and threats.

5. Describe your strategies for maintaining customer loyalty. Give reasons why you think each will work.

"My little sister decided to start a babysitting service. To tailor her business to meet client needs, she asked neighbors with children to complete an online survey regarding their child care needs. The results she compiled from the free online survey helped her put together a service and fee schedule.

How do organizations determine what services to offer? How do manufacturers determine which product features are the most important to include in a product?

Marketing research helps companies and organizations decide how to best meet the needs of their clients. Marketing research surveys provide a targeted, concise method to collect and analyze marketing data.

Employment Outlook
- Faster than average job growth is anticipated.
- Globalization, an increasingly competitive marketplace, and better educated consumers all contribute to the increased need for marketing research.
- Outsourcing will create opportunities at consulting and marketing research firms.

Job Titles
- Market Research Analyst
- Mobile Video Research Manager
- Questionnaire Development Manager
- Market Research Coordinator
- Marketing Communications Specialist

Needed Education/Skills
- A Bachelor's degree is required. Advancement may require a Master's degree or a Ph.D.

- To keep up with technology changes, continuing education is necessary.
- A blend of quantitative and qualitative coursework is helpful.

What's it like to work in Marketing Research? Sales at a local gift shop have been lagging, and the owner has contracted with Tess, a self-employed electronic marketing survey writer, to create a marketing research study. The store is an independent store with a limited budget, so Tess decides to use one of the free online survey services to gather data from existing customers. The store's mailing list will be used to send customers an electronic invitation to participate in the survey. As an incentive for participating in the survey, customers will be offered a 5 percent discount on their next purchase.

During the afternoon, Tess works on preparing a summary report for a restaurant chain. The restaurant wanted to obtain feedback on its service, the environment, and the food quality while all were still fresh on customers' minds. So Tess used a survey service that collected data via cell phones. Upon receiving their restaurant bills, clients who had cell phones were instructed how to log on to a website where they could answer a brief online survey about their dining experience. Customers can look forward to receiving a free dessert upon their next visit as a reward for survey participation.

What about you? Would you like to help a variety of businesses improve their understanding of customer preferences by developing marketing research surveys?

E-Business

To succeed in today's global market, businesses must have the ability to sell products and services to consumers via the Internet. The E-Business event demonstrates proficiency in the creation and design of web commerce sites. The event has two parts: a project and a performance component. Each year a national topic is selected by FBLA-PBL, Inc., for which participants in the event must prepare their websites. You can find the current topic on the FBLA website.

Performance Competencies

- Develop the presentation logically and systematically
- Communicate the design process effectively
- Present the tips, techniques, and tools used
- Demonstrate the ability to make a businesslike presentation
- Show self-confidence apparent through knowledge of content and articulation of ideas

Go to the FBLA website for more detailed information.

GIVE IT A TRY

Using the current national topic for the E-Business event, develop a website that meets the following project competencies:

- Document addresses topic and is appropriate for the audience
- Graphics, text treatment, and special effects show creativity and cohesiveness of design
- Selection of fonts and type sizes is appropriate
- Overall layout and design is creative and appealing
- Final product indicates a clear thought process and an intended, planned direction with formulation and execution of a firm idea
- Required information is effectively communicated

Prepare a five-minute presentation that will demonstrate and explain your E-Business website. Make the presentation to your class. Topics to discuss during your presentation should include the following: development of the topic, development and design process, use and implementation of innovative technology, use and development of media elements, and copyright issues with pictures, music, and other items. Be prepared to answer questions about your website after your presentation.

www.fbla-pbl.org

© Philip Lange, 2010/ Used under license from Shutterstock.com

Market Your Business

www.cengage.com/school/entrepreneurship/ideas

Turning Creative Fun into Dollars

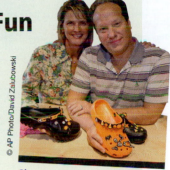

Sheri and Rich Schmelzer of Boulder, Colorado, are the founders of Jibbitz. What's a Jibbitz you may ask? Several years ago, Sheri and Rich didn't know either. Sheri was a stay-at-home mom with three children. They always had at least 12 to 15 pairs of Crocs—a type of colorful, sandal-like footwear with ventilation holes—in a pile at their back door. One day, Sheri was having

Sheri and Rich Schmelzer, founders of Jibbitz

fun experimenting with decorating the Crocs by sticking decorative pieces in the holes of the shoes. She used buttons, rhinestones, and other things she had lying around the house. Sheri showed the decorated shoes to Rich when he returned home from work, and a "light bulb" went off. Using his business experience and knowledge, the business got its start.

After experimenting with several different versions, Sheri and Rich found a secure way to attach the decorations so that they would fit snugly in the holes. Looking for a domain name for a website, they thought about using the name Flibberty-Jibbet—a nickname Rich used for Sheri. Sheri liked the word but thought it was too long for a domain name, so she shortened it, and Jibbitz was born.

Once the website was up and running, the Schmelzers were featured in a short segment on the local news. Orders began to come in like crazy. Sheri's parents came to their house every weekend to help by gluing decorations together and getting orders ready for shipment.

Once they realized how big the market for Jibbitz was, they needed to find a mass manufacturer. Along with individual orders to fill, many retailers wanted to buy their products in quantity. The Schmelzers used a home equity loan to finance their first order from a factory in China.

When the first factory shipment was delivered, they were still filling orders out of the basement of their home. They realized they needed more space, so they moved the business into a 1,000-square-foot office. They hired two people to help keep up with the wholesale side of the business so that Sheri could concentrate on new designs and Internet fulfillment. Within six months, they needed still more space, and they moved operations into a 5,000-square-foot office/warehouse.

Six months later, the Schmelzers hit it really big when Crocs, Inc. acquired their business for $10 million. Sheri and Rich still run the company. They are very proud of the company they built and plan to stay involved.

1. Why do you think Jibbitz are so popular?
2. How important do you think the decision to market Jibbitz on the Internet was to the success of the company?
3. What do you think is different for the Schmelzers since they sold Jibbitz to Crocs, Inc.?

DEVELOP THE MARKETING PLAN

Goals

- Explain the importance of marketing a business.
- Discuss how to develop a marketing strategy for a business.
- Describe what information is included in a marketing plan.

Vocabulary

- marketing
- marketing concept
- marketing mix
- marketing strategy
- marketing plan

focus **on small business**

Is a marketing plan always necessary?

Wanda loves jewelry and has spent much time studying the work of famous jewelry designers. She also has taken some beading classes at the local recreation center. She decides that she wants to open her own jewelry design business. She conducts market research and finds that there is an interest in custom-designed jewelry in the target market she defines. Now she's ready to think about how to market her business. She knows that marketing is very important and wants to be sure that she spends the money she has budgeted for marketing wisely. She contacts the SBA, and it advises her to develop a marketing plan. She is not sure that this is a wise use of her time, but she sets out to learn more about a marketing plan.

© Andresr, 2010/ Used under license from Shutterstock.com

A marketing plan lays the foundation for success.

Work as a Team Because Wanda has already found that there is a market for her jewelry designs, discuss whether she would be wise to spend time developing a marketing plan. Should she just start making jewelry and see what happens? Make a recommendation to Wanda and explain your reasoning.

What Is Marketing?

As defined by the American Marketing Association, "marketing is the activity, set of institutions, and processes for creating, communicating, delivering, and exchanging offerings that have value for customers, clients, partners, and society at large." To simplify this definition, **marketing** is all of the processes—planning, pricing, promoting, distributing, and selling—used to determine and satisfy the needs of customers and the company. This definition demonstrates the importance of the customer.

It is very important to conduct market research to discover what products or services customers want to buy. Using the primary and secondary data that is gathered through market research helps entrepreneurs develop a marketing concept for the business. The **marketing concept** uses the needs of customers as the primary focus during the planning, production, distribution, and promotion of a product or service. To use the marketing concept successfully, businesses must be able to:

© Lucian Coman, 2010/ Used under license from Shutterstock.com

How does the marketing mix for consumer products help meet consumer needs?

DEVELOP YOUR READING SKILLS

As you read this chapter, make a list of the marketing strategy components and the information you will include about each one in your marketing plan.

- Identify what will satisfy the customers' needs and wants
- Develop and market products or services that customers consider better than other choices
- Operate profitably

An important part of implementing the marketing concept is developing a marketing mix that helps meet customer needs and enables the business to earn a profit. The **marketing mix** is a blending of the product, price, distribution, and promotion used to reach a target market. For example, once you have determined what product or service meets customers' needs, you must determine the right price for it, make it available to the customers in the right places, and then let your target market know about it.

CHECKPOINT

Why is marketing important to a business?

The Marketing Strategy

As a business owner, you will need to outline the goals you want to accomplish through your marketing efforts. Once you have identified your goals, you will need to develop a **marketing strategy**, which is a plan that identifies how these goals will be achieved. In your startup marketing plan, your strategy should address:

- Product introduction or innovation
- Pricing
- Distribution
- Promotion
- Sales or market share
- Projected profitability

It is important that your marketing strategy be consistent with the overall goals you have set for your business. Be sure that the strategy will actually work for you and is within the resources you have available. Your marketing goals should be written following the SMART guidelines you learned in Chapter 1. Smart goals are specific, measurable, attainable, realistic, and timely. Your goals should reflect your short-term, medium-term, and long-term plans for your business. What do you want your marketing efforts to achieve for your business? Do you want to offer additional products or services after one year? Perhaps in three years, you want to find a larger building or add on to your current one. After five years, maybe you want to sell your product internationally. Establishing short-, medium-, and long-term marketing goals ensures that the marketing you do today fits in with the vision you have for your business tomorrow.

Short-Term Goals

Short-term goals are what you want your business to achieve in the next year. They can be stated in terms of number of customers, level of sales, level of profits, or other measures of success.

Identifying your short-term goals will help you determine how to target your marketing. If your goal is to build a customer base, you may decide to keep prices low and spend more money on promotion.

famous entrepreneur

How has the Internet provided new opportunities for entrepreneurs?

© AP Photo/Gautam Singh

SERGEY BRIN AND LARRY PAGE What would the Internet be like if there was no Google? Just what is a Google? Thanks to Sergey Brin and Larry Page, we have Google and an explanation of the name. "Googol" is the mathematical term for a 1 followed by 100 zeros. The term was coined by the nephew of Edward Kasner, an American mathematician. Brin and Page chose a variation of this term for their company. When they started their business, Brin and Page's mission was "to organize the world's information and make it universally accessible and useful!"

Brin and Page developed a new approach to online searching while they were students at Stanford University. Using that approach, they launched Google in September of 1998 as a privately held company. Today, Google is one of the world's best-known brands. Most people have learned about Google by word of mouth from satisfied users.

Google generates revenue by selling advertising space. Ads are displayed on search results pages that are relevant to the content on the page. Google tracks customer traffic to measure the cost-effectiveness of the online advertising.

Today, Brin and Page share a net worth of over $16 billion. Google handles over 2.5 billion search inquiries daily. That's not bad for a data center that started in a dorm room!

THINK CRITICALLY

Have you ever used Google? Why do you think people choose Google over other search engines?

Why is it important for entrepreneurs to set goals for their businesses?

If your goal is to have a positive cash flow, you may decide to price your products or services higher.

Luisa Ramirez, a 32-year-old entrepreneur, wants to open a gourmet food shop in her community. In the short term, Luisa wants to generate traffic into her store. Because of that goal, her marketing strategy focuses on establishing a customer base. She creates a list of short-term goals based on product, price, distribution, and promotion.

Medium-Term Goals

Medium-term goals describe what you want your business to achieve in the next two to five years. Although your marketing strategy will be determined largely by your short-term goals, you will need to make sure that the strategy you are planning will make it possible for you to achieve your medium-term goals.

Luisa wants her business to become the most successful gourmet food shop in her community by increasing her customer base and her total sales. She hopes to expand the offerings in her store to include more international foods and specialty items from local suppliers. In addition to running her store, in five years Luisa hopes to expand her business to include catering.

Long-Term Goals

Long-term goals show where your business will be 5, 10, and even 20 years from now. Thinking about what you want the business to do in the long term can help you think about how to market your business today.

Luisa eventually would like to establish a mail-order division of her business. She does not let her long-term plans for a mail-order division change her thinking about how to market her store today. Knowing what she wants in the long run, however, motivates her to work very hard to make her store a success so that she can use it as a foundation to develop a second business.

CHECKPOINT

Why is goal setting important when developing a marketing strategy?

Write Your Marketing Plan

When your goals and marketing strategy have been determined, you will be ready to write your final marketing plan. The purpose of the <u>marketing plan</u> is to define your market, identify your customers and competitors, outline a strategy for attracting and keeping customers, and identify and anticipate change. A written marketing plan will help you determine whether it is solid and all parts are consistent. Your written plan becomes a guiding document as you operate your business. You can always review it later to determine if you need to change the way you are marketing your business. The marketing plan becomes a part of your business plan. Having a marketing plan as part of your business plan is essential when you seek financing for your business. Investors will expect your marketing plan to answer the following questions:

- What product or service will I offer?
- Who are my prospective customers?
- Is there a constant demand for this product or service?
- How many competitors are providing the same product or service?
- Can I create a demand for the product or service I want to offer?
- Can I compete effectively in price, quality, and delivery of my product or service?

To effectively answer these questions, the marketing plan for your business must include information on the following topics:

1. Product or Service
2. Target Market
3. Competition
4. Marketing Budget
5. Business Location
6. Pricing Strategy
7. Promotional Strategy
8. Distribution Strategy

What kinds of information do you think should be included in a marketing plan for a small, locally owned lawn care business?

As part of your marketing plan, you should include performance standards that will help you measure your effectiveness. Researching industry norms and past performances will help you develop appropriate standards. After your marketing plan has been implemented, you should compare your actual results to your performance standards to see how well you are progressing. It is helpful to examine your performance quarterly. Questions to ask yourself include:

- Am I meeting sales forecasts?
- Is my promotional campaign reaching the target market?
- Is my company doing everything it can to meet customers' needs?
- Is it easy for my customers to find what they want at a competitive price?

 CHECKPOINT

Why is it important to put your marketing plan in writing?

5.1 ASSESSMENT

THINK ABOUT IT

1. What is the marketing mix?

2. What is the relationship between short-term goals and medium-term goals?

3. What topics should be included in the marketing plan?

MAKE ACADEMIC CONNECTIONS

4. **MATH** Akeo Goto has opened a pet grooming business. He estimates the annual sales of the pet grooming market in his community to be about $325,000. There are two pet grooming businesses in town already. If Akeo achieves his five-year goal of capturing 45 percent of the market, how much will he earn in his fifth year?

5. **COMMUNICATION** Think of a local business with which you are familiar. Make a list of questions you would like to ask the owner about the marketing plan for the business. Contact the business owner and make an appointment to discuss the questions. Report your findings to your classmates.

Teamwork

Working in a team, choose one of the following businesses: Mexican restaurant, wholesaler, health-food store, or advertising agency. Brainstorm a list of short-, medium-, and long-term goals for the business. Make a list of these goals and post them on the wall in your classroom. Discuss the goals your team set with your classmates.

THE MARKETING MIX—PRODUCT

Goals

- Explain how the marketing concept affects decisions regarding the product mix.
- Define and describe the importance of product management.

Vocabulary

- product mix
- features
- brand
- positioning

Does location affect image?

Chase has a strong interest in men's clothing. During high school and college, Chase worked at several upscale men's stores in the Seattle area. When he graduated from college with a degree in retail marketing, he decided that he wanted to open his own upscale clothing store for men. In determining the startup costs for his business, he realized that the rent for the space in an upscale mall with specialty boutiques was too expensive. In looking for space he could afford, he found a site in a medium-sized strip mall. The other stores in the mall are discount stores, but he wants to promote his business as an "upscale, specialty store."

Location can help you reach your target customers.

© Dennis Owusu-Ansah, 2010/ Used under license from Shutterstock.com

Work as a Team Do you think the location of Chase's store will affect its image and ability to attract the target customer? What do you think Chase should do? Should he change the focus of his business for this location?

The Marketing Concept and the Product

Once you have determined what kind of business you will run, you will need to make decisions about the products that you will sell. To select your products, think carefully about which products and services most appeal to your target customers. If you can convince your customers that your products satisfy their needs better than any competitor's products, then your products become a marketing tool for your business.

Consumer-Driven Market

The marketing concept is the belief that the wants and needs of customers are the most important consideration when developing any product or marketing effort. Over the past 50 years, consumers have become more educated, and competition has increased to include the global market. This has led the U.S. market to change from a product-driven market to one that is consumer-driven. The marketing concept can give small businesses an advantage over larger businesses. Small businesses can get to know their customers better than larger businesses can. They can be more responsive and have more flexibility when trying to satisfy customer needs.

In the newspaper in Luisa's community, there was a recipe for a pasta dish using a special type of cheese that Luisa did not carry in her gourmet food store, and she knew none of the local grocery stores stocked it. However, she knew that many of her customers liked to try the recipes from the paper, so she immediately placed an order with a supplier to get the cheese in stock the next day.

How does a business's product mix help to satisfy customers?

Product Mix

The different products and services a business sells are its **product mix**. In a consumer-driven economy, entrepreneurs realize that sometimes they must include products in their mix as a convenience for customers even though those products may not be profitable. This will give the appearance to customers that the store has everything they need. It has been found that often a small percentage of the product selection makes up the majority of the sales revenue.

Luisa's Gourmet Luxuries will offer hundreds of different packaged goods, such as imported Italian olive oil and pastas. Luisa will also offer a wide selection of fresh foods, including cheeses, fruits, vegetables, and baked goods. To determine her product mix, Luisa lists the various departments she plans to establish in her store and the products that each department will carry. Luisa knows that most of her customers are looking for gourmet foods, but she decides to carry a small selection of pasta-making machines and coffee makers. Although these items will not be a large source of revenue, they will show customers she can meet all their needs.

 CHECKPOINT

How does the marketing concept affect decisions made about the product mix?

Product Management

Consumers buy a product because it meets their needs. However, there is much more to a product than consumers may realize. The many aspects of a product that a business must spend time developing and managing include its features, branding, packaging, labeling, and positioning.

Select Product Features

A product includes **features**, which are product characteristics that will satisfy customer needs. Features include such things as color, size, quality, hours, warranties, delivery, and installation. You will need to consider your target market when selecting product features.

Every product has features. For instance, Luisa has many choices when she is deciding what types of olives to stock in her store. There are green and black olives and olives stuffed with pimentos, blue cheese, and almonds. There are olives that come in jars and in cans and fresh olives that are available loose. There are olives that are produced in the United States, in Italy, and in France. There are so many different types of olives that there is no way Luisa can offer every single type to her customers. She needs to decide how many types of olives she can carry and what kinds her target customer prefers.

Consider Branding, Packaging, and Labeling

Making your product stand out from all the others in the market is a challenging task. The **brand** is the name, symbol, or design used to identify your product. The package is the box, container, or wrapper in which the product is placed. The label is where information about the product is given on the package. The brand, package, and label that you choose for your product will help differentiate it from others on the market. The Nike "swoosh" has become a very recognizable brand. When you see the Nike symbol, you know about the quality of the product you have selected.

What makes a memorable brand or product name? Access www.cengage.com/school/entrepreneurship/ideas and click on the link for Chapter 5. Author Phillip Davis provides some thoughts in his e-zine article. What does Davis consider the most common naming mistake? Do you agree with him that "Apple" is a better brand name than something like "United Computer Manufacturers"? Why or why not? Provide one example of a product or business that you think has a great name and another that you think has a poor name. Explain your answers.

www.cengage.com/school/entrepreneurship/ideas

Position Your Products or Services

Different products and services within the same category serve different customer needs. For example, both Hyundai and Jaguar sell automobiles, but these two product lines are positioned very differently in the marketplace. **Positioning** is creating an image for a product in the customer's mind. Businesses position a product in a certain market to get a desired customer response. Product features, price, and quality may be used for positioning. Jaguar's pricey cars are positioned in the market to meet the needs of those consumers who desire high quality and status. Hyundai positions its products to satisfy a need for an inexpensive family automobile. Examining the competition's positioning strategy can help you determine the best positioning strategy for your target market.

Luisa knows that the other gourmet store in town is perceived as more upscale because it caters to professional cooks. Because of this, Luisa decides to position her store as the friendly gourmet store for anyone who loves to cook. To do so, she plans to offer in-store cooking classes and free samples of food items. She knows that always being cheerful and helpful to customers will help her desired image.

✓ CHECKPOINT

Why is product management important?

what went wrong?

PACKAGING MATTERS

Katharine had developed a new line of dog grooming shampoo. She spent a large amount of time researching what should go into the shampoo and had the product tested to be sure it met safety standards. Her next step was to choose a way to package the shampoo. She decided that instead of a bottle, she would have the shampoo packaged in individual foil packets. She boxed the packets six to a box and set the price.

Her initial sales were good, but she was not getting repeat sales.

After three months, her revenue decreased. She was unable to keep up with the expenses of running her business with no incoming revenue.

She decided to survey her customers to find out why they were not ordering more shampoo. The first ten customers she talked to told her that while they liked the shampoo, they found the packaging inconvenient. They could not hold their dog in the tub while trying to open the foil packet and squeeze the shampoo out. Katharine realized she had made a serious mistake in her choice of packaging, but now she had spent all her money and was stuck with a large inventory of shampoo in foil packets. She did not know what else to do, so she closed her business.

THINK CRITICALLY

1. What could Katharine have done to avoid her packaging mistake?

2. Is there anything Katharine could have done to avoid closing her business after she knew what the problem was?

© paparazzit, 2010/ Used under license from Shutterstock.com

Research the target market before introducing a new product.

How can a business position its product in the marketplace?

5.2 ASSESSMENT

THINK ABOUT IT

1. How can a small business use the marketing concept to its advantage over a larger business?

2. Choose one of your favorite products. Make a list of the features of the product.

3. In the blue jeans market, which brands are positioned to satisfy customers' need for high quality and status? Which brands are positioned to satisfy a need for inexpensive clothing? Describe the consumers who are more likely to buy each of the brands you name.

MAKE ACADEMIC CONNECTIONS

4. **RESEARCH** Choose a business in your community. Make a list of all the products and/or services it offers. Talk to the business owner about which of the products or services represent the largest revenue for the business. Find out which of the products or services are not profitable but are offered to customers as a convenience. Find out if the owner is thinking about adding any new products to the product mix or dropping some of the current products from the product mix and why.

5. **COMMUNICATION** You have created a new energy snack bar that is designed for students at your school. Design a label for the snack bar package that will brand the product. You should incorporate your school's mascot in the design of the label.

Teamwork

Working with team members, make a list of products and services you would offer if you were opening a desktop publishing business. Make a list of the features of your products and services. Write a positioning statement that differentiates your business from your competitors.

THE MARKETING MIX—PRICE

Goals

- Identify pricing objectives for a business.
- Calculate the price for products using various methods.
- Discuss factors to consider when pricing services.
- List and describe various pricing strategies.

Vocabulary

- return on investment
- market share
- demand-based pricing
- cost-based pricing
- competition-based pricing
- psychological pricing
- discount pricing

focus on small business

What price should I charge?

Marie was excited about her new business, "Straighten It Out," that offered laundry services, such as washing and ironing clothes, for busy people. She would go to the homes of her clients once or twice a week and do all of their laundry for them. She liked the work and looked forward to the opportunity to make money while home from college. But, she was not sure how much she should charge for her services. She thought about charging a flat hourly rate. She realized that some of the tasks would take longer than others and some would require extra care, such as having to treat stains, iron pleats, or handle delicates. An hourly rate might not be the fairest way to charge customers or the best way to earn money.

© Stephen Coburn, 2010/ Used under license from Shutterstock.com

Determine the best price for your product or service.

Work as a Team How should Marie decide how much to charge? What will happen if she charges too much or too little?

Set Pricing Objectives

The price is the actual amount a customer pays for a product or service. Prices you charge must be low enough so that customers will buy from you, not from your competitors. To earn a profit, though, your prices need to be high enough so that revenues exceed expenses. Before you can select a pricing strategy, you will need to establish objectives for your pricing program. What is the most important thing you want the price to do? Examples of pricing objectives include:

- Maximize sales
- Discourage competition
- Establish an image
- Increase profits
- Attract customers

Return on Investment

When setting pricing objectives, you may want to consider your return on investment. Investment refers to the costs of making and marketing a product. The <u>**return on investment**</u> (ROI) is the amount earned as a result of the investment and is usually expressed as a percentage. Entrepreneurs must identify the percentage return they want from their investment. The target percentage in the beginning may be lower than it will be as the business grows. If you invest $5,000 in your smoothie stand at a local park and you want a 15 percent return, you need to price your product so that you will earn $750, since $5,000 \times 0.15 = $750.

Market Share

Market share is another consideration when setting pricing objectives. <u>**Market share**</u> is a business's percentage of the total sales generated by all companies in the same market. The total market for a product must be known in order for a market share to be determined. For example, if people in Luisa's community normally spend $1,750,000 a year on gourmet food products and Luisa's store sells products amounting to sales of $192,500, her market share will be 11 percent calculated as follows:

Amount of sales	÷	Total market size	=	Market share
$192,500	÷	$1,750,000	=	11%

The chart below graphically illustrates Luisa's market share along with the expected market shares of her competitors.

Gourmet Market Share

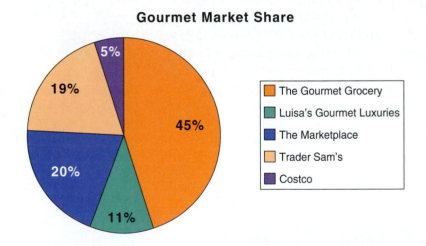

Your market share will depend on the level of competition in your market. If you create a market for an entirely new product, your market share will be 100 percent because you will be the only supplier, at least for a period of time. If you enter a market with many competitors or one in which a few large companies dominate the market, your market share will be small at first.

Companies in highly competitive environments must develop a plan to gain a higher market share. Companies can increase market

How can networking contribute to a business's success?

share in many ways. One way is to lower prices. Advertising and promotion campaigns that attract more customers can help too. You can also network with potential customers. *Networking* involves establishing informal ties with people who can help your business grow. Attending trade association meetings and other gatherings can provide good opportunities to network and gain new customers.

One of Luisa's goals is to become the most successful gourmet shop in her community by having a market share of at least 40 percent and a 10 percent return on investment. If Luisa wants a market share of 40 percent, she will need to generate annual sales of at least $700,000 ($1,750,000 × 0.40). Based on this, Luisa sets her pricing objectives carefully. She decides to set her prices low to build customer traffic. Once Luisa has increased her market share, she may raise prices slightly to increase her return on investment.

To help increase her market share, Luisa will seek out networking opportunities. As part of her networking efforts, Luisa will play softball in a local women's league in the summer. She also plans to attend Chamber of Commerce meetings monthly. She hopes that through both settings she will meet people who will become customers. She also hopes to meet other business professionals, such as lawyers, financial advisers, and other business owners, who might offer advice on ways to run her business more efficiently and, in turn, increase her return on investment.

 CHECKPOINT

Why is it important to determine pricing objectives before pricing goods and services?

Determine a Price for a Product

Once pricing objectives have been determined, the next step is to determine the possible prices for products. There will usually be more than one price that can be charged for a product. Pricing may be based on demand, cost, or the amount of competition.

Demand-Based Pricing

Pricing that is determined by how much customers are willing to pay for a product or service is called demand-based pricing. Potential customers are surveyed to find out what they would be willing to pay for the product. The highest price identified is the maximum price that can be charged.

If the bakery at Luisa's Gourmet Luxuries becomes widely recognized as the best in town, Luisa could begin charging higher prices for her baked goods. People will be willing to pay a higher price for a loaf of bread that they believe is the best available.

Cost-Based Pricing

Cost-based pricing is determined by using the wholesale cost of an item as the basis for the price charged. A *markup price* is determined by adding a percentage amount to the wholesale cost of an item.

Luisa buys artichoke hearts for $1.77 a can. To cover her operating expenses and allow for a profit, she adds 40 percent to her wholesale cost, or $0.71. The new price of $2.48 is her markup price, or retail price.

Wholesale cost	×	Percentage markup	=	Markup amount
$1.77	×	0.40	=	$0.71

Wholesale cost	+	Markup amount	=	Retail price
$1.77	+	$0.71	=	$2.48

Sometimes business owners purchase too much of a particular item and want to sell more of it quickly. To do so, they mark down the retail price of the product. A *markdown price* is determined by subtracting a percentage amount from the retail price of an item. You should be careful not to mark down an item below its cost. You do not want to lose money.

Luisa usually charges $10.50 for a large bottle of olive oil. To sell more, she decides to mark down its retail price by 20 percent.

Retail price	×	Percentage markdown	=	Markdown amount
$10.50	×	0.20	=	$2.10

Retail price	−	Markdown amount	=	Markdown price
$10.50	−	$2.10	=	$8.40

Competition-Based Pricing

Pricing that is determined by considering what competitors charge for the same good or service is called competition-based pricing. Once you find out what your competition charges for an item, you must decide whether to charge the same price, slightly more, or slightly less.

Luisa's business will compete with The Gourmet Grocery, which has been in her community for five years. She cannot charge more than her competitor for items that customers could purchase there. She decides initially to charge a few cents less than The Gourmet Grocery on all packaged goods. She will keep an eye on competitors to make sure she stays up to date on what they are charging for their products.

How can a new business compete against similar well-established businesses in the community?

CHECKPOINT

List three methods for determining the price to charge for a product.

Price a Service or an Idea

When setting the price for a service, it is important to consider not only the cost of any items used in providing the service but also the amount of time and anything that is included with the service. You may also have business ideas that you can sell to others. You should consider the different ways to structure payments for your ideas.

Time-Based Pricing

The price to charge for services can be determined by the amount of time it takes to complete the service. A plumber may charge $100 per hour. If the job takes 1½ hours to complete, the labor charge would be $100 × 1.5 = $150. A service provider must decide whether there will be a separate charge for materials or whether the materials will be included. A hair stylist charges a set amount to highlight someone's hair. The amount includes the hair stylist's time as well as all of the supplies used for the highlighting. Some service providers will negotiate the price. This is often done with legal services and construction projects.

One area in which Luisa would like to expand her business is catering. She will have to calculate prices based not only on the cost of the food but also on the time that it takes her to prepare and deliver the food. If she is responsible for serving at a catered event, she will have to charge for her time and the time of any helpers she may hire to serve guests at the event.

Bundling

Services can be *bundled*, or combined under one charge, rather than making the customer pay for each individual part of the service. When you go to a beauty salon and have your hair cut and styled, the price is bundled.

The price you pay includes the services of the hair stylist as well as the cost of the hair products, water, and towels that were used on your hair.

Pricing an Idea

Ideas can be priced in different ways. You might be acting as a consultant to another business. When consulting, you could charge an hourly rate for your time and the ideas you present during that time. You might have an idea that you want to license to another company for development. *Licensing* is the process of selling your idea to a company for the development and launch of a new product. When licensing your idea, there are different ways you can be paid.

1. *Up-front payment.* The licensee pays you a fee before development or sales begin. This may be the only amount you receive, or it could be an amount that is applied to future royalties.
2. *Royalties.* The licensee makes payments to you based on a percentage of the product sales. For example, you may be paid royalties of 2 percent of the total sales of a product developed from your idea.
3. *Annual minimum.* The licensee pays you a minimum amount each year regardless of the amount of sales.

✓CHECKPOINT

Which method would be the best for a housepainter to use to price services? Why?

Pricing Strategies

It is important to set the right price for your products and services. Pricing can make or break a business. When first introducing a product or service into the market, price skimming and penetration pricing strategies may be used. Afterwards, psychological pricing and discount pricing are two pricing strategies that you should examine and incorporate when establishing permanent pricing for your products and services.

Introductory Pricing

As a product is introduced into the market, sales will be low, marketing costs will be high, and little, if any, profit will be made. Two pricing strategies that are often used in the introductory stage of a product are price skimming and penetration pricing. *Price skimming*, which is used when a product is new and unique, starts with a high price to recover the costs involved in developing the product.

What pricing strategy might a company use for a new technology product?

Then as more competitors enter the market with similar products, the price is dropped. *Penetration pricing* uses a low introductory price with the goal of building a strong customer base. The low price also discourages competition.

Psychological Pricing

Psychological pricing is based on the belief that certain prices have an impact on how customers perceive a product. This type of pricing is most often used by retail businesses. Strategies used in psychological pricing include the following:

- *Prestige pricing* is selling at a high price in order to create a feeling of superior quality and social status.
- *Odd/even pricing* suggests that buyers are more sensitive to certain ending numbers. Studies have shown that prices ending in odd numbers are perceived to be bargains while those ending in even numbers suggest higher quality. For example, $29.99 sounds like a bargain compared to an even $30.00.
- *Price lining* involves offering different levels of prices for a specific category of product based on features and quality. A jeweler might offer three price lines of diamond necklaces and display them in different cases so that shoppers can go straight to the price level they can afford.
- *Promotional pricing* is offering lower prices for a limited time to increase sales. This type of pricing is temporary, and prices will return to normal when the promotion ends.
- *Multiple-unit pricing* involves pricing items in multiples, such as 10 for $10. This type of pricing suggests a bargain. People will buy more items than they would if the items were priced individually.

Discount Pricing

Discount pricing offers customers a reduced price. Discount pricing is used to encourage customers to buy. Markdowns are a type of discount pricing. Other discount pricing strategies include the following:

- *Cash discounts* are offered to customers to encourage early payment of invoices. When this is done, the terms of an invoice will include the amount of the discount, the number of days in the discount period, and when the invoice is due if the discount is not taken. For example, terms of "2/10, net 30" mean that a 2 percent discount may be taken if the invoice is paid within 10 days. If no discount is taken, the net or total amount of the invoice is due within 30 days of the date of the invoice. To find the last date available for the discount, add the number of days in the discount period to the date of the invoice. If the invoice is dated April 1, you would add 10, and the last day of the discount period would be April 11.

BE YOUR OWN BOSS

You plan to open a pizza delivery service near the University of Florida in Gainesville. Your target market includes students who live in dorms and houses on and near the main campus. You know that the price you charge is going to be critical to the success of your business as there are several restaurants in the area with which you will be competing. Develop a psychological pricing strategy for the pizza delivery service.

- *Quantity discounts* are reductions in price based on the purchase of a large quantity. This is also called a volume discount. Selling a large quantity at once reduces a business's selling expenses.
- *Trade discounts* are reductions on the list price granted by a manufacturer or wholesaler to buyers in the same trade.
- *Seasonal discounts* are used for selling seasonal merchandise out of season. Barbecue grills are in high demand in the spring and summer months but not in the fall and winter. Manufacturers offer discounts to customers who purchase grills out of season.

 CHECKPOINT

Name two strategies used in introductory pricing and provide an example of each.

5.3 ASSESSMENT

THINK ABOUT IT

1. What pricing objectives are most important to a new business?

2. What do you need to consider when pricing services?

3. Why is discount pricing used?

MAKE ACADEMIC CONNECTIONS

4. **COMMUNICATION** Look through advertisements in newspapers and magazines and find examples of introductory, psychological, and discount pricing. Prepare a poster of the advertisements and label each pricing strategy.

5. **MATH** You have a large inventory of small appliances in your hardware store that have not sold during the past year. You decide to mark them down by 30 percent. Access www.cengage.com/school/entrepreneurship/ideas. Click on *Activities* and open the file *Pricing Products*. Calculate the markdown price for each item. After two weeks, you still have some of these items, so you decide to mark them down an additional 25 percent. Find the new markdown price.

Teamwork

You and your teammates are going to open a home entertainment store. Access www.cengage.com/school/entrepreneurship/ideas. Click on *Activities* and open the file *Home Entertainment Store*. Print a copy and complete the activity. Locate distributors, wholesalers, and manufacturers of three products you would like to sell. Choose at least two brands for each item. Contact the distributor to obtain information about pricing and delivery. What is the wholesale price of each product? Find the same product in a local store. What is the retail price? What is the markup percentage?

Sharpen Your 21st CENTURY ENTREPRENEURIAL SKILLS

Breakeven Point

As an entrepreneur, you will have to make decisions about pricing your products. Knowing how to calculate the breakeven price will help ensure you do not price products below your cost. You do not want to lose money!

The lowest price identified in a price range is based on the costs of the product to the seller. All production, marketing, and administrative costs should be considered when determining the minimum price. The minimum price can be calculated through breakeven analysis. The breakeven point is the point at which sales revenue equals the total cost of acquiring or producing a product or service and selling it. At the breakeven point, a business has no profit and no loss—it simply breaks even. A business can use the breakeven point in units to analyze whether it is charging an appropriate price.

To calculate the breakeven point in units, a business must determine the selling price, fixed costs, and variable costs for one unit. Then, total fixed costs are divided by the selling price minus the variable costs.

Luisa's Gourmet Luxuries sells stainless steel pasta pots. Luisa determines that her fixed costs are $35,000 a year and her variable costs per unit are $9. Luisa wants to determine how many pasta pots

she would have to sell to break even if the price is set at $150. Her breakeven point for the pasta pots would be calculated as follows:

Total fixed costs ÷
  (Selling price − Variable cost) =
  Breakeven point
$35,000 ÷ ($150 − $9) = 248.23

The breakeven point in units would be approximately 249 units. Luisa must determine if she can sell 249 pasta pots. If she can, she can set the price at $150. If she wants to make a profit on the pasta pots, she will have to sell more than 249 units. Luisa can make additional calculations to determine the relationship between price and breakeven point.

Try It Out

You own AAA Audio/Video Repair. You make service calls to customers' homes to repair their audio/video equipment such as television sets and home theater systems. Your fixed costs are $10,000 a year and your variable costs for each service call are $20. If you charge $75 for each service call, how many service calls will you have to make in order to break even?

© Kurhan, 2010/ Used under license from Shutterstock.com

CHAPTER ASSESSMENT

5.1 Develop the Marketing Plan

1. Marketing is all of the processes—planning, pricing, promoting, distributing, and selling—used to determine and satisfy the needs of customers and the company. Businesses that follow the marketing concept use the needs of customers as the primary focus.

2. A marketing strategy identifies how you will achieve your marketing goals. For a new business, a marketing strategy should address, product introduction or innovation, pricing, distribution, promotion, sales or market share, and projected profitability.

3. A marketing plan should include information on the product or service, target market, competition, marketing budget, business location, pricing strategy, promotional strategy, and distribution strategy. Putting it in writing helps you determine whether your marketing plan is solid and all parts are consistent.

5.2 The Marketing Mix—Product

4. The different products and services a business offers are its product mix. The marketing concept keeps you focused on meeting the wants and needs of customers as you develop a product mix.

5. Product features are the characteristics of the product that will satisfy customer needs. Branding is the name, symbol, or design that identifies your product. The brand, package, and label will differentiate your product from others. Positioning is creating an image for a product in the customer's mind.

5.3 The Marketing Mix—Price

6. A business may set pricing objectives aimed at maximizing sales, increasing profits, discouraging competition, attracting customers, or establishing an image.

7. Pricing may be based on demand, cost, or competition.

8. Services may be priced based on time, materials used, and bundling. Ideas can be licensed and priced in different ways.

9. Introductory pricing strategies include price skimming and penetration pricing. Psychological pricing techniques include prestige pricing, odd/even pricing, price lining, promotional pricing, and multiple-unit pricing. Discount pricing includes cash discounts for early payment, quantity discounts, trade discounts, and seasonal discounts.

Read *Ideas in Action* on page 125 again. Then answer the questions a second time. Have your responses changed? If so, how have they changed?

VOCABULARY BUILDER

Match each statement with the term that best defines it. Some terms may not be used.

1. All of the processes—planning, pricing, promoting, distributing, and selling—used to determine and satisfy the needs of customers and the company
2. Uses the needs of customers as the primary focus during the planning, production, distribution, and promotion of a product or service
3. A blending of product, price, distribution, and promotion used to reach a target market
4. Identifies how marketing goals will be achieved
5. Amount earned as a result of an investment
6. Product characteristics that satisfy customer needs
7. The name, symbol, or design used to identify your product
8. A business's percentage of total sales generated by all companies in the same market
9. Creating an image of a product in the customer's mind
10. The different products and services a business sells
11. Pricing that is determined by how much customers are willing to pay for a product or service
12. Pricing that is determined by using the wholesale cost of an item as the basis for the price charged
13. Pricing that is based on the belief that certain prices have an impact on how customers perceive a product
14. Pricing that offers a reduced price to encourage customers to buy

a. brand
b. competition-based pricing
c. cost-based pricing
d. demand-based pricing
e. discount pricing
f. features
g. market share
h. marketing
i. marketing concept
j. marketing mix
k. marketing plan
l. marketing strategy
m. positioning
n. product mix
o. psychological pricing
p. return on investment

REVIEW YOUR KNOWLEDGE

15. To successfully use the marketing concept, a business must do which of the following?
    a. identify what will satisfy the customers' needs and wants
    b. develop and market products or services that customers consider better than other choices
    c. operate profitably
    d. all of the above
16. List six elements that should be addressed in a company's marketing strategy.
17. A marketing strategy should be consistent with the business's overall __?__.
18. **True or False** Opening two more restaurants in other locations around the city would be an example of a short-term goal for the owner of a new restaurant.
19. Which of the following would be a good addition to the product mix for a health club?
    a. diamond rings
    b. chocolate-chip cookies
    c. fitness apparel
    d. photo print service

20. The branding, packaging, and labeling of your product should accomplish all of the following *except*
    a. identify your product
    b. describe the company's product mix
    c. differentiate your product from others on the market
    d. provide information about the product
21. Which of the following is *not* a pricing objective?
    a. to maximize sales   c. to attract customers
    b. to increase profits   d. to decrease expenses
22. A new touch-screen tablet computer that lets you surf the Internet, send and receive e-mail, watch television, listen to music, and read books has just been released. There are people who want this device so badly they are willing to pay any price for it. This telephone should be priced using
    a. demand-based pricing   c. competition-based pricing
    b. cost-based pricing   d. time-based pricing
23. During late summer, Nordstrom's Department Store offers fall and winter clothes at a discounted price for a short period of time. After that time, the price of this clothing goes up and is not reduced again until the end-of-season clearance. This is an example of
    a. prestige pricing   c. promotional pricing
    b. price lining   d. multiple-unit pricing
24. You own an office supply store. You purchase desk lamps at a wholesale cost of $14 each. You use a markup of 45 percent to determine the selling price. At the end of the season, you offer a discount price using a markdown of 20 percent of the selling price. The discount price for desk lamps is
    a. $20.30   c. $16.24
    b. $17.50   d. $11.20
25. Which of the following pricing strategies is often used when introducing a new product into the market with the goal of developing a strong customer base while discouraging competition?
    a. price skimming   c. prestige pricing
    b. penetration pricing   d. price lining

APPLY WHAT YOU LEARNED

26. You want to open a gardening business. You plan to offer planting, weed pulling, and watering services to busy homeowners in your neighborhood. Write a positioning statement for your business.
27. You think that networking would be a good way to increase your market share for your gardening business described above. Outline a networking strategy to follow.

MAKE ACADEMIC CONNECTIONS

28. **MATH**   The annual sales of home entertainment equipment in your area is $23 million. You want to capture 15 percent of the market. How much will you have to sell to achieve your goal?

29. **COMMUNICATION**   Write a paragraph describing how psychological pricing has affected one of your purchasing decisions.

30. **PROBLEM SOLVING**   Your sporting goods store sells fitness equipment. Included in your product mix is a treadmill that is not selling well, and you do not understand why. List some possible causes. Outline strategies for determining the reason behind low sales.

31. **MATH**   You want to download some special relaxation music that you will play in the nail salon you are going to open. The site from which you download music is offering a multiple-unit price on music downloads this month. For every 3 songs you download, you pay only $2.50. If you download only one or two songs, the price is $0.99 per song. You download 38 songs. How much will you have to pay for the downloads?

What Would YOU Do?

You offer a math tutoring service for children at the elementary and middle schools in your neighborhood. You normally charge $15 per hour. You recently received a message from the mother of a fifth grader inquiring about your services and pricing. She got your name from the mother of another student you tutor. You recognize her name as being from a family that owns a very large business in your town. You would like to charge her more than $15 per hour because you know the family is wealthy.

What would you do? Is it fair for you to raise your price just because you know the family has more money? What problems do you think you might experience if you charge customers different prices? Under what circumstances would you be justified in charging customers different prices?

build your
BUSINESS PLAN PROJECT

This activity will help you get started on the development of a marketing plan for your business idea.

1. Define short-, medium-, and long-term marketing goals for your business.
2. Determine the product mix for your business and the features of each product. How do you plan on positioning your products?
3. Decide how you will develop brand recognition for your business. Design any logos, symbols, and/or product labeling and packaging you will use.
4. Determine your pricing objectives and how you plan to achieve them.
5. Develop a pricing strategy for your products and/or services. What price will you charge? How did you decide on this price?
6. Calculate the breakeven point based on your selling price. Is your breakeven point realistic? Do you need to adjust the selling price?

Planning a Career in

E-MARKETING

"My boss gave me one hour to surf the Web to research a potential business he might develop. The time limit was to encourage me to stay focused. Each website had multiple links to other sites. Some sites were informational with pages of text, while other sites were more visually appealing by using color and graphics. Some sites had movie-quality commercials, while other sites offered free products. When the hour was up, my summary report included the assigned topic and additional information about related topics."

Why do websites contain links to other sites? Why are some websites easier to navigate than others?

E-marketing is an expanding field that helps companies reach consumers via the Internet. Website designers help companies and organizations develop websites that inform potential customers about products and services offered.

Employment Outlook
- Faster than average growth is anticipated.
- As businesses increase their dependence on the Internet for the efficient distribution of product and marketing information, demand for these jobs will continue to grow.

Job Titles
- Online Marketing and Outreach Coordinator
- Website Template Designer
- Web Page Developer
- Portal Designer
- Website Marketer

Needed Education/Skills
- A Bachelor's degree is recommended.
- Strong problem-solving and analytical skills are required.
- Computer science and business courses are helpful.
- Experience in content management, HTML, and assorted web-related software is required.

What's it like to work in E-marketing? This morning Lev, a freelance website designer, is meeting with a small group of investors who want to build a dozen windmills on property bordering a huge lake. As part of a public relations campaign to encourage community support for the project, the investors want to develop a website about the project. Lev has been contracted to develop a website that will list all of the benefits of the windmill farm. The website needs to include photos of the windmill farm's proposed design, statistics on the number of homes that can be powered from wind energy, and data reflecting flight patterns of local birds. The site also needs to provide links to similar small-scale projects that have been successful.

In the afternoon, Lev will meet with a farmer's association that wants to provide support via a website for independent farmers who want to convert corn to ethanol. This meeting will focus on the site's content and possible links to other informational sites. In addition, the group will be making design decisions related to color, icon graphics, and editorial style. To help make the project more appealing to farmers, Lev must ensure that the website is easy to navigate.

What about you? Would you like to design websites that are informative, easy to navigate, and profitable for their sponsors?

Global Marketing Team Event

Teams will develop a written international marketing plan that identifies the customer base. The participating team must demonstrate oral communication skills to market a new product. The written marketing plan must not exceed ten pages. The completed written plan must include the Title Page; Table of Contents; Synopsis; Company Goals; Description of Customers and Their Needs; Description of Pricing Strategy; Competition; Marketing Mix; Economic, Social, Legal, and Technological Trends; Human Resource Requirements; Marketing Timeline; Methods of Measuring Success; and Supporting Documentation. The length of the oral presentation must not exceed ten minutes. BPA selects a new topic for the Global Marketing Team Event every year.

TOPIC: You are the Marketing Director for Flower Power. Your flower farm, located in southern Texas, raises fresh, reasonably-priced flowers that are sold throughout the United States. Most of your customers are wholesalers and supermarkets that sell fresh flowers at affordable prices. Research indicates that the global economy offers numerous markets for your fresh flowers. Your company has recently developed a revolutionary packaging system that will ensure the delivery of fresh flowers to international customers. The package also meets all international standards, making it more likely to clear another country's customs, which are restrictions imposed on imported products.

Your presentation must explain your marketing plan for conducting business globally.

Performance Indicators

- Demonstrate knowledge and understanding of management and international business concepts
- Communicate research in a clear and concise manner, both orally and in writing
- Demonstrate teamwork skills needed to function in a global marketing environment
- Demonstrate successful price selection methods
- Demonstrate effective persuasive and informative communication and presentation skills

Go to the BPA website for more detailed information.

THINK CRITICALLY
1. Why is the packaging so important for fresh-cut flowers?
2. Why is it important for the product to clear customs?
3. Why must Flower Power understand customs (cultural traditions) in other countries?
4. Why is it important to have a reasonably-priced package in this case?

www.bpa.org

Digital Vision/Getty Images

CHAPTER 6

Distribution, Promotion, and Selling

6.1 The Marketing Mix—Distribution

6.2 The Marketing Mix—Promotion

6.3 Selling and Promoting

 www.cengage.com/school/entrepreneurship/ideas

A "FUNK-tional" Fix for Footwear

Photo courtesy of Katie Shea and Susie Levitt

Katie Shea and Susie Levitt, creators of CitySlips

If you have ever worked a job where you have to constantly be on your feet, then you can probably relate to Katie Shea and Susie Levitt's aches and pains. The two friends lived in high-heeled shoes while working summer internships on Wall Street as seniors at New York University. After months of high-heel agony, Katie and Susie knew they had to create a sensible footwear alternative.

Katie and Susie co-founded FUNK-tional Footwear and created CitySlips, a split-sole pair of flats that fold into a pouch for easy on-the-go carrying. After combining $10,000 worth of savings, months of research, and feedback from friends and family on a final design, Katie and Susie had to find a manufacturer. They used an online portal that connects entrepreneurs with factories around the world. They made their decision based on price, quality, and delivery time.

Katie and Susie began selling shoes on the CitySlips website, but they were determined to find other modes of distribution. They researched retailers that sold similar functional fashion products and called to see if they would be interested in their product. They emphasized in phone calls and press releases how versatile CitySlips could be for places such as weddings and airports. Because Katie and Susie received a lot of good press early on, retailers such as Rickey's NYC were eager to buy their merchandise. They also gained interest by offering pairs as giveaway items on fashion blogs. Their persistence in reaching out to retailers and buyers was one of their keys to success.

"When we hear a 'no' from someone, we try to turn it into a 'maybe.' And then we try to turn that 'maybe' into a 'yes,'" Katie said. "It works if you are persistent."

In the past year Katie and Susie sold more than 500,000 pairs of CitySlips, and the shoes can be found in more than 500 retail locations. They have since created new footwear and currently have a flip-flop line in the works. Katie and Susie follow their "Three 'I' Mantra" when creating new products. They must be irresistible, intelligent, and innovative. Katie encourages young entrepreneurs to not discard any ideas that might seem too easy or unglamorous. Katie says, "A good spot to start is to think of a daily annoyance and imagine a way to fix it."

1. What factors did Katie and Susie consider when choosing retailers for their product?
2. How did Katie and Susie use the Internet and social media to gain interest in CitySlips?
3. Can you think of an everyday annoyance that you would like to fix?

what do you know?

THE MARKETING MIX—DISTRIBUTION

Goals

- Describe the four basic options of channels of distribution.
- Apply channels of distribution to the specific needs of various types of businesses.
- List factors to consider in the physical distribution of products.

Vocabulary

- supply chain management
- distribution
- channels of distribution
- direct channel
- indirect channel
- physical distribution

focus on small business

Avoid distribution mixups.

Dustin owns a small hardware store in south Florida. During the winter, he placed an order for swimming pool supplies to be delivered in early spring. He knew that pool usage and maintenance needs would increase for his customers in the spring. He wanted to be sure he had everything in stock in time. His supplier processed the order and assured Dustin it would be delivered in late February. Imagine Dustin's surprise when he opened the box from the supplier and found a product used to melt snow on walkways and driveways!

Digital Vision/Getty Images

Distribution problems can negatively impact a business.

Work as a Team What do you think happened to Dustin's order? How do you think Dustin should handle this situation?

Supply Chain Management

Supply chain management is the coordination of manufacturers, suppliers, and retailers working together to meet a customer need for a product or service. Distribution is an important component of supply chain management that involves the locations and methods used to make products and services available to customers. As you develop a distribution strategy for your business, you will determine how you will get your goods and services to your customers. You must be sure you have the right product in the right place at the right time.

Luisa Ramirez, who is opening a gourmet food shop and catering business in her community, knows that she must consider distribution in the marketing of her business. She will need to consider how to get the goods to sell, as well as how to actually get them into the customers' hands.

Channels of distribution are the routes that products and services take from the time they are produced to the time they are consumed. Choosing the right channel of distribution for a product includes finding the most efficient way to ship it to desired locations. Using the right distribution channels saves time and lowers costs for both buyers and sellers.

Direct and Indirect Channels

Channels are either direct or indirect. A **direct channel** moves the product directly from the manufacturer to the consumer. An **indirect channel** uses *intermediaries*—people or businesses that move products between the manufacturer and the consumer. Agents, wholesalers, and retailers serve as intermediaries.

Getting a product to the market in a timely manner is an important component of the distribution phase. If a farmer in South Georgia grows strawberries, the value of the strawberries will be maximized if they can be moved to northern markets quickly while they are fresh. Because there is a lack of fresh strawberries in northern markets, the demand will be higher, and they will command a better price. The strawberry farmer must determine whether to use a direct or indirect channel of distribution to get the product to customers.

Channel Options

Entrepreneurs should examine the different options for channels of distribution and choose the one that best meets the needs of their business. The four basic options are illustrated and described below.

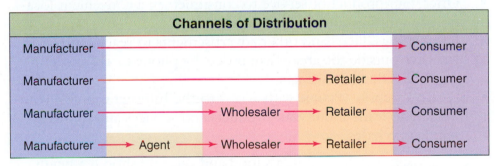

1. **Manufacturer to Consumer**   The product can be sold by the manufacturer directly to the consumer using various methods, such as the Internet, direct mail, or television shopping channels. There are no intermediaries involved in this option, and it is the most cost-effective. However, sales opportunities are limited because it is more difficult for a manufacturer to reach the final consumer.
2. **Manufacturer to Retailer to Consumer**   A sales force can sell manufactured goods to retail stores, and the retail stores can sell to the consumers. This is a more expensive option than selling directly from the manufacturer to the consumer, but it offers more sales opportunities.
3. **Manufacturer to Wholesaler to Retailer to Consumer**   To reach a large market, the manufacturer can sell large quantities

Make a list of all of the chapter key terms. Write a definition for each key term before reading the chapter. When a key term is introduced in the chapter, compare the definition to the one you wrote and correct your definitions as needed.

to a wholesaler, also called a distributor, who will then store and sell smaller quantities to many retailers. Even though more intermediaries are involved in this method, prices can be lower because the manufacturer is producing mass quantities of the product, resulting in lower production costs.

4. **Manufacturer to Agent to Wholesaler to Retailer to Consumer** With this option, the manufacturer does not get involved in selling. Selling is handled by an agent. This option is often used in international marketing.

What are the four basic options of channels of distribution?

Distribute Goods and Services

Retail businesses, service businesses, and manufacturing businesses will choose different channels of distribution based on the needs of their businesses. Those needs can vary based on the size of the market, the type of product or service, and customer needs and wants.

Retail Businesses

Retail businesses have many ways of selling products. As the owner of a retail business, you can distribute products in various ways.

- Offer your product or service to consumers in a convenient location and during convenient hours.
- Use catalogs, fliers, and other advertisements to reach customers who live outside the area. Take orders by phone or fax and ship them directly to customers.
- Create a website. People with access to the Internet can visit your website to learn about your products and services and to make online purchases.

Luisa's food and catering shop is a neighborhood business that caters to local residents, so she does not think she would get much benefit from catalogs. As a convenience for customers, Luisa decides to stay open until 8:00 on weeknights and have hours from 10:00 until 4:00 on Saturdays and 12:00 to 4:00 on Sundays. She also creates a website that contains product descriptions, menus, and order forms for customers wanting to place catering orders.

Service Businesses

Most entrepreneurs who own service businesses sell their services directly to customers. These businesses have a single, direct channel

BE YOUR OWN BOSS

You plan to open a kite shop in a beach resort town. You will sell custom-made kites as well as kites you plan to import. You know that you will have customers during the spring and summer when families are visiting the beach, but you are looking for ways to increase sales during the off-season when there are very few visitors to the area. Describe ways that you could distribute your products that would increase sales during the off-season.

of distribution because the production and consumption of a service happens at the same time. For example, electricians, restaurant owners, and lawyers deal directly with the people who purchase their services. It is important for a service provider to offer the service when it is needed by the customer to maximize the value of the service. If the service cannot be provided when needed, the customer will look for another provider. Some service businesses, such as film developers, use retail stores to distribute their services.

Manufacturing Businesses

Manufacturers usually don't sell directly to customers. Instead, they make their products and then sell the products to other businesses, such as retailers. The retail store then sells to the final consumer.

Some manufacturers distribute their products very broadly and use all possible channels of distribution. Other manufacturers distribute their products through selected outlets only. For example, high-priced cosmetics usually are sold in exclusive department stores. Inexpensive cosmetics are sold in discount stores and drugstores.

CHECKPOINT

> Why are channels of distribution different for different types of businesses?

Physical Distribution

Physical distribution includes not only transportation but also storage and handling of products and packaging within a channel of distribution. A product may move through several channel members by various forms of transportation to get to the point where it will ultimately be sold to consumers. As the product is transported, it will be stored at various points along the channel before being moved to the next channel member. It is important that storage facilities along the channel provide safe and adequate space to protect the product.

Transportation

There are many choices when transporting goods. Products can be moved by airplane, pipeline, railroad, ship, truck, or a combination of methods. You must determine which method is best and most cost efficient for your products. Factors to consider in making a transportation decision include what you are shipping and where it is being shipped. If you are shipping a small product to someone in your city, you would probably choose a parcel delivery service. If you are shipping a large item to another country, you would probably send the item by ship or air and use a truck to get the product to and from the shipyard or airport. If the product is perishable, you may need to choose a carrier that provides refrigeration or that can move the product very quickly to its destination.

Product Storage and Handling

Efficient storage allows channel members to balance supply and demand of products. However, this adds to the cost of the products and also adds the risk that products may be damaged or stolen while stored. Most products are stored in warehouses at various points through the channels of distribution. An automobile manufacturer in Japan selling autos in the United States stores them in Japan at the factory and at the shipyard until they are shipped. Once they arrive in the United States, they will be stored at the port until they can be loaded onto automobile carriers to be distributed to the dealers. Dealers have to provide storage for the automobiles until they are sold to the consumer.

Packaging

Packaging is designed to protect the product from the time it is produced until it is consumed. If the product is not protected during the distribution phase, it could be damaged or destroyed, resulting in a loss of money to channel members. Packaging requirements will vary depending on the product, the way it is shipped, and where it is being shipped. The automobile manufacturer in Japan would package a small accessory item being shipped to the United States differently than the autos it ships.

Receiving Goods to Sell

All types of businesses must receive goods from suppliers. Whether or not they sell goods to customers, all businesses need paper, computers, raw materials, and more to be able to function. Retailing businesses need to obtain goods to sell. A service business that grooms pets needs to buy cat and dog shampoos and flea combs. A blanket manufacturer must buy cotton.

You can use various sources to locate distributors, wholesalers, and manufacturers. Your public library and the Internet will have research materials you can use. Some helpful sources include the following:

Why is product storage and handling an important part of the distribution process?

- The *American Wholesalers and Distributors Directory*, which lists suppliers in a wide range of industries
- The ThomasNet website, which lists all manufacturing companies
- Trade magazines that may include articles or advertisements pertaining to the suppliers for your industry

Luisa needs to create relationships with wholesale distributors. She must find companies she can trust to deliver high-quality products quickly. Luisa will purchase products directly from companies that produce them and through distributors. Her pastries come from a local baker. Distributors will supply her with imported and domestic canned goods as well as meats, fruits, and vegetables.

 CHECKPOINT

> What factors are important to consider in the physical distribution of products?

6.1 ASSESSMENT

THINK ABOUT IT

1. Which channel of distribution would be the best for a fruit and vegetable farm with limited production of a few products to be sold to a small group of local customers?

2. How does distribution add value to goods, services, and ideas being sold?

3. How is it possible to add intermediaries to the distribution channel and at the same time increase profits?

MAKE ACADEMIC CONNECTIONS

4. **GEOGRAPHY**   Think of a product that would have to be shipped from another country to the United States. Research the route that the product would follow while being shipped. Write a paragraph describing the places the product would pass through and describe the method of transportation that would be used for shipping. Research and estimate the total costs associated with shipping the product.

5. **COMMUNICATION**   Make a list of products that are sold directly to consumers by the manufacturer. Share the list with your classmates.

Teamwork

Working in a team, choose one of the following products: apples, MP3 players, magazines, milk, motor oil, t-shirts, CDs, or DVDs. Draw flow charts tracing all the possible channels of distribution for the product.

6.2 THE MARKETING MIX—PROMOTION

Goals
- List the many forms of advertising and discuss advantages and disadvantages of each.
- Define publicity and describe ways to use publicity as a promotional tool.

Vocabulary
- advertising
- publicity
- press release
- public relations

focus on small business

Know the costs of promotion.

From the moment she got the idea to open her own spa, all Chachi could think about was Grand Opening Day! But she knew that there were many things to do before she was ready to open. She took her time and worked through all the details, preparing her business plan and securing financing for the business. Now Chachi is ready to get the word out to her target market. She wants to be sure that the information she shares motivates customers to visit the spa. She considers offering a free spa service with the purchase of a spa service on opening day. This promotion could cost her up to $120 per free service. Chachi has a staff of four, but only two of them are certified to perform certain spa services. So she knows she must consider any staffing problems that could occur on opening day as a result of the promotion.

There are many factors to consider when developing promotions.

©Katarzyna Krawiec, 2010/ Used under license from Shutterstock.com

Work as a Team Do you think Chachi's idea for an opening day promotion is a good one? Why or why not? Can you suggest some alternative promotions that Chachi might use?

Promotion Strategies

No matter how wonderful your products, distribution methods, and pricing, you will not succeed as an entrepreneur if customers do not know about your business. You will have to promote your business to make customers aware of the benefits of buying from you. Promotion takes many forms including advertising, publicity, personal selling, and sales promotion. The strategy created by adopting a blend of some, if not all, of these techniques is called your *promotional mix*.

Advertising

Service industries, manufacturers, and retailers all advertise. **Advertising** is a paid form of communication sent out by a business about a product or service. It keeps your product or service in the public's eye by creating a sense of awareness. Advertising should help a business convey a positive image.

Advertising can be very important for small businesses, particularly new ones. Advertising helps you communicate with potential customers. It lets them know what kinds of products and services your company offers and why they should buy from you. Large companies generally use advertising agencies to create their advertisements. Using an advertising agency usually results in highly creative and effective ads, but it can be costly. As a small business owner, you probably will handle your own advertising.

Your advertising should clearly communicate your message and image. If, for example, your marketing strategy is to have low prices, advertisements should highlight your prices. If your aim is to target customers who are willing to pay higher prices for excellent service, advertising that describes your well-trained staff would fit your image.

Once you choose a message, you will need to decide which advertising medium to use. To choose a medium, you will have to consider both cost and effectiveness in reaching your target audience.

Online Advertising

As Internet use has increased, online advertising has become widely used by businesses to promote their products and services. This is a cost-effective way for businesses to get information to potential customers. Ongoing changes and advancements in online advertising technology make it easier for customers to get the information they need. Potential customers can use keyword searches and browse through online catalogs by category to find information about available products and services.

Online technology lets businesses interact with customers through online chat rooms, blogs, and e-newsletters. A well-designed website can enhance customers' experiences by giving them easy-to-navigate pages that contain up-to-date information on products and services.

TYPES OF ONLINE ADVERTISING   Online advertising combines color, imagery, animation, and other elements to attract the reader's attention. Some common types of online advertising include the following:

- **Banner Ad**   A graphic image or animation displayed within a rectangular box across the top or down the side of a web page
- **Floating Ad**   An ad that moves across the screen or floats above the page content
- **Wallpaper Ad**   An ad that changes the background of the page being viewed

- **Trick Banner** A banner ad that looks like a dialog box with buttons, often appearing like an error message or an alert
- **Pop-Up Ad** A new window that opens in front of the current one, displaying an advertisement
- **Pop-Under Ad** A new window, similar to a pop-up ad, that loads behind the current window and does not appear until the user closes one or more active windows

PAYING FOR ONLINE ADVERTISING It is easier to accurately determine the effectiveness of online advertising than it is to determine the effectiveness of other, more traditional forms of advertising. As a result, new methods of charging for online advertising have been developed, based on the effectiveness of the ads. Three of the most common ways online advertising is purchased are as follows:

- **Cost per Mil (CPM)** The charge to the advertiser is based on the exposure of the message to a specific audience. CPM costs are priced per thousand viewers reached with the message.
- **Cost per Click (CPC)** The charge to the advertiser is based on the number of user clicks on the advertisement. This method offers an incentive to the publisher of the ad to target the ad correctly. It will appear when certain keywords are used in visitors' searches that correspond with the content of the ad. Payment to the publisher is dependent upon viewers actually responding to the ad by clicking on the hyperlink within the ad.
- **Cost per Action (CPA)** The charge to the advertiser is based on the user completing a form, registering for a newsletter, or taking some other action that will lead to a sale. The publisher assumes all the risks in running this type of advertisement. Advertisers prefer this type of charge for banner advertisements.

DISADVANTAGES OF ONLINE ADVERTISING Many marketers have abused the Internet and its ease of use with excessive *spamming*, which involves sending mass e-mails to Internet users. Excessive use of pop-ups, flashy banners, and spam has caused people to use pop-up blockers, spam control, and spyware to block promotions.

Luisa creates a website that provides information about her gourmet food shop and catering services. Because her customers are local, Luisa decides not to use any other forms of online advertising.

Television Advertising

Promotions on television reach millions of people every day. It is the best way to reach a large number of people quickly. Television advertising usually comes in the form of commercials and paid advertisements. Commercials are usually less than a

Why might some people overlook Internet ads?

minute in length and are run during breaks in television programming. They are very short promotions about a product or business. Infomercials can last a half hour or more and go into depth about the product being offered. Television promotion allows businesses to communicate through both sight and sound. It can be creative, entertaining, and informative.

Television advertising expenses include the fee you have to pay the station to air the commercial. This fee is based on the amount of time your advertisement or commercial plays. In addition, you must also consider the costs of producing the commercial. If a one-minute commercial costs $25,000 to produce, you pay the television station $2,000 for each minute it airs, and you plan to have it aired 30 times, the cost per minute would be [$25,000 + ($2,000 × 30)] ÷ 30 = $2,833.33.

DISADVANTAGES OF TELEVISION ADVERTISING   Advertising on television is very expensive. Producing even a low-budget commercial can cost thousands of dollars. You will need to seek the help of video and production professionals when developing a television ad. In addition, you will have to pay a network or cable station to broadcast the commercial.

Television reaches too broad an audience to be effective for most businesses. If, for example, only one percent of the viewing audience is interested in a particular product, advertising on television is not likely to be cost-effective.

Because of the excessive costs and the fact that she may not reach her target customer very effectively, Luisa decides that television advertising is not right for her business.

Radio Advertising

Radio advertising can be effective for small businesses. It is less expensive than television promotion. You can also be more certain you are reaching your target market. Radio stations tend to attract a particular kind of listener. Pop rock stations target teenagers and young adults. Classical or talk radio stations usually attract older listeners. Selecting a station whose listeners share the same demographics as your target market can increase the effectiveness of your advertising. You can contact stations and ask for a demographic profile of their listeners to make sure it fits your target market profile.

The costs of radio advertising are determined in the same way as the costs of television advertising. You must pay for air time and production costs.

Radio is a purely audio message and cannot visually show your product. Radio listeners may not remember what they hear. They may tune out or even "surf the airwaves" during the commercial spots. You may need professional help when developing a radio ad, which can be costly.

Luisa is targeting middle-aged, upscale customers. To reach this audience, she decides to advertise on the classical music station in her community. She receives a demographic profile of the radio station's listeners and determines that her business targets a similar type of person.

Newspaper Advertising

Newspapers have been the single largest form of advertising in the United States. However, as more people are looking to the Internet for news and information, newspaper circulation has dropped in many cities. Small businesses may choose to promote their products and services in the newspaper for the following reasons:

- It is relatively inexpensive.
- It targets a limited geographic area.
- It reaches large numbers of people.

Luisa decides to advertise in several local newspapers. She places quarter-page ads in the morning paper serving the citywide area. She also puts half-page ads in all of the free newspapers that serve her community. The community papers reach a much smaller audience than the large city newspaper, but they target the local audience Luisa is trying to reach. Advertising in newspapers represents a cost-effective way for Luisa to reach her target market.

DISADVANTAGES OF NEWSPAPER ADVERTISING Newspapers reach a large audience, but much of that audience may not be interested in your business. If, for example, you own a small gift shop that caters to people only in your immediate area, advertising in a large city newspaper with a wide circulation may not make sense. You would be paying to reach thousands of people who are outside of your target market.

Another disadvantage of newspaper advertising is the fact that your advertisement will compete with many others. Newspapers carry so many advertisements that readers may overlook yours.

Telephone Directory Advertising

Telephone directories list the phone numbers of people and businesses in a certain area. Directory ads usually appear on a page close to the listing and phone number of the business placing the ad. Directory ads can be similar in appearance to newspaper ads. Customers look in telephone directories again and again, making them a good advertising medium.

A disadvantage of directory advertising is that people look in the directory only when they are already in search of a particular type of business. With directory advertising, it is not easy to persuade customers to try your business instead of a competitor's business. But, knowing how important the phone book can be, Luisa decides to place a quarter-page ad in the commercial directory distributed in her area.

Direct-Mail Advertising

Direct-mail advertising includes fliers, catalogs, letters, and other correspondence sent to target customers through the mail. Mailing lists for target markets are available for purchase. If your business sells hospital beds, you can purchase targeted mailing lists of people who would purchase your product. You can also get lists of people based on the geographic area. Companies that specialize in maintaining targeted mailing lists can provide almost any kind of list for any kind of business.

Direct-mail advertising can be effective if people read it, but many people throw out direct-mail advertising, calling it "junk mail." If you use this method of advertising, you will want to come up with an attention-grabbing design or other means of making people want to read it.

Luisa decides to use direct mail to target residents living in four zip code areas near her store. She creates an attractive brochure with a catchy slogan on the outside cover, and she mails it to residents in the neighborhoods she is targeting.

Magazine Advertising

Magazines are an excellent way to aim products and services at specific markets. Fitness magazines are full of advertisements for athletic apparel and equipment. Magazines targeting teenage girls are full of advertisements for products that appeal to them, such as cosmetics and clothing.

Most magazines are nationally distributed. This can make them inappropriate for businesses that sell in a limited geographic area. Some large cities have local magazines, which would be an effective way to target a certain area.

Why are magazines an effective advertising medium when you are trying to reach a specific target market?

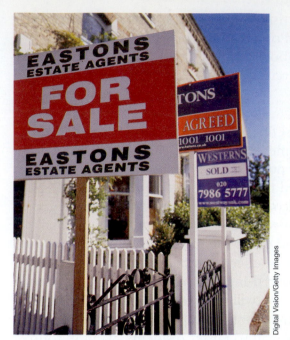

The city in which Luisa will be opening her gourmet store has two local magazines. One focuses heavily on restaurants and entertaining. Luisa checks the demographics of the magazine's readership and finds that it targets the same market she is trying to reach. She decides to advertise in the magazine every other month.

How can outdoor advertising be used effectively?

Outdoor Advertising

Outdoor advertising includes billboards and signs. Such advertising can be effective in keeping the name of your business in a place where many people can see it. But because people view such advertising quickly as they drive by, it cannot include much information. Also, outdoor advertising may not project the image you are trying to convey for your business.

Transit Advertising

Transit advertising consists of signs on public transportation. Transit advertising can provide more information than is typically seen on a billboard. Such advertising can be effective if the market you are trying to reach includes many people who use public transportation.

Luisa's target market lives in the suburbs and rarely uses public transportation. For this reason, she rules out transit advertising, which would not help her reach her target market.

Social Networking Sites

E-mail has become a necessity for most business owners today to communicate with employees, shareholders, suppliers, and customers. Now social networking is entering the business scene. Business owners are beginning to find new and creative ways to use these sites for business promotion.

Twitter allows users to send very short messages called tweets that are no more than 140 characters long. Business owners find it a good way to keep their name in front of people who have a connection with or interest in their business. Some businesses also use it to announce special offers.

LinkedIn is a social networking site aimed specifically at businesses. It can be used to search for consultants and contractors. It has also become a major source for posting job openings.

YouTube is a great way to get information out to prospects and customers. You can make a short promotional video demonstrating your product or service or have current customers provide testimonials about it. A short e-mail can direct prospective customers to your YouTube video.

did you KNOW?

Forrester Research's Interactive Marketing Forecast for the next five years estimates that social media marketing will grow at an annual rate of 34 percent, which is faster than any other form of online marketing and double the average growth rate of 17 percent for all online mediums.

Facebook is used to set up web pages promoting your business. Customers and prospective customers can view company information on your Facebook page and become a fan of your business. Once they become a fan, any posts you make will go on their own Facebook Wall.

Blogging is used by companies to highlight new products and share company information. A blog can combine text, images, and links to other web pages. It is an interactive format in which readers can add comments on a particular topic, such as a company's products or services.

Budgeting for Promotion

Once you determine your promotional mix, you must obtain the approximate costs for all forms of advertising media that you plan to use. Using the estimated costs, calculate a projected promotional budget. Compare this amount to your projected sales and decide what percentage of the budget promotion represents. Determine whether this budget is realistic for your business. Compare your percentage to the industry average, which you can obtain from trade associations,

what went *wrong?*

DENTAL PROMOTION LEAVES BAD TASTE

Dr. George Nilsson, a periodontist, had built his practice through dentist referrals and word of mouth and by speaking at conferences. As a way to expand his business, he decided to develop a program for dentists that graphically tracked gum disease. It would take the guesswork out of whether or not a patient should go to a specialist. Dr. Nilsson designed a step-by-step program, including a video and printed guide. He started the PerioDent Company, investing $150,000 in developing the program components, another $40,000 for initial inventory, and $80,000 more for advertising and public relations.

PerioDent sent out mailings to dentists, periodontists, and schools. It took out full-page ads in professional journals. Unfortunately, after six months, sales were not as expected. There was a backlash of bad press from Dr. Nilsson's peers. The majority of dentists resented the PerioDent program because they believed it criticized the way they had been diagnosing gum disease.

Additionally, dentists accused it of having a negative impact on their income because it prompted some patients to visit periodontists instead of dentists. At the same time, some periodontists accused Dr. Nilsson of blatant self-promotion and greed.

THINK CRITICALLY

1. What could Dr. Nilsson have done differently to advertise and promote the program?
2. How might publicity or public relations activities help improve PerioDent's image?

Plan your promotions carefully.

business publications, or business owners. Be sure your promotional budget is in line with similar businesses.

Why is promotion important to a business?

Publicity

Publicity is a nonpaid form of communication that calls attention to your business through media coverage. Publicity may be good or bad. Good publicity can be as helpful as advertising. Publicity is free, but staging an event or bringing in a celebrity to generate publicity usually is not. A **press release**, which is a written statement meant to inform the media of an event or product, is a good way to promote an event.

While there are things you can do to attract positive media attention, publicity is largely out of a business's control. Publicity can be negative if the media coverage is unfavorable. For example, some community newspapers publish listings of restaurants that have violated health code laws. Customers may see this publicity and stop eating at those restaurants.

Luisa plans to have an open house to mark her first day in business. She hopes that the media will do a story on her grand opening. To increase this chance, Luisa hires a popular local jazz band to perform. She also invites her community's leaders and personalities. She writes and sends a press release to all of the local newspapers, magazines, and radio and television stations as well. Luisa's press release is shown on the next page.

To keep her name in the news, Luisa volunteers to write a weekly cooking column for one of the free newspapers in her community. She likes the opportunity to educate the public about gourmet cooking and to increase her store's visibility as a seller of gourmet foods.

Public Relations

Public relations is the act of establishing a favorable relationship with customers and the general public. Public awareness and positive public relations can be generated for your business when you show your community that you are involved and committed to it. There are many ways to support your community, including the following:

- Sponsor a community sports team.
- Make a donation to a local charity or relief effort program.
- Get involved with the work-based program at your local high school or community college.
- Become active in the local chapters of the Big Brothers or Big Sisters organizations.
- Organize community programs such as cleaning up neighborhood parks.

FOR IMMEDIATE RELEASE

GALA OPENING OF LUISA'S GOURMET LUXURIES

Come celebrate the opening of Luisa's Gourmet Luxuries on Friday, September 20, at 8:00 P.M. Hors d'oeuvres, imported champagne, and French pastries will be served at the event. Music will be provided by Glendale's leading jazz ensemble, Jazz Expressions.

The opening of Luisa's Gourmet Luxuries marks the realization of a dream by owner Luisa Ramirez. "As a specialty cook," she says, "I could not always find the products I needed. And I was never happy with the selection of produce and baked goods in town." Luisa decided to open a store that would offer the kinds of products she could not find elsewhere in town.

Luisa's Gourmet Luxuries offers an astounding selection of products, including 14 different kinds of olive oil, 12 different kinds of rice, and pasta products from several different countries. "Everyone's taste is different," says Luisa, "so I offer a large selection."

For more information contact:

Luisa Ramirez, Proprietor

Luisa's Gourmet Luxuries

1610 Marbury Road, Glendale, CT

(275) 555-3983

Self-Promotion

A business should try to keep its name visible and in the forefront of people's minds. Self-promotion is a good way to do this. It's a simple way to generate "free" publicity. Self-promotion may include activities such as:

- Giving away t-shirts and hats displaying your company name and logo.
- Distributing pens, notepads, coffee mugs, and other useful items printed with the name, telephone number, website address, and logo of your business.

 CHECKPOINT

What are the advantages and disadvantages of publicity?

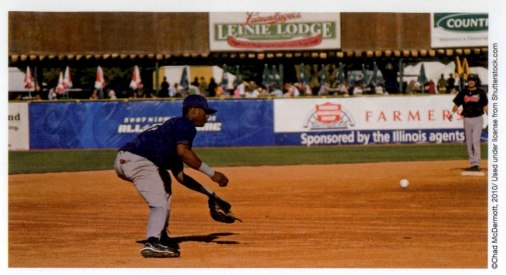

How can a company create public awareness and make its name more visible?

6.2 ASSESSMENT

THINK ABOUT IT

1. Why is it important for a business to consider its target market when selecting an advertising medium?

2. Describe some public relations activities businesses in your area have performed.

3. How would you decide which method of advertising is the best and most cost-effective for your business?

MAKE ACADEMIC CONNECTIONS

4. **PROBLEM SOLVING**   You are opening a new gardening service business in your community. You will help your customers plan their flower and vegetable gardens and shop for the plants for them. You will also provide planting services if your customers need them. Use the six-step problem-solving method to determine how to advertise the grand opening of your business.

5. **MATH**   You have produced a one-minute television commercial for $20,000. You plan to air it on a local television station for a cost of $1,000 per minute. You plan to air the commercial 20 times. What is the advertising cost per minute?

Teamwork

Working with team members, plan the grand opening activities for Fit For U, a fitness center that offers fitness equipment, exercise classes, and personal trainers for all clients along with a personalized fitness plan. Describe all of the promotional activities that you will conduct for the business. Write a press release to inform the local media of the opening.

SELLING AND PROMOTING

Goals

- Explain the role of selling in a business.
- Determine how to meet customer needs and wants.
- Discuss other types of promotional activities.
- Evaluate the effectiveness of promotional campaigns.

Vocabulary

- personal selling
- rational buying decisions
- emotional buying decisions
- sales promotion
- rebate
- telemarketing
- visual marketing

focus on small business

Expand the business.

JoJo started her dance studio five years ago. Over the years, many of her clients have expressed a desire for JoJo to sell dance attire and shoes at her studio. She looks into the idea of adding a clothing line and thinks that it would be a good addition to her business. She decides to hire Claire to run the clothing side of the business. Claire has worked in retail sales for over ten years and is very customer-oriented. By adding Claire to her staff, JoJo will be able to offer her clients other products and services to meet their needs. In addition to her dance clients, JoJo wants to make the clothing line available to the general public.

Photodisc/Getty Images

Work as a Team Do you think that JoJo is making a good decision by adding a retail clothing line to her dance studio? Why or why not? What kinds of promotions do you think JoJo should use to try to attract new customers?

Businesses must create the right promotional mix to attract customers.

Selling

Good selling skills are important to an entrepreneur. You will be selling your business ideas to potential investors in the beginning stages of developing your business, and you will be selling products or services to customers once you open your business. You may need to hire others with good selling skills to assist you with your business.

To many customers, the salesperson is the business. This may be the only representative of the company the customers ever come in contact with, so it is important for the salesperson to create a positive image for the company. Selling is the way a business makes money, so a salesperson plays a very important role.

Why is personal selling an important component to the success of a business?

Personal Selling

Personal selling is direct communication between a prospective buyer and a sales representative in which the sales representative attempts to influence the prospective buyer in a purchase situation. It is important for the salesperson to uncover and identify the customer's needs, issues, and concerns so that they can be addressed throughout the sales process.

Product Knowledge

To be successful at selling a product or service, a salesperson must have thorough knowledge of the features and benefits of the product or service. *Features* are the physical characteristics or capabilities of the product or service. *Benefits* are the advantages that could result from those features. Customers are mainly interested in the benefits they will receive from purchasing a product or service. Many times a salesperson builds a sales presentation around the features alone. However, customers who see the benefits of purchasing the product or service will be less likely to object to the price of the item as the sales transaction progresses.

It is important for a business to spend time training salespeople about the product or service being sold as well as the industry in which they are working and the market in which they are selling. They should also be familiar with their own company as well as their company's competition. The more salespeople know about the internal and external environment in which they are working, the more effective they will be.

CHECKPOINT

Why is selling important to a business?

Determine Customer Needs and Wants

Customers purchase goods and services in order to satisfy needs. The need may be as basic as food, water, or shelter. Or, it may be a more complex need, like the need for esteem. A salesperson must determine what need the customer is seeking to satisfy in order to sell a product or service to meet the need. To satisfy lower-level needs, customers do not usually need the assistance of a salesperson. Selling skills become more important as customers try to meet upper-level needs.

Needs Assessment

When an individual customer goes shopping, it is up to the salesperson to find out as much as possible about the customer's situation by conducting a needs assessment. This involves interviewing the customer to determine his or her specific needs and wants. The salesperson can then help identify the range of product or service options to satisfy those needs and wants.

Some customers will know exactly what they want. In this case, the fulfillment of their needs is referred to as *need satisfying*. Even though the customer knows what he or she wants, the salesperson must be flexible and willing to commit company resources and selling time in order to better satisfy needs. When the need is not identified, the process of satisfying the need is called *problem resolution*. Problem resolution requires the salesperson to adopt the prospect's point of view, ask questions to assess the nature of needs, and act as a consultant to assist the prospect in solving the problem.

Buying Decisions

Customers are influenced by rational and emotional buying motives. **Rational buying decisions** are based on the logical reasoning of customers. Customers evaluate their options and make a purchase only after careful thought. Rational buying motives include safety, simplicity, quality, reliability, economy, convenience, service, durability, knowledge, money gain, and ease of operation. **Emotional buying decisions** are based on the desire to have a specific product or service. Feelings, beliefs, and attitudes can influence buying decisions. Often, little thought or time is spent making an emotional decision. Some emotional buying motives include fear, protection, appearance, recreation, improved health, comfort, recognition, pride of ownership, imitation, prestige, and popularity.

Customer Decision-Making Process

Following a problem-solving process is the best way to make a decision. This is also true with customers when they are making a decision to purchase a product or service. The steps are to define the problem, gather information, identify various solutions, evaluate alternatives and select the best option, take action, and evaluate the action. A salesperson can assist customers through this process by helping them define their need, showing them the products or services that could meet the need, explaining the features and benefits of the various options, making the sale, and following up.

 CHECKPOINT

Why is it important to meet customer needs and wants in the selling process?

Other Types of Promotion

Advertising, publicity, and personal selling are not the only ways to draw attention to your business. You can also offer sales promotions, use telemarketing, and develop a visual marketing strategy to promote your business.

Sales Promotions

A **sales promotion** is the act of offering an incentive to customers in order to increase sales. Examples of sales promotions include contests, free samples, rebates, coupons, special events, gift certificates, and frequent-buyer rewards. A **rebate** is a refund offered to people who purchase a product. Customers who purchase a $12 bottle of olive oil may be entitled to a $2 rebate from the manufacturer.

As part of her sales promotions, Luisa plans to give away a $25 gift certificate each month. She also offers free samples and distributes discount coupons for selected merchandise. Luisa makes customers aware of all product rebates by posting a list in her store.

famous entrepreneur

ANNE BARGE Playing with paper dolls as a child led Anne Barge to her multimillion dollar business selling bridal gowns. Internationally known as an expert in the field of bridal wear, her designs are rooted in research and inspired by vintage culture. Anne is involved in the development of each gown bearing her name and offers three distinctive brands that can satisfy any customer's taste and budget. Customer service is her top concern, and she helps each customer create a unique style for her special day.

Anne began her career in the fashion field by working for others. In 1996, Richard Branson, owner of Virgin Records music label, asked Anne to set up a bridal store in London for him. As manager of Virgin Bride, she introduced British brides to a totally new look. Even the British tradition of having only children as attendants changed when Anne introduced adult bridesmaid gowns to the United Kingdom.

In 1999, Anne decided to become an entrepreneur. She opened a bridal store in Atlanta, Georgia, and launched the Anne Barge Bridal Collection. Her collection

© Chris Nicholls

Do you think working for others before becoming an entrepreneur contributed to Anne's success?

combined classic designs in the finest of silks with museum-quality beading and embroidery never seen before in the worldwide bridal market. Now her line is represented in more than 100 of the finest stores in the United States, the United Kingdom, Spain, and Japan. The designing dreams of a little girl have come true in a big way!

THINK CRITICALLY

How important is Anne's commitment to customer service to the success of her business? Why do you think brides would choose one of Anne's gowns over those of another designer?

Telemarketing

Telemarketing is using the phone to market your product or service. It can be an inexpensive, effective way to let people know about your business or about special offers. Keep in mind that some consumers consider telemarketing to be annoying.

Visual Marketing

Visual marketing involves the use of visual media to promote, sell, and distribute a product or service to a targeted audience. Visual images help a company build an identity in the mind of consumers. It begins with the company's identity materials—its logo, signage, promotional tools, company vehicles, and uniforms. Every point at which the company's identity is viewed by the public should create an image that is unique. Visual marketing spans across all company communications, including advertisements, promotions, and websites. Having a well-planned visual marketing strategy can help establish brand awareness, which can lead to customer loyalty and repeat sales.

CHECKPOINT

What is the purpose of sales promotions?

Evaluation Strategies

An important part of your promotional plan is to evaluate the effectiveness of the promotional strategies you use. Some factors to consider include:

1. **Is the volume of sales increasing?** In addition to an increase in sales volume, you might also check the number of new leads or appointments being generated or determine if there is an increase in customer traffic in a retail establishment.
2. **How are you getting new customers?** Ask your clients/customers where they learned about your business.
3. **Does your advertising and/or promotional activity produce direct responses?** Be sure you are advertising in the right media. Choose media that your target market uses.
4. **Do your networking activities create new opportunities for you?** To measure the effectiveness of your networking activities, track the source of incoming business and inquiries.
5. **Do your marketing tactics make it easier to sell your services?** Your marketing activities and materials should do the following:

   - Attract customers who have shown a specific interest in your services and who have the resources to pay for them.
   - Anticipate and answer potential questions from customers.
   - Be easy to use in the personal selling process.
   - Focus on your customer/client needs.

6. **What is your sales conversion rate?** Review your records and determine whether the number of sales has increased. Selling is an important part of the marketing function, so make sure you evaluate your success rate at closing the sale rather than focusing only on new leads.

7. **Does your plan have a positive return on investment (ROI)?** Does your promotional plan bring in enough new/repeat business to justify the expense? Instead of looking at the marketing budget as a whole, evaluate the cost-effectiveness of each specific marketing activity. Even if you think you're getting a great ROI overall, you might improve your rate by changing or eliminating unproductive promotion tactics.

 CHECKPOINT

How can you determine the effectiveness of promotional activities?

6.3 ASSESSMENT

THINK ABOUT IT

1. Why is personal selling used in a business?

2. What is the purpose of the needs assessment?

3. Name some sales promotions that an entrepreneur might use. Can you think of examples in addition to the ones listed in the lesson?

MAKE ACADEMIC CONNECTIONS

4. **MARKETING**   Customers are more likely to purchase a product if they see its benefits. When selling products, you must learn to sell benefits rather than features. Access www.cengage.com/school/entrepreneurship/ideas. Click on *Activities* and open the file *Turn Features into Benefits*. Print a copy and complete the activity.

5. **COMMUNICATION**   You plan to use telemarketing to market your pressure washing business to people in your local community. You can wash driveways, walkways, patios, decks, vinyl siding, and lawn furniture. Write a script you will use when making the sales calls.

Teamwork

Working in a team, choose a business in your community. Make a list of all the marketing efforts that this business uses. Outline what you think the marketing plan for this business would look like.

Marketing and Technology

Many people believe that using the Internet for marketing a business is essential to its success. There are many technology tools available, and you will need to analyze them to be sure you are using the right tools for your business. As an entrepreneur, it will be up to you to evaluate the best way to use technology tools to market your business.

Some of the advantages of using technology tools include:

- **Cost savings**   It is much cheaper to send an e-mail or a tweet containing marketing information than it is to print and mail advertisements.
- **New customers**   Websites, social networking sites, and blogs can attract new customers from all over the world to your business.
- **Networking Opportunities** You can use social networking sites, blogs, message boards, and online discussion groups to network with many people without ever leaving your home or office.

There are some disadvantages of using technology to market your business. Be aware of the following:

- **Ineffective e-mails**   If someone does not already know about your business, e-mail might not be the best way to reach him or her. Many people delete mail from senders they do not know and use spam filters to keep such mail from reaching their inbox.

- **Loss of personal contact**   You lose personal contact with your customers if you rely only on technology to communicate with them. Many people hesitate to do business with someone they have not met.
- **Expense**   Developing and maintaining an effective website or social networking site can be very expensive and time consuming.
- **Inefficient use of time**   Responding to numerous general inquiries that people post on your site can be very time consuming. If you take time to answer all of these inquiries, you can waste valuable time that you could be spending with "real" customers. It would be more efficient to have a FAQs (Frequently Asked Questions) page on your site that provides answers to commonly asked questions.

Try It Out

You are starting a bake shop specializing in cupcakes. You are trying to decide on the best technology to use to promote your business. Make a list of the goals for your promotional activities. Then determine the advantages and disadvantages of using different technology tools for the purposes you listed. Describe the promotional plan you would use incorporating various types of technology.

Brand X Pictures/Getty Images

SUMMARY

6.1 The Marketing Mix—Distribution

1. The four basic options for channels of distribution are: (1) manufacturer to consumer, (2) manufacturer to retailer to consumer, (3) manufacturer to wholesaler to retailer to consumer, and (4) manufacturer to agent to wholesaler to retailer to consumer.
2. Entrepreneurs should examine the different options for channels of distribution and choose the one that best meets the needs of their business and their customers.
3. Transportation, product storage and handling, and packaging needs are all factors that play an important role when choosing methods of physical distribution.

6.2 The Marketing Mix—Promotion

4. Advertising may be done on the Internet, on television, on radio, in the newspaper, in a telephone directory, through direct mailings, in magazines, on billboards and signs, and through social networking sites. The best option for a business is the one that reaches the desired target market in the most cost-effective way.
5. Publicity is a nonpaid form of communication that generates media coverage. A business may capture media attention by submitting a press release and through public relations activities.

6.3 Selling and Promoting

6. A salesperson must identify the customer's needs, issues, and concerns so that they can be addressed throughout the sales process. To be successful, a salesperson must have a thorough knowledge of the features and benefits of the product or service.
7. Needs assessment involves determining the customer's needs and wants. Customers' buying decisions may be rational or emotional. Customers often use the problem-solving process to make buying decisions. The salesperson can assist customers during this process.
8. Offering an incentive to customers in order to increase sales is called sales promotion. Telemarketing is another way to let people know about your business. Visual marketing creates brand awareness.
9. Evaluate promotional activities by looking at the volume of sales, direct responses to promotional activities, sales conversion rate, and return on investment.

what do you know now?

Read *Ideas in Action* on page 153 again. Then answer the questions a second time. Have your responses changed? If so, how have they changed?

VOCABULARY BUILDER

Match each statement with the term that best defines it. Some terms may not be used.

1. Routes that products and services take from the time they are produced to the time they are consumed
2. Moves the product directly from the manufacturer to the consumer
3. Uses intermediaries that move products between the manufacturer and the consumer
4. A paid form of communication sent out by a business about a product or service
5. The act of establishing a favorable relationship with customers and the general public
6. Direct communication between a prospective buyer and a sales representative
7. Purchase decisions based on the logical reasoning of customers
8. The act of offering an incentive to customers in order to increase sales
9. Involves the use of visual media to promote and sell a product
10. A written statement meant to inform the media of an event or product
11. Purchase decisions based on the desire to have a specific product or service
12. A refund offered to people who purchase a product

a. advertising
b. channels of distribution
c. direct channel
d. distribution
e. emotional buying decisions
f. indirect channel
g. personal selling
h. physical distribution
i. press release
j. public relations
k. publicity
l. rational buying decisions
m. rebate
n. sales promotion
o. supply chain management
p. telemarketing
q. visual marketing

REVIEW YOUR KNOWLEDGE

13. Which of the following types of business is *least* likely to distribute its products or services directly to consumers?
    a. retail business
    b. service business
    c. manufacturing business
    d. none of the above directly distributes products to consumers
14. Which channel of distribution would be best for someone who makes and sells pottery at his or her home?
    a. manufacturer to consumer
    b. manufacturer to retailer to consumer
    c. manufacturer to wholesaler to retailer to consumer
    d. manufacturer to agent to wholesaler to retailer to consumer
15. **True or False** Agents and wholesalers are intermediaries that facilitate the flow of goods through direct channels of distribution.
16. Goods that arrive at their destination damaged probably have a problem with the _?_ in the physical distribution process.
17. Examples of promotion include
    a. advertising   c. sales promotion
    b. publicity   d. all of the above
18. **True or False** Publicity is always good for a business.
19. An online ad that changes the background of the page being viewed is a
    a. banner ad   c. wallpaper ad
    b. floating ad   d. trick banner

20. If you have a local business that offers a service to consumers in your neighborhood, which of the following would be the best way for you to advertise?
    a. a commercial aired during the Super Bowl
    b. an advertisement on satellite radio
    c. an advertisement in the local newspaper
    d. a billboard on a major interstate highway

21. Which of the following is the *least* important in the sales process?
    a. customer's needs   c. customer's concerns
    b. customer's issues   d. customer's income

22. Which of the following would be the best way for you to promote your pressure washing business?
    a. free sample   c. contest
    b. discount coupon   d. gift with purchase

23. A salesperson who approaches all customers the same way is leaving out which important part of the sales process?
    a. needs assessment   c. rational buying decisions
    b. product knowledge   d. none of the above

APPLY WHAT YOU LEARNED

24. You are a home improvement contractor. What role will channels of distribution play in your business? Which form of promotion will work best for you? Why? How can you assist your customers in their decision-making process?

25. You are going to open a retail store that will offer gifts and accessories. Your target market is 13- to 15-year-old girls. Describe the promotional mix you will use for your business.

MAKE ACADEMIC CONNECTIONS

26. **MARKETING**   When creating advertisements and promotions for your products, you must know who your target market is in order to create a message that will be effective. Access www.cengage.com/school/entrepreneurship/ideas. Click on *Activities* and open the file *Who Is the Target Audience?* Print a copy and complete the activity.

27. **COMMUNICATION**   You are opening a bowling alley and video arcade business. Write a press release to local newspapers and radio and television stations. You are also buying time on a local radio station. Write the commercial that will air on the radio. List some public relations activities that could promote your business.

28. **RESEARCH**   Many companies have reward programs for their customers. Research the reward program of a company with which you are familiar. Prepare a presentation about the program, including information on who is eligible, how customers participate, and the rewards available to participants. How does the reward program help build customer loyalty. Present your findings to the class.

29. **MATH** You have placed an ad on the Internet that is going to be charged using the CPA method at a rate of 50 cents per registered visitor. During one week, your website received 75,345 hits from visitors linking from the advertisement, 12,000 of those inquired about your product, and 7,432 of them registered their personal information with your website. How much will you have to pay the publisher of your ad?

What Would YOU Do?

You are the owner of Cookies For You. You have been selling your cookies in gift baskets designed for adults. Recently, you decided to start offering cookie gift baskets for children as well. You are thinking about doing a promotional activity at a local day-care center in which you will give free cookies to all of the children. However, with all of the recent news reports and stories about childhood obesity, you are not sure that you should be promoting cookies to children. You are concerned that your marketing strategy will be viewed negatively.

What would you do? Is it your responsibility to monitor the eating habits of children, or is this something for which only their parents should be responsible? How can you promote your cookie gift baskets in a positive way?

build your
BUSINESS PLAN PROJECT

This activity will help you complete the marketing plan for your business idea.

1. Determine the channels of distribution that you will use for your business. Include information on how you will get products from your suppliers as well as how you will distribute your products or services to your customers.
2. Develop selling strategies and company policies to ensure that the internal environment of your business promotes good customer relations.
3. Get advertising rates for a local radio station, television station, and newspaper. Also obtain rates for Internet advertising. Choose the medium that is best for your business and write an advertisement for that medium.
4. To generate publicity, write a press release that you will send to the media.
5. Determine what types of promotional activities you will use and how you will evaluate the effectiveness of these activities.
6. After you have completed your marketing plan, review it to be sure that the questions listed on page 130 in Chapter 5 are answered. If necessary, revise your marketing plan as needed to ensure that all of these questions are addressed.

"My dad's girlfriend is excited about starting a business with her new business partner. Although she likes her prospective partner, she has hired a reputable private investigator to do a complete background check. She wants to be sure there's nothing in this person's background that could impede the progress of their business."

How do individuals check the backgrounds of household employees? How do corporations, within the confines of the law, determine their employees are honest?

Private investigators provide a variety of services to individuals and corporations including child support investigations, employee background checks, and corporate asset protection.

Employment Outlook

- Faster than average job growth is expected.
- The need to protect confidential and proprietary information will drive an ongoing need for private investigators.
- About one-quarter of private investigators are self-employed.

Job Titles

- Insurance Fraud Investigator
- Surveillance Operative
- Assets Protection Investigator
- Loss Prevention Detective
- Certified Legal Investigator
- Hotel Detective

Needed Education/Skills

- Many private investigators are retired military or law enforcement professionals.
- A degree in criminal justice can be helpful.
- Most states require licensing.

- Investigators often have prior work experience in fields related to their investigative area of expertise.

What's it like to work in Public Safety? Otto, a self-employed private investigator, has spent the early part of his day performing hidden surveillance. His client, an industrial manufacturing firm, suspected fraudulent filing of a workers' compensation claim by an employee. The employee claimed that a recurring on-the-job back injury prohibited her from reporting to work. Otto has just finished his final surveillance of the employee. Today, she was playing tennis at a local park. Otto now has photos and video coverage of the employee in multiple scenarios performing physical activities that a back injury would prevent. With this information, Otto's client will be able to prove fraudulent filing of workers' compensation claims.

Otto is looking forward to dinner this evening as the client is buying! The client, who is the owner of a local restaurant chain, hired Otto to investigate potential employee theft. Otto has been collecting data through hidden video cameras. Tonight, as he dines at the restaurant, he will focus his observation on one of the servers who is suspected of undercharging friends and family for their meals.

What about you? Would you enjoy lawfully tracking down information that could help individuals and companies do a better job of protecting their rights?

The Entrepreneurship Promotion Project provides students an opportunity to demonstrate the skills needed in planning, organizing, implementing, and evaluating a campaign to educate chapter members and other individuals about entrepreneurship opportunities. Chapter members will utilize their knowledge of entrepreneurship and marketing skills to communicate the benefits of entrepreneurship to the target audience. Participants will share the information with a selected audience in the community (examples: middle school students, elementary students, civic organizations).

This project can be completed by one to three students. The written event must be limited to 30 numbered pages, including the appendix but excluding the title page and the table of contents. The written plan must follow the outline provided by DECA. Major sections in the body of the written plan include the Executive Summary, Introduction, Management of Activities to Inform Chapter Members, Management of Activities Targeted at Outside Audience, Evaluation and Recommendations, Bibliography, and Appendix (optional).

The 15-minute oral presentation will include 10 minutes to explain the project followed by 5 minutes for questions from the audience.

Performance Indicators

- Demonstrate knowledge and understanding of entrepreneurship
- Engage in activities that clarify and enhance understanding of entrepreneurship
- Plan and implement presentation/activities to educate and promote entrepreneurship to targeted groups
- Derive facts from data, findings from facts, conclusions from findings, and recommendations from conclusions
- Demonstrate critical-thinking skills
- Develop a concept from an idea to reality
- Plan, organize, and conduct a group project
- Determine priorities and set deadlines

Go to the DECA website for more detailed information.

THINK CRITICALLY

1. What are the benefits of presenting this project to elementary or middle school students?
2. Why is it important to explain risks involved with entrepreneurship?
3. Who are popular examples of entrepreneurs?
4. What are three characteristics of successful entrepreneurs?

www.deca.org

CHAPTER 7

Creatas/Getty Images

Select a Type of Ownership

7.1 Decide to Purchase, Join, or Start a Business

7.2 Choose a Legal Form of Business

7.3 Legal Issues and Business Ownership

www.cengage.com/school/entrepreneurship/ideas

Capitalize on Youth Marketing

The corporations of today were started as small businesses—often with single owners—at some time in the past. Such is the case with Buzz Marketing Group®. Tina Wells started The Buzz, her first business, when she was just 16 years old. Ten years later, she found herself named as one of *Entrepreneur* magazine's "Young Millionaires" and the CEO of Buzz Marketing Group.

Tina Wells, CEO of Buzz Marketing Group

Tina has been able to build a career doing what she loves. She always had a love for fashion and a fascination with pop culture. At 16, she began writing reviews of companies and their products that targeted teens for *The New Girl Times,* a newspaper for young girls. For her work, she received free products from more than 40 companies. After three months, she called on ten of her friends to help her, and they started The Buzz. Tina noticed that companies were not really connecting with the teens they were targeting as customers, so she began submitting her reviews directly to the companies. She was amazed by the positive response she received from the companies. A marketing director at one company told her that she had just paid someone $25,000 for the same type of information but that Tina's report was better! This was when Tina realized she could get paid for doing what she loved. And so, Buzz Marketing Group was born. She got her first paying client while she was a freshman in college.

Tina went on to earn her B.A. in Communication Arts from Hood College. She felt that her degree gave her more credibility as a businesswoman. She currently is in a graduate program for marketing management at the Wharton School of Business. Today, Buzz Marketing Group is headquartered in Tina's hometown of Voorhees, New Jersey, and employs nine people. In addition to the staff, over 9,000 teenage and young adult "buzzspotters" are out researching what their peers are thinking and doing. The buzzspotters help Tina stay in touch with what's happening.

Tina realizes that the profits from her business must be reinvested in the business in order to keep it growing. She invests profits into training seminars for the "buzzspotters" and other things that will contribute to the success of her business.

Today Tina speaks regularly to professional audiences across the country. She has been quoted and featured in numerous business publications, including *O Magazine, New York Times, Ebony,* and *Entrepreneur.*

1. What unmet need did Tina find that led to her first business?
2. Tina set up her business as a corporation. What is a corporation?
3. Name some of today's successful corporations that started out as a small business owned by one or two people.

DECIDE TO PURCHASE, JOIN, OR START A BUSINESS

Goals

- List advantages and disadvantages of purchasing an existing business.
- Describe how to evaluate a franchise opportunity.
- List advantages and disadvantages of joining a family business.
- List advantages and disadvantages of starting a new business.

Vocabulary

- franchise
- initial franchise fee
- startup costs
- royalty fees
- advertising fees
- Franchise Disclosure Document

How can we get this dough rising?

After graduating from the culinary arts institute, Midori and Crystal wanted to realize their dream of owning a bakery. Midori found an ad for a bakery that was for sale. "If we purchase it, we would have the equipment and supplies needed to get started right away," she told Crystal. "If that's the Holcombe family bakery, we'd better stay away," Crystal warned Midori. "I was in there last week, and Mrs. Holcombe and her daughter were fighting about something. No one was waiting on the customers, and everyone was getting upset." "That's good to know," Midori replied. "If we bought that bakery, we would have to do something to change people's opinions about the service, and who knows what other problems we might find!"

There are many ways to begin a business venture.

"We could always start our own bakery 'from scratch,'" Crystal suggested. "Very funny!" Midori replied. "But that could be hard too. We would have to find a location, buy everything we need, and build a customer base." "Well," Crystal said, "maybe we should buy a franchise." "That's a possibility, but we'd have to follow the rules and regulations set by the franchise company," Midori said. "Gosh, it's not easy to get the dough rising, is it?" Crystal replied.

Work as a Team   What do you think would be some of the advantages and disadvantages to Midori and Crystal of starting a business from scratch, buying an existing business, or buying a franchise?

Purchase an Existing Business

When most people consider going into business for themselves, they think about starting a new business. But purchasing an existing business could be a good option. Owners sell their businesses for a variety of reasons. Reasons can include insufficient sales or profits, new competition, fear of changing economic conditions, retirement, a dispute among partners, death or illness of a partner, and the owner's desire to do something different.

There are many ways to find businesses that are for sale. You may find advertisements in the local newspaper. You might decide to use a business broker who sells businesses for a living. Other people in your industry might know of businesses for sale. You might also learn about available businesses through leasing agents, lawyers and bankers, management consultants, the Small Business Administration, the Chamber of Commerce, and bankruptcy announcements.

DEVELOP YOUR READING SKILLS

Before reading the chapter, make a list of questions you have about the different types of business ownership and the legal issues facing business owners. Try to find answers to your questions as you read the chapter.

Advantages of Buying an Existing Business

There are many advantages to buying an existing business.

1. **The existing business already has the necessary equipment, suppliers, and procedures in place.** It may also have built up *goodwill*, or customer loyalty. You may want to change some of the policies and procedures established by the former owner, but fine-tuning existing systems is likely to be much easier than creating systems from scratch.

2. **The seller of a business may train a new owner.** The previous owner or experienced employees may be willing to help the new owner learn about the company.

3. **There are prior records of revenues, expenses, and profits.** This means that financial planning will be easier and more reliable than it would be for a completely new business.

4. **Financial arrangements can be easier.** The seller of the business may accept an initial partial payment and allow the rest to be paid off in monthly installments. If bank financing is needed, getting it may be easier because banks are more likely to lend to an established business.

Disadvantages of Buying an Existing Business

Buying an existing business sounds like an easy way to become an entrepreneur, but it can be risky. There are disadvantages.

1. **Many businesses are for sale because they are not making a profit.** Owners often try to sell businesses that are not financially profitable.

2. **Serious problems may be inherited.** Businesses can have poor reputations with customers, have trouble with suppliers, be poorly located, or have other problems that may be difficult to overcome.

3. **Capital is required.** Many new entrepreneurs just do not have the money to purchase a mature business. Starting small may be their only option.

Steps in Purchasing a Business

Buying a business is a complicated process that requires serious thought. If you are considering buying a business, you will want to follow these steps:

What can you learn by visiting a business during its business hours?

1. **Write specific objectives about the kind of business you want to buy, and identify businesses for sale that meet your objectives.** This will help you find the right business for what you want to do.

2. **Meet with business sellers or brokers to investigate specific opportunities.** Ask about the history of the business, the reason for its sale, its financial performance, and the price the owner is asking for it.

3. **Visit during business hours to observe the business in action.** Inspect the facility closely to make sure that it meets your needs. Observe how the business operates when it is open to customers.

4. **Ask the owner to provide you with a complete financial accounting of operations for at least the past three years.** Analyzing these reports will help you see how much profit you can make and how much you will probably be paying out in expenses.

5. **Ask for important information in written form.** Get a list of all assets to be transferred to the new owner, a statement about any past or pending legal action against the business, a copy of the business lease or mortgage, and a list of all the suppliers. Have an accountant and a lawyer help you review all of the material. Be suspicious if the owner refuses to provide all of the information you request.

6. **Determine how you would finance the business.** Contact lending institutions and ask the seller if he or she would be willing to finance part or all of the purchase.

7. **Get expert help to determine a price to offer for the business.** An accountant or a *valuator*—an expert on determining the value of a business—can help. Present the offer in writing to the seller. If an agreement is reached, have a lawyer draw up a sales contract.

 CHECKPOINT

What are some of the advantages and disadvantages of buying an existing business?

Franchise Ownership

Purchasing a franchise is another route by which you can become an entrepreneur. A **franchise** is a legal agreement that gives an individual the right to market a company's products or services in a particular area. A *franchisee* is the person who purchases a franchise agreement. A *franchisor* is the person or company that offers a franchise for purchase.

More than 909,000 franchises are operating in the United States, and the number is growing. Franchising opportunities are available in virtually every field, from motels to pet stores to restaurants. *The Franchise Opportunities Handbook*, a publication of the U.S. Department of Commerce, lists more than 1,500 franchise opportunities by category. It also provides information about the costs and capital requirements. Additional sources for finding out about franchise opportunities include the following:

- *Buying a Franchise: A Consumer Guide*, published by the Federal Trade Commission
- Resources on the Internet, which can be located by searching for *franchise opportunities*
- Books on franchising available at your public library
- *The Wall Street Journal*
- Magazines such as *Forbes, Barron's, Entrepreneur*, and *Inc.*

Operating Costs of a Franchise

If you decide to purchase a franchise, you will have to pay an initial franchise fee, startup costs, royalty fees, and advertising fees. The **initial franchise fee** is the amount the local franchise owner pays in return for the right to run the franchise. The fee can run anywhere from a few thousand to a few hundred thousand dollars. It is usually nonrefundable. **Startup costs** are the costs associated with beginning a business. They include the costs of renting a facility, equipping the outlet, and purchasing inventory. **Royalty fees** are weekly or monthly payments made by the local owner to the franchise company. These payments usually are a percentage of your franchise's income. **Advertising fees** are paid to the franchise company to support television, magazine, or other advertising of the franchise as a whole.

Jim Saurbrey purchased a Subway restaurant franchise. For the right to use the Subway name and logo, Jim paid a franchise fee of $15,000. In addition, Jim spent $70,000 renting restaurant space, purchasing equipment and supplies, and obtaining legal and accounting services. During its first year, Jim's franchise earned $36,000 in profits. He paid 12.5 percent, or $4,500, to Subway in royalty fees (8 percent) and advertising fees (4.5 percent). During Jim's second year in business, his restaurant earned $51,000, and he paid $6,375 in royalty and advertising fees.

Investigate the Franchise Opportunity

The Federal Trade Commission (FTC) regulates franchises and has established certain guidelines to assist those interested in buying a franchise. If you decide to purchase a franchise, you will have to complete an application to give to the franchisor. Once the franchisor has approved your application, you should receive two documents— the Franchise Disclosure Document and the franchise agreement. The **Franchise Disclosure Document** (FDD), formerly known as the Uniform Franchise Offering Circular (UFOC), is a regulatory document describing a franchise opportunity that prospective franchisees must receive before they sign a contract. State and federal laws require that the franchisor provide these documents at least 14 days before the franchisee signs a contract. To help ensure that the franchisee is able to make a knowledgeable purchase, the FDD includes the following information:

- A brief history of the franchise, documenting who founded the company, when it began doing business, when and if it was incorporated, and when it first started franchising
- A brief summary of the officers, directors, and other executives
- The franchise fees and royalties
- An approximation of the initial costs of starting the franchise in addition to the franchise fees, including equipment, inventory, operating capital, and insurance
- The name, address, and phone number of at least 100 current franchisees, the number of franchises it anticipates selling in the next year, and the number of franchises that were sold, terminated, or transferred over the past three years
- A brief description of any major civil, criminal, or bankruptcy actions that the officers and executives have been involved in or that the franchise company is a party to
- The terms of the franchise agreement, such as initial terms of five to ten years with or without the option to renew for additional periods
- The reasons a franchisor may terminate before the contract expires, such as poor condition of the location, failure on the part of the franchisee to pay royalties in a timely manner, and excessive customer complaints
- The franchisor's responsibilities to the franchisee, such as providing a training manual, picking a suitable location, training the franchisee and/or an employee, helping plan or attending the grand opening, offering some sort of continuing assistance with advertising and managing the store, and licensing the use of certain trademarked symbols and names
  - The franchisee's principal obligations under the franchise agreement and other related agreements

Before you sign a contract, you should review the franchise manual and meet the franchisor's personnel who are going to assist you. Be sure to verify everything with an attorney, a business adviser, and your accountant.

Evaluate a Franchise

Some of the things you should do when evaluating a franchise include the following:

1. **Study the disclosure document and proposed contract carefully.** Make sure all of the information listed above is included in the disclosure document. All costs and royalty fees should be provided.

Why is it important to research a franchise before you buy it?

© Kzenon, 2010/ Used under license from Shutterstock.com

2. **Interview current owners listed in the disclosure document carefully.** Ask them if the information in the disclosure document matches their experiences with the company. Be aware of *shills*, people listed in the document that are paid to give favorable reports.

3. **Investigate the franchisor's history and profitability.** Determine how long the franchisor has been in business and review its financial performance.

4. **Investigate claims about your potential earnings.** The company should provide you with the written basis for any claims made about potential earnings. Determine the projected demand for the franchised product or service in the area where you will locate. Does the demand match the potential earnings?

5. **Obtain from sellers in writing the number and percentage of owners who have done as well as they claim you will.** Sellers are required by law to provide this information.

6. **Listen carefully to sales presentations.** Be cautious of any sales presentation that pressures you to sign up immediately. A seller with a good offer does not use high-pressure sales tactics. Don't fall for a promise of easy money. Remember that success usually requires hard work.

7. **Shop around.** Compare franchises with other business opportunities. Different companies offer different benefits. Choose franchises that interest you and request disclosure documents. Find out what services the franchisor offers. For example, will the franchisor help with marketing, merchandising, and site selection?

8. **Get the seller's promises in writing.** All promises made should be included in the written contract that you sign. Remember, the contract is a legally binding document.

9. **Determine what will happen if you want to cancel the franchise agreement.** Buying a franchise is a major investment, so you should determine the financial risks of canceling the franchise agreement.

10. **Remember that it is okay to ask for advice from professionals.** Lawyers, accountants, or business advisers can review the disclosure document and contract and give you their professional opinions about them. The money you spend for this service could save you from making a bad decision about investing in the franchise.

Advantages of Owning a Franchise

When deciding whether to buy a franchise, you should also consider the advantages and disadvantages of it. There are four main advantages.

1. **An entrepreneur is provided with an established product or service.** This allows entrepreneurs to compete with large, well-known companies.

2. **Franchisors offer management, technical, and other assistance.** This may include onsite training or classes, aid with starting the new business and handling daily operations, and tips on crisis management. Some franchisors even offer help on everything from site selection and building design to equipment purchase and recipes. Most also maintain toll-free telephone numbers that franchisees can call for advice.

3. **Equipment and supplies can be less expensive.** Large franchises may be able to purchase in huge quantities. Some of the savings they enjoy as bulk purchasers are passed on to the franchisee.

4. **A guarantee of consistency attracts customers.** A franchise contract mandates a certain level of quality. Consumers know that they can walk into a franchise anywhere in the country and receive the same product or service. The cheeseburger sold at a Wendy's in Long Beach, California, will be very similar to the cheeseburger sold in Toledo, Ohio.

Disadvantages of Owning a Franchise

Although franchising sounds like a great idea, there are some disadvantages that you need to consider.

1. **Franchise fees can be costly and cut down on profits.** The initial capital needed to purchase a franchise business often is high. Also, some of the profits you earn as a franchise owner are returned to the franchisor as royalty fees.

2. **Owners of franchises have less freedom to make decisions than other entrepreneurs.** Many business decisions that entrepreneurs generally make themselves have already been made for franchisees. Franchisees must offer only certain products or services, and they must charge prices set by the franchisor. Many entrepreneurs object to this control because it inhibits the freedom they sought as independent business owners.

3. **Franchisees are dependent on the performance of other franchisees in the chain.** A franchisee can benefit from the success of other franchisees. But if other franchisees run sloppy operations, customer opinions of the chain will decline. As a result, customers may stop going to a franchise, even if a particular store maintains high standards.

4. **The franchisor can terminate the franchise agreement.** If the franchisee fails to pay royalty payments or meet other conditions, the investment in the franchise can be lost. Similarly, when the franchise expires, the franchisor can choose not to renew the agreement.

Breadsmith is a growing bakery franchise specializing in European-style breads and rolls. Access www.cengage.com/school/entrepreneurship/ideas and click on the link for Chapter 7. Read about the Breadsmith franchise. When did the first Breadsmith franchise store open? What is the minimum amount a franchisee can expect to invest to open a Breadsmith store? What royalty fees must be paid to the franchisor? Is previous baking experience required?

www.cengage.com/school/entrepreneurship/ideas

CHECKPOINT

What should you consider when evaluating a franchise opportunity?

Enter a Family Business

The U.S. economy is dominated by family businesses. According to some estimates, as many as 90 percent of all businesses, including the vast majority of small- and medium-sized companies, are owned by families. Many large companies, such as Walmart and the Ford Motor Company, continue to be owned largely by people who are related to the company founder.

Advantages of a Family Business

Entrepreneurs who work for their family businesses enjoy the pride and sense of mission that comes with being part of a family enterprise. They also enjoy the fact that their businesses remain in the family for at least one more generation. Some enjoy working with relatives and knowing that their efforts are benefiting family members.

Josh Morgan runs Morgan's, a restaurant that has been in his family for three generations. In his grandfather's time, Morgan's was a simple coffee shop, catering to people in the neighborhood. Thanks to changes made by Josh's mother, Mary, Morgan's became a fashionable lunch spot for people from all over town. When Josh took over, he carried on some of Morgan's traditions and implemented some new ideas, such as a gourmet take-out service. Josh takes great pride in seeing how the restaurant has evolved. He enjoys the thought that one day his grandchildren may hang pictures of him on the walls of the restaurant that will then belong to them.

Disadvantages of a Family Business

Family businesses have several drawbacks. Family members, regardless of their ability, often hold senior management positions. This sometimes means that poor business decisions are made. It also makes it difficult to retain good employees who are not members of the family. Family politics often enter into business decision making. Also, the distinction between business life and private life is blurred in family-owned businesses. As a result, business problems end up affecting family life as well.

Entrepreneurs who do join their family business must be prepared to make compromises. Unlike individuals who start or buy their own companies, people who work for their families cannot make all decisions themselves. They may also be unable to set policies and procedures as they like.

Another challenge for a family-owned business is what to do when there is no family member to take over the business. This leaves the family with a decision to make regarding continuing the business or selling it to a nonfamily member.

CHECKPOINT

What are some of the advantages and disadvantages of entering a family business?

Starting Your Own Business

For one reason or another, joining a family business or operating a franchise may not be possible for you, or you might not be able to find a business to purchase. This means that to be an entrepreneur you will have to establish a business of your own. You need to consider the many advantages and disadvantages of starting your own business.

Advantages of Starting Your Own Business

Entrepreneurs who start their own business get to make decisions about everything from where to locate the business to how many employees to hire to what prices to charge. They are completely independent and create their own destinies. Many entrepreneurs find great satisfaction in starting their own businesses. Many are attracted to the challenge of creating something entirely new. They also get a feeling of triumph when their business turns a profit.

David Srivastava started his mail-order business, In a Jam, from his home. David started by selling dried fruit, which he sold through the mail. After a year and a half of disappointing sales, David began offering preserves and jams, products he felt had greater sales potential. He also put more effort into packaging, and he designed the labels for the jars himself. His instincts proved to be correct. Eight years after starting out alone in his basement, David now has accounts with several large retail stores, and his company has 14 full-time employees.

Disadvantages of Starting Your Own Business

There are many risks to consider when you start your own business. You must estimate demand for your product or service. There is no certainty that customers will purchase what you offer. Entrepreneurs who join family businesses, buy an existing business, or buy into franchises do not have this uncertainty because it is already known that customers will buy the product or service.

Entrepreneurs who start their own business must also make decisions that other types of entrepreneurs need not make. These decisions include what product or service to offer, where to locate the business, what equipment to buy, and so forth. What may seem to be good decisions at the time may not always have positive results.

What things should you take into consideration before you start a business?

Creatas/Getty Images

Lucy Chang realized how difficult it is to start a new business when she opened a kitchen accessories store. Lucy had considered purchasing a store franchise but had ruled it out because of the high franchise fee. Lucy's problems began when she discovered that her customers considered her location to be inconvenient. As a result, fewer customers shopped in the store than Lucy had projected. Contacting suppliers was more difficult than Lucy anticipated, and many of them proved to be unreliable. The high-priced items Lucy purchased in the hope of increasing profits did not sell well.

 CHECKPOINT

> **Why is it more difficult to start a new business than to take over an existing business or purchase a franchise?**

 **7.1 ASSESSMENT**

THINK ABOUT IT

1. When you purchase an existing business, why is it important to know the owner's reason for selling?

2. What extra expenses could you expect to pay when operating a franchise as compared to operating a nonfranchised company? Could you save money in expenses by operating a franchise? If so, how?

3. Your family owns a successful business that distributes flowers from around the world to local florists. Both of your parents work full time in the business. They have offered you a position in the company after you graduate from college. Will you accept their offer? Explain.

4. What would be the greatest advantage of starting a new business from scratch? What would be its greatest disadvantage? Do you think the advantages outweigh the disadvantages? Why or why not?

MAKE ACADEMIC CONNECTIONS

5. **RESEARCH** Using local newspapers, periodicals, and the Internet, find advertisements for franchises. Make a list of the type of information that is included in the advertisements.

6. **COMMUNICATION** Locate a locally owned family business. Interview one of the family owners or employees to learn about the history of the business, the number of family members employed, and the pros and cons of working in a family business. Write a one-page report on what you learn.

Teamwork

Form teams. Brainstorm a list of reasons business owners may decide to sell their businesses. Put a check mark next to the reasons that could negatively affect the buyer's chance for success.

CHOOSE A LEGAL FORM OF BUSINESS

Goals

- List advantages and disadvantages of a sole proprietorship.
- List advantages and disadvantages of a partnership.
- List advantages and disadvantages of a corporation.

Vocabulary

- sole proprietorship
- partnership
- corporation
- share of stock
- board of directors
- dividends

focus **on small business**

Establish ownership.

Cheryl and Grayson are going to open a camp for dirt bike riders. It will be a place where people can come and ride their dirt bikes and camp out overnight. Their long-range plan includes building cabins on the property that can be rented to the bikers.

Grayson asked Cheryl, "Do you think we should operate our business as a partnership or a corporation since we can't be a sole proprietorship?" Cheryl thought about it a while and said, "You know, Grayson, there is a chance that someone could get hurt, and we would be responsible if the accident was on our property. Let's choose the form of ownership that would help protect us and others too!"

"Good idea, Cheryl. Let's start investigating and see what we can find!"

Work as a Team Why do you think the possibility of someone getting hurt would be a big concern for Cheryl and Grayson? What other considerations do you think business owners should have when choosing a legal form for their business?

© Marcel Jancovic, 2010/ Used under license from Shutterstock.com

There are several forms of business ownership to consider.

Sole Proprietorship

Once you decide to start your own business, you must decide what type of ownership the business will have. A business that is owned exclusively by one person is a **sole proprietorship**. Sole proprietorships enable one person to be in control of all business aspects. Sole proprietorships may be very small businesses with just a few employees, or they may be large businesses with hundreds of employees.

Advantages of a Sole Proprietorship

The government exercises very little control over sole proprietorships, so such businesses can be established and run very simply. Accurate tax records and certain employment laws must be met, but these are usually the only forms of government regulation for a sole proprietorship. For this reason, the sole proprietorship is the most common form of ownership in the United States. As a sole proprietor, you get to make all of the business decisions and keep all of the profits the business earns.

Disadvantages of a Sole Proprietorship

It can be difficult to raise money for a sole proprietorship. You often are the only person investing money in the business. You also bear the burden of all of the risks. If a sole proprietorship fails and debts remain, the entrepreneur's personal assets may be taken to pay what is owed.

Rachel Gibson learned this lesson the hard way. Last year, her clothing store went out of business, leaving $42,000 in debt. Because Rachel had set up the business as a sole proprietorship, she had to sell some of her personal assets, including her car, to pay off the debt of the business.

 CHECKPOINT

Why are sole proprietorships the most common form of business ownership?

Partnership

A business owned by two or more people is a **partnership**. Many entrepreneurs prefer to go into business with one or more partners so that they have someone with whom to share decision-making and management responsibilities as well as the risks involved with entrepreneurship.

Advantages of a Partnership

Running a business as a partnership means that you will not have to come up with all of the capital alone. It also means that any losses the business incurs will be shared by all of the partners. Partners may offer different areas of expertise and knowledge, which can strengthen the business. Like sole proprietorships, partnerships face very little government regulation.

Disadvantages of a Partnership

Some entrepreneurs do not like partnerships because they do not want to share responsibilities and profits with other people. They fear being held legally liable for the errors of their partners. Partnerships can also lead to disagreements and can end bitterly.

Partnership Agreement

When two or more entrepreneurs go into business together, they generally sign a *partnership agreement*. The purpose of the partnership agreement is to set down in writing the rights and responsibilities of each of the owners. A sample partnership agreement is shown on the next page.

The sample partnership agreement identifies the following:

1. Name of the business or partnership
2. Names of the partners

GENERAL PARTNERSHIP AGREEMENT FORMING
"SUNNY SIDE UP"

By agreement made this 21st day of September, 20—, we, Ana Ortiz, Keesha Gentry, and Thomas Chase, the undersigned, all of Palm Harbor, Florida, hereby join in general partnership to conduct a food service business and mutually agree to the following terms:

1. That the partnership shall be called "Sunny Side Up" and have its principal place of business at 2013 Sand Drive, Palm Harbor, Florida, at which address books containing the full and accurate records of partnership transactions shall be kept and be accessible to any partner at any reasonable time.

2. That the partnership shall continue in operation for an indefinite time until terminated by the death of a partner or by 90 days' notice, provided by one or more of the partners indicating his, her, or their desire to withdraw. Upon such notice, an accounting shall be conducted and a division of the partnership assets made unless a partner wishes to acquire the whole business by paying a price determined by an arbitrator whose selection shall be agreed to by all three partners. Said price shall include goodwill, and the paying of same shall entitle the payor to continue the partnership business under the same name.

3. That each partner shall contribute to the partnership: $22,000 for initial working capital and the supplies and equipment.

4. That in return for the capital contribution in item 3, each partner shall receive an undivided one-third interest in the partnership and its properties.

5. That a fund of $75,000 be set up and retained from the profits of the partnership business as a reserve fund, it being agreed that this fund shall be constituted on not less than 15 percent of the monthly profits until said amount has been accumulated.

6. That the profits of the business shall be divided equally between the partners, that the losses shall be attributed according to the subsequent agreement, and that a determination of said profits and losses shall be made and profit shares paid to each partner on a monthly basis.

7. That the partnership account shall be kept in the First Florida Bank and that all withdrawals from same shall be by check bearing the signature of at least one of the partners.

8. That each partner shall devote his or her full efforts to the partnership business and shall not engage in another business without the other partners' permission.

9. That no partner shall cause to issue any commercial paper or shall enter into any agreements representing the partnership outside the normal conduct of the food service business without notice to the remaining partners and the consent of at least one other partner, and further that all managerial and personnel decisions not covered by another section of this agreement shall be made with the assent of at least two of the partners.

IN AGREEMENT HERETO, WE ARE

Ana Ortiz   Keesha Gentry   Thomas Chase

_Ana ortiz_____   _Keesha Gentry_____   _Thomas Chase_____

3. Type and value of the investment each partner contributes
4. Managerial responsibilities to be handled by each partner
5. Accounting methods to be used
6. Rights of each partner to review and/or audit accounting documents
7. Division of profits and losses among the partners
8. Salaries to be withdrawn by the partners
9. Duration of the partnership
10. Conditions under which the partnership can be dissolved
11. Distribution of assets upon dissolution of the partnership
12. Procedure for dealing with the death of a partner

 CHECKPOINT

Name some of the advantages and disadvantages of a partnership.

what went **wrong?**

PARTNERSHIP WOES

Stan and Peter met while working at a video production company. Stan was in charge of editorial and production. Peter ran the sales force. Stan decided to begin his own company and invited Peter to join him. SP Communications seemed like a perfect partnership. Peter would handle sales and administration while Stan managed clients and directed production.

Things seemed to be going well until Peter decided he wanted to be a part of the creative process. He spent most of his time producing videos rather than looking for new business. Because of their friendship, Stan trusted that Peter was taking care of his side of the business.

As it turned out, Peter wasn't very good at the creative tasks he attempted. He made mistakes that reduced expected profits. In addition, he wasn't making new sales

Choose your partners wisely.

contacts, which was supposed to be his main job.

By the time Stan realized what was happening to the business, it was too late. There weren't any new sales. What Stan thought were profits were the result of Peter not paying their bills. Stan was left with more than $150,000 in unpaid bills and other debts. Peter left the business. It took Stan three years to dig out of the financial mess and get his new company up and running successfully.

THINK CRITICALLY

1. How might Stan and Peter have avoided the problems that led to the end of their partnership?

2. Why is this situation a good example of the difficulty in maintaining partnerships between friends?

3. What types of things should be spelled out completely between partners at the beginning of the partnership?

Corporation

A <u>corporation</u> is a business that has the legal rights of a person but is independent of its owners. A <u>share of stock</u> is a unit of ownership in a corporation. There may be many owners, who are called *shareholders* or *stockholders*. The corporation, not the owners, pays taxes, enters into contracts, and may be held liable for negligence.

Jim Munroe set up his company, Munroe Office Supply, as a corporation. He created 100 shares of stock worth $1,000 each. Jim then issued 15 shares to each of three outside investors, which means they gave $45,000 total to be shareholders in his company. Jim kept the remaining 55 shares himself. This means that Jim owns 55 percent of his company while outside investors own a total of 45 percent of the company. The individual or group that owns the most shares maintains control of the company.

Every corporation has a <u>board of directors</u>, which is a group of people who meet several times a year to make important decisions affecting the company. The board of directors is responsible for electing the corporation's officers, determining their salaries, and setting the corporation's rules for conducting business. The board of directors also decides how much the corporation should pay in dividends. <u>Dividends</u> are distributions of corporate profits to the shareholders. The company's officers, not the board of directors, are responsible for the day-to-day management of the corporation.

Disadvantages of a Corporation

Setting up a corporation is more complicated than setting up a sole proprietorship or a partnership. To incorporate, you will need the assistance of a lawyer, who will help you file *articles of incorporation* with the state official responsible for *chartering*, or registering, corporations. Because of this, establishing a corporation can be costly. Articles of incorporation must fully detail the purpose of the business. If the articles are not well written, the corporation's activities can be limited.

Digital Vision/Getty Images

What role does the board of directors play in a corporation?

Corporations are subject to much more government regulation than are sole proprietorships or partnerships. Another drawback of incorporation is that income is taxed twice. A corporation pays taxes on its income, and shareholders pay taxes on the dividends they receive from the corporation. This means that the corporation's profits are taxed as corporate income and again as individual income. This is known as *double taxation*.

Advantages of a Corporation

If the corporate form of ownership is complicated and costly, why do entrepreneurs set up corporations? Liability is the main reason. Liability is the amount owed to others. The shareholders' liability is limited to the amount of money each shareholder invested in the company when he or she purchased stock. The personal assets of shareholders may not be taken to pay the debts of the corporation.

Munroe Office Supply has gone bankrupt, leaving $150,000 in debt. Each shareholder can lose only the amount he or she invested in the corporation, so the outside people who invested $45,000 would lose their investment. Jim would also lose his investment of $55,000. If Jim had set up his business as a sole proprietorship, he would have been liable for the $150,000 solely. If the business had been set up as a partnership among Jim and his friends, all four partners would have been liable for the $150,000.

Another advantage of corporations is that money can be raised by selling stock. Also, lenders are more willing to lend money to corporations than to sole proprietorships or partnerships. Finally, because shareholders do not directly affect the management of a corporation, the main shareholder of the company can change through the buying and selling of stock without disrupting the day-to-day business operations.

S Corporation

A small corporation can elect to be treated as an S corporation. An *S corporation* is a corporation organized under Subchapter S of the Internal Revenue Code. Unlike regular corporations, an S corporation is not taxed as a business. The individual shareholders are taxed on the profits they earn, as they would be in a partnership. However, S corporations must follow the same formalities and recordkeeping procedures as regular corporations. They are also managed by a board of directors and officers. Many companies establish themselves as S corporations because they lose money in their early years. The owners can use any losses suffered from the S corporation to offset other sources of personal income and receive a tax break.

Chanda Patel runs Forever Yours, a wedding consultant business. Like many new businesses, Forever Yours lost money in its first year when its expenses exceeded its revenues by $12,000. Since Chanda set up her company as an S corporation, she was able to reduce her taxable income from other sources by $12,000.

BE YOUR OWN BOSS

You have decided that you are going to start a new business giving horseback riding lessons. You need to decide which legal form you will use for your business. Choose a sole proprietorship, partnership, or corporation. Write a paragraph explaining why you chose the legal form you did and the advantages and disadvantages of your choice.

Limited Liability Company

A *limited liability company* (LLC) is a legal form of business that goes further than an S corporation in providing the benefits of partnership taxation and limited personal liability for all the owners of the business. The LLC is not subject to the rules for an S corporation so it is simpler to operate. Owners of LLCs are known as members—not shareholders. Unlike shareholders, members can participate in the management of the business. The disadvantages are that the type of businesses that can be set up as an LLC may be limited by state law, a single owner cannot establish an LLC, and some states limit the life of an LLC.

✔ CHECKPOINT

What is the main benefit of setting up your business as a corporation?

7.2 ASSESSMENT

THINK ABOUT IT

1. Which do you think is more risky: a sole proprietorship or a partnership? Why?

2. What would be the advantages and disadvantages of forming a partnership with a friend? Would you consider forming a business this way? Why or why not?

3. Why do you think the government regulates corporations more closely than it does sole proprietorships or partnerships?

MAKE ACADEMIC CONNECTIONS

4. **MANAGEMENT**   You and a friend plan to open a business. Negotiate the terms of a partnership agreement. Access www.cengage.com/school/entrepreneurship/ideas. Click on *Activities* and open the file *Partnership Agreement*. Print a copy and complete the activity.

5. **MATH**   Caren McHugh opened Best Foot Forward, a shoe store catering to women. To raise money, she organized her business as a corporation. She created 500 shares of stock, each worth $75. Caren held 260 of the shares for herself. She sold the rest in even amounts to six investors. How many shares does each investor own? If Best Foot Forward fails and leaves $65,000 in debt, for how much would each investor be liable?

Teamwork

Working with teammates, create a chart listing all the forms of business ownership and the advantages and disadvantages of each one.

LEGAL ISSUES AND BUSINESS OWNERSHIP

Goals

- Recognize how laws promote competition.
- Describe how entrepreneurs protect intellectual property.
- Identify regulations that protect the public and how they affect businesses.
- Describe when and how a business owner should seek legal advice.

Vocabulary

- intellectual property
- patent
- copyright
- trademark
- contract

focus on small business

Why are there regulations?

James and Katie were starting an apparel company specializing in sportswear. They were trying to decide what they wanted their company logo to look like. "Let's put a 'swoosh' in our logo like the one Nike uses," James suggested.

"James, we can't use that logo. It's a Nike trademark," Katie responded. "See the ™ symbol next to it. That means it's protected by a trademark and no one else can use it."

"Well, I guess we'd better keep thinking about what we want our trademark to be," answered James. "That's a good idea," Katie said. "And while we're at it, we'd better look into all the rules and regulations we need to follow. We don't want to start off on the wrong foot by unintentionally doing something illegal."

Photodisc/Getty Images

Business owners must follow certain laws and regulations.

Work as a Team Did you realize that businesses have to follow rules and regulations? Do you think it's fair for government to regulate business?

Regulations That Promote Competition

As an entrepreneur, you will learn that there are laws affecting almost every aspect of your business. Even the competition that businesses face is regulated by the government. To make sure that competition is fair, federal, state, and local governments have enacted various laws to help protect businesses.

Antitrust Legislation

Beginning in 1890, laws were created that made monopolies in certain industries illegal. A monopoly is also called a trust, so these laws were called antitrust laws. Antitrust laws also ban other types of business activities that do not promote competition. It is important to become familiar with these laws to determine how they affect your business.

SHERMAN ACT   This law makes it illegal for competitors to get together and set prices on the products or services they sell. This means that you and your competitors cannot jointly decide to keep prices at a certain level. Discussing prices with competitors is illegal. For example, if the owner of one business decides to raise his prices, he cannot ask the owner of a competing business to raise her prices by the same amount.

CLAYTON ACT   This law states that it is illegal for a business to require a customer to buy exclusively from it or to purchase one good in order to be able to purchase another good. A distributor of computers, for example, cannot force customers to purchase software when they purchase a computer. Customers must be free to buy only the products or services they want from whom they want.

How does antitrust legislation affect pricing?

ROBINSON-PATMAN ACT   This law protects small businesses from unfair pricing practices. It makes it illegal to discriminate by charging different prices to customers. A manufacturer, for example, may not sell its products at different prices to similar customers in similar situations when the effect of such sales will reduce competition. Differences in price may only be justified based on differences in quantities purchased (volume discounts), special distribution or legal requirements in different locations, or other economically sound reasons. If your business sells to other businesses, you must offer the same terms to all of those businesses. The law does not apply to retail stores where certain groups may be targeted by special promotions, such as giving discounts to senior citizens.

WHEELER-LEA ACT   This law bans unfair or deceptive actions or practices by businesses that may cause an unfair competitive advantage. False advertising is an example. Under this act, businesses are also required to warn consumers about possible negative features of their products. Drug companies, for example, must let people know of any side effects they may experience from using a medication.

Government Agencies that Protect Competition

The Antitrust Division of the Justice Department and the Federal Trade Commission are two government agencies that work to make sure competition among businesses remains fair. Other agencies, such as the Federal Aviation Administration and the Food and Drug Administration, oversee business practices in particular industries.

JUSTICE DEPARTMENT   The Justice Department's Antitrust Division takes legal action against any business it believes has tried to monopolize an industry. It also prosecutes businesses that violate antitrust laws, which can lead to large fines and jail sentences.

FEDERAL TRADE COMMISSION   The Federal Trade Commission (FTC) deals with issues that touch the economic life of every American. The FTC administers most of the laws dealing with fair competition and pursues vigorous and effective law enforcement. Some of the activities the FTC monitors include false or misleading advertising, price setting by competitors, price discrimination, and misrepresentation of the quality, composition, or place of origin of a product. It is the only federal agency with both consumer protection and competition jurisdiction in broad sectors of the economy. In addition, the FTC does the following:

- Advances consumers' interests by sharing its expertise with federal and state legislatures and U.S. and international government agencies
- Develops policy and research tools through hearings, workshops, and conferences
- Creates practical and plain-language educational programs for consumers and businesses in a global marketplace with constantly changing technologies

CHECKPOINT

How do laws promote competition?

Intellectual Property

Intellectual property is the original, creative work of an artist or inventor and may include such things as songs, novels, artistic designs, and inventions. Such works may be registered for special government protections—including patents, trademarks, trade names, and copyrights—that provide business owners with the exclusive use of the intellectual property in the United States and many foreign countries. Registration gives businesses or individuals the exclusive right to profit from what they have created. No one else can use their creations to make money. If you violate another person's patent, copyright, or trademark, you could be sued.

Patents

A **patent** is the grant of a property right to an inventor to exclude others from making, using, or selling his or her invention. The intent of a patent is to give the developer of a new product time to recover the development costs without having to worry about competition. Patents are issued by the U.S. Patent and Trademark Office and last for 20 years. During this period, no business or individual can copy or use the patented invention without the patent holder's permission. A *provisional patent application* allows an inventor one year to investigate the feasibility, marketability, and potential license interest of an invention before deciding to file a formal patent application. This allows the inventor to use the term *patent pending*, giving him or her a head start on other inventors who may file for the same invention.

Copyrights

A <u>copyright</u> is a form of intellectual property law that protects original works of authorship, including literary, dramatic, musical, and artistic works. Copyright law does not protect facts, ideas, systems, or methods of operation. All books must have a copyright. A copyright lists the publisher of the work and the year in which the work was published. Copyrights remain in effect for 70 years after the death of the author. A copyright allows the author to license the use of the material for a royalty payment.

famous entrepreneur

What led to Eli Whitney's success as an entrepreneur?

ELI WHITNEY is best known as the inventor of the cotton gin, but a problem with intellectual property rights kept him from making his fortune from this invention. Whitney obtained a patent for his invention but decided not to sell the machine to farmers. Instead, Whitney decided to install cotton gins throughout the south and charge farmers a hefty fee for processing the cotton himself. Resentful farmers made their own versions of the cotton gin and claimed they were "new" inventions. Due to a loophole in the 1793 patent act, Whitney was unable to win any lawsuits against the other cotton gin owners.

Without exclusive rights to the cotton gin, Whitney built another factory and began to make muskets (guns) in a new way. Whitney invented tools and machines so that any worker could turn out standardized parts. The government was waiting for guns, and Whitney amazed everyone when he assembled guns from random piles of parts. Whitney had become the father of mass production in America! Eventually the arms factory made him rich, completing a success story for the boy who had shown mechanical aptitude by making a violin when he was 12 and selling handmade nails in his teens.

THINK CRITICALLY

What do you think would have happened if Eli Whitney's patent for the cotton gin had prevented others from copying his machine?

Trademarks

A trademark is a name, symbol, or special mark used to identify a business or brand of product. Products that are trademarked are identified by the ™ or ® symbol. Examples include Band-Aid® and Kleenex®. You could not invent a new bandage and use the term Band-Aid in the product name. Nor could you use the "swoosh" mark that is trademarked by Nike in any product or business promotion you conduct.

 CHECKPOINT

> **How can entrepreneurs protect intellectual property rights?**

Laws that Protect Consumers

The government also has regulations that protect consumers. They include licenses, zoning regulations, and consumer protection laws.

Licenses

State and local governments require some businesses to have licenses. Beauty salons, restaurants, and health and fitness centers are just some of the companies that must carry licenses. If you own a business that requires a license, you and your employees may need to complete training requirements. You may also need to have regular inspections by state and local authorities. Failure to meet certain standards could mean the loss of your license and the closing of your business.

Zoning Laws

Local governments often establish zoning regulations that control what types of buildings can be built in specific areas. In many communities, certain areas are zoned for residential use only. This means that business buildings may not be built in those areas. Other areas may be zoned as commercial for retail businesses, as industrial, as agricultural, as multipurpose, and so on. All businesses must obey zoning regulations. Before you choose a location for your business, you will have to make sure that the area you have selected allows your type of business to operate there. Zoning laws help keep neighborhoods safe for its residents.

Consumer Protection Laws

A variety of laws and government agencies protect the public from harmful products. You will have to make sure that the products you manufacture or sell meet all consumer protection standards.

THE FEDERAL FOOD, DRUG, AND COSMETIC ACT OF 1938
This law bans the sale of impure, improperly labeled, falsely guaranteed, and unhealthful foods, drugs, and cosmetics. The Food

How does the information found on a food label help protect consumers?

and Drug Administration (FDA) enforces this law. The FDA has the power to force producers to stop manufacturing products that are unsafe.

THE CONSUMER PRODUCT SAFETY ACT OF 1972

This law sets safety standards for products other than food and drugs. When the Consumer Product Safety Commission determines that a product is unsafe, it can force businesses to recall the product and stop selling it.

THE TRUTH-IN-LENDING ACT OF 1968

This law requires all banks to calculate credit costs in the same way. When a consumer gets a loan, the lender must provide two types of information about the loan's cost—the finance charge and the annual percentage rate. The finance charge is the total cost a borrower must pay for a loan, including all interest and fees. The annual percentage rate is the finance charge calculated as a percentage of the amount borrowed. These numbers help consumers evaluate alternatives and determine the best option.

THE FAIR CREDIT BILLING ACT OF 1974

This law is part of the Truth-in-Lending Act and helps consumers correct credit card billing errors. Consumers who feel they have been charged incorrectly must write to the credit card issuer and explain why they think the charge is wrong. The company must reply within 30 days and resolve the dispute within 90 days. While the disputed charge is being investigated, it cannot accrue interest.

This law also gives the consumer a method for resolving problems relating to product quality. The first step in dealing with a product of inferior quality purchased with a credit card is to try to resolve the problem with the merchant. If it cannot be resolved, the consumer can withhold payment to the credit card company until the matter is settled.

 CHECKPOINT

What laws protect the public?

Legal Issues Affecting Business

It is helpful to learn some basics about legal issues affecting businesses so that you can handle minor legal issues yourself. In other instances, you may want to obtain the services of a lawyer.

Contracts

A contract is a legally binding agreement between two or more persons or parties. As an entrepreneur, you will enter into contracts as you start and operate your business. For a contract to be considered legally binding, certain elements must be included.

- *Offer and acceptance* occurs when one party offers to do something and the other party accepts or agrees. If the second party makes a counteroffer, however, there is no agreement.
- *Consideration* is what is exchanged for the promise. For example, a payment is consideration and causes the contract to be binding.
- *Capacity* means the parties are legally able to enter into a binding agreement. Minors, intoxicated persons, and insane persons cannot enter into a binding contract.
- *Legality* means that a contract cannot have anything in it that is illegal or that would result in illegal activities.
- *Genuine assent* means that the agreement is not based on deceit on the part of either party, certain mistakes of fact, or the use of unfair pressure exerted to obtain the offer or acceptance.

In addition to the elements described above, some contracts must be in writing to be fully enforceable in court. In many cases, however, an oral contract would be enforceable.

Torts Relating to Business Enterprises

A *tort* is a wrong against people or organizations for which the law grants a remedy. If someone commits a tort, the person injured as a result can sue and obtain compensation for damages. Torts may occur when manufacturers make defective products that injure users. Certain elements are common to most torts and must be proved in a court of law to establish liability.

- *Duty*—A legal obligation to do or not to do something
- *Breach*—A violation of the duty
- *Injury*—A harm that is recognized by the law
- *Causation*—Proof that the breach caused the injury

Agency Relationships

An *agency* is a relationship that allows one party to act in a way that legally binds another party. The *principal* is the person who authorizes another person, the *agent,* to enter into legal relationships on the principal's behalf. One of the most common forms of agency occurs when a salesperson for a business makes a contract with a customer on behalf of the business's owner.

Hire a Lawyer

At some point, you probably will need to hire a lawyer to assist you with legal issues affecting your business. Your Chamber of Commerce may have a list of lawyers who specialize in small businesses. Other community business owners may also be able to suggest a lawyer.

HOW LAWYERS CAN HELP YOU

Assist you in choosing a legal structure for your business	Create documents such as lease and purchase agreements and contracts	Develop partnership agreements
Inform you of regulations and licenses	Give advice on insurance coverage	Advise you on taxes
Prepare and file patent applications	Help you plan for your future (a will, retirement plans)	Defend you in a lawsuit or file one on your behalf

 CHECKPOINT

Name legal issues of which entrepreneurs should be aware.

7.3 ASSESSMENT

THINK ABOUT IT

1. Think of three examples of how a business might misrepresent a product it sells. Explain each example.

2. Besides Band-Aid, Kleenex, and Nike, name at least three other products that are trademarked.

3. Explain the elements of the Fair Credit Billing Act of 1974.

MAKE ACADEMIC CONNECTIONS

4. **RESEARCH**   Use the Internet, the newspaper, or your local library to find information on the process for applying for a patent. Also, find out how much a patent costs, how many patents have been issued to date, and what the criteria are for obtaining a patent. Prepare a short report on your findings.

5. **COMMUNICATION**   Research a company that has violated one or more of the laws or regulations discussed in this lesson. Prepare a report describing the legal issues facing the business and the impact of the violation on both the business and the individual or group who experienced the violation.

Teamwork

Gather in teams. Create several business scenarios that involve violation of antitrust laws. Role-play scenarios for the rest of the class and let them tell which antitrust law is being violated.

Effective Telephone Conversations

As you research business opportunities, you will need to make telephone calls to gather information. Once you become a business owner, you will conduct much of your business over the telephone. The way you present yourself over the telephone will have a big impact on the people with whom you deal. It is also important to use good listening skills when talking on the telephone. Use the following tips to make the most of your telephone conversations.

1. **Speak clearly and talk directly into the receiver.** If you are using a headset, be sure that the microphone is in the correct position so that the person you are talking to will not have difficulty hearing you.

2. **Be cheerful.** Everyone prefers to deal with a happy person rather than someone who is sad or angry.

3. **Always speak politely.** Do not use foul or unprofessional language. Be respectful.

4. **Think about what you are going to say before you make a call.** Write down the questions you want to ask or the points you want to make. Consult your notes as you are talking to make sure you cover everything.

5. **Focus your attention on the person with whom you are talking.** Concentrate exclusively on what the person is saying.

Ask questions to confirm you correctly interpreted what is being said.

6. **Eliminate all distractions.** Background noises, such as the radio and other people talking, should be held to a minimum.

7. **Take notes to summarize what you are hearing.** You may forget important details unless you write them down.

Try It Out

You found an advertisement for a candy store business that is for sale in a local mall. You want to call the real estate broker to find out more information about the business. Make a list of all the questions that you want to ask the broker. Role-play the phone call with a classmate and make an appointment to visit the business and meet with the owner. Follow the tips listed above to ensure your telephone conversation is effective.

7.1 Decide to Purchase, Join, or Start a Business

1. An existing business has an established customer base and relationships with suppliers. The seller may train you, and prior records can make financial planning easier.

2. When evaluating a franchise opportunity, study the disclosure document, interview current owners, investigate the franchisor's history, investigate potential earnings claims, compare opportunities, get promises in writing, learn the risks of canceling the franchise, and seek advice from professionals.

3. Joining a family business has advantages, such as pride in the business and enjoyment of working with relatives. However, family politics can negatively affect the business.

4. Entrepreneurs who start entirely new businesses are completely independent and create their own destinies. However, there is increased risk because there is no established demand for the product or service and you must make all the decisions.

7.2 Choose a Legal Form of Business

5. A sole proprietorship is the easiest form of business ownership, but the owner may have trouble raising money for the business. Personal assets are at risk if the business fails.

6. A partnership is easy to start, faces little government regulation, and shares the risk with others. But a partner can be held legally liable for the actions of the other partner(s).

7. A corporation is more difficult to start, but it is easier to raise capital by issuing shares of stock. Owners' personal assets are not at risk.

7.3 Legal Issues and Business Ownership

8. Antitrust laws were developed to promote fair competition in business. The Antitrust Division of the U.S. Justice Department and the Federal Trade Commission are government agencies that work to ensure fair competition.

9. Entrepreneurs can protect intellectual property by registering for patents, copyrights, and trademarks.

10. Laws that protect consumers include licensing, zoning, and consumer protection laws.

11. Legal issues affecting a business include contracts, torts, and agencies. Lawyers can assist in handling these and other issues.

Read *Ideas in Action* on page 185 again. Then answer the questions a second time. Have your responses changed? If so, how have they changed?

VOCABULARY BUILDER

Match each statement with the term that best defines it. Some terms may not be used.

1. The original, creative work of an artist or inventor
2. Paid to the franchise company to support television, magazine, or other advertising of the franchise as a whole
3. The grant of a property right to an inventor to exclude others from making, using, or selling his or her invention
4. A business that has the legal rights of a person but is independent of its owners
5. Distributions of corporate profits to shareholders
6. A legal agreement that gives an individual the right to market a company's products or services in a particular area
7. A regulatory document describing a prospective franchise opportunity
8. A unit of ownership in a corporation
9. Weekly or monthly payments made by the local owner to the franchise company
10. A form of intellectual property law that protects original works of authorship, including literary, dramatic, musical, and artistic works
11. A business that is owned exclusively by one person
12. A business owned by two or more people
13. A name, symbol, or special mark used to identify a business or brand of product
14. The costs associated with beginning a business
15. A legally binding agreement between two or more persons

a. advertising fees
b. board of directors
c. contract
d. copyright
e. corporation
f. dividends
g. franchise
h. Franchise Disclosure Document
i. initial franchise fee
j. intellectual property
k. partnership
l. patent
m. royalty fees
n. share of stock
o. sole proprietorship
p. startup costs
q. trademark

REVIEW YOUR KNOWLEDGE

16. Which of the following is *not* an advantage of buying an existing business?
    a. existing customer base
    b. seller can provide training
    c. seller may work out financing agreement
    d. capital is required
17. **True or False**   A franchise is an inexpensive way to get into business quickly.
18. The legal form of business that is the simplest to establish is the
    a. sole proprietorship
    b. partnership
    c. S corporation
    d. limited liability company
19. **True or False**   The board of directors of a corporation is responsible for the day-to-day management of the corporation.
20. You and several business owners in your area agree to raise the price of the paint you sell by $1.50 per gallon. You are in violation of the
    a. Sherman Act   c. Robinson-Patman Act
    b. Clayton Act   d. Wheeler-Lea Act

21. You want to advertise a special price on a product that you do not have just to get customer traffic into your store. If you do so, you will be in violation of the
    a. Sherman Act
    b. Clayton Act
    c. Robinson-Patman Act
    d. Wheeler-Lea Act
22. For a contract to be legally binding, it must have which of the following elements when it is created?
    a. offer and acceptance, cooperation, capacity, legality
    b. offer and acceptance, consideration, capacity, legality
    c. genuine assent, consideration, cooperation, and legality
    d. amendment, consideration, capacity, and legality
23. **True or False**   The U.S. Justice Department administers all of the laws dealing with fair competition.
24. **True or False**   A patent grants property rights to an inventor for 70 years.

APPLY WHAT YOU LEARNED

25. You are meeting with the owner of an ice cream shop you would like to purchase. What specific questions are you going to ask her? What documents do you want to see? How will you evaluate whether or not to purchase this business?
26. You decide to start a business selling a new video game you have developed. You plan to sell the game over the Internet. What intellectual property right issues should you consider?
27. You want to purchase a cleaning service franchise. The franchise fee is $19,500 and startup costs are $15,200. Advertising fees are $1,500. The royalty fee is 8 percent. If your estimated sales for the first year of operation are $56,500, how much is your profit after paying all costs and the royalty fee?

MAKE ACADEMIC CONNECTIONS

28. **MATH**   Marta Vasquez is one of three partners in a car dealership. The division of profits and losses as specified in the partnership agreement is 60 percent for Marta, 25 percent for the second partner, and 15 percent for the third partner. The dealership has recently lost a lawsuit and must pay damages of $1,200,000. What is Marta's liability? What is the liability of each of the other two partners?

29. **RESEARCH**   Use the Internet, newspaper, magazines, and other materials to research business opportunities. Find two businesses for sale that interest you. Access www.cengage.com/school/entrepreneurship/ideas. Click on *Activities* and open the file *Businesses for Sale*. Print a copy and complete the activity. Which business would be the better investment? Why?
30. **RESEARCH**   Use the Internet to research FTC requirements and your state's requirements for disclosure documents prior to the purchase of a franchise. Write a paragraph outlining the requirements.
31. **HISTORY**   Research one of the antitrust laws listed in Lesson 7.3. Write a brief history of what led to its passage. Describe any amendments that have been made to the law since its original passage.

32. **GEOGRAPHY** China is a major source of intellectual property theft. Many counterfeit products are produced in China. Research the extent of this problem and learn how U.S. businesses can better protect themselves. Write a two-page report on your findings.

What Would YOU Do?

You receive a new iPod and $50 iTunes gift card for your birthday. You sign onto iTunes and download many of your favorite songs, quickly spending $50. One of your friends tells you about some websites where you can download all the music you want for free. You decide to talk to your parents about these sites. They explain that iTunes is a legal site and that the music artists receive royalties when you download from its site. The websites your friend told you about do not pay the artists the royalties due to them. When you tell your friend this, he still sees no harm in getting the music for free because he believes the artists have already made enough money. Will you continue to pay and use only iTunes or will you use the free websites? Why? Recording artists are entrepreneurs. If you were an entrepreneur, how would you feel if you did not get the money that was owed to you?

build your
BUSINESS PLAN PROJECT

This activity will help you continue with the development of a business plan for your business idea.

1. Contact your state and local governments and obtain information about licensing and zoning regulations. How will these regulations affect your business?
2. To expand your business, you have decided to purchase similar businesses in your area. List the businesses in your area that compete with you. Write the reasons you would or would not consider buying each business.
3. Investigate a franchise opportunity available in your business field. Gather information about it, such as franchise fees, royalties, projected earnings, and operating costs.
4. You have a friend who is interested in being your business partner. Write the partnership agreement for the two of you.
5. Make a list of all the advantages and disadvantages of organizing your business as a corporation. Determine how much stock to sell and the value of each share.
6. How will you become an entrepreneur? Will you buy an existing business, enter a family business, purchase a franchise, or start your business from scratch? Determine which form of business organization you will use—sole proprietorship, partnership, corporation, S corporation, or limited liability company. Write the Ownership and Legal Structure section of your business plan as described in Chapter 3.

Planning a Career in FRANCHISING

Business Management & Administration

"This weekend my family was really startled when we walked into a new restaurant to order sub sandwiches for lunch. Our former babysitter was behind the counter. She had bought the restaurant from a franchisor. The franchisor taught her how to run the restaurant. It provided the training and support materials she needed. She said that, although the hours were long, the work was gratifying and profitable."

Why do people decide to purchase a franchise? How do they decide which type of franchise is best for them?

By helping individuals evaluate their personal and professional goals, Franchise Coaches help potential franchisees determine which franchise will best meet their needs. Coaches are usually compensated by the franchisors after a franchise is purchased by one of the coach's clients.

Employment Outlook
- Faster than average growth is expected.
- Career changes, as a result of an evolving business environment and downsizing, will increase the need for business counselors.

Job Titles
- Franchise Business Coach
- New Business Sales Leader
- Franchise Business Consultant
- Franchise Performance Coach

Needed Education/Skills
- A Bachelor's degree is recommended.
- Strong interpersonal and problem-solving skills are needed.

- Prior management experience in training or sales is helpful.
- A desire to help others and an ability to gain trust is important.

What's it like to work in Franchising? Jasmine, a Franchise Consultant, is on the phone with a prospective new client. The client recently lost her job due to downsizing and is eager to purchase a franchise. By collecting data through informational interviews, structured assessments, and coaching sessions, Jasmine can help the client match her business objectives to an appropriate franchise.

Jasmine's next two phone calls are to two different windshield repair franchisors. Jasmine has a client whose testing results revealed that a windshield repair franchise is a strong match for his interests and business objectives. Jasmine is setting up a meeting between the franchisors and her client. After her client talks with both franchisors, Jasmine will coach him through the decision-making process. Jasmine will receive compensation from the franchisor her client selects.

On the way home from work, Jasmine stops by a tutoring franchise that she helped one of her clients establish. She has a brief chat with the franchise owner to see if there are any business issues she can help resolve. By staying in touch with clients, Jasmine can help ensure the ongoing success of their franchise.

What about you? Would you like to provide structured testing and coaching to clients to help them match their interests, goals, and resources with an appropriate franchising opportunity?

The Team Decision Making Event requires participants to analyze one or a combination of elements essential to the effective operation of a business. This Business Law and Ethics Team Decision Making Event will require students to understand copyright laws, trademarks, and royalties paid to protected entities.

Your team has decided to open a sporting goods/gift shop in a popular university city. You want to sell merchandise that bears the emblem, logo, mascot, and name of the university. You have scheduled a meeting with the university's attorney (judge) to present your proposal for selling the merchandise. Your team must explain the pricing strategy for merchandise and demonstrate an understanding of royalties from merchandise sales to the university, college conference, and the National Collegiate Athletic Association (NCAA). You must also describe the type of merchandise you will sell and explain how it is different from university merchandise sold by competitors. You must convince the attorney that your business offers competitive advantages that will result in strong sales and good royalties for the university.

You have 30 minutes to prepare your presentation, 10 minutes to present to the attorney (judge), and 5 minutes to answer the attorney's questions about your proposal.

Performance Indicators

- Explain the nature of business law
- Describe legal issues affecting businesses
- Describe strategies used to protect a business's copyrights
- Explain legal strategies used to protect trademarks
- Make an effective oral presentation
- Explain legal considerations for pricing
- Explain business ethics in product/service management

Go to the DECA website for more detailed information.

THINK CRITICALLY

1. Why is it important to consider copyright and trademark laws when selling merchandise?
2. Why are copyright and trademark laws hard to enforce in other countries?
3. How can you determine the royalty percentage to be paid to a university for the use of its emblem, logo, or mascot?
4. Why does a university need an attorney who specializes in copyright laws?

www.deca.org

© mangostock, 2010/ Used under license from Shutterstock.com

Locate and Set Up Your Business

8.1 Choose a Location

8.2 Obtain Space and Design the Physical Layout

8.3 Purchase Equipment, Supplies, and Inventory

www.cengage.com/school/entrepreneurship/ideas

Finding Fitness and Fun on the Go

Brent Teal and Bryan Pate, inventors of ElliptiGO

Photo courtesy of Bryan Pate

When searching for a site for a business, entrepreneurs are often told the tried and true mantra of "location, location, location." The location of a business can have a big effect on its success and can increase the product's value. As the alleged birthplace of the triathlon and a city with year-round ideal weather, San Diego is the perfect location to maintain a healthy lifestyle. Bryan Pate and Brent Teal used these factors and their adventurous spirits to break into the action sports industry.

As a retired Marine and longtime distance runner, Bryan felt his body could no longer take the strain of intense outdoor workouts, but he hated being forced to use gym equipment to maintain his fitness. Bryan thought of the idea to combine a gym-style workout with his love of nature by creating an outdoor elliptical bicycle. With Bryan's idea and Brent's mechanical engineering background, they made a prototype of what would become the ElliptiGO.

Less than a year later, Bryan and Brent have sold more than 250 ElliptiGO bikes to outdoor enthusiasts in California and beyond. Having the headquarters in sunny Solana Beach, San Diego has been a boon to business. The two owe much of their early success to the vibrant and fit location. To garner attention for the cycles, Bryan, Brent, and friends take the ElliptiGO devices on rides typically reserved for bicycle cyclists. Rides such as the 129-mile "Death Ride" through the California hills draw close to 4,000 riders per year, making California a perfect spot to showcase the product.

Once a potential buyer's interest is sparked, the ElliptiGO can be purchased at the company store, at fitness retailers in California, and on the website. In order to keep up with demand, Bryan and Brent use a projected sales model when determining inventory. They try to keep 100 machines in stock to minimize an inventory shortage. They follow this model because there is a four-month turnaround for the finished product. If the product is in stock, a potential customer can buy when desired.

Bryan emphasizes that in order to open and run a successful business, entrepreneurs need to have a broad understanding of "how the world works." He stresses the importance of having a general knowledge of subjects such as math, public policy, tax structure, and communication.

1. Why is San Diego a good location to open a business in the action sport industry?
2. Why is it important for ElliptiGO to closely track its inventory?
3. What kind of businesses would be a good addition to your neighborhood?

CHOOSE A LOCATION

Goals

- Identify options for locating a retail business.
- Discuss factors to consider when choosing a location for a nonretail business.
- Identify the benefits of locating a business online.
- Describe steps to take in selecting a site.

Vocabulary

- industrial park
- enterprise zones
- e-commerce
- trade area

focus on small business

Good locations come at a price.

Gail worked very hard to get just the right product mix for her company, Fitness for You, which offers creative branding strategies and products to the fitness industry. Business was good, but profits were still not at the level she wanted. She examined her expenses and realized that a large portion of her monthly expenses was for rental of her office space. She was located in an upscale office complex in Palm Beach, Florida. When she started looking at her customer base, she realized that most of her customer interaction was by phone or e-mail and at trade shows and business meetings held away from her office. Many of her customers were located in other states.

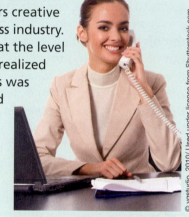

Carefully consider your location needs.

© vgstudio, 2010/ Used under license from Shutterstock.com

Work as a Team   How important do you think Gail's location is to the success of her business? What would you advise her to do about her location?

Locating a Retail Business

Your location plan will help ensure that your product is available in the right location to reach your target customer. If you want to open a retail business, choosing the location for it will be one of the most important decisions you will make as an entrepreneur. The wrong location could spell disaster, but the right location will help your business succeed from the start. The right location for your business depends on the kind of business you plan to operate and the type of customer you want to reach.

Another factor to consider is whether you will sell your products or services through inside sales or outside sales. If you are selling a product through inside sales, customers will come to your place of business to purchase the product. If you are using outside sales to sell your product, you will travel to the customer's residence or place of business. The way you offer your product or service will affect the location of your business.

Downtown Areas

In some communities, the downtown area represents an easily accessible, central location. Workers from downtown offices and professional businesses may shop at your business on their breaks or on their way to and from work. Rents vary widely from city to city, so you will want to do some research if you are thinking of using a downtown location.

Some downtown areas have lost business to neighborhood, community, and regional shopping centers. But many cities are revitalizing their downtown shopping districts and are offering incentives to attract businesses back into the area. Issues faced in many downtown areas include a higher crime rate, traffic jams, lack of free or convenient parking, and a lack of customers in the evening.

Neighborhood Shopping Centers

Neighborhood shopping centers are small shopping centers that serve a certain neighborhood. They are often called strip malls and consist of 3 to 15 stores. They are typically anchored by a supermarket, which is supported by other stores offering convenience goods (food, pharmaceuticals, and miscellaneous items) and personal services. Examples of supporting stores include drugstores, dollar stores, and dry cleaners.

Neighborhood centers represent good locations for stores selling goods or services that people need to purchase frequently. Rent is usually low in these centers, making them ideal for small businesses. Customers of neighborhood shopping centers are mainly residents of the surrounding area who shop at these centers because of their convenience. However, it could be a disadvantage for your business if the only customers you have come from the immediate area.

Community Shopping Centers

Community shopping centers have more square footage than neighborhood centers and are designed to serve residents from many neighborhoods. Apparel, furniture, toy, sporting goods, and electronic stores are often located in community shopping centers. Community centers usually have one or two major anchor stores. Anchor stores can include the following:

- Small department stores (Kohl's, JCPenney)
- Discount department stores (Walmart, Kmart, Target)
- Large supermarkets (Kroger, Food Lion, Safeway, Publix)
- Super drugstores (Walgreens, Rite Aid, CVS)
- Home improvement stores (Home Depot, Lowe's)

Although rent in community shopping centers is generally higher than in neighborhood shopping centers, it is usually still affordable. Stores in community shopping centers can earn higher profits. Anchor stores advertise heavily and attract customers from throughout

DEVELOP YOUR READING SKILLS

As you read, make a chart showing the advantages and disadvantages of each type of location for retail, service, home-based, industrial, and online businesses.

What are the advantages and disadvantages of locating a business in a shopping mall?

the community. Other businesses in the shopping center typically benefit from the advertising. Customers shop at the anchor store and then may browse and buy at the smaller stores located in the shopping center as well.

Regional Shopping Centers

Regional shopping centers are designed to attract customers from an entire region. These large shopping areas usually have 40 to 100 stores and are anchored by two or more large department stores, such as JCPenney and Nordstrom. The majority of the stores sell apparel. Many regional shopping centers are malls. Regional shopping centers offer depth and variety of products and services.

If your business requires a large amount of walk-in traffic to be successful, you may want to locate in a regional shopping center. Rents at these centers are high, however, making it more difficult to earn profits. Also, the distance to the shop may be too far for some consumers. For convenience, they may decide to patronize businesses closer to their homes.

Super-Regional Shopping Centers

Super-regional shopping centers are the largest classification of shopping centers. They house more than 100 stores that offer an extensive variety of merchandise and services. They are typically anchored by three or more large department stores. They serve a larger population base than the other types of shopping centers. Two of the largest super-regional centers are the West Edmonton Mall in Edmonton, Canada (with over 800 stores), and the Mall of America in Bloomington, Minnesota (with over 500 stores).

Most tenants in these centers are large chain stores that can afford the very high rents charged. If convenience is a factor for your target market, customers may not be willing to travel a great distance to come to your store. Such centers usually are not recommended for new businesses because of the competition that exists among many similar businesses.

Stand-Alone Stores

Stand-alone stores can be located just outside of shopping centers or far away from other businesses. These stores often depend on drive-by traffic. They must have plenty of parking, good signs, and effective lighting if they are to be successful.

Businesses locate in stand-alone locations because rent is often less expensive than it is elsewhere. Also, a competing business is less likely to be right next door. Advertising is often necessary to earn a profit because people must have a specific reason to come to your business. Large jewelers, auto parts stores, and flower and garden centers are often operated as stand-alone stores. A recent trend shows that department stores and large drugstores are opening up stand-alone stores.

Warehouses

Some retail stores, such as appliance dealers or furniture sellers, operate in warehouses. Warehouses are generally one of the cheapest rental facilities because they are of basic construction with few frills inside or out. Locating your business in a low-rent warehouse may allow you to charge lower prices than your competitors. This can work to an appliance store's advantage because customers are usually more concerned about getting the best price than about the appearance of the business. However, locating away from other retailers can also mean that potential customers will not notice or be aware of you. For this reason, businesses that operate out of warehouses generally advertise heavily.

What are the main options for locating a retail business?

Locating a Nonretail Business

Location can be very important for nonretail businesses, which include service, wholesale, and manufacturing businesses. Owners of these types of businesses face different considerations when choosing a location.

Service Businesses

For some service businesses, such as restaurants and hair salons, location considerations are the same as for many retail businesses because they are offering an inside service. Owners of these types of businesses have to be very careful when choosing a location. Convenience can be an important factor for the business's customers.

Location is much less important for other types of service businesses. Customers never actually visit businesses that offer outside services, such as plumbing or carpet-cleaning companies. Locating these kinds of businesses in expensive areas does not make sense. Being close to customers may be important, however, because customers are more likely to call a company located nearby. For example, a computer-repair service might choose to locate downtown to be closer to its customers—the businesses in the downtown area—so it can respond quickly to emergency calls.

Industrial Businesses

Industrial businesses, such as manufacturing and wholesale companies, ship their products directly to their customers, so customers rarely see their facilities. Industrial businesses do not need to operate in upscale locations that attract lots of consumer traffic. Availability of good employees and low cost are the key factors in determining where an industrial business locates.

Nonretail businesses sometimes locate in industrial parks. An **industrial park** is a section of land that is zoned for industrial businesses only. They are usually located where space is less expensive, away from housing developments and downtown areas. Communities sometimes subsidize rents in industrial parks in order to attract industrial businesses.

Industrial businesses may locate in enterprise zones. **Enterprise zones** are areas that suffer from lack of employment opportunities. Entrepreneurs who set up businesses in these areas may be eligible for favorable tax treatment based on the number of jobs their businesses create.

Some businesses may find the tax benefits offered by enterprise zones attractive. Others, however, may find that these benefits do not make up for the lack of an appropriate customer base or the increased risk of crime in those areas.

Why do you think the number of home-based businesses is growing?

Photodisc/Getty Images

Home-Based Businesses

In recent years, there has been an increase in the number of home-based businesses. Some of the reasons that entrepreneurs decide to locate their business in their home include the following:

- **Cost savings** Separate rent, utility costs, and maintenance fees for the business are eliminated, so there is more capital available for promotional activities and the purchase of inventory.
- **More freedom** Home-based business owners do not have to sign a lease agreement for the business, so they are not subject to the restrictions and obligations of a lease.
- **Convenience** The owner can work more flexible hours and does not have to commute to and from another location.

Locating a business at home is a great way to save money when starting a business. If the business outgrows its space, the owner can begin to look for an appropriate location outside the home.

Although it is cheaper to operate a business from home, there are some disadvantages to operating a home-based business. Lack of space can limit the expansion of the business. It may also be hard to keep your business and family life separate. Many home business owners feel isolated from the business community and miss opportunities to network with colleagues.

✓CHECKPOINT

What are some of the factors to consider when selecting a location for a nonretail business?

Starting a Virtual or Online Business

The widespread use of technology and access to the Internet has changed the way business is conducted. For entrepreneurs, the virtual or online world has created many new business opportunities. **E-commerce**, or electronic commerce, consists of buying and selling products or services over the Internet. Virtual or online businesses offer an alternative means of conducting business transactions that traditionally have been carried out by telephone, by mail, or face to face in a traditional retail setting.

Benefits of Virtual or Online Businesses

Starting a business online allows a startup business to have an immediate presence and compete with larger, established businesses. A traditional business location limits a startup business because it can only be as big as the physical space it can afford and reach as far as its geographic boundaries. But these barriers do not exist in an online business. The cost of maintaining an online business is much less than the cost of buying or leasing a building. Rather than serving only local customers, a business can reach out to customers globally. Even time restrictions aren't a problem because e-commerce can take place 24 hours a day, including holidays and weekends.

Operating an online business can also help with the cash flow problems experienced by many startups. Marketing, customer service, order processing, inventory, and personnel costs are much lower. For example, it is much more cost-effective to use e-mail than direct mailings to reach out to hundreds of customers. Because customers enter their own orders online, employee costs are kept to a minimum. In addition, collecting and managing information about customer behavior is quick and easy for an online business. A customer's movements and selections on the website can be tracked. This information can be used to improve customer relations.

Virtual or Online Business Precautions

To help ensure success, there are some precautions to take when setting up your online business.

- Do not use free web space. Buy your own domain (web address) to get a single and specific name for your website. This is more professional.
- Use a creative website design that appeals to customers. It should reflect the image you want to project for your business. Don't use all text and no pictures.
- Be aware of the loading speed of your website. If it takes too long to load web pages, customers may get frustrated and exit the website.
- Don't leave outdated information on your website. Keep it current.

CHECKPOINT

What are some benefits of having a virtual or online business?

Selecting Your Site

Given all of the possible types of locations for different types of businesses, how do you decide where to locate? One way of identifying the options for your business location is to buy a map and mark your trade area. The **trade area** is the area from which you expect to attract customers. Indicate on the map all of the locations that might be appropriate for your business. Also indicate the location of all of your competitors. Using a different color marker or symbol, mark the locations of businesses that do not directly compete with your business but may attract the same kind of customer. For example, if you want to open a poster store that will attract mostly teens, mark the locations of other stores that appeal to this target market, such as trendy clothing stores and music stores.

Location Type and Availability

The next step is to identify which type of location is right for your business. Do you want to locate in a community shopping center? A stand-alone store? Downtown? At home? Determining which type of location you want will help narrow your search.

After deciding on the type of location, you must determine what spaces of this type are available in your trade area. The classified section of your local paper will list available sites. You can also find

what went wrong?

locations by driving around your trade area. Signs advertising an available building will often be hung in the front window or placed on the front lawn of the property. Websites and search engines may also be helpful in determining options that are open to you. Mark each possible location you find on your trade area map.

Evaluate the Location

After getting a list of possible locations, inspect each location to assess its appeal. Is the location safe? Is it attractive? Does it attract the kind of customers your business will be targeting? Is it easy to reach? Is parking adequate? Do businesses in the area seem to be thriving? By answering these questions, you should be able to identify one or two viable locations.

✓ CHECKPOINT

What are some of the factors you should consider when selecting a site for your business?

8.1 ASSESSMENT

THINK ABOUT IT

1. Why do you think rents are lower in neighborhood shopping centers than in community and regional centers?

2. Do you think advances in technology have influenced some new business owners' decision to operate from their homes? Why or why not?

3. When marking the trade area for your business, why should you indicate the locations of your competitors?

MAKE ACADEMIC CONNECTIONS

4. **PROBLEM SOLVING**   Using a map of your area, mark the potential trade area for a new furniture superstore. Then use the six-step problem-solving model to determine at least two appropriate locations.

5. **COMMUNICATION**   As a downtown business owner, you actively work to recruit other businesses to the area. Write a letter to the editor of your local newspaper about the advantages of locating a business downtown.

Teamwork

Work in teams to select an online business your group will operate. Design a website for your business by describing the content and features you would include. Use word processing software or a graphics program to create the proposed layout of the home page. If available, use web design software.

Goals

- Compare purchase and lease options.
- Describe layout considerations for different types of businesses.

Vocabulary

- tenant
- landlord
- gross lease
- net lease
- percentage lease
- visual merchandising

focus on small business

Store layout results in walking inventory.

Trying to create a fun, relaxing atmosphere in his clothing and accessories store, Justin decided to move the cash register into the far back corner of his store. That gave him more space for displays and merchandise up front. He was really excited about all he could do with the space.

Due to slow traffic in the store at times, there was often only one employee on duty. The next thing Justin knew, his inventory was "walking right out the door," and it wasn't with paying customers. Justin had created a perfect layout for shoplifters. He knew he had to make some changes.

Work as a Team What did Justin do wrong in changing the layout of his store? If Justin wants to keep the same layout, what suggestions can you make that would cut down on shoplifting?

The layout should meet the needs of the business and its customers.

©Apollofoto, 2010/ Used under license from Shutterstock

Lease or Buy Space

Unless you operate your business out of your home, you will have to lease or buy business property. There are advantages to buying space. Owning property offers a bigger tax advantage than leasing because you get a tax deduction on the interest you pay on your loan for the building. A loan payment on the building may be no more than a lease payment.

However, most entrepreneurs lack the money to purchase property for their businesses. Even entrepreneurs who can afford to purchase property generally prefer not to be locked into a particular location. Some leases require the owner of the building, not the owner of the business, to pay certain expenses, such as upkeep and maintenance of the building's exterior. For these reasons, most businesses lease space.

Commercial Leases

When leasing property, a contract is required. In a lease contract, there is a tenant and a landlord. The **tenant** is the person who pays rent to occupy space owned by someone else. The **landlord** is the person who owns and rents out buildings or space. There are three kinds of commercial leases.

1. In a **gross lease**, the tenant pays rent each month for the space occupied, and the landlord covers all property expenses for that space, such as property taxes, insurance on the building, and building maintenance.

2. A **net lease** occurs when the landlord pays building insurance, and the tenant pays rent, taxes, and any other expenses.

3. With a **percentage lease**, the tenant pays a base rent each month, and the landlord also receives a percentage of the tenant's revenue each month. The percentage lease is most common for prime retail locations. This type of lease can be beneficial for both the landlord and tenant. The landlord shares in the business's profits, and the tenant has the advantage of a lower base rent, which can make rent more affordable during slow sales periods.

Why is it important to have a contract when leasing property?

Commercial lease agreements are usually long and complex. You should never sign one without consulting an attorney. Your attorney will review your lease to make sure that it covers all conditions and costs, including the basic rent, maintenance fees, utility costs, insurance costs, and other items.

Compare Costs of Doing Business

Once you have selected some possible locations for your business, you need to compare the costs and benefits of leasing property at each location. To do so, you need to calculate how much rent you will be paying per customer.

Juan Martinez plans to open a music store. He finds two locations that meet his needs—one in a neighborhood shopping center and the other in the downtown area. To decide which location he should select, Juan determines the amount of rent he would pay and the number of projected customers for each location. Juan divides the amount of rent by the number of projected customers to determine the *rent per customer*.

	Downtown	Shopping Center
Rent per month	$ 925	$ 1,100
Projected customer traffic per month	÷ 8,500	÷12,000
Rent per customer	$ 0.11	$ 0.09

From his calculations, Juan determines that, although the total rent at the shopping center will be higher, he will be paying a lower rent per customer. Juan leases space at the shopping center.

✓ CHECKPOINT

Name three kinds of commercial leases.

Design the Layout of Your Business

After you have leased or purchased a facility, you will need to design your layout, or floor plan. Your layout must include enough space for employees, customers, merchandise, and equipment. It must also have space for restrooms, stockrooms, storage, and offices.

Create the Floor Plan

You will need to prepare a scale drawing of the layout. Graph paper will help you draw your layout to scale. To create a scale drawing, let 1 inch represent 1 foot of actual space. For example, a 4-foot-by-3-foot closet would be represented by a 4-inch-by-3-inch rectangle. Indicate the planned use of each area. Also indicate the location of furniture, display cabinets, shelves, fixtures, and equipment. Your drawing will help you identify potential problems in your layout. It will also help you communicate with the people who may be helping you organize your space.

Sample Floor Plan

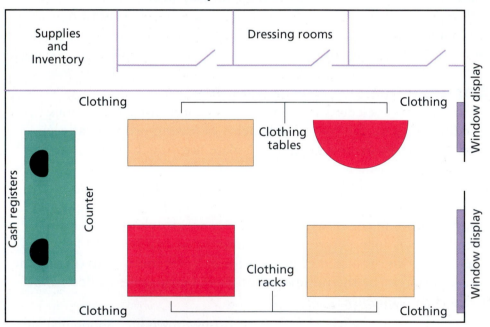

Decide on a layout, an outside sign, and window displays that match your image. If you sell expensive jewelry, you will probably decide on a sophisticated outside sign and an elegant inside design that will appeal to your target customer. If you sell outdoor equipment, you will select a very different design for your store.

Layout of a Retail Business

For a retail business, visual merchandising is very important. <u>Visual merchandising</u> is the process of combining products, environments, and spaces into an appealing display to encourage the sale of products or services. The goal of your layout should be twofold: (1) to attract customers to your store and keep them coming back and (2) to meet the needs of your business.

Here are some ways you can send a positive message about your store.

1. Choose lighting that is appropriate for the kind of merchandise you sell. Good lighting is important for any business where customers inspect merchandise closely. Avoid fluorescent lighting, which creates an unattractive glare.
2. Think carefully about window displays. Use them as a way to display new merchandise or seasonal items.
3. Make the entrance inviting. An entrance that is welcoming will draw customers into the store.
4. Use common sense when organizing the merchandise in your store. Customers should always easily find what they want. Inventory and supplies should also be well organized so that you can find things faster and serve your customers better.

famous entrepreneur

How did Rachael Ray build upon her early success?

Brad Barket/Getty Images

RACHAEL RAY Sometimes success comes from being in the right place at the right time. And it always helps to be prepared! Just ask Rachael Ray, who says her life has been "a very happy, wonderful accident that I didn't and couldn't have planned."

The truth behind that statement is that Ray had extensive training in the food service industry before she became a TV star. She grew up in a family of restaurant owners. Starting at the candy counter of Macy's, she was promoted to manager of the Fresh Foods Department. She then helped to open and was store manager and buyer for Agata & Valentina, the prestigious New York gourmet marketplace.

She was discovered by the local CBS station while working for Cowan & Lobel, a large gourmet market in Albany, New York. She had begun a series of cooking classes to increase sales during the holidays. The classes were so popular that the station signed her on to do a weekly "30 Minute Meals" segment for the evening news. She sold 10,000 copies locally of a companion book.

The Food Network soon came calling, and the *Rachael Ray Show* began in September 2006. Her likable personality and quick, tasty recipes that fit modern lifestyles appeal to her viewing audience.

THINK CRITICALLY

Even though Rachael Ray says her success was accidental, what steps did she take in her life that prepared her for her current position?

Appearance is very important for a retail business. Effective store layouts maximize the available space and create a natural flow of traffic through the store to encourage additional spending. Access www.cengage.com/school/entrepreneurship/ideas and click on the link for Chapter 8. Read the article on types of store layouts. According to the article, what three factors must a retailer consider when developing a floor plan/store layout? Name the five types of store layouts described in the article. Then think of a retail store you visit frequently. Which type of layout design does the store use?

www.cengage.com/school/entrepreneurship/ideas

5. Leave at least four feet of aisle space. This makes it easy to move around in your store.
6. Create attractive in-store displays. Customers are drawn to displayed merchandise.
7. Use wall space wisely. Wall space may be too high for customers to reach, but it can be used to display merchandise.
8. Place the cash register in a central location. Customers should not have to search for a cashier.

Layout of a Service Business

Service businesses can be divided into two categories.

- Service businesses where people come to the business location to receive a service (restaurants, hair salons, automobile repair services)

- Service businesses that travel to the customer's location and perform the service on-site (exterminators, plumbers, cleaning services)

The layout of the first type of service business should be considered just as carefully as that of a retail business. However, on-site service businesses are never visited by their customers, so an attractive layout is not important. Organization should be a major consideration of on-site service businesses so that supplies and other items are easy to find.

Layout of a Wholesale Business

Customers of wholesale businesses are concerned with price and quality, not physical appearance. For this reason, a wholesale business needs only to have an efficient and well-organized layout. Wholesalers are constantly receiving and shipping large volumes of products. Wholesale businesses can do the following to facilitate shipping and receiving:

1. Locate in a one-story warehouse.
2. Keep merchandise close to the shipping dock. This minimizes the distance it will have to be moved when it is brought into and taken out of the warehouse.
3. Store the most popular items in the most accessible locations.
4. Be sure there are areas that can accommodate merchandise of all sizes.
5. Keep walkways free of merchandise so that employees can exit the building quickly in an emergency.
6. Store items safely. For instance, do not stack too many boxes on top of one another because they may fall if they become unsteady.

Layout of a Manufacturing Business

For manufacturing businesses, the layout should facilitate the production process. Attractiveness does not count. Important considerations include the following:

1. Work teams should be situated close together.
2. Supervisors should be able to easily observe the people they supervise. Their office should be located near the employees.
3. Exits should be clearly marked and easily accessible so that employees can quickly leave in the event of an emergency.
4. Any hazardous materials should be stored safely.
5. Equipment and machinery should be positioned in a way that reduces the chance of an accident.

✓CHECKPOINT

What are the major considerations for choosing a layout for a business?

8.2 ASSESSMENT

THINK ABOUT IT

1. What are the differences between a gross lease, a net lease, and a percentage lease? Which type of lease would you prefer? Explain why.

2. Why do you think it is important to draw a floor plan of your business before you begin setting up shop?

3. For a service business that serves customers at the place of business, why are layout considerations similar to those for a retail store?

MAKE ACADEMIC CONNECTIONS

4. **RESEARCH**   You are thinking about opening a bicycle sales and repair shop. Research layouts of other bicycle shops and determine what type of equipment and supplies would be included in the layout for this shop.

5. **MATH**   Determine the rent per customer for each of the following:

Location	Rent per Month	Projected Customer Traffic per Month	Rent per Customer
Downtown	$1,200	9,500	?
Community shopping center	$2,800	18,000	?
Stand-alone store	$1,050	7,400	?

Teamwork

Working with a team, choose a business with which you are familiar. Access www.cengage.com/school/entrepreneurship/ideas. Click on *Activities* and open the file *Evaluate the Layout of a Business*. Print a copy and complete the activity to rate the effectiveness of the business's layout and to offer suggestions for improvement.

PURCHASE EQUIPMENT, SUPPLIES, AND INVENTORY

Goals

- Explain how to find and choose vendors for your business.
- List factors that determine the needed level of inventory.

Vocabulary

- inventory
- vendors
- quote
- reorder point

focus on small business

Set up shop.

Karen had operated Bear Creek Embroidery and Alterations as a home-based business for several years. Her business had grown to the point where she needed more space for equipment and new employees. She shopped around for space and found a good location near her neighborhood.

While planning the move, Karen realized that in addition to rent, she would have many other expenses now that she would no longer be operating out of her home. As she began to add up the cost of all the furnishings, equipment, supplies, and other expenses that she would incur by moving out of her home and expanding her business, she began to wonder if she could afford the move.

Work as a Team What additional expenses will Karen be paying if she moves her business out of her home? Before deciding to move her business, what should Karen have done to be sure she could afford the move?

Consider all of the expenses involved in running a business.

Photodisc/Getty Images

Obtain Equipment and Supplies

Every business needs to analyze its operational needs and select equipment, supplies, and goods and services based on these needs. Machinery, computers, cash registers, and furniture are types of equipment. Supplies include things like paper, pens, and pencils. Inventory consists of the products and the materials needed to make the products that a business sells to its customers. Without these things, a business cannot function properly. If there is no inventory, what will you sell? If there is no paper, how will you send a letter? Suppliers or vendors can provide your business with everything you need to function.

To determine the equipment and supplies you need to start your business, make a list of what you think you will need. All businesses need standard items such as furniture, lamps, and office supplies. Businesses also need goods specific to the type of business. For example, lawn-care companies and landscaping firms would need lawn fertilizer as part of their supplies and lawn mowers as part of their equipment. Your list should include standard items needed by all businesses as shown in the table below. It should also include items specific to your particular business.

Once you have listed all of the items you need, indicate how much of each item you require. Be sure to list the minimum quantity you need right now, not the amount you might need if your business succeeds. Being overly optimistic could leave you with many bills that will be difficult to pay if your sales fall short of your projections.

STANDARD EQUIPMENT AND SUPPLY NEEDS FOR MOST BUSINESSES	
Type	Items
Furniture	Desks, chairs, bookcases, filing cabinets, tables, computer stands
Fixtures	Lamps, overhead lights
Office Equipment	Computers, routers, modems, fax machines, telephones, printers, copiers, scanners
Office Supplies	Stationery, pens and pencils, scissors, tape, staplers, paper clips, binder clips, folders, calendars
Maintenance Supplies	Toilet paper, paper towels, hand soap, cleaning supplies
Kitchen Supplies	Coffee maker, small refrigerator, soft drinks, coffee, tea

Identify Suppliers

To fill the standard and special needs of your business, you will need to research vendors. **Vendors** are companies that sell products and services to businesses. Vendors are also called *suppliers*. Valuable sources of vendor information include the following:

- Telephone directory advertising section
- Trade magazines (specialized magazines devoted to a particular industry), which carry vendor advertising
- Trade associations
- The Internet
- Other companies in your industry
- SBA and SCORE

Shira Silberg wants to open an assisted-living center for senior citizens. To find suppliers of furniture, linens, and many other items, Shira looks through copies of trade magazines for advertisements from companies that target the nursing-home industry. Shira also contacts nursing-home trade associations and locates vendor websites for additional information. Finally, she contacts other assisted-living centers to find out which vendors they use.

Evaluate Proposals

Most of the items you will need to start your business will be available from a variety of vendors. How will you decide among them? Before you make a purchase, contact several vendors and ask them to quote you a price for the merchandise you are interested in purchasing. A quote is an estimate for how much you will pay for the merchandise or service. Also ask vendors about the quality of their merchandise, their financing terms, quantity discounts, and shipping and handling charges. Once you have all the information you need, compare the various proposals. Choose the vendor that provides the best combination of products at a cost that fits your budget.

Shira selects her suppliers by asking for quotes from vendors. She then compares price quotes, service, quality of merchandise, and discount options. Shira knows that the lowest price is not always the best option if paying a little more means receiving better quality and service. She decides on a higher-priced linen business because it offers additional services that best meet the needs of her business.

 CHECKPOINT

> What should you consider when selecting vendors for your business?

Purchase Inventory

Retailing, wholesaling, and manufacturing businesses must purchase inventory before they can open for business. For retail and wholesale businesses, inventory is merchandise (a finished product) purchased with the intent of reselling it to customers. For manufacturing businesses, inventory consists of the business's finished product as well as the parts that go into producing the finished product.

What kinds of inventory might a bakery have?

Purchase Inventory for a Startup Business

Determining the amount of inventory to keep in stock is difficult for all business owners. It is particularly difficult for owners of new businesses, who do not yet know what their level of sales will be.

Chris Keating wants to open an art supplies store. He wants to have enough inventory that his shelves look full. He also wants to be able to offer his customers a full line of art supplies. Not knowing how high or low his sales will be at first, Chris doesn't want to purchase too much inventory. He doesn't want to tie up his cash in inventory if he can't sell it quickly. Chris is also worried about finding space to store the inventory. Because of these concerns, Chris purchases just enough stock to fill his shelves.

Purchase Inventory for an Ongoing Business

Once your business is up and running, you will have a better idea of how much inventory you need. To make sure that you do not run out of stock unexpectedly, you should track it and establish reorder points for each product you sell. The **reorder point** is a predetermined level of inventory that signals when new stock should be ordered. How low you set the reorder point depends on how long it takes your supplier to get merchandise to you, how many units of the item you sell each month, and how important it is for you not to be out of stock.

Chris sells 150 erasers a month. Because he never wants to be out of stock, he sets his reorder point at 30. Every time his inventory of erasers falls at or below 30 units, he places an order to renew his stock of this item.

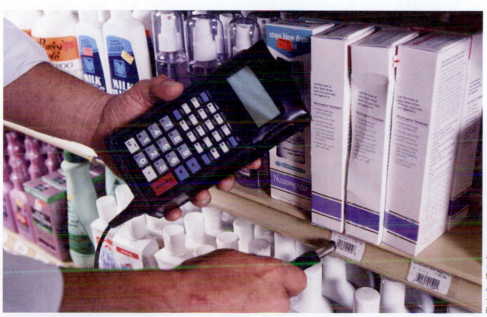

Why should you keep track of your inventory?

Photodisc/Getty Images

CHECKPOINT

How do you determine the amount of inventory to keep in stock?

8.3 ASSESSMENT

THINK ABOUT IT

1. Why should you make a list of all the equipment and supplies you need to start your business?

2. Why is it important to obtain price quotes from several different vendors before selecting a vendor? What questions should you ask potential vendors?

3. What issues should a business owner consider when purchasing inventory for the business? Explain the relationship between inventory and customer service.

MAKE ACADEMIC CONNECTIONS

4. **COMMUNICATION** You are a wholesale distributor of party supplies. A new store, Party Express, has asked you to submit a proposal for supplying its paper goods inventory. In order to prepare for a meeting with the Party Express management, make a list of questions you will ask them in order to get enough information for your proposal. Role-play the meeting with a classmate.

5. **MATH** Access www.cengage.com/school/entrepreneurship/ideas. Click on *Activities* and open the file *Equip Your Business*. Print a copy and complete the activity to calculate the cost of the equipment and supplies you would need to start your own fitness training business.

6. **RESEARCH** Use the Internet, trade magazines, newspapers, and other sources to search for suppliers of house paint for professional painters. Report your research in a short document, which could be used by a painter to help select a vendor.

Teamwork

Lee Torres is opening a retail pet store that carries high-quality pet foods, leashes, collars, coats, carriers, beds, toys, treats, grooming supplies, and flea products for dogs and cats. Lee does not plan to sell puppies or kittens but will have a large assortment of birds, tropical fish, and small animals (hamsters, guinea pigs, etc.) and the foods and accessories needed for them. The store will carry an assortment of books about selecting, training, breeding, and caring for pets. In addition, Lee will also offer grooming services for pets.

Working with teammates, make a list of all of the equipment and supplies Lee will need for his business. Use the Internet to compile a list of several vendors that sell pet products and supplies. Create a list of questions that Lee should ask the vendors. Finally, consider Lee's inventory needs. Decide which products Lee should order in large or small quantities and explain why. Compile a report to present to Lee.

E-Mail Etiquette

As you deal with vendors, suppliers, and customers, you will have the opportunity to communicate using e-mail on a regular basis. Today, many business deals are made by e-mail without the parties ever meeting or talking over the telephone. E-mail is preferred over regular mail, fax machines, and telephones as being quicker and less intrusive than a phone call. With e-mail, you can key your message, and with one stroke, your message is delivered instantly.

Although it may not be as formal, the same care should be given to e-mail as to the preparation of a business letter. You should always proofread your e-mail for spelling and grammar before sending it.

The following guidelines are important to remember when sending e-mails:

1. **Cover only one topic per e-mail.** If you have several topics to discuss, send them in separate e-mails.

2. **Use an appropriate subject line.** The subject line should appropriately describe the message. Also, because people receive numerous e-mails, try to use a subject line that will catch their attention.

3. **Your message should be brief.** Use short sentences and paragraphs. Long e-mails often go unread.

4. **Be courteous and professional in your message.** Remember, once the e-mail is sent, you cannot get it back.

5. **Remember that business e-mail is not private.** E-mail may be monitored in many companies. Also, any e-mail you send can easily be forwarded to someone else. Do not send anything that you would not want to be made public.

6. **Do not key text in all upper case.** Use of all caps is the equivalent of screaming, and it lowers readability. Use it for emphasis only.

7. **Limit the number and size of attachments.** Large files can take too much time to open and can fill up the recipient's mailbox.

When it comes to e-mail, the best habit to have is to use e-mail etiquette that will display your professionalism to others. Be sure your e-mail is worthy of a response.

Try It Out

You want to send an e-mail to a potential vendor asking for a quote for office supplies that you need for your new business. Compose the e-mail that you would send. Be sure to follow the guidelines given above.

©Michael D Brown, 2010/ Used under license from Shutterstock.com

SUMMARY

8.1 Choose a Location

1. Options for locating retail businesses include downtown areas, neighborhood shopping centers, community shopping centers, regional shopping centers, super-regional shopping centers, stand-alone stores, and warehouses.

2. When choosing a location for service businesses that customers visit, the same factors must be considered as for retail businesses. For service businesses where the service is performed on-site, the business location is not as important.

3. For industrial businesses, availability of good employees and low cost are key factors in choosing a location.

4. Operating a small business out of the home can save on costs, but it may make it difficult to separate personal and business life.

5. Starting a virtual or online business allows a startup business to have an immediate presence and compete with larger, established businesses.

6. Mapping your trade area with possible locations, the locations of competitors, and the locations of businesses that draw the same target customers can help you narrow your location options.

8.2 Obtain Space and Design the Physical Layout

7. To evaluate leases, compare the costs and expected benefits of various locations and the types of leases—gross, net, or percentage—offered. Calculating the rent per customer can help you determine which location is most cost-effective.

8. The layout of a business depends on the type of business. For retail businesses, the aim of a layout is to attract and keep customers. For wholesale businesses, the aim of a layout is to store inventory in the most efficient manner. For manufacturing businesses, the aim of a layout is to facilitate the production process.

8.3 Purchase Equipment, Supplies, and Inventory

9. Once you determine your equipment and supply needs, you will need to identify and evaluate a number of vendors by obtaining quotes.

10. To determine the amount of inventory to keep in stock and the reorder point, consider the amount of expected sales, the time it takes your supplier to get merchandise to you, and how important it is for you not to be out of stock for the item.

Read *Ideas in Action* on page 219 again. Then answer the questions a second time. Have your responses changed? If so, how have they changed?

VOCABULARY BUILDER

Match each statement with the term that best defines it. Some terms may not be used.

1. A section of land that is zoned for industrial businesses only
2. Companies that sell products and services to businesses
3. The area from which a business expects to attract customers
4. An estimate of how much you will pay for merchandise or services
5. The person who owns and rents out buildings or space
6. A lease in which the tenant pays rent each month for the space occupied, and the landlord covers all property expenses for that space
7. A lease in which the landlord pays building insurance and the tenant pays rent, taxes, and any other expenses
8. Areas that suffer from lack of employment opportunities
9. Buying and selling products or services over the Internet
10. A predetermined level of inventory that signals when new stock should be ordered

a. e-commerce
b. enterprise zones
c. gross lease
d. industrial park
e. inventory
f. landlord
g. net lease
h. percentage lease
i. quote
j. reorder point
k. tenant
l. trade area
m. vendors
n. visual merchandising

REVIEW YOUR KNOWLEDGE

11. Which of the following is *not* a location option for a retail business?
    a. downtown area
    b. industrial park
    c. community shopping center
    d. warehouse
12. Which of the following service businesses would consider the same location factors as a retail business?
    a. exterminating company
    b. lawn service
    c. hair salon
    d. on-site computer repair service
13. Which of the following is *not* a good reason to locate a business in the home?
    a. saves money
    b. more freedom
    c. limited space
    d. convenience
14. **True or False** Availability of parking would be an important consideration for the location of a coffee shop.
15. **True or False** Most entrepreneurs start out by purchasing the site where their business will be located.
16. In which type of lease does a landlord receive a portion of the tenant's revenue each month in addition to a base rent?
    a. gross lease
    b. net lease
    c. percentage lease
    d. tenant-landlord lease

17. Which of the following is the *least* important consideration when organizing the layout of a retail business?
    a. lighting
    b. window displays
    c. aisle space
    d. organization of supplies
18. Which of the following is the *least* important consideration for the layout of a wholesale business?
    a. organization
    b. efficiency
    c. safety
    d. appearance
19. **True or False** When purchasing supplies, equipment, and inventory, it is always best to purchase from the lowest-cost vendor.
20. Which of the following is *not* considered inventory?
    a. dolls for a toy store
    b. component parts of a product
    c. vacuum cleaners owned by a maid service
    d. all of the above are considered inventory
21. Which of the following is the *least* important factor in determining the reorder point for a sale item in your store?
    a. the size of the item
    b. the time it takes to receive merchandise from your supplier
    c. how many units you sell each month
    d. how important it is to you to not run out of stock

APPLY WHAT YOU LEARNED

22. You are planning to open a bakery. Identify the trade area. What types of locations are available in your community? List the advantages and disadvantages of each. Are there competing bakeries in any of these locations? Are there other businesses that do not compete directly but attract the same kind of customer? What are these businesses? Why do you think these businesses chose this particular location?
23. You want to start an online business that offers photo gifts such as photo keychains, mugs, and calendars. Customers can upload their photos to your website. Then you will assemble the products and mail them to the customers. Describe the advantages of operating your business online. What should you consider when designing your website?

MAKE ACADEMIC CONNECTIONS

24. **RESEARCH** Interview the owners or managers of three to five local businesses. What do each of them see as advantages and disadvantages of their locations? Are these businesses successful?
25. **MARKETING** Design the layout of a bookstore. Create a scale drawing of the space and show the placement of all of the fixtures, shelves, furniture, and equipment. Describe how you will use visual merchandising to help promote a positive image for your store.

26. **MATH** You are choosing between a neighborhood shopping center and a stand-alone store for your shoe store. The monthly rent for the shopping center is $3,200; the monthly rent for the stand-alone location is $2,500. The projected monthly customer traffic at the shopping center is 6,500, and the projected monthly traffic at the stand-alone location is 5,100. Which location will you choose and why? What other factors might you consider before choosing a location?

What Would YOU Do?

You are looking for a vendor to supply your new business with a computer, a printer, and a copy machine. You have contacted several vendors for quotes. One of the vendors offers you a "special" deal if you accept his quote before the end of the day.

In addition to a competitive price for the equipment, he is offering you tickets to an NFL game in a private stadium suite. He wants you to agree to the deal without signing a contract and has asked that you pay him in cash. What would you do?

build your
BUSINESS PLAN PROJECT

This activity will help you choose a location and vendors for your business idea.

1. Choose the location area that is best for your business. Why is it the best choice? Record your reasons on paper.

2. Using a local map, mark the trade area for your business. Mark the possible locations for your business and the locations of your competitors. Are there any businesses in the trade area that do not directly compete but attract a similar type of customer? If so, mark those on the map. For each area, write an evaluation that outlines why this would or would not be a good location for your business.

3. Determine if it will be more cost-effective for you to buy or lease space, to run your business from home, or to operate your business online. Consider rent-per-customer projections. Write a short paper justifying your decision.

4. Design the physical layout of your business. Create a scale drawing of the space and show the placement of all of the furniture, fixtures, and equipment. Indicate the planned use of each area. How does this layout meet your goals? Calculate the square footage requirements for the entire layout.

5. Analyze the equipment and supplies you will need to start your business. Using the telephone book, trade magazines, the Internet, and other sources, locate five vendors. Contact the vendors to obtain information about their products, pricing, financial terms, and quantity discounts. Using the prices from each vendor, calculate the total cost of all equipment and supplies you will need. How do the vendors compare? Which one will you select? Why?

"My uncle is visiting from out West. He is excited about the solar panels he recently installed at his home. His city provided a $1,000 rebate for solar panel installation. As required by the rebate, the panels annually displace 1,500 kilowatt hours of grid-based power. My uncle's utility bills have gone down. He also feels good about doing his part to improve the environment by decreasing his dependence on the grid."

How do individuals and organizations transition their energy resources from traditional sources to environmentally friendly, renewable sources?

Solar power is a renewable energy source that is rapidly increasing in popularity. Many companies are available to help individuals and corporations utilize solar energy and to assist in solar panel installation.

Employment Outlook

- Solar energy consumption is expected to grow as part of the overall growth of U.S. energy consumption.
- Workers who are trained to work with alternative energy sources may experience good job prospects.
- Individuals with college coursework in high-end technology will have the best opportunities in the utilities industry.

Job Titles

- Solar Installer
- Consultant, Solar Energy
- Solar Energy Project Manager
- Photovoltaic Lighting Designer
- Solar System Design Engineer

Needed Education/Skills

- A Bachelor's degree in science with an engineering major is required for higher-level design, production, and management jobs.
- Expertise in a variety of areas including journeyman-level electrical knowledge, plumbing, and mount racking systems is needed for solar panel installers.

What's it like to work in Architecture and Construction? Paige, a Solar Panel Installation Contractor, has obtained installation contracts from a variety of companies. The companies that have contracted for Paige's services provide their clients with on-site consulting, ranging from determining the optimal location of solar panels, to the filing of paperwork for government-based rebate and tax credit programs, to providing a six-month follow-up visit to ensure proper functioning of panels.

Since Paige has been installing panels for many years, her experience is broad-based. Given the breadth of her experience, she can install panels at residential, commercial, or industrial sites. For the larger jobs, she is often part of a team of installation contractors.

Paige is planning to attend a conference that will focus on state and federal solar energy incentive programs. Becoming more knowledgeable about these issues is part of Paige's continuing education plan to prepare her to start her own solar energy consulting business.

What about you? Would you like to help clean up the environment by actively converting energy consumers to renewable, "green" energy sources?

Buying and Merchandising Team Decision Making Event

Your team is in charge of buying merchandise and clothing bearing the university's name, logo, and trademark for a large university bookstore on a campus that has 54,000 students. The university has a highly successful football and baseball team, attracting numerous fans to the campus on game days. Your team must understand product mix, product life cycles, seasonal markdown schedules, pricing strategies, target markets, and special promotional events. You will meet with the bookstore managers to explain your proposed product mix, markdown schedule for seasonal merchandise, and special sales events to sell merchandise. Your merchandising strategy must consider the fluctuating student population during the year. You must also explain a strategy to increase Internet merchandise sales.

Your team has 30 minutes to study a business situation and organize your analysis, using a management decision-making format. Participants have ten minutes to describe the team's analysis of the situation. All members of the team must participate in the presentation. The judge has five minutes to ask questions about the presentation. Each participant must answer at least one question asked by the judge.

Performance Indicators

- Identify product opportunities
- Describe the use of technology in the selling function
- Explain the nature and scope of the product/service management function
- Identify the impact of product life cycles on marketing decisions
- Develop strategies to position product/business
- Explain factors affecting pricing decisons
- Explain the nature of a promotional plan

Go to the DECA website for more detailed information.

THINK CRITICALLY

1. Why must the clothing at the bookstore be unique from clothing carried in department stores and other retail outlets?
2. Why are scheduled merchandise markdowns important for retailers?
3. What types of special promotions could increase sales from fans and alumni attending football and baseball games?
4. Why should the bookstore consider Internet merchandise sales?

www.deca.org

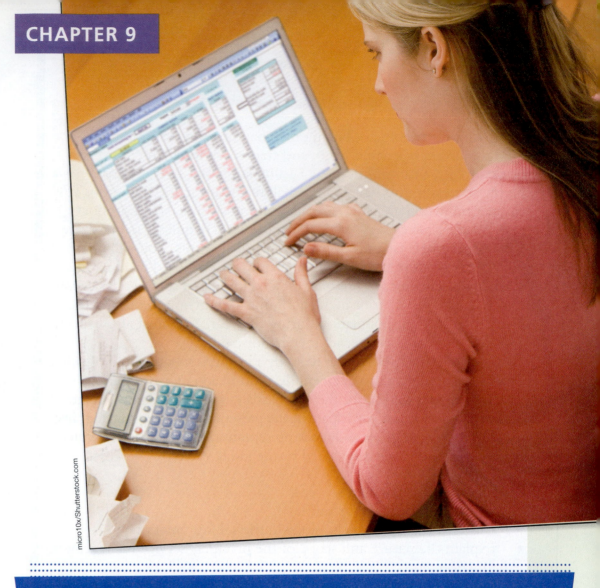

micro10x/Shutterstock.com

Plan and Track Your Finances

9.1 Financing Your Business

9.2 Pro Forma Financial Statements

9.3 Recordkeeping for Businesses

www.cengage.com/school/entrepreneurship/ideas

Making Homework Fun

Making a profit is a big motivating factor when starting a business. In order to be successful, entrepreneurs must have a firm understanding of finance and money management. When Jason O'Neill attended craft shows with his mom, he was envious of the money she made selling her items. Jason discovered at the early age of nine that if he wanted to make money, he would need to create a product of his own.

Jason O'Neill, Owner/ Founder of Pencil Bugs

Jason wanted to create a product that would make homework more fun. After brainstorming several designs, Jason came up with the idea of Pencil Bugs. Pencil Bugs are brightly colored Styrofoam bugs with googly eyes, wire antennae, and pipe cleaner bodies that wrap snuggly around a pencil. With money he had saved, Jason bought all the materials for the first batch of pencil toppers for $10 at his local craft store. After Jason's classmates saw him using the Pencil Bugs, orders started rolling in. Jason also sold Pencil Bugs outside local stores, at craft shows, and on his website. Because of the early success of the Pencil Bugs, Jason expanded his business to include t-shirts, bookmarks, and greeting cards, all with the same "buggy" theme.

Jason was dealing with a large inventory of supplies and finished products (Pencil Bugs), so it was important to closely manage his finances. His parents showed him how to organize the numbers on spreadsheets and manage the money in his bank account.

As the youngest recipient to win the Young Entrepreneur of the Year Award by Young Entrepreneurs of America, Jason has learned more valuable life and financial lessons than most high school students. Jason emphasizes that it is not just about the money he makes, but what he does with the money. Although he has tucked away most of his profits for college tuition, Jason donates to local charities and buys toys and games for local children's hospitals.

With the recent self-publication of his book, *Bitten by the Business Bug*, and a long list of speaking engagements on the horizon, Jason hopes to have a long career as an entrepreneur. Jason encourages other aspiring entrepreneurs to explore all ideas as a possible business because you never know when one will bite.

1. Why do you think Pencil Bugs was such an easy business to start?
2. If Jason did not have any money saved, what are some other ways he could have gotten money to start his business?
3. What are some ways that you keep track of your finances?

FINANCING YOUR BUSINESS

Goals

- Estimate your startup costs and personal net worth.
- Identify sources of equity capital for your business.
- Identify sources of debt capital for your business.

Vocabulary

- net worth
- debt-to-equity ratio
- equity capital
- venture capitalists
- debt capital
- collateral

focus on small business

Line up your financing.

Monty was excited about starting his own meeting planning business. He compiled a list of all the things that he would need to buy for his business. Monty realized that he was going to need some financial assistance because he did not have enough money saved to purchase everything he needed. He called his friend Sarah for some advice.

"Sarah, I need some help financing my new business. Who do you think I should ask?" Sarah had taken some business courses in school and remembered that there were many different avenues for funding a business. "Why don't you start with your friends and family and see if any of them are interested in investing in your business," Sarah suggested. "If not, I've got lots more ideas!"

Work as a Team Do you think your friends and family members would be willing to loan money or invest in your business? If not, whom else could you approach for funding?

Determine if you need financial assistance.

Assess Your Financial Needs

As you start a business, you will have many decisions to make regarding its financing. Your financial needs will vary depending on the size and type of business you start. If you are starting a very small business, you may be able to provide all the startup money you will need. If your business will be large or require special equipment, you may need to look to others for help raising the startup money.

Before you can approach a lender or investor about financing your business, you will have to prepare some financial documents. To begin, you should estimate your startup costs and create a personal financial statement. Then you will prepare pro forma financial statements of the cash flow statement, income statement, and balance sheet. Financial statements based on projections are known as *pro forma financial statements*. You will learn more about pro forma financial statements in the next lesson. These items allow potential lenders and investors to determine if your business is viable. They also help lenders decide whether the financing you are requesting is reasonable.

Startup Costs

Itemizing your startup costs is an important part of determining how much money you need to start your business. You will want to be sure you have accounted for all of the items you will need. Common startup items to be purchased include the following:

- Equipment and supplies, such as computers, printers, telephones, and paper
- Furniture and fixtures, such as desks and chairs
- Vehicles, such as delivery trucks
- Remodeling, such as electrical and plumbing expenses
- Legal and accounting fees
- Licensing fees

Felicia Walters plans to start a lighting fixture store. To help her determine how much money she will need to borrow, she calculates her startup costs. She must include her estimate of startup costs with the other documents she provides to lenders or investors.

Personal Financial Statement

In order to determine if you have the resources you need to finance your business, begin by assessing your net worth. <u>Net worth</u> is the difference between what you own, called *assets*, and what you owe, called *liabilities*. Net worth is also referred to as *equity*. To calculate your net worth, you should prepare a *personal financial statement*. On the left side, list all of your assets with their value. Include cash, investments, and any property. Total the worth of these items. On the right side, list your liabilities and total the amount that you owe. Then subtract your total liabilities from your total assets to determine your net worth.

Felicia Walters prepares a personal financial statement to help her determine whether she is able to finance her new business. She finds that her net worth is $27,800, as shown on the next page. After comparing her startup costs to her net worth, Felicia determines that she will need to seek additional financial resources for her business. Felicia will share her personal financial statement and startup cost estimates with potential lenders and investors when she seeks financing for her business.

DEVELOP YOUR READING SKILLS

As you read this chapter, list all of the key terms. Then write a sentence using the key term to demonstrate comprehension of the term.

STARTUP COSTS
Walters Electric

Item	Estimated Cost
Equipment and supplies	
Computers (3 @ $1,500)	$ 4,500
Scanner	175
Cash registers (2 @ $1,800)	3,600
Printer	400
Supplies	300
Subtotal	$ 8,975
Furniture and Fixtures	
Desks (4 @ $400)	$ 1,600
Chairs (8 @ $75)	600
Subtotal	$ 2,200
Vehicles	
Delivery truck	$10,000
Automobile	8,000
Subtotal	$18,000
Remodeling	
Drywall replacement	$ 1,000
Electrical work	2,500
Paint	1,000
Carpet	3,000
Subtotal	$ 7,500
Legal and accounting fees	$ 3,000
Total	$39,675

PERSONAL FINANCIAL STATEMENT
Felicia Walters

Assets		Liabilities	
Cash	$ 5,000	Car loan	$ 6,900
Checking account	13,500	College loan	4,000
Certificate of Deposit	6,000	Credit cards	1,300
Stock	10,000		
Computer equipment	3,000		
Coin collection	2,500		
Total assets	$ 40,000	Total liabilities	$12,200

Total assets − Total liabilities = **Net worth**

$40,000 − $12,200 = $27,800

CHECKPOINT

> **Why is the net worth of an entrepreneur important to potential investors in the business?**

Equity Capital

There are two types of financing available for your business—equity and debt financing. When obtaining financing, you must consider your company's **debt-to-equity ratio**, or the relation between the dollars you have borrowed (debt) and the dollars you have invested in your business (equity). This ratio measures how much money a company can safely borrow over time. The formula for debt-to-equity ratio is:

Total Liabilities ÷ Total Equity

A high ratio indicates that a business is mostly financed through debt, while a low ratio indicates that a business is primarily financed through equity. The debt-to-equity ratio can vary among industries, so comparisons of ratios among companies within the same industry should be made. Lenders and investors look at this ratio to assess risk. Lenders usually prefer low debt-to-equity ratios. A high debt-to-equity ratio indicates that a company may not be able to generate enough cash to meet its debt obligations. Thus, a bank runs the risk of not being repaid for its loan. Having the right mix of debt and equity will help ensure your business's sound financial future.

Equity capital is money invested in a business in return for a share in the profits of the business. Equity capital includes money invested by the owner. Entrepreneurs may seek additional equity capital when they do not qualify for other types of financing and are not able to fully finance their business out of their own savings. Other sources of equity capital include people you know or venture capitalists.

Personal Contributions

Many entrepreneurs use their personal savings to finance the start of their business. Investing personal finances can help you get a loan from a bank. By investing your own money, you demonstrate to the bank that you have faith that your business will succeed.

Friends and Relatives

Friends and relatives can be a good source of equity capital. They will already be familiar with your business idea and know whether you are trustworthy and a good risk. They may be willing to invest more money in your business than other sources in return for a share of the business profits.

Venture Capitalists

Some privately owned companies get financing through venture capitalists. Venture capitalists are individuals or companies that make a living investing in startup companies. They carefully research opportunities that they believe will make above-average profits. They are usually interested in companies that have the potential of earning hundreds of millions of dollars within a few years. The prospect of a company going public by publicly offering shares of stock for sale also attracts venture capitalists. Because of the desired criteria, many small businesses would have trouble attracting the interest of venture capitalists.

 CHECKPOINT

What are some of the ways entrepreneurs can get equity capital?

Debt Capital

Debt capital is money loaned to a business with the understanding that the money will be repaid, usually with interest. You can borrow money from friends, relatives, and banks. Bank loans may be secured or unsecured.

Friends and Relatives

If friends and relatives are not interested in investing in your business with equity capital, they may be willing to loan you money. Before borrowing from friends or relatives, consider how the loan may affect your relationship with them. Those who loan you money might also feel they can give you advice along with their money. You may decide that the risk of losing a friend if you are unable to pay back the borrowed funds is not worth taking.

If you take a loan from friends or relatives, you should prepare a formal agreement that spells out

What are the pros and cons of borrowing money from family and friends?

the terms of the loan. Be sure both you and the individuals loaning the money understand exactly how much interest and principal you will pay each month. Also, specify what your obligations are to pay back the loan if your business is not successful.

Commercial Bank Loans

Most businesses take out loans from banks. Entrepreneurs usually have an established relationship with a bank and begin looking for funds there. When a loan is obtained, it must be repaid with interest in a certain time period. There are different types of loans that banks offer their customers.

SECURED LOANS   Loans that are backed by collateral are called secured loans. **Collateral** is property that the borrower forfeits if he or she defaults on the loan. Banks demand collateral so that they have some recourse if the borrower fails to repay the loan.

Suppose you take out a $25,000 business loan and use your home as collateral. If you fail to repay the loan, the bank has the right to take ownership of your home and sell it to collect the money you owe. Banks accept different forms of collateral, including real estate, savings accounts, life insurance policies, stocks, and bonds.

Types of secured loans include the following:

1. **Line of credit**   An agreement by a bank to lend up to a certain amount of money whenever the borrower needs it is called a *line of credit*. Banks will charge a fee for this program whether or not money is actually borrowed. In addition, they will charge interest on the borrowed funds. Most businesses establish lines of credit so that funds are readily available to help them make purchases when necessary.
2. **Long-term loan**   A loan payable over a period longer than a year is a *long-term loan*. Long-term loans are generally made to help a business make improvements that will boost profits. For example, the owner of a small coffee shop may obtain a $50,000, five-year loan to increase the size of the shop to accommodate more customers.
3. **Accounts receivable financing**   Many businesses allow their customers to charge merchandise and services and pay for them later. The balances owed by customers are called the business's *accounts receivable*. A bank will loan a business up to 85 percent of the total value of its accounts receivable if it feels that the business's customers are good credit risks. As the receivables are paid, the payments are forwarded to the bank. The interest rate for accounts receivable financing is often higher than for other types of loans.
4. **Inventory financing**   When banks use the inventory held by a business as collateral for a loan, it is called *inventory financing*. Banks usually require that the value of the inventory be at least double the amount of the loan, and the business must have already paid its vendors in full for the inventory. Banks are often not eager to make this kind of loan. If the business defaults, the bank ends up with inventory it may have trouble reselling.

UNSECURED LOANS   Loans that are not guaranteed with collateral are unsecured loans. These loans are made only to the bank's most creditworthy customers. Unsecured loans are usually made for very specific purposes. They are usually short-term loans that have to be repaid within a year. A business may obtain a short-term loan to help with temporary cash flow problems during slow or seasonal periods. Unsecured lines of credit are also available for those who have good credit.

REASONS A BANK MAY NOT LEND MONEY   Banks use various guidelines to determine whether borrowers are a good risk. They reject applications that do not meet their criteria. Some of the main reasons banks turn down loan applicants include the following:

1. **The business is a startup.** Banks are often reluctant to lend money to startup businesses because new businesses have no record of repaying loans. They are more likely to default on their loans than established companies.
2. **Lack of a solid business plan.** Banks evaluate businesses based on their business plans. A company with a poorly written or poorly conceived business plan will not be able to obtain financing from a bank.
3. **Lack of adequate experience.** Banks want to be sure that the people setting up or running a business know what they are doing. You will have to show that you are familiar with the industry and have the management experience to run your own business.

famous entrepreneur

THE WRIGHT BROTHERS When you think of the Wright Brothers, you probably think of them as the first men to fly. But before they were flying a plane at Kitty Hawk, they were entrepreneurs in Dayton, Ohio. As children, Wilbur and Orville loved fixing and experimenting with machines. They sold kites to other children in their neighborhood for extra money. Wilbur invented a machine to fold papers for mailing when he was a teenager. Orville and a friend set up a small printing firm when Orville was 14 years old. Orville and Wilbur went on to publish their own newspaper, *West Side News,* in 1889. Cycling was a growing sport at that time. Because of their ability to repair things, people were always asking the Wrights to repair their bicycles. So in their early twenties, Wilbur and Orville opened the Wright Cycle Company. Using the

Science Faction/Getty Images

Why do entrepreneurs often have more than one business venture?

profits from their bicycle shop, they began to study flight and experiment with gliders and kites. These experiments led them to the powered flying machine they flew successfully on December 17, 1903.

THINK CRITICALLY
Do you think Wilbur and Orville would have been able to finance their flight experiments if they had not had income from their own business?

4. **Lack of confidence in the borrower.** Even if your business plan looks solid and you have adequate experience, you may fail to qualify for financing if you make a bad impression on your banker. Make sure you dress and behave professionally. Show up on time for appointments, and provide all information your banker requests.

5. **Inadequate investment in the business.** Banks are suspicious of entrepreneurs who do not invest their own money in their businesses. You will have to commit a significant amount of your own money if you are to receive financing from a bank.

Obtaining bank financing for a startup business is difficult but not impossible if you can show that you are confident, well prepared, and able to repay the loan. Being aware of banks' most common objections can help you prepare for the application process. For instance, you can properly prepare your business plan, wear a business suit to bank appointments, and arrive on time to make a good impression.

Other Sources of Loans

In addition to commercial banks, there are many government agencies that can assist you with debt capital loans.

1. **Small Business Administration**   Approximately 95 percent of all businesses are eligible for SBA assistance. The SBA aids entrepreneurs most often by guaranteeing loans made by commercial banks. This means if you default on the loan, the SBA will pay a certain percentage of the loan to the bank. This helps banks feel more comfortable about lending money. The SBA also makes funds available to nonprofit organizations that, in turn, make loans to eligible borrowers.

2. **Small Business Investment Companies**   SBICs are licensed by the SBA to make loans to and invest capital with entrepreneurs.

3. **Minority Enterprise Small Business Investment Companies**   MESBICs are special kinds of SBICs that lend money to small businesses owned by members of ethnic minorities.

4. **Department of Housing and Urban Development**   HUD provides grants to cities to help improve impoverished areas. Cities use these grants to make loans to private developers who must use the loans to finance projects in needy areas. The American Recovery and Reinvestment Act of 2009 (Recovery Act) includes $13.61 billion for projects and programs administered by the Department of Housing and Urban Development, nearly 75 percent of which was allocated to state and local recipients. Recovery Act investments in HUD programs will generate tens of thousands of jobs and support a broad range of housing and community development projects.

NETBookmark

The Small Business Administration (SBA) offers many loan programs to assist small businesses. Its programs offer many benefits, such as longer payment terms and larger loan amounts than might be available through a conventional commercial bank loan. Access www.cengage.com/school/entrepreneurship/ideas and click on the link for Chapter 9. Read about the various SBA loan programs and describe three of them.

www.cengage.com/school/entrepreneurship/ideas

5. **The Economic Development Administration** The EDA is a division of the U.S. Department of Commerce that partners with distressed communities throughout the United States to foster job creation, collaboration, and innovation by lending money to businesses that operate in and benefit economically distressed parts of the country. Borrowing from the EDA is similar to borrowing from the SBA, but the application is more complicated, and the restrictions are tighter.

6. **State Governments** Government assistance may also be available at the state level. Almost all states have economic development agencies and finance authorities that make or guarantee loans to small businesses.

7. **Local and Municipal Governments** City, county, or municipal governments sometimes make loans to local businesses. The loans are usually $10,000 or less.

 **CHECKPOINT**

> Where can entrepreneurs look for debt financing?

did you KNOW?

In 2009, the SBA guaranteed more than 50,000 loans in the amount of $62.2 billion to small businesses. It also approved 21,780 disaster loans for $1.2 billion.

9.1 ASSESSMENT

THINK ABOUT IT

1. What are some of the challenges you might encounter if you get equity financing from friends and/or family members?

2. Why is a secured loan easier to get than an unsecured loan?

3. Why would a bank be more willing to grant an SBA-guaranteed loan to a new business?

MAKE ACADEMIC CONNECTIONS

4. **MATH** Tisha Appleton obtained an SBA-guaranteed loan from her bank for $45,000 for her new business. The SBA guaranteed 75 percent of the loan. How much has the bank risked losing if Tisha's business fails?

5. **COMMUNICATION** When applying for a loan, most lenders will want to see a personal financial statement. Access www.cengage.com/school/entrepreneurship/ideas. Click on *Activities* and open the file *Personal Financial Statement*. Print a copy and complete the personal financial statement required by the SBA.

Teamwork

You want to start a home remodeling business. You need money to purchase remodeling equipment and a new truck. Work in small groups to identify sources of financing for the business. Role-play a scenario in which you are meeting with a potential investor. Explain your business idea and your need for funds, and make a request for funding.

PRO FORMA FINANCIAL STATEMENTS

Goals

- Prepare a pro forma cash flow statement.
- Prepare a pro forma income statement.
- Prepare pro forma balance sheet.

Vocabulary

- cash flow statement
- income statement
- balance sheet

focus on small business

Show me the money!

"So, Monty, how much money do you think your business will make?" asked Sarah. "And I'm supposed to know that how?" Monty replied. "Well, take a look at your pro forma financial statements," Sarah answered. "Well, Sarah, once again you are showing me how much I don't know!"

Financial statements show how well your business is doing.

"There are financial statements you should prepare to help you estimate the finances of your business." Sarah responded. "The pro forma income statement estimates how much money will come in, how much you will spend, and the amount of any projected profit or loss. Some people even call it a profit/loss statement. There's also a pro forma cash flow statement and balance sheet. Come on, Monty, we've got work to do."

Work as a Team Discuss the reasons you think it is important to prepare pro forma financial statements. What types of information do you think that a business owner can get from these financial statements? Why do you think pro forma financial statements should be included as part of a business plan?

Cash Flow Statement

Financial statements are important when you are trying to raise capital for your business. The financial statements you prepare for your business plan are pro forma financial statements and are based on projections. The cash flow statement, income statement, and balance sheet all tell you something different about the condition of your business.

For many, the cash flow statement is the most important financial statement. A **cash flow statement** is an accounting report that describes the way cash flows into and out of your business over a period of time. Because it deals with actual cash coming in and going out of a business, it shows how much money you have available to pay your bills and whether you have enough money to continue operating.

Forecast Receipts and Disbursements

To create a pro forma cash flow statement, you will need to estimate your monthly cash receipts and monthly cash disbursements. Cash receipts include cash sales, collected accounts receivable, tax refunds, and funds from bank loans and investors. When you forecast the amount of your cash receipts, you need to analyze the demand for each of your products and services. You also need to know the price you will charge for each item.

FORECASTED RECEIPTS
Walters Electric
January 20—

Cash sales

	Quantity Sold	Price	Total
CFL bulbs	20	$ 15	$ 300
Indoor light fixtures	10	155	1,550
Outdoor lights	6	175	1,050
Subtotal			$2,900
Accounts receivable			$ 300
Bank loan			$1,000
Total			$4,200

Felicia Walters estimates her total cash sales for her lighting fixture store by multiplying the quantity of each type of product she expects to sell by the price she has set for each item. In addition, Felicia estimates her other monthly cash receipts as shown above.

Cash disbursements may include payments for cost of goods (what you pay manufacturers or wholesalers to get products and services to sell), accounts payable (credit accounts with suppliers), rent, salaries, taxes, office supplies, utilities, insurance, advertising, loans, and other expenses. Felicia's estimated monthly cash disbursements are shown in the table to the right.

FORECASTED DISBURSEMENTS
Walters Electric
January 20—

Disbursement	Amount
Cost of goods	$2,400
Rent	900
Utilities	100
Salaries	2,000
Advertising	700
Supplies	100
Insurance	75
Payroll taxes	175
Other	50
Total	$6,500

Prepare the Cash Flow Statement

After making projections of cash receipts and cash disbursements, you are ready to prepare your cash flow statement. You should create monthly pro forma cash flow statements for the first year of operation and annual statements for the second and third years to give your lender an accurate picture of your cash flow over time.

Net cash flow is the difference between cash receipts and disbursements.

Cash receipts − Cash disbursements = Net cash flow

PRO FORMA CASH FLOW STATEMENT						
Walters Electric						
January–June 20—						
	Jan	Feb	Mar	Apr	May	June
Cash receipts	$4,200	$5,410	$5,750	$6,320	$7,375	$8,130
Cash disbursements						
Cost of goods	$2,400	$2,520	2,520	2,640	3,300	3,480
Rent	900	900	900	900	900	900
Utilities	100	100	100	100	100	100
Salaries	2,000	2,000	2,000	2,000	2,000	2,000
Advertising	700	700	700	700	700	700
Supplies	100	115	130	150	150	150
Insurance	75	75	75	75	75	75
Payroll taxes	175	175	175	175	175	175
Other	50	50	50	50	50	50
Total disbursements	$6,500	$6,635	$6,650	$6,790	$7,450	$7,630
Cash Flow	−$2,300	−$1,225	−$ 900	−$ 470	−$ 75	$ 500

If cash receipts total more than disbursements, your business has a positive cash flow. You can put this money in the bank, pay down debt, or use it to expand your business. If disbursements total more than cash receipts, your business has a negative cash flow. You may have to borrow money or ask your creditors to give you more time to pay. Preparing pro forma statements helps you to anticipate when negative cash flows will occur, so you can plan for how you will handle or avoid them. Felicia Walters' pro forma cash flow statement is shown above.

Many entrepreneurs create two cash flow statements based on a worst-case scenario and a best-case scenario. For a worst-case scenario, you should project lower cash receipts and higher cash disbursements than you think you will have. For a best-case scenario, you should project the highest cash receipts and lowest cash disbursements your business is likely to have.

Economic Effects on Cash Flow

Changes in the economy can have a dramatic effect on the cash flow of a business. During the good economic times of the 1990s, many businesses saw large amounts of cash flowing into their companies and experienced positive cash flows. However, economic slowdowns such as the one that resulted after September 11, 2001, and the one in 2008 brought on by the mortgage loan crisis, caused many businesses to experience unexpected negative cash flows. When making projections, business owners should look at economic forecasts and make conservative estimates. Remembering that changing economic conditions can affect cash flows, it is best to err on the side of caution.

CHECKPOINT

> **What does a cash flow statement show?**

Income Statement

An income statement shows the business's revenues and expenses incurred over a period of time and the resulting profit or loss. For this reason, it is sometimes called the *profit/loss statement*. An income statement can help you do the following:

1. Examine how sales, expenses, and income are changing over time.
2. Forecast how well your business can expect to perform in the future.
3. Analyze your costs to determine where you may need to cut back.
4. Identify categories of expenditures you may want to increase or decrease, such as advertising.

While the cash flow statement deals with actual cash coming in and going out, the income statement shows revenues that you have not yet received and expenses that you have not yet paid.

Suppose Walters Electric sells $5,000 worth of lighting in June. The company's monthly income statement would show income of $5,000. Felicia may not actually have received $5,000, because some customers may have paid on credit. They will not make payments until July or August. Further, some credit customers may fail to ever pay their bills.

Customers are not the only people who defer payments. Felicia may purchase $1,500 worth of merchandise to sell but wait 30 days to pay the invoice. Because no cash has been paid for this purchase, it will not appear on the cash flow statement. In contrast, the income statement will show that Felicia incurred an expense of $1,500.

Prepare a Pro Forma Income Statement

Preparing a pro forma income statement for a number of years will help lenders see the long-term growth of your business. The pro forma income statement consists of the following parts:

Why should a business estimate the amount of revenue it expects to earn?

- **Revenue** The dollar value of the goods or services a business sells to customers is called revenue.

PRO FORMA INCOME STATEMENT
Walters Electric, 20—

Item	Year 2	Year 3
Revenue	$115,000	$125,000
Cost of goods sold	55,400	60,000
Gross profit	$ 59,600	$ 65,000
Operating expenses:		
Salaries	$ 26,705	$ 27,315
Rent	10,800	10,800
Utilities	1,230	1,260
Advertising	1,200	1,200
Insurance	900	900
Supplies	600	615
Other	615	615
Total operating expenses	$ 42,050	$ 42,705
Net income before taxes	$ 17,550	$ 22,295
Taxes	7,020	8,918
Net income/loss after taxes	$ 10,530	$ 13,377

- **Cost of goods sold** The cost of the inventory a business sells during a particular period is called cost of goods sold. Only businesses that have inventory will have this item on their income statements. It is listed separately from the other expenses.
- **Gross profit** The difference between revenue and cost of goods sold is the gross profit.
- **Operating expenses** The expenses necessary to operate a business are the operating expenses. They include salaries, rent, utilities, advertising, insurance, supplies, and other expenses. All businesses pay operating expenses.
- **Net income before taxes** Net income before taxes is the amount remaining after cost of goods sold and operating expenses are subtracted from revenue. It shows how much you earned before taxes.
- **Taxes** Taxes are usually listed separately from other expenses.
- **Net income/loss after taxes** After taxes are subtracted, the result is the net income or loss for the period.

CHECKPOINT

What does an income statement show?

Balance Sheet

A **balance sheet** is a financial statement that lists what a business owns, what it owes, and how much it is worth at a particular point in time. It does so by identifying the assets, liabilities, and owner's equity of the business. It is based on the accounting equation:

Assets = Liabilities + Owner's Equity

Assets are items of value owned by a business. They include items such as cash, equipment, and inventory. Liabilities are amounts that a business owes to others. They include loans and outstanding invoices. Owner's equity is the amount remaining after the value of all liabilities is subtracted from the value of all assets. A business that has more assets than liabilities has positive net worth. A business that has more liabilities than assets has negative net worth.

Prepare a Pro Forma Balance Sheet

You must estimate the amount of assets, liabilities, uncollectible accounts, and asset depreciation when preparing a pro forma balance sheet for your business. Felicia Walters' pro forma balance sheet is shown below.

TYPES OF ASSETS Businesses usually separate assets into current assets and fixed assets. *Current assets*, often referred to as *liquid assets* because they can be converted to cash easily, include cash, inventory, and items that are used up in normal business operations, such as supplies. Another special type of current asset is accounts receivable. *Accounts receivable* are the amounts owed to a business by its credit customers. Accounts receivable are usually collected from customers within a few months and then converted into cash. *Fixed assets*, also referred to as *illiquid assets* because they cannot be converted into cash easily, are those that will be used for many years. They include buildings, furniture, and computers.

TYPES OF LIABILITIES Businesses usually separate liabilities into long-term liabilities and current liabilities. *Long-term liabilities* are debts that are payable over a year or longer. A mortgage is a type of long-term liability. *Current liabilities* are debts that are due to be paid in full in less than a year. A special kind of current liability is accounts payable. *Accounts payable* are amounts owed to vendors for merchandise purchased on credit. Businesses can usually choose to pay later for merchandise they receive now. Because a business generally pays invoices from vendors within 30 to 90 days, accounts payable are a current liability.

REDUCTIONS IN ASSETS Some customers will fail to pay for the merchandise they purchased on credit. The amount a company estimates

---

PRO FORMA BALANCE SHEET
Walters Electric
December 31, 20—

Assets		Liabilities	
Current assets		*Current liabilities*	
Cash	$1,000	Accounts payable	$12,000
Accounts receivable	8,000		
Less allowance for			
uncollectible accounts	−500	*Long-term liabilities*	
Inventory	14,000	Loans payable	$17,900
Total current assets	$22,500	Total liabilities	$29,900
Fixed assets			
Equipment	$8,975		
Less depreciation	−1,795		
Furniture	2,200		
Less depreciation	−220		
Vehicles	18,000	Owner's Equity	
Less depreciation	−3,600	Felicia Walters	$16,160
Total fixed assets	$23,560	Total liabilities and	
Total assets	$46,060	owner's equity	$46,060

---

it will not receive from customers is known as the *allowance for uncollectible accounts.* This amount should be subtracted from the assets.

Business equipment will lose value over time just as a car loses value as it gets older. The lowering of an asset's value to reflect its current worth is called *depreciation.* Estimates for uncollectible accounts and depreciation should be included to ensure that the balance sheet provides an accurate picture of the business's net worth.

CHECKPOINT

> **Name one example each of a current (liquid) asset, a fixed (illiquid) asset, a current liability, and a long-term liability.**

9.2 ASSESSMENT

THINK ABOUT IT

1. Why would you prepare both a best-case and a worst-case pro forma cash flow statement?

2. Green Golf Course has a positive cash flow only six months out of the year. What should the owner do with the extra cash during these months?

3. When making financial projections, why must a business owner consider economic conditions?

MAKE ACADEMIC CONNECTIONS

4. **PROBLEM SOLVING**   You are trying to save money to buy a new computer within the next six months. Create a pro forma cash flow statement to project your cash receipts and disbursements over the next 6-month period. Do you project a positive cash flow? If not, how can you improve your cash flow?

5. **MATH**   In May, Yoder's Bookstore had sales of $5,000, cost of goods sold of $3,000, operating expenses of $800, and taxes of $400. Calculate Yoder's gross profit and final net income or loss.

6. **MATH**   At the end of its first year of operations, Berganstein Sportswear had current assets of $13,000, fixed assets of $25,000, current liabilities of $7,000, and long-term liabilities of $14,000. What is the amount of owner's equity?

Teamwork

Working in a small group, research the state of the U.S. economy today and future forecasts of the economy. Prepare a brief presentation using visual aids to share what you have learned. Based on your findings, predict how today's economy could affect the cash flow of a new business. Then based on future forecasts, predict how the economy will affect the cash flow of a business in coming years.

RECORDKEEPING FOR BUSINESSES

Goals

- Differentiate between alternative methods of accounting.
- Describe the use of journals and ledgers in a recordkeeping system.
- Explain the importance of keeping accurate and up-to-date bank, payroll, and tax records.

Vocabulary

- cash method
- accrual method
- transaction
- journals
- account
- check register
- payroll

focus on small business

Keep it all straight.

After securing financing for his business, Monty was ready to get started. He purchased all of his equipment and supplies, sent out advertising fliers, and set up meetings with potential clients. Two months into his business, he was very surprised to find a notice from his bank informing him that he had written checks from a bank account that had no funds.

"How did this happen?" he asked Sarah. "Did you reconcile your bank statement last month? Have you been recording your business transactions and keeping your business records?" Sarah responded.

Judging from Monty's puzzled look, Sarah realized that he needed some serious help. "Monty, financial recordkeeping is one of the most important things you do as a business owner. We need to get you some help from an accountant. In the meantime, I'll give you a few lessons in basic recordkeeping! Let's get started!"

Good recordkeeping keeps everything in balance.

Work as a Team Why do you think financial recordkeeping is essential to the success of a business? What types of records do business owners need to keep? What problems could result from poor recordkeeping?

Cash or Accrual Accounting Methods

As a business owner, you will have to choose between two alternative methods of reporting your revenue and expenses: the cash method and the accrual method. The major difference between the two methods is the timing of when transactions, including sales and purchases, are recorded.

Cash Method

Under the cash method, revenue is not recorded until cash (or a check) is actually received, and expenses are not recorded until they are actually paid. If your home remodeling business installed windows in October but you did not receive the payment from the customer until December, you would not record the revenue until December. The cash flow statement is prepared using the cash method.

Accrual Method
Under the **accrual method**, transactions are recorded when the order is placed, the item is delivered, or the service is provided, regardless of when the money is actually received or paid. In other words, revenue is recorded when the sale occurs, and expenses are recorded when you receive the goods or services. You don't have to wait until you receive the money or pay money to record the transaction. If the accrual method is used in the home remodeling example above, you would record the revenue in October when you completed the work, not in December.

Choosing an Accounting Method
Typically, only very small businesses use the cash method. The accrual method is used by most companies because it offers a better picture of long-term profitability. The cash method does not report expenses that have been incurred but not yet paid and revenue that has been earned but not yet received. This distorts a company's profitability. Most small businesses (with sales of less than $5 million a year) are free to adopt either accounting method. However, a business must use the accrual method if:

- it has sales of more than $5 million a year, or
- it stocks an inventory of items that will be sold to the public and has sales over $1 million a year.

CHECKPOINT

What is the main difference between the cash and accrual methods of accounting?

Recording Transactions
A **transaction** is any business activity that changes assets, liabilities, or net worth. Accurate recordkeeping of your business transactions will help you keep track of how much money you have earned, how much you have spent, how much money you owe, and how much customers owe you. It will also help you create financial statements to determine your business's net worth and how much profit you have made.

Journals
Journals are accounting records of the transactions you make. There are five different journals that businesses use to record their transactions.

1. **Sales journal** This journal is used to record only sales of merchandise on account. Merchandise sold on account means that customers receive goods or services now that they will pay for later.

Why is it important to keep track of business transactions?

2. **Cash payments journal**   This journal is used to record only cash payment transactions. Any cash, check, or electronic payment a business makes is recorded in this journal.

3. **Cash receipts journal**   This journal is used to record only cash receipt transactions. Cash sales and cash payments received from customers on their credit accounts are recorded in this journal.

4. **Purchases journal**   This journal is used to record only purchases of merchandise on account. If you receive supplies today but pay for them later, you should record this transaction in the purchases journal.

5. **General journal**   This journal is used to record any kind of transaction. Some businesses use only a general journal. Businesses that use the four special journals described above record transactions that do not fit in the other four journals in the general journal.

Ledgers

Businesses also use a general ledger that is made up of accounts. An **account** is an accounting record that provides financial detail for a particular business item, such as for cash, sales, rent, and utilities. The general ledger will have an account for every type of asset, liability, revenue, expense, and so forth. Transactions entered into the journals are posted, or transferred, to the general ledger accounts affected by the transactions, as shown on the next page. Posting is generally done every one to two days to keep the ledger current. The balances in the accounts will help you prepare the financial statements you will need to run your business effectively.

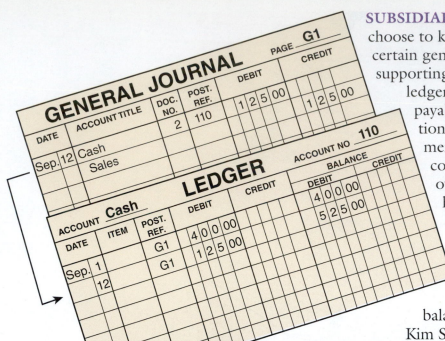

SUBSIDIARY LEDGERS Some businesses choose to keep a more detailed record of certain general ledger accounts in a separate, supporting subsidiary ledger. A subsidiary ledger is commonly used for accounts payable to show in detail the transactions with each vendor from whom merchandise is purchased on account. Each vendor will have its own account showing transaction history and the current balance owed. A subsidiary ledger is also commonly used for accounts receivable with separate accounts showing each customer's transaction history and current balance due.

Kim Smith is the owner of Photo Memories. She wants to use subsidiary ledgers for accounts payable and accounts receivable to keep detailed records of transactions with her suppliers and customers. The detailed information in these subsidiary ledgers will be summarized and transferred to the accounts payable and accounts receivable accounts in the general ledger. The subsidiary ledgers make it easy for Kim to see at a glance her transactions with suppliers and customers.

AGING TABLES An *aging table* is a recordkeeping tool for tracking accounts receivable. It shows a business how long it is taking customers to pay their bills. Because accounts receivable can affect a company's cash flow positively or negatively, the collection period should be closely monitored to identify problem customers.

Kim can see by her aging table that one customer is more than 61 days past due on a bill. She decides that she should not ship this customer any more merchandise until he has paid the outstanding bill.

Customer	Amount	0–30 days	31–60 days	over 61 days
E. Kwon	$175.23	$175.23		
P. Mossett	$106.20		$106.20	
M. Stern	$82.34			$82.34
Totals	$363.77	$175.23	$106.20	$82.34
Percent of total	100%	48%	29%	23%

CHECKPOINT

What is the difference between a journal and a ledger?

Business Records

Good recordkeeping can help you make smart business decisions. Incomplete or inaccurate records can cause you to mismanage your business or can cause serious legal problems. You will need to keep accurate banking, payroll, and tax records. These records may be kept manually or electronically.

Banking Records

You will need to open a separate checking account for your business. You will use your business account for all deposits and withdrawals related to your business.

When you open your checking account, you will receive a set of checks and a check register. A **check register** is a booklet in which you record the dates and amounts of the checks as well as the names of people or businesses to whom you have written the checks. You can also maintain a check register electronically using computer software.

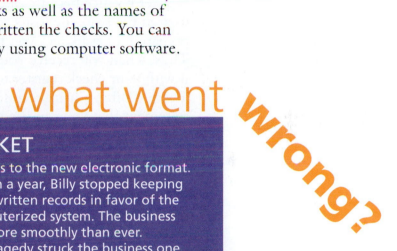

what went wrong?

ALL YOUR EGGS IN ONE BASKET

Billy Wong started Japanese Car Parts Distributors (JCP). The business grew, and in ten years it had 12 employees, thousands of parts in inventory, and hundreds of customers across the country.

Billy kept handwritten records for the business. Before long, his 18-year-old, computer-whiz son, Tommy, wouldn't let him ignore the advantages of computerizing his recordkeeping. So Billy gave Tommy the task of setting up a computer system and transferring the accounts, inventory, and financial information from his paper records to the new electronic format. Within a year, Billy stopped keeping handwritten records in favor of the computerized system. The business ran more smoothly than ever.

Tragedy struck the business one night when Tommy found robbers in the business office. Tommy was badly injured by the thieves and, sadly, he died. If this wasn't enough for Billy to handle, the thieves also stole the office computer.

Billy had left all the electronic recordkeeping to his son, and he had no idea whether Tommy had made backup copies of all the files that had been stored on the stolen computer. Billy found that it would take months of work and a large sum of money to set up a new computerized recordkeeping system.

Backing up computer files can prevent problems.

THINK CRITICALLY

1. Was Billy wrong to trust his young son with so much responsibility?

2. Would JCP's problems have been solved if they had found the computer?

BALANCE YOUR ACCOUNT   Every time you write a check or make a deposit, you should balance your check register. Balancing your check register is very important because it will prevent you from accidentally writing checks when you do not have enough money in your account to cover them. Writing bad checks is illegal! If your checks do not clear, your suppliers may stop shipping merchandise to you. Businesses and banks will charge you fees for having to deal with the bad checks. If you use a computer program to keep your checkbook register, it will automatically balance your account after each transaction is recorded.

RECONCILE YOUR ACCOUNT   Every month you will receive a bank statement that shows all of your deposits, checks paid, and bank fees. The bank statement balance will not be the same as your check register balance because of checks you have written that have not cleared the bank, deposits you have made after the bank statement was prepared, or bank fees you have not recorded in your check register. Thus, when you receive your bank statement, you should *reconcile* it with your check register to ensure your bank balance is accurate. There is often a bank reconciliation form on the back of the bank statement that you can use to reconcile your account, or you can use a computer program.

Payroll Records

If you have employees working for you, you will have to maintain payroll records. A **payroll** is a list of people who receive salary or wage payments from a business. The payroll records will show how much your employees have earned during each pay period. They will also show deductions that may have been made from those earnings for taxes and benefits. There are many computer programs that can help you maintain these records. There are also many payroll service companies with which you can contract to handle payroll processing for you.

How can you balance your checking account?

Why is it important for a business to carefully estimate its income taxes?

You will need to complete a payroll register for every pay period. The register will include the following information for each employee:

- Employee name
- Number of hours worked
- Regular and overtime earnings
- Federal, state, and local taxes deducted
- Social security and Medicare contributions deducted
- Deductions for benefits, such as health insurance, life insurance, and retirement savings plans.

After you create the payroll register, you will prepare payroll checks. Most businesses use voucher checks for their payrolls. *Voucher checks* have a statement of earnings and deductions attached to them. The statement shows employees how their pay was calculated.

Tax Records

You will have to make several different kinds of tax payments as a business owner. These include income taxes, payroll taxes, and sales taxes.

INCOME TAX Businesses that earn profits must pay income tax. These taxes are paid quarterly, or every three months. Income tax must be prepaid at the beginning of a quarter, so you will need to estimate your income taxes. If you fail to make these payments or you underestimate how much tax is due, you may have to pay a penalty. You could also be subject to criminal penalties for tax fraud.

PAYROLL TAXES AND DEDUCTIONS By law, you are required to deduct taxes from your employees' paychecks and submit these taxes to the government. As an employer, you are also required to pay unemployment insurance taxes and a portion of social security and Medicare taxes based on the earnings of your employees. Your employees may ask you to take voluntary deductions from their earnings to cover health or dental insurance. If you deduct this money from employees' earnings, you are required to send it to the companies that are providing the insurance coverage.

BE YOUR OWN BOSS

You own a home remodeling business in your community. You have one full-time employee working for you. Research the types of federal, state, and local taxes you will need to withhold from your employee's paycheck. Create a table listing the types of taxes to withhold. For each one, describe how you would determine the amount of taxes to withhold.

SALES TAX   Retail businesses are required to charge sales tax on goods or services. If you own a business that collects sales tax, every month you will have to deposit the tax you collect into a special bank account that belongs to the government. Sales taxes are based on a percentage of sales. The actual percentage charged varies from state to state and can vary within a state if the local county or city also assesses a sales tax. You will need to find out the percent of sales tax to charge in your area.

CHECKPOINT

What kinds of bank, payroll, and tax records do you have to keep?

9.3 ASSESSMENT

THINK ABOUT IT

1. Eliza Conner owns a small clothing boutique. Eliza uses her personal checking account for both business and personal needs. How would you convince Eliza that she should open a separate bank account for her business?

2. Why is it important to keep accurate and up-to-date bank, payroll, and tax records?

3. Why might a business prefer to use the accrual method instead of the cash method to record revenue and expenses?

MAKE ACADEMIC CONNECTIONS

4. **MATH**   Scott Belville, owner of Flowers on Main, completed an aging table for his accounts receivable, similar to the one found on page 266. The column totals are shown below. Complete the "Percent of total" row for Scott.

Customer	Amount	0-30 Days	31-60 Days	Over 60 Days
Totals	$6,500	$2,300	$3,100	$1,100
Percent of total	__?__	__?__	__?__	__?__

5. **COMMUNICATION**   Assume you are Kim Smith, the owner of Photo Memories. Look at the aging table on page 266. You have decided that no more orders will be filled for Mark Stern until his account balance is paid in full. Write a letter to Mr. Stern to inform him of your decision. Provide payment options to help Mr. Stern pay off his account balance.

Teamwork

Working with team members, discuss the pros and cons of maintaining electronic records versus manual records for your business. What are some ways to resolve the cons of maintaining electronic records? Which way do you think is best? Why?

Bank Statement Reconciliation

To ensure your bank balance is accurate, follow the steps below to reconcile your account:

1. Compare the bank statement with your check register. Place a checkmark in your check register by the checks that you have written that have cleared the bank. Also checkmark the deposits that you have made that have cleared the bank. Any remaining checks or deposits that are not listed on the bank statement are classified as outstanding.

2. Using the account reconciliation form on the back of your bank statement, enter the amount of your bank statement balance.

3. List outstanding deposits and add them to the bank statement balance.

4. List outstanding checks and deduct them from the bank statement balance.

5. Record the checkbook balance in the space provided.

6. If there were any deposits on your statement that you forgot to write in your check register, list them and add them to the checkbook balance.

7. Record any fees that the bank has charged your account and subtract them from the checkbook balance.

8. If your account earns interest from the bank, record the amount of interest earned and add it to the checkbook balance.

9. The bank statement and checkbook balances should now match. If they do not, check your math. Be sure all checks and deposits have been recorded in your checkbook and processed by the bank correctly.

Bank statement balance	$2,151.00	Balance from checkbook	$2,501.15
Add outstanding deposits	660.00	Add deposit not recorded	0.00
Subtotal	$2,811.00	Subtotal	$2,501.15
Deduct outstanding checks:		Deduct bank fees	12.00
#345	$ 60.00	Balance less fees	$2,489.15
#366	105.60		
#369	150.00	Add interest earned	6.25
Total outstanding checks	315.60		
Adjusted bank balance	$2,495.40	Adjusted checkbook balance	$2,495.40

Try It Out

Access www.cengage.com/school/entrepreneurship/ideas. Click on *Activities* and open the file *Bank Reconciliation*. Print a copy and complete the activity to reconcile the checkbook and bank statement.

CHAPTER ASSESSMENT

SUMMARY

9.1 Financing Your Business

1. As an entrepreneur, you must prepare a list of startup costs to determine how much money you will need to start your business. You should also prepare a personal financial statement based on the formula: Total assets – Total liabilities = Net worth.

2. Equity capital is money invested in a business in return for a share in the profits of the business. Sources of equity capital include personal contributions, friends and relatives, and venture capitalists.

3. Debt capital is money loaned to a business that must be repaid. Sources of debt capital include friends and relatives, commercial banks, and government agencies such as the SBA. Bank loans may be secured, requiring that you provide collateral, or unsecured.

9.2 Pro Forma Financial Statements

4. The cash flow statement describes the way that cash flows in and out of your business and uses the following basic formula: Cash receipts – Cash disbursements = Net cash flow.

5. The income statement shows the business's revenues and expenses incurred over a period of time and the resulting profit or loss. It can help you forecast how well your business may perform in the future.

6. The balance sheet is a financial statement that lists what a business owns, what it owes, and how much it is worth, using the accounting equation: Assets = Liabilities + Owner's Equity.

9.3 Recordkeeping for Businesses

7. Businesses can use the cash or accrual method for reporting revenue and expenses. The difference between the two methods is the timing of when the transactions are recorded.

8. Businesses initially record transactions in journals. The transactions are then posted to accounts in the general ledger. More detailed records of certain general ledger accounts, such as accounts receivable and accounts payable, are kept in a subsidiary ledger.

9. You will need to maintain accurate and up-to-date bank, payroll, and tax records. You will need to keep your bank records balanced and prepare a bank reconciliation each month. If you have employees, you will need to prepare a payroll register for every pay period. You will also have to track and pay income, payroll, and sales taxes at regular intervals.

what do you know now?

Read *Ideas in Action* on page 247 again. Then answer the questions a second time. Have your responses changed? If so, how have they changed?

Match each statement with the term that best defines it. Some terms may not be used.

1. The difference between what you own and what you owe
2. A financial statement that shows a business's revenues and expenses incurred over a period of time
3. Money invested in a business in return for a share in the profits of the business
4. A list of people who receive salary or wage payments from a business
5. A financial statement that describes the way that cash flows into and out of your business
6. Any business activity that changes assets, liabilities, or net worth
7. Property that the borrower forfeits if he or she defaults on a loan
8. Recording transactions when the revenue is actually received or the expenses are actually paid
9. Money loaned to a business with the understanding that the money will be repaid
10. The relation between the dollars you have borrowed and the dollars you have invested in your business
11. Individuals or companies that make a living investing in startup companies
12. A financial statement that lists what a business owns, what it owes, and how much it is worth at a particular point in time

a. account
b. accrual method
c. balance sheet
d. cash flow statement
e. cash method
f. check register
g. collateral
h. debt capital
i. debt-to-equity ratio
j. equity capital
k. income statement
l. journals
m. net worth
n. payroll
o. transaction
p. venture capitalists

REVIEW YOUR KNOWLEDGE

13. Which of the following would be a startup cost?
    a. computer for a business
    b. monthly utility bill
    c. monthly rent expense
    d. weekly payroll
14. Loans that are guaranteed with property are called __?__.
15. You have decided to try to finance your business with equity financing. Whom should you approach to invest in your business?
    a. local bank
    b. Small Business Administration
    c. friends and family
    d. Department of Housing and Urban Development
16. Which of the following would most likely be accepted as collateral for a secured loan for $25,000?
    a. $32,000 automobile that is paid for
    b. $12,000 of home equity
    c. $2,500 computer system
    d. apartment that you rent
17. Which of the following is *not* a reason that a bank may reject your loan application?
    a. business is a startup
    b. owner invested $30,000
    c. business plan is sloppy
    d. owner has no experience
18. **True or False** The Small Business Administration offers loans to businesses in the same way that a commercial bank does.

19. Which of the following would *not* be included on a cash flow statement?
   a. sale to customer on account
   b. payment received from a customer on account
   c. payment for new equipment
   d. funds of $4,000 received from bank loan

20. You are using five separate journals to record your business transactions. In which journal would you record a sale of merchandise if the customer pays you cash at the time of the sale?
   a. sales journal
   b. cash payments journal
   c. cash receipts journal
   d. purchases journal

21. **True or False** Taxes that you withhold from employees' paychecks are deposited into your bank account until the employee files an income tax return.

22. **True or False** If your cash receipts are less than your cash disbursements, your business has a negative cash flow.

23. A potential investor or bank would want to see all of the following financial documents *except*
   a. cash flow statement
   b. startup costs
   c. personal financial statement
   d. journal

APPLY WHAT YOU LEARNED

24. You plan to open a retail sportswear store. You will hire several employees to help run the store. What types of journals do you need to keep for such a business? Why? What kinds of bank, payroll, and tax records will you have to maintain? How could you use a computer to help you keep and manage your records?

25. You plan on opening Rashida's Beauty Salon. You have listed your projected monthly revenues, expenses, and taxes below. Prepare a pro forma income statement based on this information.

Revenue	$15,000	Insurance	$ 750
Cost of goods	2,550	Rent	1,000
Supplies	1,100	Utilities	650
Salaries	4,800	Taxes	1,050

MAKE ACADEMIC CONNECTIONS

26. **MATH** You own a store that sells video games. You owe $25,000 to video game vendors; you have a ten-year bank loan of $50,000; your bank account balance is $13,000; you own inventory worth $57,000; you have $2,000 in accounts receivable; and fixed assets are $22,000. What are your total assets, liabilities, and owner's equity? What is your debt-to-equity ratio?

27. **COMMUNICATION** Conduct a phone interview with the manager of a local bank to find out what kinds of loans the bank offers to small businesses. Specifically, ask about secured loans, unsecured loans, and SBA-backed loans. Write a one-page report on your findings.

What Would YOU Do?

You are preparing for a meeting with a loan officer to get financing for your new business. As you compile your resume, you think it might appear as if you do not have the adequate experience and skills to run your business successfully. You consider enhancing your resume by adding some additional job experiences that you haven't had in order to make it look better for potential investors and lenders. Do you think it will matter? Do you think anyone will ever actually check your job experiences or references? What might be the result if they do check? What would you do?

build your
BUSINESS PLAN PROJECT

This activity will help you continue with the development of a business plan for your business idea.

1. Estimate your startup costs for your business and prepare a personal financial statement to determine your net worth.
2. Determine how much money you need to begin your business. Decide if you will obtain equity and/or debt financing. Will you use personal contributions or borrow from friends and relatives, venture capitalists, a commercial bank, the SBA or other government agency, or a combination of these resources? Write why you think one or more of these financing methods will work for your business.
3. Determine your projected cash receipts and cash disbursements for the first year of your business. Prepare a pro forma cash flow statement. After doing so, prepare pro forma cash flow statements based on worst-case and best-case scenarios.
4. Decide if you will use the cash or accrual method of keeping records of revenue and expenses and explain why. Determine your projected revenue and operating expenses for the first year of your business. Estimate the amount of income taxes you will have to pay. Prepare a pro forma income statement.
5. Make a list of your assets and liabilities. Prepare a pro forma balance sheet.
6. Determine what types of journals you will keep for your business. For each type, give an example of a transaction that will be recorded in that journal. What accounts will your business have?
7. Contact two local banks and obtain information about commercial checking accounts. What are the rates? What types of special services or products are offered to small business owners?
8. Create a payroll register for your business. Contact your state and/ or local government to find out what taxes must be deducted from employees' pay. Find out how the taxes are calculated. Are there any other deductions that will be made? If your business collects sales tax, find out what the rate is in your state or county.

Planning a Career in

FINANCE

"My brother Boyd, an accountant, got tired of the demanding hours required while working at a large accounting firm. Tax season was particularly demanding on his family. His wife is an attorney with her own strenuous workload. They decided he should stay home with the kids and start a part-time business as an accountant for small businesses."

How do small businesses manage their finances to comply with legal requirements? How can a small business understand how changes in financial reporting laws affect them?

Accountants help individuals and corporations prudently manage their finances. Asset management, design of accounting information management systems, and tax preparation are some of the services provided by accountants.

Employment Outlook
- Faster than average job growth is anticipated.
- Changes in accounting-related legislation will fuel demand for accountants to help corporations meet regulatory requirements.
- Accountants will be needed to help prevent and circumvent financial fraud.

Job Titles
- Accounting Manager
- Controller
- Financial Auditor
- Certified Public Accountant (CPA)
- Cost Accountant
- Financial Reporting Accountant

Needed Education/Skills
- A Bachelor's degree with a major in accounting, finance, or business administration is required.
- Advancement may require a Master's degree in accounting or an MBA.
- Professional certifications in various accounting specialties for certain positions.
- Continuing education is required in most states.

What's it like to work in Finance? Boyd, an independent Certified Public Accountant, has a variety of clients. Today he has a monthly meeting with the owner of a home décor boutique store. Evaluating the financial components of the business, including inventory levels, expenditures, payroll, accounts receivable, and taxes, is a critical part of the meeting.

Boyd will also help his client assess the value of various promotions the store runs periodically throughout the year. Analyzing the success of promotions by comparing promotional costs to incremental revenue increases helps the boutique owner understand which promotions are profitable.

At the conclusion of the meeting, the client asks Boyd to evaluate whether it would be financially wise to buy a building to house the boutique or whether the store should remain in its current rented location.

What about you? Would you like to help businesses improve their financial performance by helping them manage the financial portions of their business?

Business Financial Plan

Business financial planning is paramount to the success of any business enterprise. This event is designed to recognize FBLA members who possess the knowledge and skills needed to establish and develop a complete financial plan for a business venture. The financial plan requesting a loan from a financial institution must be economically and financially sound with a realistic time frame. There are two parts to the event: a written report and a performance component. Each year a national topic is selected by FBLA-PBL, Inc., and participants in the event prepare their financial plans for this topic. You can find the current topic on the FBLA website.

Performance Competencies
- Articulate the need for the loan
- Explain the process of applying for a loan
- Explain the type of loan
- Demonstrate good communication skills
- Demonstrate the ability to make a professional presentation
- Answer questions effectively

Go to the FBLA website for more detailed information.

GIVE IT A TRY

Using the current national topic for the Business Financial Plan event, prepare a report that meets the competencies listed below:

- Identify the appropriate type of loan
- Complete an application for a loan
- Provide justification for the loan selected
- Write a report in appropriate business style
- Demonstrate correct spelling and grammar

Prepare a seven-minute presentation that will demonstrate and describe the project and the results obtained. Make the presentation to your class. Be prepared to answer questions after your presentation. During the preparation process, you will do the following:

- Learn and apply financial business decision-making skills
- Develop business contacts
- Implement written and oral skills
- Develop familiarity with procedures of financial institutions

www.fbla-pbl.org

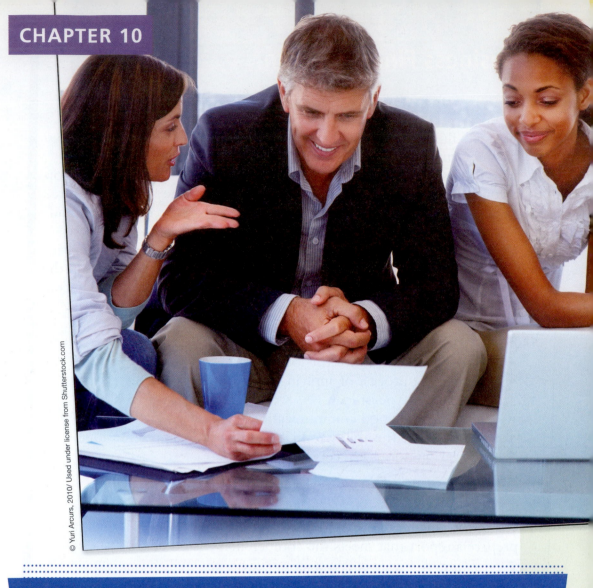

CHAPTER 10

© Yuri Arcurs, 2010/ Used under license from Shutterstock.com

Operations Management

10.1 Operating Procedures

10.2 Inventory Management

10.3 Financial Management

www.cengage.com/school/entrepreneurship/ideas

Entertaining and Planning

Twin brothers, Erik and Andrew Jensen, wanted some special entertainment for their parent's twenty-fifth wedding anniversary party. They were not able to find anyone to provide what they wanted, so they decided to DJ the party themselves, using a mix of equipment they had both purchased and rented. Soon guests from the party started requesting their services, and Twin Spin DJ Company was started!

Andrew Jensen, President and CEO, Jx2 Productions

Photo courtesy of Andrew Jensen

To accommodate changes in the business over the next year, they changed the name to Jx2 Productions. As the business continued to grow and change from a hobby to a career, the brothers found a need to develop a formal business plan. Eventually, Andrew bought out his brother's share of the business and changed the form of ownership to a limited liability corporation. The business expanded to offer video services, event planning, and bookings for hypnotists, comedians, jugglers, and other live entertainers.

As the services offered expanded, Andrew found a need for a better way of presenting the business on paper and on the Web. So, he hired a professional graphic design company to create a company logo to display in advertisements and on the company website. The logo presents a consistent, professional look and has been important to the image of Jx2 Productions.

Andrew uses the teamwork approach to running his business. He serves as the team leader and holds monthly and sometimes weekly meetings with his staff to keep everyone informed and on the same page. They work together to come up with new marketing ideas. He feels that this is important because his DJ's are also his salespeople. It is very important for them to have the right information to communicate to potential clients when they are out on assignments.

Jx2 Productions was temporarily located in the Student Business Incubator (SBI) at Springfield Technical Community College in Massachusetts. This location provided Andrew opportunities to grow the business. It offered space and a convenient location as well as networking and training sessions on finances, advertising, teamwork, and time management. After becoming more established, Jx2 moved its offices to the Shaker Farms Country Club in Westfield, Massachusetts.

Andrew encourages other students to start their own business if they feel it is right for them. His advice is to follow your dreams, your heart, and whatever drives you to get up every day.

1. What is the advantage to Andrew of forming Jx2 Productions as a limited liability corporation?
2. Do you think the image of a company is important?
3. What do you think of Andrew's teamwork approach to running his business?

OPERATING PROCEDURES

Goals

- Define the five functions of management.
- Describe five types of policies that should be included in an operations manual.

Vocabulary

- manager
- management
- organizational structure
- authoritative management
- democratic management
- operations manual

focus on small business

Make the shift from entrepreneur to manager.

Avery had been running her alterations business alone. The business grew to the point that she was able to hire three employees. Because she now had others to help operate the business, Avery was looking forward to having more free time for herself. She decided to take a vacation.

Two days into her vacation, her cell phone was ringing nonstop. The three employees were fighting among themselves about who was supposed to do what. No one wanted to answer the phone, and customers were becoming frustrated trying to find out when their clothing alterations would be completed. Avery realized she needed to return home and get her business under control!

Managers are responsible for business operations.

© Sean Prior, 2010/ Used under license from Shutterstock.com

Work as a Team   Discuss with your teammates the shift that must be made from entrepreneur to manager when the business hires employees. What skills do you think good managers should have?

Management Functions

Once you open your business and have people working for you, you become a manager. A **manager** is the person responsible for planning, organizing, staffing, implementing, and controlling the operations of a business. These are functions that all managers must perform, no matter the size or type of business that they manage. **Management** is the process of achieving goals by establishing operating procedures that make effective use of people and other resources. All functions of management work together and are continuous.

Planning

Planning involves analyzing information, setting goals, and making decisions about what needs to be done to move the business forward.

The planning activities must be performed in a timely manner. In business you often hear the saying, "time is money." If you waste time in the planning process, you can lose money for your business. There are three types of planning that should take place in any organization:

- **Strategic planning**   Setting broad, long-range objectives to achieve the long-term goals of your business is called strategic planning. You should think three to five years ahead when doing strategic planning. Envision where you want your business to be at that time and what it will take to get you there.
- **Intermediate-range planning**   Preparing detailed plans and strategies for achieving goals within a one-year period is intermediate-range planning. You should include target dates for the completion of the tasks that will lead to the accomplishment of your goals.
- **Short-term planning**   Planning for the day-to-day operations of the business to achieve the goals and objectives set in intermediate-range planning is called short-term planning. Rules, policies, procedures, and budgets are important components of short-term planning.

Planning is an ongoing process. Entrepreneurs frequently refer back to their business plan for guidance. Likewise, the planning that you do once your business is up and running will help you maintain focus and keep your business on track. Once plans are in place, it does not mean they must be followed exactly. Plans can be revised as needs change.

Organizing

Organizing is identifying and arranging the work and resources needed to achieve the goals that have been set for your business. Included in the organizing function are the following:

- **Assignment of tasks**   You will need to decide which employee will be responsible for which tasks in the business. As you start your business, you will have to determine how many employees you will need and what their duties will be.
- **Grouping of tasks into departments**   As your business grows, you will need to organize departments. You will have to decide which tasks are closely related and group them accordingly. Some of the department titles that businesses use include Accounting, Marketing, and Human Resources.
- **Organizational structure**   As your company grows, you will need an organizational structure. An **organizational structure** is a plan that shows how the various jobs in a company relate to one another. It is often represented in a chart and indicates the working relationships within the business.
- **Allocation of resources across the organization**   There will never be enough resources for all the needs and wants of everyone in your business. There must be a plan for distributing the available resources for their most efficient use across the company. This is done by creating budgets based on requests from the departments within the company.

DEVELOP YOUR READING SKILLS

Before you begin reading, skim the chapter and note the headings and boldface words. Think about what you will be learning as you read the chapter.

Staffing

Staffing includes all of the activities involved in obtaining, training, and compensating the employees of a business. Because a company is only as good as the people who work for it, the staffing function is critical to the success of a business.

Implementing

Implementing involves directing and leading people to accomplish the goals of the organization. Implementing is accomplished through communicating directions, assignments, and instructions to your employees. In order to effectively implement the work of the organization, managers must develop a management style that will motivate employees to perform at a high level. *Management style* is the way a manager behaves toward and works with employees. Managers use different styles based on the characteristics of the employees being managed, the type of work assignment, and the importance of the work being performed. An experienced and effective manager can change the style as needed.

AUTHORITATIVE MANAGEMENT A management style in which the manager is directive and controlling is called <u>authoritative</u> <u>management</u>. This style is also called *directing* or *autocratic management*. The manager makes the major decisions and closely monitors the work of the employees to be sure the work is done correctly. This management style is often used in a crisis situation when there is not enough time to let the group participate in the decision-making process. It is also appropriate when working with a new group of employees who do not have previous experience in the type of work being performed.

DEMOCRATIC MANAGEMENT A management style in which employees are involved in decision making and the manager provides less direction is called <u>democratic management</u>. This style is also called *participatory management*. A manager of a group of experienced employees who work well together does not have to be directive and controlling. Employees like to be involved in the planning and decision making that affects their work.

MIXED MANAGEMENT Combining authoritative and democratic management styles is called mixed management. Different employees prefer different management styles. Some employees prefer to be told what to do and want someone else to do the day-to-day decision making. Others feel that if they are not involved in the decision-making process, the manager does not trust them. An effective

NETBookmark

There are several other categories of management styles besides the traditional ones described in your textbook. George Litwin and Robert Stringer of Harvard Business School have identified six different managerial styles: coercive, authoritative, affiliative, democratic, pacesetting, and coaching. Access www.cengage.com/school/entrepreneurship/ideas and click on the link for Chapter 10. Read about the different styles. Do you agree with the article's assessment of the democratic style? Do any of the styles in the article seem to incorporate elements of mixed management?

www.cengage.com/school/entrepreneurship/ideas

manager should be prepared to use mixed management in order to meet the needs of the business and its employees.

Controlling

Controlling is the process of setting standards for the operation of a business and ensuring that those standards are met. Some of the ways that you can determine if standards are being met are as follows:

- Compare actual revenues and expenses with what was projected
- Observe business operations and determine if they are running effectively
- Inspect products and services to ensure they are meeting performance and quality standards

If standards are not being met, it will be necessary for managers to make changes. Changes may include hiring new employees, upgrading to higher-quality production materials, or increasing the budget for a specific area. You may also decide to change operating procedures such as work processes and work flow. As part of the control function, you will routinely review your plans and make adjustments.

CHECKPOINT

What are the functions of management?

Operations Manual

As your business grows, you will find that a detailed operations manual is an essential tool for operating your business efficiently. An **operations manual** contains all of the rules, policies, and procedures that a business should follow in order to function effectively. You can also have a separate *company* or *employee handbook* that details the rules, policies, and procedures that apply to employees. Just as you spent time developing your business plan, it is important to spend time detailing the operations of your business. By having this information in writing, it can be referenced easily and applied consistently to business operations.

Your operations manual should include the rules, policies, and procedures that guide your business practices. *Rules* outline the appropriate behavior and actions of those that work for you. All employees should be treated the same way when it comes to rules. *Policies* serve as a guideline for daily operations. They are established to make the business run efficiently and may apply to

Why does a business need an operations manual?

Why is it important for a business to establish customer service policies?

both employees and customers. *Procedures* are a series of steps and actions that employees must follow to complete an activity. They are instructions on how to perform a job task correctly. Procedures are more specific than rules.

Rules, policies, and procedures are established to make the business run efficiently. As a business owner, it is important to remember that sometimes you have to make exceptions to rules, policies, and procedures because not all situations are the same.

Operating Policies

You should set daily operating hours that are convenient for your customers. For many years, banks were open Monday through Friday from 9 a.m. to 4 p.m. when most people were working. In order to meet the needs of their working customers, many banks have extended hours to 6 or 7 p.m. and are open on Saturdays.

Customer Service Policies

Customer satisfaction is one of the main goals of any business. It is important to have a policy for customers who need to return a product or have a follow-up service. Products do not always meet the expectations of customers, and a service might not be performed to the customer's satisfaction the first time. A policy for replacements, refunds, or repairs will help maintain goodwill. Other customer service policies can include payment options regarding cash, checks, and credit cards.

Delivery Policies

Some businesses provide delivery services along with the sale of their products. Delivery may be required because of product size or for the convenience of the customer. A customer might be more likely to purchase a large appliance from a company that offers delivery, since most people are unable to transport the appliance themselves. Many restaurants offer delivery service for food as a convenience to their customers. You will need to determine whether you will offer delivery services for the products you sell, whether you will charge a delivery fee, and whether you will guarantee delivery within a certain timeframe.

Hiring Policies

A business must have a hiring policy. The policy may specify that all job applicants must complete an employment application and submit a resume and letters of reference. Testing may be required for some positions. Applicants may also have to submit to a background check or even a credit report check. The hiring policy may also specify who makes final hiring decisions.

Safety Policies

It is important that you have policies in place that provide for a safe environment for your customers and employees. Instruction in safety procedures should be part of employee training. Employees should know how to operate equipment safely and be required to wear the necessary protective gear. Employees should also be briefed on emergency plans for fires, tornadoes, and other disasters. Signs should be placed in strategic locations reminding employees of safety procedures in the workplace. You should also provide warnings to customers so that they do not enter employee-only areas. Caution cones can be placed where unsafe conditions exist.

✔ CHECKPOINT

What type of information should be included in an operations manual?

10.1 ASSESSMENT

THINK ABOUT IT

1. Why do you think it might be difficult for some entrepreneurs to become managers?

2. Why do you think it is important to develop an operations manual for a business?

MAKE ACADEMIC CONNECTIONS

3. **PROBLEM SOLVING** You have been named manager of the children's department of a retail clothing store. Sales are down in the department. You have five employees in your department. Two have been working in the department for three years. The other three are new to the store and have no retail experience. Describe the management style you will use to lead the department and increase sales.

4. **COMMUNICATION** Good customer service policies are essential to the success of a business. Think about the customer service provided by businesses in your area. Choose a business and write a paragraph describing what is good about the customer service provided and another paragraph with suggestions for improving customer service.

Teamwork

Working in a small group, describe the traits of the perfect manager. Explain why each trait is important.

INVENTORY MANAGEMENT

Goals

- Prepare a purchasing plan for inventory.
- Describe the perpetual and periodic inventory methods.
- Determine how much inventory to keep in stock.

Vocabulary

- perpetual inventory method
- stock card
- point-of-sale software system
- periodic inventory method
- stock turnover rate

focus on small business

How much to buy?

Matthew was starting his own frame store, Matt's Frames. He had previously worked part time in a framing store and had learned a great deal about the business.

Matthew considered how much inventory he would need initially. He knew from experience that the first few months of the year would be slow but that business would pick up as Mother's Day and graduations approached. Because people purchase frames as wedding gifts, business would pick up in the summer during the height of the wedding season. Another sales peak would occur during the holiday season.

Because he was opening his store in February, Matthew decided he would start out with a small inventory of basic framing supplies and focus on specialty frames that people might want for Valentine's Day. Then he would increase his inventory of frames and frame supplies for the spring and summer seasons.

© Adam Radosavljevic, 2010/ Used under license from Shutterstock.com

Business owners must carefully plan to meet inventory needs.

Work as a Team Do you think that Matthew is doing the right thing by starting out with only basic framing supplies? Why do you think he intends to increase his supplies as spring and summer approach?

Meet Inventory Needs

Inventory is the stock of goods a business has for sale. Successful inventory management involves balancing the costs of inventory with the benefits of having inventory in stock. Maintaining inventory is costly to a business, and it must be well managed if you are going to make a profit. Direct costs of inventory include storage, insurance, and taxes, in addition to the purchase price of the inventory. Some of the concerns about inventory that managers must address include the following:

- Maintaining a wide assortment of stock, but keeping adequate quantities of fast-moving items
- Increasing inventory turnover, but maintaining a high level of service
- Keeping stock levels as low as possible without sacrificing service or performance as a result of stockouts
- Obtaining lower prices by making bulk purchases, but not ending up with slow-moving inventory
- Having adequate inventory on hand, but not ending up with out-of-date items

How can a store meet both its inventory needs and its customers' needs?

Purchasing Plan

The most important aspect of inventory management is having items in stock when they are needed. This involves planning ahead to determine inventory needs, placing purchase orders for the items in advance, and scheduling deliveries to arrive at the point in time when you need the items. Inventory management also involves determining when you need the most inventory in stock, when reorders should be placed, and when you should discontinue stocking an item.

The amount of inventory you need to purchase can be calculated from the sales forecast. You must look at how many units you need to add to the inventory you already have in stock to reach your sales objective. The formula for calculating inventory needs is:

Beginning inventory + Purchases − Sales = Ending inventory

Alan has a beginning inventory worth $40,000 in his automobile parts store and expects to sell $80,000 over a period of six months. He wants to have $25,000 of inventory at the end of the six-month period. Alan uses the formula to calculate his purchases.

Beginning inventory	+	Purchases	−	Sales	=	Ending inventory
$40,000	+	?	− $80,000		=	$25,000
		?	− $40,000		=	$25,000
		?			=	$25,000 + $40,000
		?			=	$65,000

Alan must purchase $65,000 in inventory during the six-month period. He now needs to plan for the purchase and delivery of the inventory. He does not want to purchase the entire inventory and have it delivered at the same time because he does not have the cash to pay for it all at once, nor does he have the storage space. Alan decides to make his major purchases in the spring when people are beginning to get their cars ready for vacations and summer travel. He knows from past experience that he will sell more from March through June and that January and February are slower months.

Based on this information, Alan prepares a detailed purchase plan to show how much inventory he will purchase each month during the six-month period.

PURCHASE PLAN FOR AUTOMOBILE PARTS

	January	February	March	April	May	June	Total
Beginning inventory	$40,000	$33,500	$29,500	$25,300	$25,600	$25,050	
+ Purchases	4,500	4,500	10,800	16,800	14,200	14,200	$65,000
– Sales	(11,000)	(8,500)	(15,000)	(16,500)	(14,750)	(14,250)	$80,000
= Ending inventory	$33,500	$29,500	$25,300	$25,600	$25,050	$25,000	

 CHECKPOINT

What are some of the concerns managers have regarding inventory?

Track Your Inventory

Most businesses have to keep the products they sell in stock as a convenience to their customers. To avoid running out of items your customers want, you will need to keep track of your inventory levels. You will also need to determine how much you can afford to keep in stock at any given time.

Tracking your inventory can be done in two different ways. You can use the perpetual inventory method or the periodic inventory method. Regardless of the inventory method you use, you will need to take a physical inventory at least once or twice a year.

BE YOUR OWN  BOSS

You own a small hardware store located on the Gulf Coast. Weather forecasters are predicting higher-than-average hurricane activity in your region for the upcoming season. You know that if a hurricane comes to your area, there will be a high demand for plywood, generators, batteries, and other hurricane preparedness supplies. You have limited storage space and limited funds to invest in inventory, but you realize the chance to increase sales and profits. Outline a plan for managing your inventory needs. Explain your decisions.

Perpetual Inventory Method

The **perpetual inventory method** keeps track of inventory levels on a daily basis. This method can make your business more efficient. It can also ensure that you never run out of stock. This method uses stock cards or a computer to keep track of the inventory you have. A **stock card** is a paper inventory record for a single item. Regardless of whether you use stock cards or maintain electronic inventory records, you should record the following information:

- A description of the item
- A stock number for identification purposes

- Any receipt of inventory, the number of units received, and the date of the transaction
- Any sale of inventory, the number of units sold, and the date of the transaction
- The amount of inventory you currently have
- The minimum amount you want to keep in inventory, often referred to as the *reorder point* because it indicates when you should place an order to receive more units
- The maximum amount you want in inventory at any time

Lei Woo owns a toy store. Lei uses her computer to track inventory levels on a daily basis. She creates a low stock report, which shows the items she needs to reorder. It also shows how many units of each item Lei needs to order so that she can restock to the maximum level.

LOW STOCK REPORT				
ITEM	STOCK NUMBER	MAXIMUM	REORDER POINT	NEED TO ORDER
Building blocks	Q323	15	7	8
Doll houses	K393	4	2	2
Playing cards	S222	25	12	13
Stickers	S494	50	20	30

USE A COMPUTER   Businesses that sell hundreds of items usually track inventory electronically. The inventory software programs available let you track usage, monitor changes in unit dollar costs, calculate when you need to reorder, and analyze inventory levels on an item-by-item basis.

Many retail businesses use cash registers with a point-of-sale (POS) software system that updates inventory records as each sale happens. Bar-code scanners and credit card authorization systems can be integrated into the POS system. With the POS system, you will always have an up-to-date inventory balance. You will also get detailed information on sales that will assist you in the decision-making process for inventory management. You can analyze the sales data, determine how well each item you have in stock is selling, and adjust your purchasing accordingly.

Periodic Inventory Method
Some businesses use the periodic inventory method, which involves taking a physical count of your merchandise at regular intervals, such as weekly or monthly. This method will tell you how many units of each item remain in stock. You can then compare your inventory counts to your established reorder points to determine which items need to be restocked. This method is commonly used by small businesses with limited inventory.

Take a Physical Inventory
Even with the perpetual inventory method, you will need to take a physical inventory at least once or twice a year. Your actual inventory may differ from that listed in your perpetual inventory system. The difference can be caused by many things, such as failure to record sales, theft, or damage to merchandise. Taking a physical inventory means counting the number of items you have in stock. You will need

to record the date on which you are taking the inventory, the stock number of each item, a description of each item, and the actual number of units in stock.

At least two people should be involved in taking a physical inventory. One person should count the items on the shelves while the other records the information found. This information can later be entered into a spreadsheet for easy use.

CHECKPOINT

How does the perpetual inventory method differ from the periodic inventory method?

Why should businesses take a physical inventory periodically?

Digital Vision/Getty Images

Manage Your Inventory

The level of inventory you keep in stock depends on three factors:

- The costs of carrying inventory
- The costs of lost sales due to being out of stock
- Your stock turnover rate

Costs of Carrying Inventory

Holding inventory can be very costly. These costs are known as *carrying costs*. A business with inventory will always have carrying costs. Carrying costs can become too high if you have too much inventory. Costs can increase for many reasons.

- **Obsolescence**   Inventory can be held too long and become old and outdated. People do not want to buy a computer made two years ago. You may be stuck with merchandise you cannot sell.
- **Deterioration**   Inventory can deteriorate, forcing you to throw it away or sell it at a discount. If you own a garden store, some plants will need to be sold within a few weeks because they will begin to die.
- **Interest fees**   Vendors charge interest on money due to them. If you cannot pay your vendors until you sell your inventory, you will incur an extra expense.
- **Insurance**   You will need to carry insurance against theft, fire, and other disasters. Insurance premiums increase as the value of the inventory insured increases.
- **Storage**   Inventory takes up space—space that you may be leasing on a square-foot basis. If you run out of room, you will need to lease additional space.

Costs of Being Out of Stock

Being out of stock can cost you money. If you are out of the items your customers want, you will lose sales. If customers repeatedly fail to find what they are seeking at your business, you could also lose customer loyalty. You must weigh the costs of being out of stock against the costs of carrying more inventory.

Stock Turnover Rate

A supermarket might sell hundreds of cans of soft drinks every day but only 12 jars of marmalade. The **stock turnover rate** is the rate at which the inventory of a product is sold and replaced with new inventory. It shows how many times a year you sell all of your merchandise. A store that purchases inventory four times a year and sells all of its inventory in that same year has a stock turnover rate of 4.

Stock turnover rates vary from industry to industry. You should contact the trade association for your industry or talk to other entrepreneurs in your field to find out the turnover rate for the items you carry.

Why do you think Webkinz are so successful?

famous entrepreneur

GANZ FAMILY What do a stuffed animal toy and the Internet have in common? Plenty if you are in the Ganz family business. They have taken the stuffed animals children play with and made them a portal to the Internet and the Webkinz World.

Shortly after World War II, Samuel Ganz came to the United States from Romania and settled in New York. At about the same time, his sons Sam and Jack settled in Toronto, Canada. In 1950, Samuel went to visit his sons and took along a prototype for a doll. Sam and Jack asked some local toy stores if they would be willing to sell the dolls. After making a few contacts and holding family discussions, Ganz Toys began business!

In the 1980s, Ganz Toys began to focus on gift retailers and added a line of plush gift toys. Under the direction of Howard Ganz, Samuel's grandson, the privately held family company became the top toy company in Canada. It distributed several licensed products from Disney and Sesame Street that helped the company grow. Today, the company is known simply as Ganz.

In 2005, Ganz introduced the Webkinz, which quickly became a big hit. The lovable plush pets come with a unique secret code on the label. The code allows entrance into the Webkinz World on the Internet. There, an electronic version of the pet can be adopted for virtual interaction. More than 2.5 million units have been sold and 1.5 million users have registered on the Webkinz website. The Ganz family business is committed to a future filled with excitement and innovation.

THINK CRITICALLY

What inventory challenges do you think the success of Webkinz brought to Ganz?

Turnover rates can help you determine how much inventory to keep in stock. To find out how many months of inventory you should keep in stock, divide 12 (the number of months in a year) by the stock turnover rate.

Brad Wilson owns a retail store. The stock turnover rate in his industry is 6. This means that he needs to keep two months worth of inventory in stock at all times.

Months in year	÷	Stock turnover rate	=	Months of inventory to stock
12	÷	6	=	2

 **CHECKPOINT**

What three factors determine the amount of inventory a business keeps in stock?

10.2 ASSESSMENT

THINK ABOUT IT

1. Why do you think a purchasing plan is essential to good inventory management?

2. What do you think are the benefits of using the periodic inventory method? The perpetual method?

3. Do you think you could still manage your inventory well if you did not know the turnover rate for a product? Why or why not?

MAKE ACADEMIC CONNECTIONS

4. **TECHNOLOGY**   Your business uses the perpetual inventory method. Use spreadsheet software to create an inventory tracking report for at least five inventory items a grocery store would carry.

5. **MATH**   Access www.cengage.com/school/entrepreneurship/ideas. Click on *Activities* and open the file *Inventory Management*. Print a copy and complete the activity to help evaluate the inventory needs of Elizabeth's Kitchen Warehouse.

Teamwork

Working with teammates, make a list of items that you would sell in a hobby store that caters to teenagers. This is a new business with no inventory on hand. Decide how many of each item you think you could sell in a six-month period (July–December). Based on this information, make a purchasing plan for the hobby store showing how much inventory you would purchase each month.

FINANCIAL MANAGEMENT

Goals

- Describe strategies for managing cash flow.
- Evaluate a business's performance through financial statement analysis.

Vocabulary

- cash budget
- gross sales
- net sales

Cash flows in and out.

Lars is an independent contractor in the construction business. He has a good handle on his finances and has built cash equity in his business. He has recently completed two big contracts and is eagerly awaiting his next. Lars realizes that demand for his services will be less in the winter months and could also decrease as a result of changes in the economy.

Realizing that there could be months when he does not have money coming in, Lars begins to think about the cash in his bank account. Although he has cash in the bank today, he knows he has to plan for tomorrow. He needs to manage his cash flow to ensure he can cover his expenses during slower months. Lars understands that when he gets a big construction contract, he needs to set aside some of the money for a time when he doesn't have any contracts lined up.

Seasonal businesses must plan their cash flow.

Work as a Team   Why do you think cash flow is important to a business owner? List the kinds of businesses that you think might have cash flow issues similar to those in Lars' business.

Manage Your Cash Flow

As the owner of your own business, you will need to make sure that you have enough cash to make purchases and pay expenses. To do so, you will have to create a cash budget. You will also have to learn how to manage your cash flow.

Create a Cash Budget

A cash budget should show the projections of your cash coming in and going out. To ensure accuracy, it should be based on actual past revenues and operating expenses. A cash budget looks very similar to a cash flow statement, but it has slight differences. Three columns are used to show the estimated cash flow, the actual cash flow, and the difference between the two. This information can help you budget your financial resources. If your cash budget shows you will be short of cash in six months, you can begin arranging financing or generating capital now. If your cash budget shows you will have a surplus of cash two years from now, you might use that information in planning how to expand your business.

Many companies use spreadsheets to prepare their cash budgets. The spreadsheet will automatically perform calculations on the amounts you provide. This allows you to see the outcomes of changes in your cash flow instantly.

Mark Matson owns a snow removal business that he runs from his home. He uses a spreadsheet to create a budget for the first three months of the coming year, which is shown below.

CASH BUDGET MARK'S SNOW REMOVAL SERVICE Month One, 20—

	A	B	C	D
		Estimated	Actual	Difference
1	**Cash receipts**			
2	Cash sales	$2,000	$4,000	$2,000
3	Accounts receivable payments	$11,150	$13,150	$2,000
4	Tax refund	$850	$850	$0
5	**Total cash receipts**	**$14,000**	**$18,000**	**$4,000**
6	**Cash disbursements**			
7	Salaries	$4,500	$5,500	−$1,000
8	Gasoline	$2,500	$3,125	−$625
9	Vehicle maintenance	$350	$400	−$50
10	Utilities	$50	$50	$0
11	Advertising	$150	$300	−$150
12	Insurance	$500	$500	$0
13	Other	$250	$250	$0
14	**Total cash disbursements**	**$8,300**	**$10,125**	**−$1,825**
15	**Net cash increase/decrease**	**$5,700**	**$7,875**	**$2,175**

Improve Your Cash Flow

Two businesses with the same level of sales and expenses may have very different cash flows. One business may have a positive cash flow while the other may have a negative cash flow and be unable to cover its expenses. The difference may reflect a different pattern of cash receipts and disbursements.

If your cash receipts will not cover required cash disbursements, you will need to take action to improve your cash flow. You can increase cash receipts, decrease cash disbursements, or perform both actions.

INCREASE CASH RECEIPTS One way to improve your cash receipts is to decrease your accounts receivable by getting customers who owe you money to pay more quickly. To encourage faster payment, you can do the following:

- Offer discounts on bills paid right away.
- Establish tighter credit policies (decrease the amount of time your customers have to pay their bills from 60 days to 30 days).
- Establish a follow-up system for collecting unpaid accounts receivable. Consider hiring a collection agency to track down customers who are considerably late with their payments.
- Hold shipments to customers with large unpaid bills or insist that such orders be paid in advance.

Businesses can have cash flow problems if they start off with too little capital. If your cash flow is inadequate, you may want to increase cash receipts by obtaining more capital. This means securing a loan, investing more of your own money in the business, or finding investors who will provide you with capital in return for a share of your future profits.

DECREASE CASH DISBURSEMENTS Another way of improving the cash flow of your business is to reduce your disbursements. This

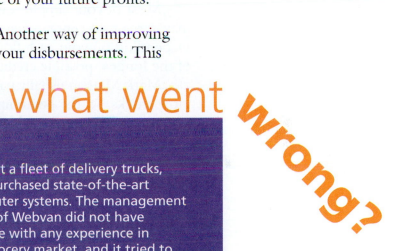
what went **wrong?**

TOO BIG, TOO FAST

Webvan was founded in the late 1990s by Louis Borders. Webvan was an online grocery ordering and delivery service. Initially, customers were excited about this service that was offered in nine U.S. markets. The company's long-range plans included expansion into 26 cities. The company started with hundreds of millions of dollars from private investors and then raised $375 million in its initial public offering of stock. At one time, Webvan was worth $1.2 billion, but all was not well in the Webvan world. Customers did not sign up as founders hoped they would. But the biggest problem Webvan faced was rapidly disappearing cash reserves. It placed a $1-billion order to build high-tech warehouses,

Too many cash disbursements can lead to business failure.

bought a fleet of delivery trucks, and purchased state-of-the-art computer systems. The management team of Webvan did not have anyone with any experience in the grocery market, and it tried to get too big, too fast. Even though customers were not happy with long lines and the quality of products in traditional supermarkets, they did not flock to the online grocery store. In less than two years after its successful initial public offering, Webvan announced it was closing.

THINK CRITICALLY

1. What are some of the problems Webvan faced during its short-lived operation?

2. Webvan started with a large amount of cash reserves. What caused Webvan to end up with cash flow problems?

3. What changes in operations do you think Webvan could have made that might have helped it be successful?

can be done by gaining better control over your inventory and payroll, slowing the rate at which you pay your bills, or reducing your expenses.

Inventory is a large business expense over which you have some control. Reducing this expense will improve your cash flow. You know that carrying inventory is costly. If your business has cash flow problems, check to make sure that you are not holding too much inventory. Reducing your inventory will reduce your accounts payable because you will not be purchasing as much.

Payroll is another large category of expense for businesses. Reducing your payroll can improve your cash flow. Payroll expenses can be decreased by reducing the size of your workforce or reducing the number of hours employees work. It is important to determine your workforce needs before you start making reductions in this area.

Most of your suppliers will offer credit terms. This means that they may agree to accept payment at a later date if you pay interest charges. Depending on your cash flow needs, you may want to take advantage of the longest possible credit terms or use a credit card for purchases.

Mark Matson usually pays cash for gasoline and oil for his snowplow trucks. At the beginning of the winter season in December, his expenses are particularly high and cash receipts low, so he charges his expenses to his credit card. By delaying payment until the following month, Mark improves his cash flow in December. When the credit card bill comes in January, he will have received payment from his customers for the work he did in December and will not have a problem paying the bill.

Other expenses, such as rent, are fixed, so you cannot reduce them. But you can reduce variable expenses, such as advertising, to help improve your cash flow.

CHECKPOINT

What are some ways you can improve your cash flow?

Prepare and Analyze Financial Statements

To run your own business, you have to be able to understand and analyze financial statements to determine how well your business is performing. Businesses keep many kinds of records and create different kinds of financial statements. Your records and statements can help you analyze your profits, debts, and equity. They also can assist you in making management decisions.

Prepare Financial Statements

When you are starting a business, you will prepare pro forma financial statements based on projections. Once your business is up and running, you will prepare financial statements that show actual financial performance. These financial statements will contain more detailed financial information than the pro forma statements because the business's finances will change as the business grows.

CASH FLOW STATEMENT The cash flow statement shows the cash inflows (receipts) and cash outflows (disbursements) for a business during a specific period of time. This statement shows the actual cash a business receives and how that cash is used. Unlike the income statement, which reports revenues not yet received and expenses not yet paid, the cash flow statement reports actual amounts, making it the most valuable financial statement for many business owners.

INCOME STATEMENT The income statement reports revenues, expenses, and the net income or loss over a specific period of time, such as a month, a quarter, or a year. Many businesses will prepare an income statement monthly in order to closely monitor revenues and expenses.

BALANCE SHEET The three most important elements of a company's financial strength are its assets, liabilities, and owner's equity. The value of assets, liabilities, and owner's equity on a specific date is reported on the balance sheet. The balance sheet is usually prepared monthly and at year-end.

What kind of information is contained on each of the financial statements?

Analyze Sales

You must know how to use the information in your financial statements to determine the level of sales you need to achieve to earn a profit. Your sales records show sales trends and patterns. You can use these records to forecast future sales and make good business decisions.

ANALYZE SALES BY PRODUCT Analyzing your sales by product can help you make decisions about the kind of inventory to stock. It can help you increase sales and profits.

Emily Lee owns a garden and patio store. Her store has four departments: outdoor furniture, outdoor grills, plants, and garden tools. Emily's sales figures show that almost 57 percent of her annual sales come from the outdoor furniture department, as calculated below.

DEPARTMENTAL SALES • LEE GARDEN AND PATIO

Department	Sales	Percent of total*
Outdoor furniture	$110,000	56.7
Outdoor grills	37,000	19.0
Plants	24,000	12.4
Garden tools	23,000	11.9
Total	$194,000	100.0

*Rounded

Sales of outdoor furniture	÷ Total sales	= Percent of sales
$110,000	÷ $194,000 =	56.7%

The plants department accounts for only a little over 12 percent of sales. Based on these data, Emily decides to reduce the size of the plants department and increase her inventory of outdoor furniture.

Analyze Net Profit on Sales

Your income statement shows whether or not your business is earning a profit. It also tells you how profitable your business is. This information can be very useful in helping you set and meet profit goals. The rate of profit a business earns is often shown as the ratio of its net profit to its sales. This ratio is calculated by dividing net income after taxes by net sales.

Net income after taxes ÷ Net sales = Net profit on sales

In order to calculate net profit on sales, a business must first perform calculations to determine net income after taxes and net sales. All of these calculations are found on the income statement, as shown on the next page.

CALCULATE NET SALES   Jack Hendrick owns a retail store that sells automotive supplies. He wants to find out his net profit on sales. First he must determine his gross sales and net sales. **Gross sales** is the dollar amount of all sales. **Net sales** is the dollar amount of all sales with any returns subtracted. Jack sold $235,000 worth of merchandise and had $3,200 worth of merchandise returned. Therefore, his net sales amount is $231,800.

Gross sales − Returns = Net sales
   $235,000 − $3,200 = $231,800

CALCULATE NET INCOME AFTER TAXES   Three calculations must be performed to determine your net income after taxes. You must calculate the (1) gross profit, (2) net income from operations, and (3) net income before taxes.

Gross profit is profit before operating expenses are deducted. Last year, Jack spent $150,000 for merchandise that he sold. This amount represents his cost of goods sold. Jack subtracts his cost of goods sold from his net sales to find his gross profit.

Net sales − Cost of goods sold = Gross profit
   $231,800 − $150,000   = $81,800

Jack's operating expenses include rent, salaries, and similar business expenses. Last year his operating costs were $39,900. Gross profit minus operating expenses equals net income from operations.

		Operating		**Net income from**
Gross profit	**−**	**expenses**	**=**	**operations**
$81,800	−	$39,900	=	$41,900

To calculate net income before taxes, Jack has to subtract one more expense that has not yet been taken into account: interest on loans he has obtained. Last year, Jack paid $2,400 in interest. He subtracts this from his net income from operations to get his net income before taxes. If a company has no additional expenses, such as interest expense, the net income from operations equals the net income before taxes.

$$
\begin{array}{ccc}
\text{Net income} \\
\text{from} & \text{Interest} & \text{Net income} \\
\text{operations} - & \text{expense} = & \text{before taxes} \\
\$41,900 - & \$2,400 = & \$39,500
\end{array}
$$

To compute his after-tax income, Jack subtracts the amount he paid in income tax last year, $12,245, from his net income before taxes. This gives him his net income after taxes for his automotive supply business.

$$
\begin{array}{ccc}
\text{Net income} & \text{Income} & \text{Net income} \\
\text{before taxes} - & \text{tax paid} = & \text{after taxes} \\
\$39,500 - & \$12,245 = & \$27,255
\end{array}
$$

CALCULATE AND ANALYZE NET PROFIT ON SALES

After all of the above calculations have been performed, the net-profit-on-sales ratio can be calculated. This calculation helps determine how profitable your business is. Jack determines that his profits represent 11.8 percent of his net sales.

$$
\begin{array}{ccc}
\text{Net income after taxes} \div & \text{Net sales} = & \text{Net profit on sales} \\
\$27,255 \div & \$231,800 = & 11.8\%
\end{array}
$$

Jack can use this figure to assess his profits in two ways. First, he can compare his profit ratio this year with his profit ratio in previous years. If his profit ratio has declined, his business has become less profitable. If the ratio has increased, his business has become more profitable. Jack can also compare his profit ratio with average profit ratios in his industry. If his ratio is lower than the industry average, he may want to figure out what he can do to improve his profitability.

Set and Meet Profit Goals

To run your business effectively, you will need to set profit goals. These goals will reflect the amount of profit you hope to earn from your business during a particular year.

Jack Hendrick would like to increase his profit ratio to 15 percent. He decides to try to increase his sales and reduce his expenses. He begins a frequent-buyer program and offers discounts on bulk purchases. Jack will talk to suppliers with the hope of reducing his cost of goods sold.

Jack would like to increase his profits even more by opening several more stores. He hopes that purchasing his inventory in large quantities will lower his costs significantly.

INCOME STATEMENT
Hendrick's Auto Supplies, 20—

Revenue from sales	
Gross sales	$235,000
Returns	3,200
Net sales	$231,800
Cost of goods sold	150,000
Gross profit	$ 81,800
Operating expenses	
Salaries	$ 26,200
Rent	8,400
Utilities	1,500
Advertising	1,100
Insurance	1,000
Supplies	700
Other	1,000
Total operating expenses	$ 39,900
Net income from operations	$ 41,900
Interest expense	2,400
Net income before taxes	$ 39,500
Taxes	12,245
Net income/loss after taxes	$ 27,255

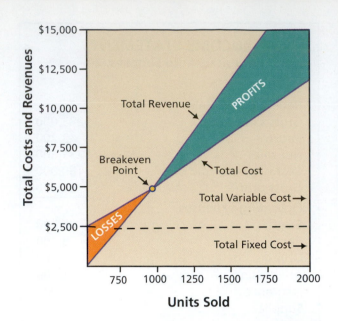

Perform Breakeven Analysis

As you learned in Chapter 5, breakeven analysis is a useful tool for determining how increases in sales will affect your profits. The breakeven point is the volume of sales that must be made to cover all of the expenses of a business. Below the breakeven point, your expenses will exceed your revenues and you will be losing money. Once you reach the breakeven point, your sales will equal all of your expenses. This means that at this level of sales, you will neither make nor lose money. Once you exceed the breakeven point, you will begin to earn profits, as shown in the graph.

Analyze Debt and Equity

When analyzing a company's financial health, it is important to look at its mix of debt and equity. The balance sheet, as shown on the next page, contains most of the data needed for this analysis. There are four key areas an entrepreneur should review using data from the balance sheet:

1. *Ability to pay debt as it comes due.* Does the company have enough money to meet its short-term commitments?
2. *Return on assets.* Is the company providing a good rate of return on assets?
3. *Amount of debt the company is using.* Using debt increases the risks a company faces, but it could also increase the expected return on owners' equity investment.
4. *Rate of return by the owners on their equity investment.* All decisions ultimately affect the rate of return earned by the owners on their equity investment in the business.

ABILITY TO PAY DEBT   A business that has enough money to pay off any debt owed is described as being liquid. The liquidity of a business depends on the availability of cash to meet debt obligations. The current ratio is used to measure a company's liquidity. The ratio compares a company's current assets to its current liabilities.

Current assets   ÷   Current liabilities   =   Current ratio

Speedy Print Shop has current assets of $125,410 and current liabilities of $59,610. Its current ratio equals 2.10. This means that it has $2.10 in current assets for each $1 in current liabilities. A standard current ratio is close to 2, meaning that the company has twice as many assets as liabilities.

RETURN ON ASSETS   A very important factor for a company to consider is its return on assets (ROA). The ROA indicates how profitable a company is relative to the total amount of assets invested in the company. It is usually expressed as a percentage. Assets are invested in a company for the purpose of producing net income. A comparison

BALANCE SHEET
Speedy Print Shop
December 31, 20—

Assets			Liabilities		
Current assets			*Current liabilities*		
Cash		$ 24,720	Accounts payable		$ 37,390
Accounts receivable		47,400	Notes payable		22,220
Less allowance for			Total current liabilities		$ 59,610
uncollectible accounts		−1,500			
Inventory		54,790	*Long-term liabilities*		
Total current assets		$125,410	Loans payable		$ 42,000
			Total liabilities		$101,610
Fixed assets					
Equipment		$ 37,975			
Less depreciation		−3,975			
Furniture		32,280			
Less depreciation		−3,320			
Vehicles		24,000	**Owner's Equity**		
Less depreciation		−5,600	Faith Jackson		$105,160
Total fixed assets		$ 81,360	**Total liabilities and**		
Total assets		$206,770	**owner's equity**		$206,770

of net income to total assets reveals the rate of return that is being earned on the entire company's assets.

$$\text{Net income} \div \text{Total assets} = \text{Return on assets}$$

Speedy Print Shop has net income totaling $22,230, and its total assets equal $206,770. Its ROA is .1075, or 10.75%, which means that the company earned over $0.10 for each $1 of assets. The higher the ROA, the better. A higher number indicates a company more effectively used its assets to generate profits. It is important to compare your return on assets with similar companies and your competition.

DEBT RATIO   The amount of debt (total liabilities), relative to total assets, used to finance a business should be examined. The more debt a business has, the more risk it is taking. Because debt is a fixed cost, it has to be repaid no matter how much profit the company earns. The debt ratio is calculated using the following formula:

$$\text{Total debt} \div \text{Total assets} = \text{Debt ratio}$$

Speedy Print Shop's total debt (liabilities) is $101,610, and its total assets are $206,770. Its debt ratio is .4914. This means that it has approximately $0.49 in debt for each $1 of assets. For good financial health, the ratio should be 1 or less, which indicates the company has more assets than debt.

RETURN ON EQUITY   The owner's (or shareholders') profitability can be measured by the return on equity (ROE). The ROE is the rate of return the owners are receiving on their equity investment. It reveals how much profit a company earned in comparison to the total amount of owner's equity reported on the balance sheet. It is usually expressed as a percentage. A business that has a high ROE is likely to be more capable of generating cash internally. The formula for return on equity is as follows:

Net income ÷ Owner's equity = Return on equity

Speedy Print Shop's net income totals $22,230, and its owner's equity totals $105,160. Its ROE is .2114, or 21.14%. It is considered a good sign if a company's ROE is at least as good as the average ROE for other companies in the same industry. If the industry average is 24.5%, then the owners of Speedy's are not receiving a return on their investment equivalent to that of owners of comparable businesses.

CHECKPOINT

Why is it important for an entrepreneur to analyze the financial statements of the business?

10.3 ASSESSMENT

THINK ABOUT IT

1. How will constructing a cash budget using an electronic spreadsheet make this financial report more helpful?

2. What would be the benefit of preparing an income statement monthly instead of once a year?

3. Which goals do you think are more important to meet: sales goals or profit goals? Explain your answer.

MAKE ACADEMIC CONNECTIONS

4. **PROBLEM SOLVING**   If your business is experiencing a negative cash flow, how might you use the six-step problem-solving model to help find a solution?

5. **MATH**   Using the following data, calculate the current ratio, return on assets, debt ratio, and return on equity for Hallman Printers. Current assets = $170,000; Current liabilities = $100,000; Net income = $50,000; Total assets = $450,000; Total liabilities = $150,000; Owner's equity = $300,000.

6. **MATH**   Access www.cengage.com/school/entrepreneurship/ideas. Click on *Activities* and open the file *Cash Budget*. Print a copy and complete the activity by preparing a cash budget for your school store and determining ways to increase cash flow.

Teamwork

Working in a small group, use the Internet to locate a copy of an annual report for a business. Review all of the financial statements that are included in the annual report. Calculate the following: net profit on sales, current ratio, debt ratio, return on assets, and return on equity. Based on your calculations, write an analysis of the financial condition of the business.

Internal Accounting Controls

As an entrepreneur, you will have to establish internal accounting controls to promote and protect sound management practices. Internal controls help prevent and detect fraud. Following internal accounting control procedures will significantly increase the likelihood of the following:

- Financial information is reliable so that it can be used for decision making.
- Assets and records of the business are not stolen, misused, or accidentally destroyed.
- The company's policies are followed.
- Government regulations are met.

The most important areas for control activities include:

1. **Segregation of duties**   Different individuals should be assigned responsibility for different elements of related activities, especially those involved with recordkeeping. There should be a system of checks and balances. For example, the person who writes the checks should not be the person who signs the checks.

2. **Proper authorization**   Transactions and activities must follow established procedures. For example, a company's return policy may serve as an official authorization to refund money to a customer.

3. **Adequate documentation and records**   There must be documentation and records for all transactions to ensure that financial information is reported correctly. Checks should be numbered and all checks should be accounted for. There should also be documentation to back up each check that is written.

4. **Physical control**   Having physical controls helps protect the company's assets and records. These may include electronic or mechanical controls (a safe, employee ID cards, security system) or computer-related controls (file backup and recovery procedures).

5. **Independent checks**   Audits should be performed by personnel who did not do the work being audited. For example, a supervisor may verify the accuracy of a retail clerk's cash draw at the end of the day.

Try It Out

Internal accounting controls will vary from company to company depending on the type of business. Interview a business owner in your local community to find out what type of internal controls the company has in place. Ask the business owner to identify an instance when an internal control was not followed and to describe the result of that action.

© Paul Matthew Photography, 2010/ Used under license from Shutterstock.com

SUMMARY

10.1 Operating Procedures

1. Managers are responsible for planning, organizing, staffing, implementing, and controlling the operations of a business.
2. A detailed operations manual is essential for a business's success. It should include rules, policies, and procedures. Policies may include operating policies, customer service policies, delivery policies, hiring policies, and safety policies.

10.2 Inventory Management

3. A purchasing plan will assist with inventory management by ensuring you have items in stock when they are needed. It helps you calculate ending inventory needs based on beginning inventory, purchases, and sales.
4. You can track inventory using the perpetual or periodic inventory methods. The perpetual inventory method tracks inventory levels on a daily basis. The periodic inventory method involves taking a physical count of merchandise at weekly or monthly intervals.
5. The level of inventory you keep in stock depends on three factors: the costs of carrying inventory, the costs of losing sales due to being out of stock, and your stock turnover rate.

10.3 Financial Management

6. To manage cash flow, begin by creating a cash budget. You can increase cash receipts by offering credit customers discounts for prompt payment, establishing tighter credit policies, establishing a follow-up system for collecting unpaid accounts receivable, and obtaining additional capital for your business. You can decrease cash disbursements by gaining better control over inventory and payroll, slowing the rate at which you pay your bills, and reducing your expenses.
7. When starting a business, you prepare pro forma statements based on projections. Once your business is operating, you will prepare financial statements based on actual performance. The three financial statements most commonly prepared by businesses are the balance sheet, income statement, and cash flow statement.
8. You can examine your business's finances by analyzing your sales by product; calculating your net profit on sales, current ratio, return on assets, debt ratio, and return on equity; and performing a breakeven analysis.

what do you know now?

Read *Ideas in Action* on page 279 again. Then answer the questions a second time. Have your responses changed? If so, how have they changed?

VOCABULARY BUILDER

Match each statement with the term that best defines it. Some terms may not be used.

1. The process of achieving goals by establishing operating procedures that make effective use of people and other resources
2. The rate at which inventory of a product is sold and replaced with new inventory
3. A management style in which the manager is directive and controlling
4. The dollar amount of all sales with any returns subtracted
5. A plan that shows how the various jobs in a company relate to one another
6. Keeps track of inventory levels on a daily basis
7. Involves taking a physical count of your merchandise at regular intervals, such as weekly or monthly
8. A management style in which employees are involved in decision making
9. Shows the projections of your cash coming in and going out
10. Contains all of the rules, policies, and procedures that a business should follow in order to function effectively
11. A system that updates inventory records as each sale happens
12. The person responsible for planning, organizing, staffing, implementing, and controlling the operations of a business

a. authoritative management
b. cash budget
c. democratic management
d. gross sales
e. management
f. manager
g. net sales
h. operations manual
i. organizational structure
j. periodic inventory method
k. perpetual inventory method
l. point-of-sale software system
m. stock card
n. stock turnover rate

REVIEW YOUR KNOWLEDGE

13. Which of the following functions of management would apply when grouping tasks into departments?
    a. planning
    b. organizing
    c. implementing
    d. controlling
14. Jorge is supervising new employees with no experience in food service at a concession stand in an amusement park. Which management style should he use?
    a. authoritative management
    b. democratic management
    c. mixed management
    d. participatory management
15. **True or False** The organizational structure outlines all of the rules, policies, and procedures that a business must follow.
16. Preparing detailed plans that will provide strategies for achieving goals and objectives in a one-year period is
    a. strategic planning
    b. intermediate-range planning
    c. short-term planning
    d. none of the above
17. A small specialty store that has a very limited inventory should use the __?__ inventory method.
18. The level of inventory you keep in stock depends on all *except*
    a. the costs of carrying inventory
    b. the costs of lost sales due to being out of stock
    c. your stock turnover rate
    d. your net-profit-on-sales ratio

19. **True or False** A point-of-sale inventory system makes it easier to analyze your inventory records at the end of the day.

20. **True or False** Generally, employees do not like to be involved in the planning and decision-making process.

21. If you want to improve your cash flow by increasing cash receipts, which of the following strategies could you try?
    a. offer discounts on bills paid right away
    b. establish tighter credit policies
    c. hold shipments to customers with large unpaid bills
    d. all of the above

APPLY WHAT YOU LEARNED

22. You received a $500 payment from one of your customers in the form of a check. You deposited the check into your bank account. Several days later, you received a notice from your bank that the check was returned because your customer's checking account did not have the funds to cover it. You were counting on that money to help you cover your monthly rent. What will you do?

23. You want to analyze your sales by product for your hardware store. Your total sales are $140,750. The sales of each department in your store are given below. What percent of sales does each department generate for your store?
    Seasonal merchandise $25,525
    Lumber   40,211
    Tools   38,524
    Lighting   15,235
    Kitchen cabinets   21,255

MAKE ACADEMIC CONNECTIONS

24. **MATH** You own a bookstore. The stock turnover rate in the bookstore business is 4. How many months worth of inventory must you keep on hand?

25. **COMMUNICATION** You and a partner own a kitchen equipment store. You would like to implement a point-of-sale inventory system using a computerized cash register, but your partner is not convinced this is the best method for your business. Write a letter to persuade your partner to implement a new POS inventory system. Identify advantages of using a POS system.

26. **MATH** You own a pet-supply business. Last year, you sold $42,000 in dog food and $53,000 in cat food. Returns totaled $5,000. The cost of goods sold on the dog food was $13,000, and the cost of goods sold on the cat food was $14,000. Operating expenses for the business were $13,000 for salaries, $4,500 for rent, $1,200 for insurance, $1,000 for utilities, $900 for advertising, and $600 for other. Taxes were $10,500. What is your net income after taxes? What is your net-profit-on-sales ratio?

27. **PROBLEM SOLVING** Managers must make operations decisions. Access www.cengage.com/school/entrepreneurship/ideas. Click on *Activities* and open the file *Management Problem Solving*. Print a copy and work with a partner to come up with solutions for Katrina's management issues.

What Would YOU Do?

You asked two of your employees to work extra hours over the weekend to perform a physical inventory. You are certain that there were three plasma television sets in stock prior to having the employees take inventory. However, when the inventory was completed, the list showed only two plasma television sets in stock. You checked the stockroom, and you found only two. You have always trusted your employees. What would you do? Will you confront the employees? If so, how will you approach them? Working with a partner, role-play the conversations you will have with the employees.

build your BUSINESS PLAN PROJECT

This activity will help you plan the operations management of your business.

1. Describe the management style you will use for managing your business. Will you always use the same style? How will you determine when to use a different style?

2. Locate and contact two professionals in your area who specialize in strategic planning. What are their credentials? What are their fees? Do you think it would be helpful to utilize the services of a strategic planner? Why or why not?

3. Develop an operating procedures manual for your business. Include the rules, policies, and procedures that your business will follow to run effectively.

4. If your business has an inventory, list all of the items you will have in inventory and your cost for each. Create a purchasing plan for your inventory.

5. Set up inventory records for your business using either a paper system or an electronic system. Be sure to list all of the items discussed in Lesson 10.2. How did you determine your reorder point? What inventory carrying costs are relevant to your business? How can you reduce your carrying costs?

6. Analyze your sales by creating a table that lists each of your products and the total sales (or estimated sales) for each. What is the percentage of total sales for each product? Based on this information, will you make any changes to your inventory?

7. Develop internal controls for your business. Explain why you chose the controls you did.

"My stepsister, who is a high school senior this year, has become our household computer expert. She recently attended a summer technology camp sponsored by a national computer retailer that provides a variety of computer support services. The camp was established as a way to help fulfill future labor needs. After completing camp, she's become the household 'go to' person for any high-tech gadget issues."

How do individuals and small businesses solve computer-related technology problems?

Computer service specialists, who make on-site visits to homes and businesses, help resolve a variety of complex technological issues that affect computer efficiency and reliability. As computers and personal gadgets have become more complex, the need for these service specialists has increased.

Employment Outlook
- Faster than average growth is anticipated.
- The use of the newest forms of technology, which are often complex, will help fuel demand.
- Growing demand for computer specialists will be somewhat offset by the trend to outsource computer support to foreign countries with lower labor costs.

Job Titles
- Software Support Specialist
- Help Desk Analyst
- Application Specialist
- Technical Support Associate
- MIS Support Technician

Needed Education/Skills
- Degree requirements vary between an Associate degree and a Bachelor's degree in computer-related areas.
- Sometimes relevant computer experience or professional certification can serve in lieu of a degree.
- Strong analytical, problem-solving, and interpersonal skills are needed to resolve technical issues among a wide user group.

What's it like to work in Information Technology? Milo is a self-employed PC service specialist who helps his customers solve their computer problems.

Today, Milo is updating the rates on his company website. These rates include the trip charge to arrive at a client's home or place of business, the one-hour minimum labor charge, and the additional fees for a partial hour beyond the one-hour minimum.

After receiving a call from a frantic client, Milo dashes off to the client's home. The client, who has a home-based consulting business, has a hard drive that is failing. The client had accidentally dropped his flash drive into a cup of coffee, and he had no backup for his files. Consequently, he needed help retrieving critical files from his hard drive.

After saving the files to a new flash drive, Milo suggests to his client that he consider investing in an automated data backup service. For a monthly fee, designated data would be automatically saved to a personalized website that would be password accessible for security purposes.

What about you? Would you like to help a variety of individuals and businesses solve their computer technology problems?

The Partnership with Business Project recognizes FBLA chapters that develop and implement the most innovative, creative, and effective partnership plan. The purpose of this project is to learn about a business through communication and interaction with the business community. This project can be completed by one to three students.

This event consists of two parts: a report and a performance component. The report should describe the planning and implementation of activities that build a partnership between business leaders and chapter members for the purpose of learning about a business. The performance should address the business partnership, member involvement, and results of the project. You can find complete guidelines on the FBLA website.

Performance Competencies

- Demonstrate good communication skills
- Describe project development and implementation
- Describe the partnership
- Demonstrate the ability to make a professional presentation
- Answer questions effectively

Go to the FBLA website for more detailed information.

GIVE IT A TRY

Plan and implement a partnership with a business that meets the guidelines of the FBLA competitive event. Prepare a written report that includes the following sections.

- Development (description of the partnership goals, description of planning activities used to build a partnership, and roles of business leaders and chapter members in developing the partnership)
- Implementation (description of activities, level of involvement from business leaders, and roles of business leaders and chapter members)
- Results (description of concepts learned from the project and the impact of the project)
- Degree of Involvement (hours spent and contacts made)
- Evidence of Publicity (description of the recognition received as a result of the partnership)

Prepare a seven-minute presentation that will describe the project and the results obtained. Make the presentation to your class. Be prepared to answer questions after your presentation.

www.fbla-pbl.org

CHAPTER 11

© Adam Gregor, 2010/Used under license from Shutterstock.com

Human Resource Management

www.cengage.com/school/entrepreneurship/ideas

Happy Employee, Happy Customer

Doug Burgoyne, founder of Frogbox

Moving to a new office or home can be a cumbersome task that often involves wasteful cardboard boxes. Doug Burgoyne set out to find a moving supply business with an eco-friendly twist. Doug knew there was a market for a reusable alternative to cardboard boxes, but there were still many decisions to be made before the business could take off.

First, the company needed a name. With Doug's tech background, he knew he wanted an Internet-based company with an easy-to-remember domain name. And since the moving boxes are green, Doug wanted a name that would catch the interest of environment-friendly consumers. After careful consideration, the company was named Frogbox. Although it's true many frogs are green, it was not the only reason for choosing the amphibian as the namesake. Because the company believes strongly in giving back and because the frog species is decreasing at an astonishing rate, Frogbox plans to donate 1 percent of its gross revenues to frog habitat restoration.

Next, Frogbox needed employees. The company decided to hire trustworthy employees that believed in the company's mission of environmental conservation. "If you hire happy and dedicated employees, then you will have happy and dedicated customers," Doug said.

Because the business is so customer-focused, Doug believes strongly in comprehensive training for new employees. The majority of Frogbox's 15 employees are delivery drivers who pick up and drop off the moving boxes. The drivers' training includes a week-long drive along with a trainer. The drivers average ten trips per day, giving them ten times a day to help ease customers' moving angst.

Frogbox is currently located in three cities—Vancouver, Seattle, and Toronto—but Doug has big plans for the future. The company will soon start full-scale North American expansion. Doug wants the new Frogbox locations to be more about the people running the business than the location. He wants to make sure future franchises will have the same eco-friendly and customer-service focus.

Photo courtesy of Doug Burgoyne

what do you know?

1. Frogbox.com is an easy domain name to remember. Why do you think this is important?
2. Besides dedication and trustworthiness, what are some other characteristics you would look for in an employee?
3. Why do you think employee training is essential for so many businesses?

IDENTIFY YOUR STAFFING NEEDS

Goals

- Explain how to determine staffing needs for a business.
- Describe options for recruiting employees.
- Identify alternatives to hiring permanent employees.

Vocabulary

- staffing
- job description
- job analysis
- chain of command
- recruit
- freelancers
- interns

Hire help.

Emanuel started his contracting business six months ago. He specialized in excavation work and had more business than he could handle. He decided he needed help and posted a "Help Wanted" sign along with his phone number in front of his business. People began calling and stopping by, continually interrupting his work. They wanted to know what type of work he had and how much it would pay. Emanuel didn't really know what to tell them. He had not thought through the details of the posted position.

Think about your staffing needs before posting a Help Wanted sign.

Emanuel took down his sign to determine exactly what type of help he needed. In addition to his excavation work, Emanuel had a large amount of paperwork to do. He realized that if he had help with the administrative tasks, he would have more time to devote to other areas of his business. He could also use someone else with excavation experience to help him.

Work as a Team What do you think Emanuel should have done before posting the "Help Wanted" sign? What types of positions could Emanuel add? Do you think using a sign in front of his business is the best way for Emanuel to attract qualified job applicants?

Staffing

The management functions of staffing, implementing, and controlling can be directly applied to the people who work for your business. The people who work for your business are your *human resources*. You may not need to hire employees when you first start your business. But as your business grows, you will find the need for employees. Good employees and a well-run human resource management program are as important to your business as are capital, equipment, and inventory.

What staffing needs might a hair salon have?

Staffing involves determining the number of employees you need and defining a process for hiring them. To find out your staffing needs, ask yourself these questions:

- What kinds of employees do I need?
- What skills am I missing?
- What skills do I need daily?
- What skills do I need occasionally?

To **answer** these questions, list all the duties in your business. Then try to identify how much time is needed to perform each of these duties. Your list should help you identify whether you need part-time, full-time, or temporary workers. You can also determine whether you need managers or assistants and how many employees you need.

DEVELOP YOUR READING SKILLS

Make an interactive notebook for this chapter. Before you read, divide your paper into two columns. In the left column, record notes about what you are reading. In the right column, write notes that will help you relate what you are reading to your everyday life.

Job Descriptions

A *job* is a collection of tasks and duties that an employee is responsible for completing. A *task* is a specific work activity that is performed, such as answering the telephone or answering e-mail. Many positions include a variety of tasks that are sometimes referred to as *functions*. A **job description** is a written statement listing the tasks and responsibilities of a position. Job descriptions also include to whom the position reports, educational and professional experience required, and salary range.

Job descriptions are written after conducting a **job analysis**, which is the process of determining the tasks and sequence of tasks necessary

---

SAMPLE JOB DESCRIPTION

Title: Account Executive
Tasks and Responsibilities: Plans, coordinates, and directs advertising campaigns for clients of advertising agency. Works with clients to determine advertising requirements and budgetary limitations. Coordinates activities of workers engaged in marketing research, writing copy, laying out artwork, purchasing media time and space, developing special displays and promotional items, and performing other media-production activities.
Qualifications: College degree with courses in marketing, leadership, communication, business, and advertising; sales experience; interpersonal and written communication skills; neat professional appearance; characteristics of self-motivation, organization, persistence, and independence
Reports to: Marketing Manager
Salary Range: $30,000 to $50,000, depending on experience

---

to perform a job. You will need to understand exactly what every job involves so that you can determine how much money to offer job applicants. A detailed job description will make clear the job responsibilities. If a sales assistant objects to answering phones, you can refer that employee to the job description that lists this task as part of the job. Job descriptions also can be used to measure how well an employee performs a job.

Organizational Structure

Once your company has several employees, you will need an organizational structure. An *organizational structure* is a plan that shows how the various jobs in a company relate to one another. Many businesses use a chart to represent the organizational structure. The organizational chart can also help you analyze your staffing needs. Using the chart during planning can help you identify the number and types of employees you need. When planning, you can list positions and primary responsibilities of each. Then as employees are hired, you can fill in the names.

The organizational chart shows the <u>chain of command</u>, or who reports to whom in the company. In a small business, all employees may report directly to the company owner. In large companies, lower-level employees usually report to a supervisor. This kind of organizational structure ensures that the owner is not called upon to deal with relatively unimportant issues that could be handled more efficiently by a lower-level manager.

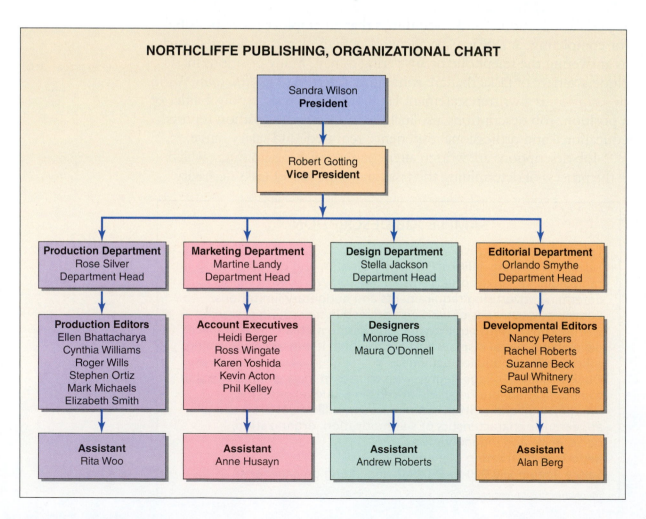

NORTHCLIFFE PUBLISHING, ORGANIZATIONAL CHART

Sandra Wilson
President

Robert Gotting
Vice President

Production Department	**Marketing Department**	**Design Department**	**Editorial Department**
Rose Silver	Martine Landy	Stella Jackson	Orlando Smythe
Department Head	Department Head	Department Head	Department Head

Production Editors	**Account Executives**	**Designers**	**Developmental Editors**
Ellen Bhattacharya	Heidi Berger	Monroe Ross	Nancy Peters
Cynthia Williams	Ross Wingate	Maura O'Donnell	Rachel Roberts
Roger Wills	Karen Yoshida		Suzanne Beck
Stephen Ortiz	Kevin Acton		Paul Whitnery
Mark Michaels	Phil Kelley		Samantha Evans
Elizabeth Smith			

| **Assistant** | **Assistant** | **Assistant** | **Assistant** |
| Rita Woo | Anne Husayn | Andrew Roberts | Alan Berg |

How do you determine staffing needs for your business?

Recruiting

To **recruit** is to look for people to hire and attract them to the business. As the owner of a small business, it may be difficult for you to attract experienced employees to work for your business. They will have opportunities to work for larger, established businesses that can offer them higher pay and better benefits. You can use a variety of resources for recruiting, including online career and employment sites, employment agencies, college placement centers, in-store advertising, classified advertisements, and referrals.

Online Career and Employment Sites

Many people now use the Internet to look for a job, so many employers are advertising with online career and employment sites. Most online employment services allow you to post a job and then search the resumes that are sent in response to the posting. Some online employment services have a database of resumes that you can review when you are looking for someone to fill a specific job. More than 23 million unique visitors visit CareerBuilder.com every month to check out the opportunities in every industry, field, and job type. Online recruiting can be very expensive, so you should compare alternatives and be sure that this is the best method for your business.

Employment Agencies

Employment agencies find employees for businesses and other institutions. These firms try to match people looking for jobs with businesses looking for employees. They charge businesses and/or the

Why are online career websites becoming a popular way to recruit employees?

job seekers a fee when they are successful in making a match. Some businesses may use a *headhunter*, which is an employment specialist who seeks out highly-qualified professionals to fill positions. Seeking applicants through an employment agency or a headhunter saves time for the employer in screening applicants, but the cost is higher than placing a classified advertisement.

College Placement Centers

Most colleges and universities operate job placement centers. These offices collect information on career and employment opportunities, which they make available to their students and graduates. Generally, they do not charge a fee for their services. Contact local colleges and universities and ask them how you can list your business with their placement center.

In-Store Advertising

Have you ever walked into a store and seen a sign that says "Help Wanted" or "Now Hiring"? This is another method of advertising that businesses use. When you post a sign, interested applicants will come into your business and fill out an application form. Before placing a sign in the window, be sure you will have time to deal with the many people who may stop to inquire about the position. You can interview them at that time or call them later for an interview.

Classified Advertisements

Using the local newspaper for advertising is a good way to attract a large number of applicants. The advertisement that you place in the newspaper is called a *want ad*. It should briefly describe the position and the education and experience requirements. It should also identify any special job requirements, such as a willingness to travel or to work evenings. You should request resumes and cover letters from applicants interested in the position. Sometimes employers ask for specific information in the cover letter, such as salary requirements, date of availability, or other useful information. You should screen the resumes to determine which applicants you want to interview.

Referrals

One of the best ways entrepreneurs find employees is by acting on referrals from friends, acquaintances, or other employees. If you consider the person making the recommendation reliable, a referral may require very little screening. However, some business owners do not like to hire friends or relatives of current employees because it can sometimes create other problems.

Alternatives to Adding Staff

Adding employees to your payroll is costly. It takes time and money to recruit staff and to track, report, and pay their salaries, benefits, and tax withholdings. In many cases, you may need help but not have sufficient work to keep a permanent full-time employee busy. For these reasons, you may want to consider alternatives to permanent employees, such as hiring freelancers, interns, and temporary workers.

Freelancers

Freelancers are people who provide specialty services to a number of different businesses on an hourly basis or by the job. Freelancers are also called *independent contractors*. Examples of freelancers include bookkeepers, accountants, lawyers, graphic designers, window display artists, and advertising copywriters. Business owners use freelancers when they need to have a job done but do not have enough of the required type of work to warrant hiring a permanent employee. A freelancer is different from an employee, because the business does not have control over the actions of the freelancer. The freelancer can decide what methods to use to accomplish a task as long as the completed job meets the business's specifications.

Interns

Interns are students who will work for little or no pay in order to gain experience in a particular field. To find out whether interns are available in your community, contact local colleges and high schools.

Do you think a want ad in a newspaper is a good way to find job candidates? Why or why not?

If you hire an intern, you will most likely have to work with a college or high school intern coordinator to ensure certain program requirements are fulfilled. It is your responsibility to provide a valuable learning experience for the intern.

Temporary Workers

Businesses that need additional help often use temporary workers. Some temporary workers are seasonal employees. Other temporary workers are substitutes for employees who are sick or on a leave of absence. Temporary employment agencies provide trained workers for various kinds of businesses. A business that uses a temporary employee pays a fee to the agency. The agency in turn manages the worker's salary and benefits.

 CHECKPOINT

What are some alternatives to hiring permanent employees?

11.1 ASSESSMENT

THINK ABOUT IT

1. Why is it important for a company to have an organizational structure that allows the owner to focus on long-term issues?

2. List some advantages of using an employment agency to fill job openings.

3. What would be some disadvantages of hiring freelancers and temporary workers?

MAKE ACADEMIC CONNECTIONS

4. **PROBLEM SOLVING**   Create an organizational structure for a 30-person local package delivery service. First determine all the types of employees the business would have. Then create the chart based on your decisions.

5. **RESEARCH**   Create a resource guide containing names of online career and employment websites, employment agencies, and college placement centers that you could use to help meet the staffing needs of your business. Include contact information such as URLs, addresses, and phone numbers.

Teamwork

Form teams and choose a business in your community. Discuss the various job positions that may be held at this business. Select one position and develop a recruiting plan to hire a new employee. Design a job advertisement that could be used for the recruiting method you select. If you select referrals as the best recruiting method, design a referral request form that could be sent to friends, acquaintances, and current employees.

STAFF YOUR BUSINESS

Goals

- List and describe the steps in the hiring process.
- Describe compensation packages for employees.
- Identify laws protecting employee rights.

Vocabulary

- wages
- salary
- bonus
- profit sharing
- commission
- benefits

focus on small business

Who to hire?

Emanuel took a good look at his business needs and decided that he would hire an administrative assistant to help him. If he had someone in the office to answer the phone, schedule work, and handle the billing, it would allow him to spend more time at excavation job sites. He put an ad in the local newspaper and had several candidates contact him. Now he had to decide whom to interview.

Emanuel's sister, JoAnna, had run her own business for several years, so he went to her for advice. JoAnna recommended that he have candidates complete an application form. He could review the provided information and check their references to determine who is really qualified for the job. Then he could set up interviews with the best candidates.

"So, JoAnna," Emanuel asked, "do you have an application form lying around here anywhere?"

Consider the skills needed to improve your business.

© Flavio Masssari, 2010/ Used under license from Shutterstock.com

Work as a Team   Do you think that JoAnna gave Emanuel good advice about selecting candidates to interview? Why or why not?

The Hiring Process

Hiring the best people available and retaining them is important for the success of your business. Working conditions in a small business are different from those in a large corporation. Employees in a small business are closer to the founder and owner of the company, and there is usually more variety and freedom in the work environment. However, there are also drawbacks to working for a small company. Mistakes are more obvious, and there is less support for legal and human resource issues.

Hiring employees is often difficult because it requires making very important decisions based on fairly limited information.

How should you decide whom to hire? The four-step hiring process involves (1) screening candidates, (2) reviewing and verifying information on job applications, (3) interviewing the best candidates, and (4) making a job offer.

Screen Candidates

The first step in the hiring process is to screen candidates to remove people who are not right for the job. This allows you to focus on the most qualified candidates. The job description identifies the specific qualifications needed to perform a particular job. You need to match the job candidate's experience and skills with the job description. You should also look for personal characteristics that would make a person a desirable employee.

Michael Johnson, owner of Johnson's Medical Supply, ran a want ad in the local newspaper. He was looking for a person with at least five years of experience selling medical equipment. He received more than 150 responses to his ad. However, 120 of the resumes he received were from people with no experience in the field. Michael immediately removed those from the stack of possibilities. Next, he carefully examined each resume and cover letter and selected ten candidates to interview based on their experience.

Review and Verify Information on Job Applications

You will need to have potential candidates complete an application. There are standard application forms that you can use, or you can design one that will meet your specific needs. The application allows you to gather information that might not be included on a resume. If you decide to design your own application, you can use the job description as a guide to gather the information you need about the candidate's experience.

Once you have applications and resumes from candidates, you need to verify that the information provided is correct. The first thing you should do is check references. Call previous employers to make sure the applicant held the positions listed on the resume. Ask what they can tell you about the person. Describe the job opening and ask the previous employers if the candidate

Why is it important to check the references provided by a job applicant?

© Yuri Arcurs, 2010/ Used under license from Shutterstock.com would perform well in such a position. Other questions can revolve around the personal qualities of the candidate, such as interpersonal skills and punctuality. Request that the candidates provide an official transcript from schools they attended to verify education and training.

Interview the Best Candidates

The job interview provides you with the opportunity to determine whether a prospective employee would improve your ability to meet customer needs. It is also your chance to make your small business appealing to a prospective employee. Making the most of the job interview is as important for you as it is for the job candidate.

SELL YOUR BUSINESS   During the interview, make your small business appear inviting and appealing to prospective employees.

- **Share your values and plans for the business.** Help the applicant understand your vision for the business.
- **Talk about the significance of working in a new business.** Emphasize the importance of the contributions the applicant would make in the development and growth of a new business.
- **Explain the atmosphere in which the candidate would work.** Make sure the applicant understands that a small business can foster an environment of flexibility and caring. Some people would rather work in a small business that is not as structured as a large corporation.
- **Describe your bonus system.** With a small startup business, you may not be able to pay a large salary, but you can offer an attractive bonus or benefits package. Explain that if the business does well, you will share some of the profits with those who help you succeed.

MAKE THE INTERVIEW EFFECTIVE   To ensure that you use your time during the interview effectively, follow these basic rules:

1. **Be prepared.** Make a list of open-ended questions you want to ask. Review the job candidate's resume and application again just before the interview begins.
2. **Be courteous.** Do not be late for the interview. Avoid taking phone calls during the interview. Try to put job candidates at ease by offering them something to drink. Make them feel welcome in your office.

> ### SAMPLE INTERVIEW QUESTIONS
> 1. What interests you about the job?
> 2. How can your skills and experience benefit the company?
> 3. What are your career plans? How does this job fit in with those plans?
> 4. What other positions have you held? What did you like and dislike about those positions?
> 5. What were your achievements at your previous jobs?
> 6. Why did you leave your last job?
> 7. How do you think your education has prepared you for this job?
> 8. What kind of work do you enjoy most? What makes a job enjoyable for you?
> 9. Describe a situation where you had to manage conflicting priorities.

3. **Avoid dominating the interview.** Remember that the interview is your opportunity to get to know the job candidate. To do so, be sure to allow the applicant plenty of time to speak.
4. **Take notes.** Throughout the interview, jot down your impressions of the candidate as well as any interesting information he or she reveals.
5. **Look for warning signs.** Signs that a person may not be a good worker include frequent job changes, unexplained gaps in employment, and critical comments about previous employers.
6. **Don't make snap judgments.** Don't rule out a candidate until the interview is over.
7. **Remain pleasant and positive throughout the interview.** At the end of the interview, thank the candidate for coming and let him or her know when you plan to make a decision.
8. **Write a summary of your impressions of the candidate.** Write your summary immediately after the interview while your thoughts are still fresh. Put this document in the candidate's file.

Make a Job Offer

When you have decided to make a job offer, contact the person by phone. Let the person know you were impressed with his or her credentials. Be sure to emphasize how much you would like the applicant to join your company. Clearly state the starting salary, benefits, and terms of employment. If the first applicant declines your offer, extend the offer to your second choice and then to your third choice, if necessary.

Once a candidate accepts your offer, contact the remaining candidates. Thank them for interviewing with your business and politely let them know that you have given the job to another applicant.

CHECKPOINT

What are the four steps in the hiring process?

Compensation Package

As an entrepreneur with paid employees, you will need to create a compensation package. The package will include some type of pay and may also provide a variety of benefits. The benefits package can influence a candidate's decision on whether or not to take a position with a company.

Types of Pay

There are many ways you can choose to pay your employees. The terms "wages" and "salary" are often used interchangeably, but there is a difference. **Wages** are payments for labor or services that are made on an hourly, daily, or per-unit basis. The paycheck for a person earning a wage will vary depending on how many hours are worked or how many units are manufactured. A **salary** is an amount paid for a job position stated on an annual basis. Regardless of the number of hours the person filling the position works, the amount of money the salaried employee is paid does not vary. Wages and salaries can be paid weekly, biweekly, or monthly. Employees may also receive a **bonus**, which is a financial reward made in addition to a regular wage or salary. Bonuses usually hinge on reaching an established goal. **Profit sharing** is another compensation arrangement in which employees are paid a portion of the company's profits.

Some employees are on commission-based salary plans. A **commission** is a percentage of a sale paid to a salesperson. A commission-based salary varies from month to month depending on sales. Those receiving this type of salary may be paid using a commission-only plan or a combination plan.

COMMISSION-ONLY PLAN   Some employees, especially those in sales, receive all of their salaries in commission. Commission-only plans are good for employers because commissions are paid only when sales are made. Some employees may not want to accept a commission-only position, because they are not comfortable with the uncertainty of not knowing what their actual pay will be from pay period to pay period.

Lyn Kovacs works entirely on commission. Last year, Lyn sold $490,000 worth of electronic devices. She received ten percent of her sales as commission. Her annual salary was $49,000, as calculated below.

Amount sold	×	Percent of commission	=	Amount of commission
$490,000	×	0.10	=	$49,000

COMBINATION PLAN   An employee may be on a combination plan. A combination plan includes a base salary plus commission. Employees may feel more comfortable accepting a position that offers this type of payment plan.

Hector Marquez sells men's clothing at a local department store. He earns $6.75 an hour, plus ten percent of whatever he sells. Last month, Hector worked 158 hours and sold $11,500 worth of

Digital Vision/Getty Images

Why are many salespeople paid using a commission plan?

clothing. His total monthly compensation was $2,216.50, calculated as follows:

Base Pay	+	Commission	=	Total Pay
(Hours × Hourly wage)	+	(10% × Sales)	=	Total Pay
(158 × $6.75)	+	(0.10 × $11,500)	=	Total Pay
$1,066.50	+	$1,150.00	=	$2,216.50

PAY COMPETITIVELY In most markets, wages and salaries are competitively determined. This means that an employer who offers much less than the going wage or salary rate is not likely to find qualified workers. To offer competitive wages or salaries, you will have to find out how much similar businesses in your area are paying their employees. You should also find out what people are earning in jobs with similar qualifications. Once you know the going wage or salary rate, you will have to decide whether you want to offer more than, less than, or about the same as other businesses. Offering more than other businesses will attract the best employees.

Eva Aylward owns a limousine service. She knows that finding and keeping good drivers is difficult. To make sure her compensation package is attractive, she regularly finds out what other limousine companies are offering. She then sets a starting salary that is three percent higher. She also offers a few more days of paid vacation than her competitors. Eva hopes that these things will attract drivers who will stay with her company for many years.

Benefits

Benefits are rewards, other than cash, given to employees. They may include paid leave, insurance, and a retirement plan.

PAID LEAVE Almost all employers offer paid vacation and sick time. Both kinds of leave represent costs to employers because employees are paid while they are not working. Be aware that some employees may abuse paid leave. You or someone in your business should keep a record of the paid leave employees take and watch for patterns that might indicate abuse.

Businesses handle vacation in various ways. Many offer one or two weeks of paid vacation a year to new employees. Employees usually gain more vacation time the longer they work at a business. Some businesses let employees carry over unused vacation days from year to year while others require employees to use their vacation time each year.

Sometimes your employees will not be able to work because of

Why do you think employers offer their employees paid vacation time?

illness. The number of days of sick leave provided varies from business to business. Some businesses offer only five sick days a year. Others allow employees unlimited sick leave. You will have to develop a sick leave policy that is fair to your employees but not excessively costly to you.

INSURANCE   Many businesses offer health insurance as a benefit to full-time employees. The cost to small businesses to provide insurance coverage can be quite high. Large businesses receive discounted group rates but may still require employees who opt for this benefit to pay a portion of the cost. Businesses may also offer other kinds of insurance, such as dental insurance, life insurance, and accident and disability insurance.

RETIREMENT PLANS   Some businesses help employees save for retirement by offering 401(k) plans. Employees that participate in 401(k) plans have a percentage of their earned income withheld by the employer to be deposited into a professionally managed

famous entrepreneur

J. K. ROWLING Ask successful people how to succeed, and they will always tell you to do what you love. For a fortunate few, that formula works. Such is the case with J. K. Rowling, creator of *Harry Potter* and one of the most successful writers in the world today.

Rowling always wanted to be a writer and eventually became one, but before Harry and success came a young adulthood full of indecision. Her favorite subject in school was English, and she liked studying languages too. Rowling went to Exeter University and studied French. Her parents thought languages would lead to a career as a bilingual secretary. She discovered that she liked nothing about being a secretary and spent time working on stories at the computer when she thought no one was looking. Such misbehavior eventually got her fired, so Rowling went abroad to teach English as a foreign language in Portugal. With her mornings free, she began work on her third novel after giving up on two others when she realized how bad they were.

AP Photo/Alastair Grant

What can you learn about entrepreneurship from J. K. Rowling's experiences?

When she left Portugal, her suitcase was filled with stories about Harry Potter. She settled in Edinburgh and decided to finish the novel and try to get it published before starting work as a French teacher. A publisher bought the book one year after it was finished. The road to success for J. K. Rowling had begun!

THINK CRITICALLY
J. K. Rowling found great success as a writer, but her experience as an employee was not very successful. Why do you think this is often the case with entrepreneurs?

investment account. Some employers will match employees' 401(k) contributions as much as 50 cents per dollar invested. The funds will continue to grow tax-free until they are withdrawn by the retiree upon reaching retirement age. Pension plans are another type of employer-sponsored retirement savings plan, but they are not as common because they are more costly to a company.

> **What may be included in a compensation package for employees?**

Regulations that Protect Employees

There are many laws designed to prevent discrimination and promote health and safety in relation to employment. It is important to consider these regulations as you develop your staffing plan. Small businesses often run into human resource management issues because the person doing the hiring is not a trained personnel specialist who is familiar with these laws.

National Labor Relations Act (NLRA) of 1935

Congress passed the National Labor Relations Act (NLRA) to protect the rights of employees and employers in the process of negotiating employment contracts. It guarantees workers the right to join a *union*, which is an organization that represents employees and bargains on their behalf for better working conditions and terms of employment. The contract negotiation process between the employer and the union is known as *collective bargaining*. The National Labor Relations Board (NLRB) supervises and controls all aspects of labor relations including formation of a union and the implementation and carrying out of collective bargaining agreements.

Entrepreneurs prefer to operate independently and usually are not unionized. However, some small businesses do negotiate labor contracts and employ unionized personnel.

Fair Labor Standards Act (FLSA) of 1938

The FLSA defines the employment relationship between an employee and employer. It distinguishes between an employee and an independent contractor, who has a business of his or her own. An employee is dependent on the business for which he or she works. When an employee relationship exists as defined by the FLSA, the employee must be paid at least minimum wage. The act established the national minimum wage. Congress reviews the minimum wage every few years and makes adjustments when warranted.

The FLSA also establishes the maximum number of hours employees can work. It requires that employees earn overtime pay for hours worked in excess of 40 hours a week. In addition, the act includes rules for workers under the age of 16.

Civil Rights Act of 1964

Title VII of the Civil Rights Act prohibits discrimination on the basis of race, color, religion, sex, or national origin in hiring, promotion, discharge, pay, fringe benefits, job training, classification, referral, and other aspects of employment. This law is enforced by the Equal Employment Opportunity Commission (EEOC), a government agency established by Congress in 1972 to regulate labor laws. The Civil Rights Act also includes protection against sexual harassment. Businesses should incorporate the following strategies in the workplace to avoid sexual harassment and liability claims:

- Establish clear policies and procedures and communicate them to employees
- Require employees to report incidents of harassment immediately
- Investigate all complaints thoroughly
- Take action against violations and maintain confidentiality
- Contact an attorney if a lawsuit is likely to be filed

Age Discrimination in Employment Act of 1967

The purpose of this act is to promote employment of older persons (40 and over) based on their ability rather than their age. It prohibits arbitrary age discrimination in employment and helps employers and workers find ways of resolving issues that arise from the impact of age on employment.

Occupational Safety and Health Act (OSH Act) of 1970

The OSH Act requires that employers maintain safe working conditions for their employees. To comply with the act's regulations, you must keep records that show the steps you have taken to protect the welfare of your workers and to keep your workplace safe. If employees have to work with dangerous equipment or substances, you must provide them with special training. If the Occupational Safety and Health Administration (OSHA) suspects that your business has unsafe practices, its inspectors will examine your facility and may require you to make changes.

What is the purpose of the Occupational Safety and Health Act?

Immigration Reform and Control Act of 1986

This act requires that employers check the identification of employees hired after 1986 to ensure that they are legal citizens of the United States. It also established the Office of Special Counsel for Immigration-Related Unfair Employment Practices to enforce antidiscrimination provisions.

Americans with Disabilities Act (ADA) of 1990

The ADA bans discrimination against employees based on disabilities. It requires businesses with 15 or more employees to accommodate the needs of employees with disabilities, even if the firms currently do not have disabled employees. The intent of the ADA is to protect job applicants and employees who are legally disabled but are qualified for a specific job. An employee is qualified if he or she can carry out the necessary functions of the job with some type of reasonable accommodation.

Family and Medical Leave Act of 1993

This act requires businesses with more than 50 employees to provide employees up to three months of unpaid leave if a serious health condition affects the employee, the employee's child, or the employee's parent or spouse. This act also makes it possible for male and female employees to take leave in the event of a birth or adoption of a child. To be eligible, an employee must have been employed by the business for at least one year.

 **CHECKPOINT**

Why do we need laws to help protect the rights of employees?

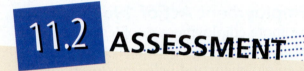

THINK ABOUT IT

1. How are employee relationships in a small business different from those in a large corporation?

2. Why is the compensation package important to potential employees?

3. Why is it important for you as a small business owner to have an understanding of the laws designed to protect employees?

MAKE ACADEMIC CONNECTIONS

4. **RESEARCH**   Find and compare three advertisements for the same type of job. Are the qualifications requested the same? How are they different? Is any mention of compensation made? If so, how is it structured? Using the library or Internet, research the going wage for this position. What do you think is a fair wage for this job?

5. **MATH**   You have an open sales position in your company. You plan to offer a salary of $23,000 per year. You discover that another company with a similar sales position offers a combination plan of $12,000 per year plus a commission of 15 percent of sales. Average sales are $90,000. Which job has the potential for higher earnings? Do you need to adjust your salary? Why or why not?

Teamwork

When interviewing job candidates, there are questions you cannot legally ask. Access www.cengage.com/school/entrepreneurship/ideas. Click on *Activities* and open the file *Interview Questions* to print a copy. Working with a partner, review the list of interview question guidelines. Then think of a position in a company and make a list of interview questions adhering to the guidelines. Role-play an interview for the position.

DIRECT AND CONTROL HUMAN RESOURCES

Goals

- Explain how to implement your staffing plan.
- Discuss ways to motivate your employees.
- Describe the control function of management as it applies to human resources.

Vocabulary

- delegate
- performance evaluation

focus on small business

You've hired someone, now what?

Emanuel carefully screened the applicants for administrative assistant, interviewed a couple of candidates, and offered the position to Vivian. Vivian reported to work bright and early on a Monday morning. Emanuel reviewed her job description with her, showed her how the phone system worked, and then headed out to do some excavation work.

He hadn't been gone 20 minutes when his cell phone started ringing. It was Vivian. She was in a panic because she had received several calls about excavation services. Customers wanted to know the costs and when they could be scheduled for service. Vivian didn't know what to tell them, and some customers became impatient and demanding. Emanuel quickly turned his truck around and headed back to his shop. On the way there, he tried to figure out what to do.

© Iodrakon, 2010/ Used under license from Shutterstock.com

Well-trained employees help a business succeed.

Work as a Team   What mistakes do you think Emanuel made after hiring Vivian? What does he need to do now?

Implement Your Staffing Plan

Once you have people working for you, you become a manager. This means that you will no longer focus all of your efforts on doing your own job. You will be *implementing*, which involves directing and leading people to accomplish the goals of the organization. As a manager, you will have to exhibit leadership and motivate your employees.

To manage your staff effectively, you need to understand the levels of management and develop good leadership qualities. This will help you create a workforce that is dedicated to meeting customer needs and increasing sales.

Understand the Levels of Management

There are three basic levels of management: supervisory level, middle level, and top-management level. The amount of responsibility varies with the level of management. As the manager moves up, the amount of responsibility increases. The number of managers at each level will vary depending on the size of the company. In a new business venture, the entrepreneur may serve in all levels of management. A large corporation may have many individuals working as middle and supervisory-level managers.

Supervisory-level managers work directly with the workers on the job and are responsible for implementing the plans of middle management. Middle managers serve as a liaison between the supervisory-level and the top-level managers. They are responsible for implementing the goals of top management. Top management is responsible for establishing the vision for the company and has the highest level of responsibility.

Apply Leadership Styles

As you learned in Chapter 10, managers will develop a style or way of working with those whom they supervise. Leadership styles have changed over the years as the workplace has changed. Successful managers today often empower their employees and give them the authority to make decisions without supervisory approval. Empowerment gives employees a sense of responsibility and pride in accomplishment. It also reduces delays in the flow of work and reduces the workload of the manager.

However, not all managers use this style. There are many different leadership styles. Some managers use fear and intimidation and manage their employees as if they are lazy and cannot be trusted. They are called *Theory X managers* and use the authoritative management style. Other managers trust and respect their employees and value their contributions. They are called *Theory Y managers* and use the democratic management style. *Theory Z managers* place more emphasis on group decision making and teams. In your working career, you will encounter many different leadership styles. When you become a manager, incorporate the qualities you like in other leaders into your leadership style.

Enforce Employee Policies

As the owner of your own business, you will establish policies concerning vacations, holidays, hours, acceptable dress, and other issues affecting your workers. You will need to make sure that all of your employees are familiar with these policies. You may need to gently remind employees of policies if they fail to follow them.

BE YOUR OWN BOSS

You own a floral design studio. Last year, you promoted Philip, one of your designers, to manager of the studio. Philip had shown excellent design skills and was eager to take on new responsibilities. Recently, Philip has become increasingly protective of information regarding the day-to-day management of the floral shop. Several major problems with important customers have surfaced that Philip knew about but had not shared with you. Business from two of these customers has decreased during the last quarter. Also, several staff members have come to you privately with complaints about Philip's management practices. Tina, who has worked for you for over ten years, is threatening to quit. Use the six-step problem-solving method to determine how you will handle the issues with Philip.

Many companies communicate policies to staff by creating an employee handbook. These handbooks can be just a few pages long or they can fill a small binder, depending on the size of the company and the number of policies.

Train Your Employees

You will need to develop a training program for your new employees. This program should begin as soon as they are hired. Training should not end when the employee learns how things are done. Continuous training ensures that employees are always knowledgeable and up to date on changes affecting the business.

There are many ways to provide training to employees. You may use different techniques for different job responsibilities. You will need to decide which is best for you, your business, and the employee.

- **On-the-job training** Employees learn new responsibilities by actually performing them at their place of business.
- **Coaching** Employees receive feedback and instruction from their manager on a constant basis.
- **Mentoring** One employee teams up with another more experienced employee to learn a job.
- **Conferences and seminars** Employees attend conferences and seminars to learn about new techniques and trends from an expert in the field. These are usually held off-site.

After training, you need to make sure employees are using the training and that the training was effective. Justin Reynolds needs to train his employees on the new computerized inventory system he wants to use. He brings in a representative from the software company to provide a training session. Justin will know the training was effective if employees understand the software and are able to use it.

Why are conferences and seminars valuable training methods?

> **What should be included in the implementation of a staffing plan?**

Motivate Your Employees

To get the most out of your employees, you will have to motivate them. You can do so in several ways.

1. **Pay employees well.** When employees feel they are compensated well, they will be happier. They will perform to the best of their ability.
2. **Treat employees fairly.** Everyone wants to be treated well. Be sure to treat everyone the same.
3. **Recognize employees for the work they do.** Offer public recognition for a job well done. Praise employees frequently.
4. **Give employees adequate responsibility.** Employees who are allowed to make decisions on their own often work harder. They take pride in the fact that their input makes a difference.

Delegate Responsibility

Many entrepreneurs have difficulty delegating responsibility. To **delegate** is to let other people share workloads and responsibilities. Employees who are given more responsibility are better motivated and contribute more to the company. Delegating responsibility to them allows you to make the most of their experience, talents, and skills.

As a business owner, delegating allows you to focus on important items, such as expanding into new markets or offering new products. Assigning paperwork and other duties that can be performed by someone else will free up your time.

© bikeridrenlondon, 2010/ Used under license from Shutterstock.com

Why should a manager encourage employees to share their opinions and ideas?

Finally, delegating responsibility is essential if a company is to grow. When your business is small, you may be able to handle all areas of its management. If the company is to expand, you will have to let managers take on more and more responsibility.

Listen to Employees

Some entrepreneurs fail to listen to their employees. In doing so, they miss out on an opportunity to take advantage of valuable ideas and resources that can help them increase profits.

The people who work for you are very familiar with your business and may be able to offer fresh ideas. Listening to new points of view may help you come up with new, creative solutions. If you value the opinions of your employees, they will feel they are a valuable asset to your company. This feeling of importance will keep them motivated to do a good job for you.

 CHECKPOINT

How can you motivate employees?

what went wrong?

WHOM DO YOU TRUST?

Sandy Warren formed Motiva International, a sales motivation and consulting company. Sandy felt it was very important to involve her employees in all business operations. At weekly meetings, she shared and discussed confidential company details with the company's 18 employees. Sandy soon learned that there were some things that should not be shared.

The company was experiencing some cash flow problems, and Sandy discussed this with the employees. Employees became concerned that they would not get paid, which distracted them from their job

Carefully consider what information to share with employees.

duties. Because work wasn't getting done, customer relations suffered. At another meeting, Sandy told her employees about a deal she was about to close with a new client. One excited employee told someone outside the company about the new client. This leak of information enabled a competitor to develop a stronger proposal and steal away the new client. Losing that deal forced Sandy to lay off employees, go deeper into debt, and finally dissolve the company.

THINK CRITICALLY

1. How do you determine what company information should be reserved for management and withheld from employees?

2. Would you have fired the employee who leaked the information regarding the potential new client? Why or why not?

© Flashon Studio, 2010/ Used under license from Shutterstock.com

Why are performance evaluations important to both the employer and employee?

Control Human Resources

The controlling function of management involves setting standards for the operation of a business and ensuring those standards are met. In the area of human resources, it is necessary to establish performance standards for employees and then evaluate employees periodically to be sure they are meeting the performance standards. This process can help you identify outstanding employees who should be promoted and problem employees who should be dismissed.

Evaluate Employees

Most businesses perform an employee review once or twice a year in which they analyze each employee's performance and determine the increase in the employee's salary. The job description should be used when evaluating how well an employee has fulfilled all of his or her job responsibilities. Some of the items that are usually evaluated include dependability, punctuality, attitude toward job and coworkers, and success in achieving predetermined objectives.

A **performance evaluation** serves as a management control tool that helps determine whether the objectives for a particular job are being met. The evaluation process is also useful to the employee. It helps the employee recognize strengths and see where there is room for improvement. As part of the process, plans for mentoring, training, and practice should be put in place to help improve the employee's performance in areas where needed.

During the performance review, the reviewer should focus on the positive aspects of the employee's performance. Productivity should be reviewed, and the employee and reviewer should work together to set new objectives for the upcoming period. The review should be recorded on an appraisal form, as shown on the next page. The form should include the employee's name and job title as well as the manager's name, the date range the review covers, job responsibilities and attributes, comments, goals for the next year, and a section outlining plans for employee development. A ranking method can be used to rate how well the employee has performed.

Performance reviews should be conducted face to face. A written summary of the review should be kept in the employee's file.

Promote Employees

Promoting good employees will help ensure that they remain interested in working for your business. Employees often compete with one another, so promoting one over the other may cause problems. Be sure you make all decisions fairly. Base your decisions on solid reasons, such as volume of sales and quality of customer service.

PERFORMANCE APPRAISAL

DATE: January 21, 20--
NAME: Daniel Tisdale
JOB TITLE: Marketing Director

Reports To: Laureen Stiles
Review Period: 1/1 to 12/31

ATTRIBUTE	WELL ABOVE STANDARD	ABOVE STANDARD	STANDARD	BELOW STANDARD	FAR BELOW STANDARD
Quantity of work		✓			
Knowledge of work		✓			
Ability to organize			✓		
Ability to meet deadlines			✓		
Dependability			✓		
Judgment			✓		
Initiative	✓				
Communication				✓	
Management of others			✓		
Teamwork			✓		

COMMENTS

You have done an outstanding job of increasing sales. Your hard work, dependability, and initiative are very much appreciated.

AREAS FOR IMPROVEMENT:

1. Increase technical knowledge to improve the quality and quantity of work.

2. Improve written communication skills by enrolling in a business writing course.

3. Improve management skills, in particular by delegating more responsibility to your marketing assistants.

4. Increase ability to participate as part of team.

GOALS FOR COMING YEAR:

1. Increase store sales 12 percent.

2. Oversee completion of company website.

3. Generate online sales of $75,000.

Employee: Daniel Tisdale

Manager: Laureen Stiles

Daniel Tisdale

Laureen Stiles

Dismiss Employees

Some employees may not work out. In fact, they may end up hurting your business. How will you handle such situations? As soon as you notice an employee not performing well or causing problems, discuss the situation with him or her. If performance does not improve, issue a written warning. If there is still no improvement, you will need to dismiss that employee. Once you decide to dismiss an employee, do so immediately. Record the reasons for the dismissal in the employee's file.

 CHECKPOINT

Why is it important to conduct employee performance evaluations at regular intervals?

11.3 ASSESSMENT

THINK ABOUT IT

1. What is the difference between a Theory X manager and a Theory Y manager? Which leadership style do you think is more effective? Why?

2. Why do many entrepreneurs find it difficult to delegate?

3. Why do you think it is important to keep a written summary of a performance evaluation?

MAKE ACADEMIC CONNECTIONS

4. **PROBLEM SOLVING**   You own a clothing store and currently employ two sales assistants. You have just hired a new sales assistant. Develop a training program for your new employee so she will learn all aspects of the business, including operating the cash register, assisting customers, and opening and closing the store. Consider whether to use on-the-job training, coaching, mentoring, or conferences and seminars.

5. **COMMUNICATION**   Access www.cengage.com/school/entrepreneurship/ideas. Click on *Activities* and open the file *Performance Evaluation*. Print a copy. With a partner, role-play an employee and employer participating in a performance review. Assume the employee is a good worker who deserves a promotion. Make up the employer and job. Complete the performance evaluation form.

Teamwork

You manage a department in a business that is in the midst of change. Your employees have heard many rumors about job changes, possible layoffs, and pay reductions. Morale in the department is at an all-time low. Working with teammates, develop a plan to motivate your employees to achieve high performance standards and keep a good attitude in the midst of all the changes. Share your motivational plan with the rest of the class.

Leadership Skills

As an entrepreneur and a manager, you need to demonstrate good leadership skills. If you want your business to grow, you must be able to lead and influence others to help you carry out your business vision. A manager who can get individual employees and groups to work well together to accomplish objectives is considered to be an effective leader.

Being a good leader is more than just being nice to people. Characteristics of effective leaders include the following:

1. **Understanding**   Respect the feelings and needs of fellow workers.

2. **Initiative**   Have the ambition and motivation to see a project through to the end.

3. **Dependability**   Follow through on commitments.

4. **Judgment**   Make decisions carefully, objectively, and fairly.

5. **Objectivity**   Look at all sides of an issue before making a decision.

6. **Confidence**   Make decisions and take responsibility for the results.

7. **Consistency**   Do not be too emotional or unpredictable.

8. **Cooperation**   Work well with others.

9. **Honesty**   Behave ethically and be truthful.

10. **Courage**   Be willing to take reasonable risks and make unpopular decisions.

11. **Communication**   Listen, speak, and write effectively.

12. **Intelligence**   Have the knowledge, understanding, and skills needed to perform well.

Try It Out

Leadership styles vary from person to person. Choose two individuals who have played leadership roles in history and research their leadership styles. Prepare a report that illustrates how they exhibited each of the characteristics described above.

Digital Vision/Getty Images

SUMMARY

11.1 Identify Your Staffing Needs

1. To determine staffing needs, list all the duties in your business, identify how much time is needed to perform each one, determine the skills and qualifications employees need, and write job descriptions that list the specific responsibilities of each position. You should also create an organizational structure to show the relationships between the various jobs in the company.

2. To recruit new employees, you may use online career and employment sites, employment agencies, college placement centers, in-store advertising, classified advertisements, and referrals.

3. In addition to hiring permanent employees, you can also hire freelancers, interns, or temporary workers.

11.2 Staff Your Business

4. The four steps in the hiring process include (1) screen candidates, (2) review and verify information on job applications, (3) interview the best candidates, and (4) make a job offer.

5. A compensation package should include a method of pay and may provide a variety of benefits. Types of pay include wages, salary, commission only, or a combination of salary plus commission. Bonuses and profit sharing are other compensation methods. Benefits may include paid leave for vacation and sickness; medical, dental, life, and accident and disability insurance; and retirement plans.

6. Employers must follow all laws and regulations that are created to protect employees from unfair labor practices.

11.3 Direct and Control Human Resources

7. Implementing your staffing plan effectively requires that you have good management and leadership qualities. By enforcing policies and offering training, you will help your employees perform better.

8. There are several ways to motivate employees, including paying them well, treating them fairly, recognizing them for good work, and giving them adequate responsibility.

9. You should create a procedure for evaluating employees. Outstanding employees should be promoted when opportunities become available, and problem employees should be dismissed.

what do you know now?

Read *Ideas in Action* on page 311 again. Then answer the questions a second time. Have your responses changed? If so, how have they changed?

VOCABULARY BUILDER

Match each statement with the term that best defines it. Some terms may not be used.

1. A written statement listing the tasks and responsibilities of a position
2. The process of determining the tasks and sequence of tasks necessary to perform a job
3. A management control tool that determines whether objectives for a job are being met
4. To look for people to hire and attract them to the business
5. People who provide specialty services to a number of different businesses on an hourly basis or by the job
6. Payments for labor or services that are made on an hourly, daily, or per-unit basis
7. An amount paid for a job position stated on an annual basis
8. A percentage of a sale paid to a salesperson
9. Financial reward for employment service in addition to salary
10. To let other people share workloads and responsibilities

a. benefits
b. bonus
c. chain of command
d. commission
e. delegate
f. freelancers
g. interns
h. job analysis
i. job description
j. performance evaluation
k. profit sharing
l. recruit
m. salary
n. staffing
o. wages

REVIEW YOUR KNOWLEDGE

11. **True or False** Good employees and a well-run human resource management program are as important to your business as are capital, equipment, and inventory.
12. A collection of tasks and responsibilities that an employee is responsible for completing is a
    a. job
    b. job description
    c. job analysis
    d. duties and task list
13. Which of the following is *not* a way to motivate employees?
    a. pay them well
    b. treat them fairly
    c. recognize them for good work
    d. make all decisions for them
14. **True or False** The job analysis helps people in a company understand who reports to whom.
15. Which of the following would *not* be included in a job offer?
    a. job analysis
    b. starting salary
    c. terms of employment
    d. benefits package
16. **True or False** During the screening process, you determine which candidates are most qualified for the position you are trying to fill.
17. If you live in a very small community with a limited pool of available workers, what would be the *best* way to recruit employees from nearby communities?
    a. online advertisement
    b. in-store advertising
    c. classified ad in the local paper
    d. college placement center for a university 300 miles away
18. Offering an employee the opportunity to participate in your group health insurance plan is an example of a
    a. wage
    b. salary
    c. bonus
    d. benefit

19. You interviewed a candidate for a sales position in your swimming pool sales and installation business. Sales are usually high in the spring and summer and then drop off in the fall and winter. The candidate has a family and needs a steady income but likes the idea of earning more pay if he makes a large number of sales. Which payment method do you think he would prefer?

    a. wage
    b. salary
    c. commission only
    d. combination plan

20. **True or False** The Occupational Safety and Health Act establishes the maximum number of hours employees can work.

21. **True or False** The Family and Medical Leave Act makes it possible for both men and women to take leave in the event of a birth or adoption of a child.

22. A __?__ manager works directly with the workers on the job and is responsible for implementing the plans of middle management.

23. **True or False** As long as a job candidate has the appropriate skills needed, it is not necessary to check his or her references.

24. Which of the following would be the most effective training method to use for an employee who needs to learn about the latest technology trends for today's modern office?

    a. on-the-job training
    b. coaching
    c. mentoring
    d. conference or seminar

APPLY WHAT YOU LEARNED

25. You have decided to hire three people to help in your custom drapery business: an administrative assistant, an interior designer/salesperson, and a sewer. What qualifications and skills must each of these employees possess? Write a job description for each position. Also, establish a compensation package for each position describing the type of pay and the benefits included. Using Internet resources, plan a training session to educate the employees about sexual harassment and medical or family leaves of absence.

26. For each of the positions in your custom drapery business above, describe how you will recruit these employees. Create a want ad and prepare a list of interview questions for each position.

MAKE ACADEMIC CONNECTIONS

27. **MATH** Jayne Smith sells vacuum cleaners and is compensated under a combination plan. She earns $9.25 per hour plus 15 percent of whatever she sells. Last month, Jayne worked 160 hours and sold 9 vacuum cleaners. Five of the vacuum cleaners were top-of-the-line models with a price of $1,100 each. The remaining vacuum cleaners were $450 each. What is Jayne's compensation for last month?

28. **PROBLEM SOLVING** One of your employees is upset that another employee received a promotion. She thinks she should have received the promotion because she has worked there longer and has always had good performance evaluations. What are some reasons that a newer employee would receive the promotion? How will you handle the situation?

What Would YOU Do?

You want to hire a new sales assistant for your company. You checked with the local college placement office, and it sent several qualified applicants for an interview. You are really impressed with one of the candidates, and you want to hire him for the position. Before making the job offer, you decide to check the Internet to see if the candidate has a personal web page that might provide you with more information regarding his background and interests. You quickly find his personal web page and are shocked at some of the pictures he has posted and at some of the activities in which he has participated. What would you do? Would you hire him anyway, or would this change your impression of him?

build your
BUSINESS PLAN PROJECT

This activity will help you determine staffing needs for your business. This information will help you develop the Operations section of your business plan.

1. Assume your business will grow over the next year and you will need to add employees. Make a list of at least five jobs that need to be filled. Is each job a full-time job, part-time job, or temporary work? For each job, write a detailed job description. Create an organizational chart for your business based on these new positions.

2. Write a classified advertisement for each of the jobs you will need to fill. What employee characteristics and qualifications are you seeking? Write the interview questions that you will ask the candidates for each position. Write a list of questions you will ask their references.

3. For each position, create a complete compensation package that outlines wages or salary and any nonsalary benefits. Explain why you have structured the compensation package as such.

4. Add employee policies concerning vacation, holidays, hours, acceptable dress, and any other employee issues to the operating procedures manual you previously created in Chapter 10.

5. Create a sample performance appraisal form. Will this form be the same for each position? Why or why not?

6. Determine the ways you plan to motivate your employees. Create at least one method of publicly acknowledging employees for good work. Record your ideas.

7. In what ways will you train new and existing employees for your business? What aspects of your business require training, and what type of training is the best for each aspect? Write a short report about your decisions.

Arts, A/V Technology & Communications

"My aunt got married last weekend, and the wedding was a blast. Both a photographer and a videographer were at the wedding. During the reception, the photographer set up a laptop on a table that had photos of the ceremony streaming on screen. It was really fun to see pictures of the ceremony while we were still celebrating the wedding."

How do people determine the best way to record significant events in their lives? How do companies develop portfolios of their products for use in printed catalogs or on websites?

Photographers take pictures of people, events, and products. Photographers often specialize by topic. Areas of specialization include news, commercial, fine arts, portrait, or special event photography.

Employment Outlook
- Average growth is anticipated.
- Competition for positions is fierce as many people find this field appealing.
- Individuals who keep current with technological changes in equipment and processing will have the most opportunities.

Job Titles
- News Photographer
- Children's Photographer
- Soft Goods Photographer
- Online Photographer
- Event Photographer
- Portrait Photographer

Needed Education/Skills
- Creativity and a solid understanding of the photographic process are essential.
- Strong interpersonal skills are required—especially for portrait photographers who work with a diverse client base.
- Independent photographers should be Internet savvy to facilitate direct marketing to clients.
- Strong computer skills are necessary for digital photo manipulation.

What's it like to work in Audio-Video Technology? On Sunday afternoon, Keisha, a freelance photographer, went to a local park to take a combination of candid and posed pictures for a family reunion.

Sunday evening Keisha loaded the family reunion photos on her website. Although Keisha earned a fee for taking photos at the reunion, she will generate additional revenue when family members purchase either individual photos or customized albums.

Monday morning, Keisha met with a newly engaged couple who were potential clients. After discussing the logistical details of the wedding, Keisha showed the couple a few albums from prior weddings. She then walked the couple through her website. By providing digital copies of the photos online, categorized by various stages of the wedding, it was easy for couples to review photos. Album viewers could simply click a tab like "Ceremony" or "Reception" to view the photos of most interest.

What about you? Would you like to help a variety of individuals record special events through the use of photography?

Business plans are an effective tool for evaluating, organizing, and selling a new business concept. A well-developed business plan can be a key component for a successful business startup. Participants must demonstrate an understanding and mastery of the process required in developing and implementing a new business venture. The project may be completed by teams of two to three members. The business plan must include the following sections: Executive Summary, Company Description, Industry Analysis, Target Market, Competitive Analysis, Marketing Plan and Sales Strategy, Operations, Management and Organization, Long-Term Development, and Financials. Many business plans also include copies of key supporting documents such as certifications, licenses, tax requirements, and codes in an appendix.

Proposals may describe a proposed business venture or a current business operation. The business idea must be currently viable and realistic. The *Build Your Business Plan Project* that you have been working on could be used in this competitive event.

Performance Competencies

- Demonstrate good verbal communication skills
- Articulate the need for the proposed business
- Explain the process of preparing a business plan
- Identify obstacles for the owner or business
- Explain the lessons learned
- Answer questions effectively

Go to the FBLA website for more detailed information.

GIVE IT A TRY

Using the FBLA competitive event guidelines for the Business Plan event, prepare a business plan that contains all of the required components for the business proposed in the *Build Your Business Plan Project* or another business venture you would like to pursue. Prepare a seven-minute presentation describing the business plan. Make the presentation to your class. Visual aids and samples specifically related to the project may be used in the presentation. Be prepared to answer questions about your business plan.

www.fbla-pbl.org

CHAPTER 12

© StockLite, 2010/ Used under license from Shutterstock.com

Risk Management

12.1 Business Risks

12.2 Insure Against Risks

12.3 Other Risks

www.cengage.com/school/entrepreneurship/ideas

Growth Is Risky

Scott Alterman, The Icebox

Scott Alterman started making money at an early age. In high school, he had a lawn mowing business and a car detailing business, and he collected and sold baseball cards. After college, Scott joined his brother, Greg, who was running Gagwear, a small company in Atlanta that served the corporate market with customized apparel.

The Alterman brothers began manufacturing edgier and higher-quality apparel than what was typically offered in their target market. They started with caps that included their own label with a phone number on them. They took a risk by importing thousands of caps before they had sold one. Their customers took notice. Ironically, they had many inquiries from competitors wanting to buy the blank hats, so they decided to start a "blanks" division. This was the beginning of Alternative Apparel, the wholesale division. Scott concentrated his efforts on Gagwear while Greg developed Alternative Apparel.

Gagwear's customer base was small- to medium-sized corporate customers. Scott wanted to grow Gagwear by calling on retailers and larger customers but needed to continue to serve the current customer base. So another company, The Icebox, a full-service advertising-specialty company serving small- to medium-sized companies, was born. The Alterman brothers brought in a partner, Jordy Gamson, to run The Icebox. Later, Scott and Jordy decided to merge Gagwear and The Icebox divisions and operate both under The Icebox name. Greg is now running Alternative Apparel while Scott and Jordy run The Icebox.

Meanwhile, Alternative Apparel had begun to experience serious growth. The decision was made to completely separate Alternative Apparel and The Icebox to let them grow properly. The businesses quit sharing employees, and each got financing to evolve on its own.

The growth of The Icebox did not come without risks. With a $2 million note for his new building along with a $1.2 million line of credit, Scott realized the financial risk he faced. He also knew he would face risk every time he extended credit to a customer. Scott wanted to be customer-friendly by extending credit to customers most other businesses would consider too risky. On the other hand, after The Icebox became a separate company, Scott was able to eliminate some of the risks associated with the production side of his business. Rather than incur the financial risks of buying and repairing equipment and hiring production employees, The Icebox decided to use contract companies for screenprinting and embroidery.

1. What unmet need did the Alterman brothers uncover?
2. How does Scott take a risk by extending credit to customers?
3. Why is contracted work less risky for The Icebox

BUSINESS RISKS

Goals

- List and explain steps involved in preparing to face risks.
- Discuss types of theft and security precautions to take to protect your business.

Vocabulary

- risk
- risk management
- risk assessment
- shoplifting
- bounced check

focus on small business

What if disaster strikes?

"Kristin," Ty asked his partner, "what do you think would happen to our web hosting business if our computers or computer data were stolen or hacked into?"

"Wow, Ty, we've never really thought about that. We just come in every day and do our work. We do back up our work periodically, but we just put the CDs in our file cabinet."

Businesses must address computer security risks.

"I know," Ty responded, "I started thinking about it after I read about a business that had all of its computers stolen one night. And I realized we have no emergency plan in place."

"We sure don't, but I bet we will have something figured out by tomorrow!" Kristin said.

Work as a Team What risks do you think Ty and Kristin would face if all their computers were destroyed or computer data were compromised? What steps do you think they should take to be prepared in case this would happen?

Dealing with Business Risks

As an independent businessperson, you will face many risks. **Risk** is the possibility of some kind of loss. Risks can be categorized as human risk, natural risk, and economic risk. **Risk management** is taking action to prevent or reduce the possibility of loss to your business. You can avoid risk, assume risk, or transfer risk.

Identifying Risks

Human risks are those caused by the actions of individuals, such as employees or customers. Examples include shoplifting, employee theft, robbery, credit card fraud, and bounced checks. *Natural risks* are caused by acts of nature. Examples are storms, fires, floods, and earthquakes. The occurrence of any of these could bring about tremendous loss to a business. *Economic risks* occur because of changes in business conditions.

Preparing to Face Risks

As an entrepreneur, you must be prepared to face all kinds of risks. You will need to decide the best strategy for dealing with risks. You may decide to avoid the risk. For example, if you think a product you are developing will not meet market needs, you may decide to avoid financial risks caused by low sales by halting production of the product.

You may decide to assume the risk if you determine the risk is low. If your market research indicates the product you are developing will be successful with your target market, you will most likely produce and sell the product even though there is still a chance of lower sales than expected.

Transferring the risk is another option. You will be able to protect yourself against the financial losses from some risks by purchasing insurance. Insurance transfers the risk of financial loss to the insurance company.

You never know when a disaster may strike, but you should have a plan of action in place when it does. When Hurricane Katrina struck New Orleans in 2005, many business owners were not prepared for the loss of property and income that occurred. You need to have a plan in place so that if something does happen, you can recover and restart business operations quickly. To prepare for risks, you should do the following:

1. Determine what can go wrong.
2. Develop a plan.
3. Communicate your plan.

DETERMINE WHAT CAN GO WRONG   As a business owner, the first thing you need to do is conduct a risk assessment. A **risk assessment** involves looking at all aspects of your business and determining the risks you face. During this assessment, you should:

- Learn the risks your business faces.
- Decide how the risks would affect your business.
- Prioritize the risks by the impact they will have on your business.

DEVELOP A PLAN   Once you have identified the risks that could affect your business, you should develop a written plan for dealing with them. When developing a risk management plan, you may have to comply with certain laws. For example, OSHA (Occupational Safety and Health Administration) requires businesses to have an evacuation plan for emergencies. There are many good sources available to help you establish an effective risk management plan. If you are developing an emergency action plan, the National Safety Council, a nongovernmental organization that promotes safety, is a good source. It recommends that the following items be included in your emergency action plan.

- Chain-of-command information, including names and job titles of the people responsible for making decisions, monitoring response actions, and recovering back-to-normal operations

DEVELOP YOUR READING SKILLS

As you read, use the SQ3R method:
- Survey the chapter to get an idea of what you will be reading.
- Make a list of Questions about the chapter that come to mind as you survey.
- Read the chapter.
- Recall what you have read.
- Review the material by discussing it with a classmate.

Why is it important to have a plan for handling risks?

- The names of individuals responsible for assessing the degree of risk to life and property and who should be notified for different types of emergencies
- Preferred method for reporting fires and other emergencies
- Specific instructions for shutting down equipment and other business activities and procedures for employees who must shut down equipment before they evacuate the facility
- Facility evacuation procedures, including maps showing the best and alternate exit routes
- Specific training for those who are responsible for responding to emergencies

Be sure to have a recovery plan in place if you suffer a setback. A *recovery plan* will enable you to get back to business as quickly as possible. If you suffer a loss due to a fire, have a plan for temporarily relocating, getting replacement equipment, and retrieving lost data. If one of your suppliers is out of stock of a component needed in the production of your product, have another supplier lined up. A recovery plan will help you continue to meet your customers' needs.

Review your risk management plan periodically. As your business develops and grows, risks facing your business may change. Revise your risk management plan to accommodate your changing needs.

COMMUNICATE YOUR PLAN   Let your managers and employees know about your plan for handling risks. To ensure your plan is carried out properly, assign activities and responsibilities to the appropriate people. For example, to protect against the risk of a faulty product, assign the production manager the task of checking the quality of the finished product. If you plan to run an advertisement for an upcoming sale, make sure someone is responsible for placing the ad in the appropriate media at the appropriate time to avoid the risk of lost sales. If you want to protect your computer system from the risks of viruses and computer hackers, you can work with a computer security expert. To address the risks related to emergencies, provide training for all employees to show them what to do in the event of any type of emergency. Work with your managers and employees to be sure all risks are addressed.

CHECKPOINT

What should you do to prepare for business risks?

Types of Theft

One of the biggest risks that businesses face is theft. Shoplifters and employees may steal your merchandise. Burglars may break into your business and steal your equipment. Customers may use stolen credit cards or write checks when they don't have money in their account. Once you have identified the theft risks you face, you can determine what security precautions you need to take.

Shoplifting

Shoplifting is the act of knowingly taking items from a business without paying. Customers shoplift millions of dollars in merchandise every year. The problem exists in virtually every type of retail business.

If you own a retail business, you will have to take steps to prevent or reduce shoplifting. Some of the things you can do include the following:

- Instruct your employees to watch for customers who appear suspicious.
- Hire security guards or off-duty police officers to patrol your store.
- Post signs indicating that you prosecute shoplifters.
- Ask incoming customers to leave their bags behind the counter.
- Install electronic devices, such as mounted video cameras, electronic merchandise tags, and point-of-exit sensors, to detect shoplifters.

Employee Theft

Most employees are hard working and honest, but there are a few who will take things from your business, such as office supplies, equipment, merchandise, and even money. These employees can negatively impact your business financially.

As an entrepreneur, you need to be aware of the possibility of employee theft. You need to take steps to prevent the problem from occurring. You also need to know how to detect the problem and to handle it once it is detected.

Some businesses, such as restaurants and retail stores, are more vulnerable to employee theft than others. If you own such a business, you may need to adopt the following procedures:

1. **Prevent dishonest employees from joining your company.** Screen job applicants very carefully. Consider using a company that specializes in verifying job applicants' educational backgrounds and searching their criminal records, driver's license reports, civil court records, and credit reports.
2. **Install surveillance systems.** Often the mere knowledge that they are being

NETBookmark

Shoplifters can be male or female, any race or color, children or senior citizens. Anyone who deliberately takes merchandise from a store without paying for it is a shoplifter, no matter the value of the item taken. The Kansas Bureau of Investigation has created a pamphlet that discusses the various types of shoplifters and how retailers can identify them. Access www.cengage.com/school/entrepreneurship/ideas and click on the link for Chapter 12. Read more about shoplifters. What are the six types of shoplifter? Which do you think is the hardest for retailers to spot? What are some of the signs to look for when trying to spot shoplifters?

www.cengage.com/school/entrepreneurship/ideas

filmed by a video camera deters employees from stealing.

3. **Establish a tough company policy regarding employee theft**. Your company policy should detail the consequences of employee theft. Make sure that all employees are aware of the policy.

4. **Be on the lookout**. Watch for cash discrepancies, missing merchandise or supplies, vehicles parked close to loading areas, and other signs that something may be wrong. Keep an eye on employees who seem to work at odd hours, perform their jobs poorly, or complain unreasonably. Make inquiries if an employee has an unexplained close relationship with a supplier or customer or has a personal lifestyle that seems inconsistent with his or her salary.

How can a surveillance system help a business owner reduce risk?

© Tom Pingel, 2010/ Used under license from Shutterstock.com

Robbery

Almost all businesses are vulnerable to robberies. You can choose what is considered a safe area of town to locate your business to guard against being robbed. You can also install dead-bolt locks and burglar alarms. To limit losses in the event of a robbery, many businesses keep a minimal amount of cash in the cash register. Once more than a certain amount is received, the cash is transferred to a safe. Some businesses also use surveillance cameras, which deter prospective robbers from entering the business in the first place. Be aware that you may be robbed regardless of the number of preventative measures you take. It is simply a risk of being open for business.

Credit Card Fraud

Business owners lose millions of dollars every year because of stolen credit cards. If a purchase is made on a stolen credit card, a business may not be able to collect the money. To prevent stolen credit cards from being used to purchase goods, you can install an electronic credit authorizer. This machine checks to see if a credit card is valid. If the card has been reported stolen or if the cardholder has exceeded the credit limit, authorization will not be granted.

Bounced Checks

A **bounced check** is a check that the bank returns to the payee (the person or business to

BE YOUR OWN BOSS

You are the owner and manager of a diner located along a busy interstate highway. You do a good business with travelers passing through as well as locals who eat with you regularly. Recently, there have been several robberies during operating hours in nearby businesses. Your local customers are beginning to get a little scared about coming to your business. Outline a plan to minimize your risk of robbery. Include ways to make your customers feel safe.

whom the check is made payable) because the check writer's checking account has insufficient funds to cover the amount. Bounced checks are also called *bad checks*. Preventing losses from bad checks is difficult. To minimize losses, you can establish a policy of accepting checks drawn on in-state banks only. You can also charge a fee if a customer writes a bad check to your business. Asking for identification, such as a driver's license, can help you track down a person who writes you a bad check so that you can collect the money due. If bad checks are a serious problem in your area, you may decide not to accept checks at all.

✓ CHECKPOINT

How can you protect your business from theft?

ASSESSMENT

THINK ABOUT IT

1. What are the categories of business risk? Provide three examples of each.

2. What are some steps that you can take to minimize employee theft?

3. You own a pizza shop. You suspect that one of your delivery people is charging customers more than what they actually owe and keeping the difference. How would you handle this situation?

MAKE ACADEMIC CONNECTIONS

4. **MATH**   At closing, the Old World Café's cash register receipts totaled $884. The cash in the register equaled $534, and the credit card slips equaled $237. How much of the proceeds are not accounted for? What might explain the difference?

5. **COMMUNICATION**   Think about your school as if it were a business. How can your school identify and deal with the risks it faces? Access www.cengage.com/school/entrepreneurship/ideas. Click on *Activities* and open the file *Risk Management Plan*. Print a copy and complete the activity. Share your plan with the class.

Teamwork

Last year, the holiday season profits at Ray's Sporting Goods were reduced significantly because of shoplifting. Form teams and brainstorm ways to approach the problem this year. Put together a proposal containing your recommendations for Ray. Share your recommendations with the rest of the class.

INSURE AGAINST RISKS

Goals
- Identify risks faced by business owners.
- Explain why some business risks are uninsurable.
- Determine the different types of insurance you need for your business.
- Explain how to approach an insurance purchase.

Vocabulary
- premium
- pure risk
- speculative risk
- controllable risk
- uncontrollable risk
- insurable risk

focus on small business

A river runs through it.

Carlos thought he had found the perfect location for his new restaurant. He wanted to have a large outdoor patio with a great view, and this location had exactly what he wanted. The patio looked out over a river, and there were many beautiful shade trees. Carlos decided to talk to the owner of the previous restaurant that had occupied the site. He told Carlos that his restaurant had flourished until the river flooded and caused extensive water damage. The owner made the repairs but was never able to recover financially, so he went out of business. This concerned Carlos and made him wonder if this was really the ideal spot.

Without taking precautions, some businesses may be forced to close.

Photodisc/Getty Images

Work as a Team What do you think Carlos should do? If he decides to locate here, what can he do to protect his investment?

Classification of Risk

As a business owner, you are at risk from more than just criminal activity. A fire could destroy your building. An accident could injure an employee. A broken water pipe could ruin your inventory. One precaution you can take to protect against financial loss is to purchase insurance. A payment made to an insurance company to cover the cost of insurance is a **premium**. It is the price paid to cover a specified risk for a specific period of time.

Business owners face many types of risk. The classifications of risk are based on the result of the risk, controllability of the risk, and insurability of the risk.

Result of the Risk

A **pure risk** presents the chance of loss but no opportunity for gain. If you have a vehicle that is used in your business, every

What are some ways that a jewelry store could control the risks it faces?

did you KNOW?

According to the Bureau of Economic Crisis (BEA), the overall economic impact of Hurricane Katrina was estimated to be about $150 billion, which was the most costly natural disaster in United States history.

time it goes out on the road there is the risk of an accident. If there is an accident, a loss will likely be suffered. However, if an accident is avoided, there is no opportunity for gain.

A speculative risk offers you the chance to gain as well as lose from the event or activity. Investing in the stock market is a good example of a speculative risk. When you invest money, you have the chance to make money if the stock price rises. However, if the stock price falls, you risk the chance of losing money.

Controllability of the Risk

A controllable risk is one that can be reduced or possibly even avoided by actions you take. Installing a security system in your business could lessen the risk of your business being robbed.

An uncontrollable risk is one on which actions have no effect. The weather cannot be controlled, but it can have a tremendous effect on some businesses. If a hurricane hits a resort town, a dramatic decrease in business and loss of profit will result. But if the weather is sunny and warm, tourism will flourish and business owners may make a profit.

Insurability of the Risk

A risk is an insurable risk if it is a pure risk faced by a large number of people and the amount of the loss can be predicted. Buildings that house businesses are susceptible to fire. Nearly all businesses face this risk, and past statistics can help insurance companies predict the amount of loss and percentage of businesses that will suffer fire losses annually. Insurance companies can sell fire insurance to help cover losses. The premiums of all those insured are pooled and used to help those who incur losses.

If there is a risk that a loss will occur and the amount of the loss cannot be predicted, the risk is *uninsurable*. An insurance company would have no way of determining the premiums to charge or the amount of funds to pool to cover unpredictable losses. A business may move to a new location, and customers may not follow. The loss of income that could result cannot be predicted and, thus, is not insurable.

CHECKPOINT

What is the difference between a pure risk and a speculative risk?

Uninsurable Risks

Sometimes things happen in the business world that are not covered by insurance, which can be very costly to a business. Insurance does not cover risks that cannot be reasonably predicted or for which the financial loss to the business cannot be calculated. These risks are tied to economic conditions, consumer demand, competitors' actions, technology changes, local factors, and business operations.

Economic Conditions

Managers must constantly study economic conditions. Changes in economic conditions can result from an increase or decrease in competition, shifts in population, inflation or recession, and government regulations. World events can also result in economic changes. The terrorist acts of September 11, 2001 caused a dramatic downturn in the U.S. economy, resulting in major cutbacks and layoffs by businesses. This decreased the amount of disposable income for many Americans, which resulted in losses for many entrepreneurs. When the economy takes a downward turn, a business must respond quickly by cutting production and expenses.

Consumer Demand

Businesses produce products and services that they think consumers want to buy. Business owners must research consumer needs and wants. If they can predict a change in demand, they may be able to profit by producing and selling a new product or service. However, if consumer demands change suddenly, the company may end up with products in its inventory that it cannot sell.

Competitors' Actions

Business is competitive. As a business owner, you must be aware of your competitors and their actions. A major advertising campaign or a drop in price by your competitors may result in a change in your volume of sales. You must be ready to respond to actions by your competitors to minimize the risk to your business.

Technology Changes

Changes in technology bring about changes in business. As a business owner, you need to stay up to date on technology trends. Evaluate new

How might the actions of one computer manufacturer pose a risk to another computer manufacturer?

Digital Vision/Getty Images

technology and see if it can help your business. Updates to technology can be a major expense but can alternatively provide efficiencies and help you serve customers better. If customers view your business as outdated, you may lose customer loyalty and sales to your competition.

Local Factors

Businesses can suffer due to activities that occur in their local community. If there is an increase in local taxes or a change in local business regulations, it can affect your business. If a local government makes improvements to the infrastructure, such as road or utility improvement, it can help your business in the long term. In the short term, it may result in a loss of business because ongoing construction could cause customers to detour around your business.

Business Operations

The management of a business contributes directly to the success or failure of the business. A business that is poorly managed can have high employee turnover, poor customer service, higher expenses, and other problems. Poorly trained employees can also cause operational problems. Managers and employees must work together to ensure the success of the business.

 CHECKPOINT

Why are some risks uninsurable?

Types of Insurance

Purchasing insurance is one of the best ways you can prepare for the unexpected. There are many options for insurance. You will have to examine the risks you identify and their potential impact on your business to determine if you need to insure against the risk.

Business Insurance

Insurance companies selling business insurance offer policies that combine protection from all major property and liability risks in one package. These coverages are also sold separately. Package policies are created for businesses that generally face the same kind and degree of risk. Large companies might purchase a commercial package policy or customize their policies to meet the special risks they face. Many small and mid-sized businesses purchase a package known as a business owner's policy (BOP), which typically includes the following:

- **Property insurance** This type of insurance provides coverage for damage to buildings and the contents inside the buildings, such as furniture, fixtures, equipment, and merchandise owned by the business.

- **Business interruption insurance**   This type of insurance covers the loss of income resulting from a fire or other catastrophe that disrupts the operation of the business. It can also cover the extra expense of operating out of a temporary location.
- **Liability protection**   This type of insurance covers your company's legal responsibility for the harm it may cause to others as a result of what you and your employees do or fail to do in your business operations. Harm may involve bodily injury or property damage due to defective products, faulty installations, and errors in services provided.

BOPs do not cover auto insurance, workers' compensation, or health and disability insurance. They also do not cover professional liability, which involves claims of negligent actions by business professionals such as doctors. You will need separate insurance policies to cover these items.

Life Insurance

Life insurance is paid in the event of the death of the insured. It is intended to provide financial support for families should the income earner die. A business owner may buy life insurance so that his or her heirs have enough money to continue the business.

Other Kinds of Insurance

Other types of insurance that you may want to purchase include flood, crime, and renter's insurance. Flood protection is not standard with property insurance, so you may have to purchase it separately. Crime insurance protects against losses resulting from crime, such as robbery, computer fraud, or employee theft. Renter's insurance covers the contents owned by the renter inside the leased space. The actual owner of the building would purchase insurance for the building. Depending on your business and its location, you may or may not decide to purchase these additional kinds of protection.

 CHECKPOINT

What types of insurance can you purchase for your business?

Buy Insurance

Buying insurance can be complicated. Is it possible to have too much or too little insurance? A good insurance agent can help you make decisions about insurance coverage.

Choose an Insurance Agent

Insurance is sold by agents. An agent can be independent and represent many different insurance companies or work for a single insurance company. Before selecting an insurance provider, talk to an agent who represents more than one insurer or ask representatives of several different companies to talk with you about their policies.

The market for insurance is competitive, so many agents will be eager to sell you insurance. To get the best price, contact a few agents and compare prices and policies. Then consider how you feel about the agents. Remember that the person who sells you the policy will be involved in processing your claim should you ever need to collect on your policy. It is therefore important to choose someone whom you trust. You may already have an agent you trust with your car insurance or other types of insurance. That agent can be a good starting point in your research.

Determine How Much Coverage You Need

To determine the kinds and amounts of coverage you need, start by making a list of the property you own. Include equipment, inventory, vehicles, and other significant assets, and put a value next to each. Then think about the kinds of risk you would like to insure against. If, for example, your business is located near a river, you may want to purchase flood insurance. If you live in a low-crime area, you may decide against insurance that covers break-ins. Understand, however, the implications of not having insurance if something should happen.

The next step is determining how much coverage you need. Be sure you have enough insurance to cover any and all debts you may have incurred while starting your business. Li-Li Tang, owner of Computer Systems, has a $50,000 bank loan on her business as well as two small loans

what went *wrong?*

GOODBYE, GORGEOUS!

Edie opened her beauty salon "Hello, Gorgeous!" by taking out a $40,000 loan to help pay for the renovations and equipment she needed. She had two hair stylists working in the salon as contract employees. They paid her monthly rent to use space in the salon. The combined rent they were paying helped cover about 50 percent of the monthly operating expenses.

Edie took out a business owner's insurance policy for $20,000 worth of coverage. Edie was making enough money to pay her monthly expenses, but not enough to save at this point. After six months of being in business, there was a fire in the salon. Hello, Gorgeous! was completely destroyed. The cause of the fire was a curling iron that Edie left on over the weekend.

Edie still owed over $35,000 on the business loan she obtained. Her contracted employees immediately moved to another salon. Suddenly, Edie was all alone without any income or savings and not enough insurance to cover her loan. She was forced to close Hello, Gorgeous! and take a job working at another salon to pay off her debt.

THINK CRITICALLY

1. Do you think Edie was prepared to deal with business risks?

2. What mistake did Edie make when purchasing insurance?

Don't trim costs by buying less insurance coverage than you need.

for $5,000 each. She wants to get at least $60,000 worth of property insurance to cover these outstanding debts in the event of a problem.

Insurance agents earn commissions on the amount of coverage they sell. To make sure you need all the coverage your agent suggests, talk to other business owners in your area or counselors from SCORE or the SBA.

CHECKPOINT

How can you determine how much insurance you need?

12.2 ASSESSMENT

THINK ABOUT IT

1. What factors must be considered when classifying risks?

2. Provide three examples of risks that are uninsurable.

3. Tim Stanton has just opened a surf shop on the beach in South Florida. He has purchased property insurance to cover possible losses against his building, fixtures, equipment, merchandise, and other assets. Against what additional risks should he consider insuring his business?

4. What factors should you consider when choosing an insurance agent?

MAKE ACADEMIC CONNECTIONS

5. **MATH** You have taken out a loan for $50,000 to start your business. As a condition of the loan, your bank requires you to carry property insurance for at least the amount of the loan. Your property is valued at a total of $100,000. Your agent recommends you carry property insurance covering at least 80 percent of your property's value. If annual insurance premiums are $15 per $1,000 of coverage, how much will you pay for insurance to satisfy your bank loan requirement? How much will you pay if you follow your agent's recommendation?

6. **COMMUNICATION** You have just opened an insurance agency that specializes in insuring businesses. Write a sales letter to prospective customers introducing yourself and your services.

Teamwork

Choose a partner. One partner should assume the role of an entrepreneur who just took out a loan to open a roller skating rink. The other should play the role of an insurance agent who must educate the new owner about the types of insurance available. Working together, use the Internet and other resources to research information about the types of insurance a skating rink should carry. Then role-play the conversation between the insurance agent and the business owner.

OTHER RISKS

Goals

- Identify risks associated with credit.
- Explain how to manage risks at work.
- Describe strategies to reduce the risks of doing business internationally.

Vocabulary

- trade credit
- consumer credit
- Federal Employees' Compensation Act (FECA)
- exchange rate

focus on small business

Risks are everywhere!

Dale realized that there were many risks he would face as the business owner of a new sporting goods store. He called his friend Monica for some advice. Monica had been in business for almost two years and had gained valuable business experience.

"Dale, it's good that you came to me," Monica replied. "I've got lots of information for you. I know you have learned about insurable and uninsurable risks, but there are some hidden risks you might not think about. I thought I could increase sales and provide customers a convenient service by offering them a store credit account, but you wouldn't believe how many people never paid the first bill! Then my maintenance employee fell off a ladder while painting. He had to spend two weeks in the hospital. I could go on and on."

"Yes, Monica, I think you have given me plenty to think about. There are many more risks to consider than I was aware of!" Dale replied.

Beware of hidden risks.

Photodisc/Getty Images

Work as a Team What do you think Dale can learn from Monica's experiences? What can Dale do to minimize the risks Monica mentioned?

Risks of Credit

As a business begins operation, there will be costs that will be too expensive for the entrepreneur to pay all at once. Credit makes it possible for the entrepreneur to make these costly purchases. The business owner will also have to make decisions about extending credit to customers. When a business extends credit to customers, it is entering into a voluntarily created debtor-creditor relationship. For example, when a person purchases an appliance and finances the cost, the business and purchaser now have a debtor-creditor

Why would a business offer a credit card if it risks not being paid?

relationship. Examples of voluntarily created debtor-creditor relationships include loans of all types, credit lines, and the use of credit cards. Involuntarily created debtor-creditor relationships also exist. For example, if the delivery driver of a small business is at fault in a traffic accident and injures someone, the business can be required to compensate the injured person. These types of risks can be minimized through insurance, however.

Debtor-creditor relationships that involve extending credit can help increase a business's sales. However, a business will need to decide if extending credit will result in an overall increase in income. Although credit is useful to a business when buying or selling, there are risks involved. It is important for you as an entrepreneur to understand these risks.

Types of Credit

Credit can be categorized according to whom the credit is offered. Like bank loans, the credit a business offers its customers can be secured or unsecured.

TRADE CREDIT   When one business allows another business to buy now and pay later, it is offering trade credit. Many purchases a business owner will make from other businesses will be made with trade credit. The negotiated price of products purchased on trade credit will often be higher than the cash price. This is necessary because there is a lapse of time that occurs from when the sale is negotiated to when the products are actually delivered and the supplier is paid. Because of this delay in receiving payment, the supplier charges a higher price. As the business owner, you will need to be sure that you have the money to cover your expenses when they are due in order to protect your credit record.

On March 29, Raul Gomez places an order with Bear Creek Embroidery for three-dozen golf shirts with his company logo embroidered on them. On April 1, Bear Creek Embroidery negotiates the purchase of three-dozen shirts from Alternative Apparel on credit. The shirts are delivered to Bear Creek on April 15. Two weeks later, Bear Creek ships the shirts with the logos to Raul. It takes one week for the shirts to arrive and one week for Raul to process and pay Bear Creek's invoice.

The trade credit that Alternative Apparel extends to Bear Creek allows 60 days for payment. This enables Bear Creek to receive the shirts, add the logo, ship the shirts, and receive payment from Raul in time to send payment to Alternative Apparel.

Why do many businesses offer installment loans on certain products, such as appliances?

CONSUMER CREDIT

When a retail business allows its customers to buy merchandise now and pay for it later, it is offering consumer credit. Consumer credit is offered in two basic forms: loans and credit cards. A loan gives the individual a lump sum of money to spend and pay back over time with interest. If a loan is secured, it is backed by something of value that can be taken and sold if the loan is not repaid. One type of secured loan offered by retail establishments is an *installment loan* that is paid back with interest in equal monthly amounts over a specified period of time. Many cars and home appliances are financed with installment loans, with the financed item serving as the collateral.

An unsecured loan is granted based on the credit history of the individual. This type of loan is not backed by collateral. Most credit cards are considered unsecured loans. When a business offers its own credit card to customers, it will not receive payment for a month or more after the sale is made. Therefore, the business will need to make other arrangements to ensure it has money to cover expenses associated with the sale of the merchandise. If the customer does not pay, then the business owner can attempt to collect the money or take back the goods that were purchased.

Collection difficulties are one reason a business chooses to accept credit cards that are issued by banks or credit card companies, such as Visa, Discover, or MasterCard. The credit card company will pay the business for the amount of the purchase. The business is charged a fee by the credit card company that is a percentage of total credit sales. The credit card company is then responsible for collecting the amount charged from the customer.

If Raul Gomez offers a credit card to his customers, then Raul is responsible for collecting payment from the customer. However, if the customer pays with a Discover card, Raul gets his money from Discover, and Discover bears the burden of collecting payment from the customer.

Credit Policies

Once an entrepreneur decides to offer credit, policies must be established to help reduce risks. Policies should specify to whom credit will be extended, what products may be purchased on credit, and what the terms of the credit will be. The terms include the amount of credit, the rate of interest charged, and the length of time before payment is required.

It will be very important for the entrepreneur to determine what type of customer will be approved for credit. Most businesses offering credit cards have customers complete a credit application to determine whether they are *creditworthy*, or able to pay. Some things to consider in determining who is creditworthy include the following:

- Previous credit history
- Employment record
- Assets owned
- Money available for making payments (checking and savings accounts)
- Financial references

Even though a business is careful about deciding which customers are creditworthy, there is still the risk that some customers will not pay their account balances, resulting in *uncollectible accounts*. If credit is extended to individuals who are not able to pay, the business loses all the money invested in the product. If the product is recovered, money will still be lost because used merchandise cannot be resold at the original selling price.

Businesses and credit card companies usually charge the customer interest on the balance due to cover the cost of the credit service. When accounts are paid on time, the interest is income for the business. However, uncollectible accounts are an expense to the business and decrease net income. Collection procedures must be established and followed carefully. This will ensure that customers are billed on time. Procedures should state how to handle customers who do not pay on time or do not pay at all.

CHECKPOINT

How can a business owner reduce the risks of offering credit?

Risks on the Job

Different occupations have different risks associated with them. Due to the nature of the work that is performed, some workplaces are considered to be dangerous. Some of the most dangerous occupations in America include timber cutters and loggers, commercial pilots, construction and iron workers, trash collectors, farmers and ranchers, roofers, electrical power line installers, and cab drivers. Other occupations, although not classified as dangerous, do have risks associated with them. Individuals who work in hospitals can be exposed to viruses and bacteria that can cause disease or infection. Night clerks can be a target for a robbery. Even using a computer for long stretches of time can cause injury. *Repetitive stress injuries* result from performing the same activity repeatedly for long periods of time. They can be very painful and cause disabling injuries. With some exceptions, any harm suffered by employees at the workplace is considered to be a work-related injury.

Federal Employees' Compensation Act

The **Federal Employees' Compensation Act (FECA)** is a law that provides benefits to employees who have suffered work-related injuries or occupational diseases. These benefits include payment of medical expenses and compensation for lost wages. The FECA also provides for payment of benefits to dependents of employees who die from work-related injuries or diseases.

Employers are required by law to carry insurance to protect against these risks. This insurance is called workers' compensation. The expense for this insurance is entirely the employer's responsibility. No part of this insurance expense is paid by an employee.

Workers' Compensation

Workers' compensation laws vary from state to state but generally provide for the payment of medical bills, a percentage of lost wages, and vocational retraining if an employee is unable to resume his or her former job. Workers' compensation will also pay a death benefit to compensate survivors if an on-the-job injury results in the death of a worker.

Why are employers responsible for carrying insurance on their employees?

Once employees accept workers' compensation benefits, they cannot sue their employer unless there is proof that the employer knew about the unsafe condition causing the accident and did not do anything to fix it.

In some states, small businesses are exempt from workers' compensation requirements, and employees working for them are not covered. Also, business owners, independent contractors, occasional workers, domestic workers in private homes, agricultural workers, and unpaid volunteers are not covered by workers' compensation in some states.

Employers must notify employees of their right to compensation for work-related injuries and diseases. Employees must also be notified that they cannot be fired for filing a claim and that workers' compensation premiums cannot be deducted from their pay. Most employers display a poster in the workplace containing this information.

COVERAGE PROVIDED Medical expenses for employees injured on the job should be covered by workers' compensation. If an employee is out of work for more than a few days, a percentage

How does workers' compensation benefit employees?

of lost wages may also be covered. Lost wage payments are usually about two-thirds of the employee's income, not to exceed state limits. If an employee is left permanently disabled from a work-related injury, the employee may be eligible for a lump-sum payment or long-term benefits. This depends on whether the employee can perform other work that pays as well as the former position. If a worker cannot earn as much as before the injury, the worker may be eligible for a long-term payment. If the worker is completely and permanently disabled, the worker may be eligible for social security benefits.

INJURIES NOT COVERED   Although laws vary from state to state, generally, the following injuries would not be covered by workers' compensation insurance:

- Injuries individuals afflict on themselves
- Injuries suffered under the influence of alcohol or illegal drugs
- Injuries suffered during a fight that the injured employee started
- Injuries suffered while disobeying orders or violating employer policy
- Injuries suffered while committing a crime
- Injuries suffered while not on the job

FILING A CLAIM   There are certain steps that must be followed in the event of an injury or illness at the workplace. Be sure that you are familiar with these steps so that you know what you and your employee should do in the event of an accident at your business.

1. **The injured employee must notify the employer.** The employer must be notified immediately after the accident. Check your state law to determine the time limit that employees have for reporting an accident or illness.
2. **The employee must follow doctor's orders.** If the employee does not follow the doctor's orders, it could be grounds for denying workers' compensation coverage. The doctor should put any special requirements for the employee in writing. Be sure the employee goes to the doctor that handles the workers' compensation cases for your business.

3. **The employee must file the claim.** The employer must provide the employee with the proper forms, but it is the employee's responsibility to file the claim.

CHECKPOINT

What is the purpose of workers' compensation insurance?

Risks in International Business

When you start working with businesses and customers in other countries, there are risks that you may face. The stability of the economic system in other countries depends on the government's management of its economy. An unstable government can negatively impact businesses within its borders. It can also lead to difficulties for foreign companies doing business there. The cultural and social environments of these countries will also have a great influence on your international business activities. Doing business in a foreign country can present challenges for several reasons.

1. **You may not speak the language of the countries you are targeting.** If you cannot communicate with buyers or consumers, how can you sell your service or product? Misunderstandings are likely to occur.

2. **You may not be familiar with the laws, customs, and cultures of foreign countries.** In the United States, looking directly at people while speaking to them is a sign of respect. In some other countries, it is a sign of disrespect. If you fail to recognize these

When doing business in another country, why should you learn about its customs and culture?

differences, you risk offending those with whom you are trying to do business.

3. **You may have to change your products or services to meet the needs of global trade.** Consumers abroad have different needs and wants than do consumers in the United States. What sells in this country will not necessarily appeal to foreign customers. You will need to consider this when you sell products or services in other countries.

4. **You will have to deal with different currency systems.** The amount of one country's currency that can be traded for one unit of currency in another country is the **exchange rate**. These rates change daily depending on the country's economic and political stability. The value of currency is affected by supply and demand. If a country's money is believed to have a solid value, people will accept it as payment, and its value will increase. However, if a country is having financial difficulties, its currency will lose value compared to the currency of other countries.

famous entrepreneur

Why do you think creativity is an important attribute for entrepreneurs?

© Entertainment Press, 2010/ Used under license from Shutterstock.com

MARY J. BLIGE Having sold over 65 million records worldwide, Mary J. Blige is considered one of the greatest singers of all time. She has received nine Grammy Awards. In addition to her achievements as a singer, she is also making her mark in the business world.

Although her singing career has been extensive and includes albums, tours, and performances, she also has produced and written songs and has worked with artists like Sean "Puffy" Combs, her first manager. She has performed duets with a wide range of musicians including Ludacris (a rapper) and Andrea Bocelli (a classical music artist). In addition to singing, she has acted on the stage, screen, and television as well as in a web cartoon!

Mary was 17 when she recorded a song at a recording booth in the Galleria Mall in White Plains, New York. The recording passed through several hands before it reached the president and CEO of Uptown Records, Andre Harrell. He met with Blige and signed her to the label in 1989. She was the youngest and first female artist of the company.

In 2004, Blige began her own record label, Matriarch Records. In 2010, she launched her first perfume, My Life, on the Home Shopping Network (HSN) and an eyewear line, Melodies. She has had endorsement contracts with Reebok, Air Jordan, and many other businesses. Mary has also established the foundation FFAWN (Foundation for the Advancement of Women Now), which inspires women to reach their individual potential.

THINK CRITICALLY

What risks has Mary J. Blige taken to further her career?

5. **Your travel and shipping expenses may be high.** International flights can be very expensive. Sending or receiving packages overseas can also be costly.

Strategies for Dealing with International Markets

If you decide to conduct business globally, you should develop a plan that outlines your goals and identifies your risks. Analyze the foreign target market and perform research to learn more about the risks of doing business abroad.

Strategies recommended for dealing with the risks of international business include the following:

Why is it important to create a strategy for conducting business internationally?

1. **Seek government assistance to answer your questions about international business.** Government agencies such as the Small Business Administration and the International Trade Administration can provide counseling, locate buyers overseas, and promote U.S. products and services.

2. **Conduct business in many different countries.** If you are doing business in only one country and something happens in that country, such as political upheaval, you run the risk of losing all sales and profits.

3. **Work with local business partners.** If you partner with a company that is located in the country you are targeting, your company will be better received by locals in that country.

4. **Comply with international labor standards.** Many Americans feel that the United States should require compliance with international labor standards as part of international trade agreements. Americans consider unfair labor practices in other countries morally wrong and believe that low labor standards create unfair competition for U.S. labor. Many also believe that the United States should not allow products to be imported when they have been produced under conditions that violate international labor standards. A strong majority of Americans have indicated they would pay higher prices for products to ensure that the products are not manufactured in substandard conditions.

5. **Employ local management.** If you hire managers from the country you are targeting, they will have a better understanding of the cultural and political scene of the country. They will be able to assist you in any product modifications or changes in business practices you need to make to work with the foreign market. Local management also can assist with labor issues such as how much to

pay employees, whether or not to work with a labor union, how to establish trust with employees, and how to deal with the ethical issues of the country.

6. **Learn about the other country's culture.** Research the country's cultural customs and beliefs. Develop cultural sensitivity.

 CHECKPOINT

What are some of the challenges of competing internationally?

12.3 ASSESSMENT

THINK ABOUT IT

1. What are the risks involved in using and extending credit?

2. Why are some workplace injuries not covered by workers' compensation insurance?

3. What are some strategies you can use to reduce the risks involved with international business?

MAKE ACADEMIC CONNECTIONS

4. **COMMUNICATION** Working with a partner, role-play situations in which voluntary debtor-creditor relationships are created.

5. **MANAGEMENT** You are planning to open a retail store that will sell home appliances and furnishings. Decide what type of consumer credit you will offer and develop a credit policy. Present your decisions to the class.

6. **RESEARCH** Choose three countries with different currency systems. Research online the exchange rate for each country's currency in relation to the U.S. dollar. Prepare a chart showing how they compare. Research the reasons why the value of the currency is such in relation to the U.S. dollar. Write a summary explaining what factors influence the exchange rates.

Teamwork

Many employers think workers abuse workers' compensation insurance. They may hire people to investigate workers who are on medical leave to determine if they are conducting themselves in any way that is not consistent with the injuries they have claimed. Suppose a worker claims he has hurt his back and cannot work. If he is seen lifting heavy objects or climbing a ladder at his home, then the employer may have a case for discontinuing the employee's workers' compensation claim. Working with teammates, discuss whether you think it is ethical for employers to spy on employees. What can be done to keep workers from abusing workers' compensation insurance?

Respect Cultural Diversity

In today's global economy, you will come in contact with all kinds of people. Many of these people will be from cultures different from your own. You may work with people of different cultures. You may also buy from and sell to people of different cultures. As an entrepreneur, you need to appreciate different cultures for the following reasons:

- You need to be comfortable with your customers. If you are open to other cultures, you can attract more customers.

- People from different cultures may have different needs and wants. Understanding these can help you market your business more effectively.

How can you develop good relationships with everyone you do business with? There are at least five things you can do to enhance these relationships:

1. **Avoid stereotyping people.** Don't assume that all people from a particular ethnic or cultural group hold the same values and opinions, behave the same way, or like the same things.

2. **Focus on similarities rather than differences.** Most people, regardless of their culture, want the same things in life.

3. **Learn about different cultures.** Learning about a different culture will make you more comfortable around people from that culture. Learn how people in a different culture live and work.

4. **Make friends with someone from a different culture.** The friendship will help you begin to appreciate other cultures.

5. **Try to understand and identify with other people's feelings.** Try to see the world through the eyes of people from different cultures. Try to understand cultural views that are different from your own.

Try It Out

Before conducting business in another country, you will have to answer many questions. Will your product sell well in another country or will you have to make modifications to it? What aspects of the country's culture could affect your business? What is the value of the foreign currency in relation to the U.S. currency? Access www.cengage .com/school/ entrepreneurship/ ideas. Click on *Activities* and open the file *Competing in the Global Economy*. Print a copy and complete the activity.

© Yuri Arcurs, 2010/ Used under license from Shutterstock.com

SUMMARY

12.1 Business Risks

1. To prepare for risks, you should (1) determine what can go wrong, (2) develop a plan, and (3) communicate your plan to employees and first responders.

2. Theft is one of the biggest risks faced by business owners. Types of theft include shoplifting, employee theft, robbery, credit card fraud, and bounced checks. Business owners can take precautions to prevent these risks.

12.2 Insure Against Risks

3. Classifications of risk faced by businesses are based on the result of the risk (pure or speculative), controllability of the risk (controllable or uncontrollable), and the insurability of the risk (insurable or uninsurable).

4. Insurance does not cover risks that cannot be reasonably predicted or risks in which the financial loss cannot be calculated. These risks are tied to economic conditions, consumer demand, competitors' actions, technology changes, local factors, and business operations.

5. You will have to analyze the risks your business faces to determine the types of insurance you should purchase. A typical business owner's policy (BOP) covers property damage, business interruption, and liability. Depending on your situation, you may also want to purchase life, flood, crime, or renter's insurance.

6. Before committing to an insurance purchase, compare prices and policies and seek advice from experienced business owners.

12.3 Other Risks

7. Although useful to you as a business owner and to your customers, credit has risks associated with its use. You must analyze the potential risks of credit to determine if it is wise for you to use and/or extend it.

8. Workers' compensation insurance covers employees' medical expenses and lost wages incurred as a result of workplace injuries and occupational illnesses.

9. To reduce international business risks, companies should seek government assistance, conduct business in many countries, involve local business partners, comply with international labor standards, employ local management, and learn about the culture.

what do you know now?

Read *Ideas in Action* on page 345 again. Then answer the questions a second time. Have your responses changed? If so, how have they changed?

VOCABULARY BUILDER

Match each statement with the term that best defines it. Some terms may not be used.

1. The possibility of some kind of loss
2. Taking action to prevent or reduce the possibility of loss to your business
3. Looking at all aspects of your business and determining the risks you face
4. The act of knowingly taking items from a business without paying
5. A payment to cover the cost of insurance
6. A risk that presents the chance of loss but no opportunity for gain
7. A risk on which actions have no effect
8. A pure risk faced by a large number of people and for which the amount of loss can be predicted
9. When one business allows another business to buy now and pay later
10. A law that provides for benefits to employees who have suffered work-related injuries or occupational diseases
11. A risk that can be reduced or possibly even avoided by actions you take
12. A risk that presents the chance to gain as well as lose from an event or activity

a. bounced check
b. consumer credit
c. controllable risk
d. exchange rate
e. Federal Employees' Compensation Act (FECA)
f. insurable risk
g. premium
h. pure risk
i. risk
j. risk assessment
k. risk management
l. shoplifting
m. speculative risk
n. trade credit
o. uncontrollable risk

REVIEW YOUR KNOWLEDGE

13. **True or False**   Businesses can avoid all possible risks by purchasing insurance.
14. Conducting a risk assessment involves all of the following actions *except*
    a. learn the risks your business faces
    b. decide how risks will affect your business
    c. prioritize the risks by the impact they will have on your business
    d. communicate your plan
15. **True or False**   Credit card fraud is an example of an economic risk.
16. If there is a risk that a loss will occur and the amount of the loss cannot be predicted, the risk is __?__.
17. **True or False**   A credit card offered by a home furnishings center is an example of an installment loan.
18. Which of the following is *not* a risk associated with doing business in another country?
    a. language barriers
    b. different laws, customs, and cultures
    c. high travel and shipping costs
    d. all of the above are risks
19. A __?__ plan will enable you to get back to business as quickly as possible after a disaster and help you continue to meet customer needs.
20. Which of the following types of insurance would cover the cost to repair your office building if it were damaged by fire?
    a. property insurance
    b. business interruption insurance
    c. liability protection
    d. life insurance

21. A change in the way websites are accessed that requires new, expensive computer equipment is an example of a risk related to
    a. economic conditions
    b. consumer demand
    c. competitors' actions
    d. technology changes
22. Which of the following types of insurance would cover losses your business incurred as a result of selling a faulty product that injured someone?
    a. property insurance
    b. business interruption insurance
    c. liability protection
    d. life insurance
23. **True or False**   A speculative risk is classified as uninsurable.
24. **True or False**   The credit that a retail business extends to customers is called trade credit because they are trading money for goods.
25. **True or False**   When you extend credit to a customer, you are guaranteed that you will receive payment for the goods or services sold.
26. **True or False**   All injuries that occur at work are covered by workers' compensation insurance.
27. Which of the following is *not* a strategy for dealing with a global risk?
    a. conduct business in only one country to minimize the risk
    b. seek government assistance
    c. work with local business partners
    d. employ local management
28. **True or False**   If you are leasing a building for your business, you do not need to carry renter's insurance because the owner of the building is required to carry insurance.

APPLY WHAT YOU LEARNED

29. You plan to open a horseback riding training center with a horse boarding facility. Make a chart and list the types of risk you will face. Categorize the risks as human, natural, or economic. Classify risks as controllable or uncontrollable and insurable or uninsurable. If the risk is insurable, list the type of insurance that you could purchase to protect against the risk.
30. Make a list of accidents and injuries that workers in a hospital could experience. Write "yes" next to the accidents and injuries that would be covered by workers' compensation insurance. Write "no" next to those that would not be covered.
31. You own a clothing boutique and have recently expanded into catalog sales. Many of your products will be sold abroad. As your business expands, you will need additional manufacturing sources. You are looking in other countries. Explain the labor issues that will be of concern to you.

32. **MATH**   You are trying to decide whether to purchase security equipment for your business or hire a security guard. You research the cost of the security equipment you will need and find that it will cost $15,000 and has a useful life of 3 years. You have looked into hiring a security guard through an agency and find that it will cost you $50 per hour to hire a guard for 3 hours per day. Calculate and compare the annual cost of each and decide which will be the most cost-effective for your business.

33. **COMMUNICATION**   Interview a business owner in your community to find out what type of controls the owner has in place for handling cash to minimize losses due to theft. Prepare a presentation and share your findings with the class.

What Would YOU Do?

Your business is growing and you have recently hired five new employees. Your business has been exempt from paying workers' compensation insurance premiums, but with the addition of new employees, you will no longer be exempt. You do not agree with the workers' compensation program because of the added expense to your business. You are thinking about not paying the premiums. Would this be fair to your employees? What would happen if one of your employees had a serious injury on the job and you did not have workers' compensation insurance?

build your BUSINESS PLAN PROJECT

This activity will help you continue with the development of a business plan by outlining your risk management strategy.

1. Identify risks faced by your business and establish a plan for dealing with them. Describe how the business will prevent shoplifting, employee theft, robberies, credit card fraud, and bad checks. Research how much it will cost to buy special security equipment or hire a guard. Present your proposal to the class. Prepare to defend your strategies.

2. Contact an insurance agent to obtain information on insuring your business. What types of insurance do you need? How much coverage should you buy?

3. Research workers' compensation laws for your state. Explain how you will meet your responsibilities under these laws.

4. What are some other cultures you will be exposed to in your business? Research one of these cultures and find out information about the lifestyle and business practices associated with this culture. What cultural issues will affect your business? How will you market your product or service to this and other cultures?

Planning a Career in
INSURANCE

Finance

"After returning from the grocery, our neighbor came home to a big mess. The laundry he had tossed into the machine prior to leaving the house had been off-balance. During the spin cycle, the water hose became loose and caused a huge water leak. Although he did his best to dry out the floors, he ultimately had to replace the hardwood flooring in the rooms bordering the laundry room. Fortunately his homeowner's insurance covered the costs."

How do individuals and businesses protect their assets from unexpected mishaps that result in financial expenses? How is insurance coverage matched to particular levels of need?

Insurance agents sell and service insurance policies. The agent is an intermediary between the insurance provider and the insurance buyer. Agents are responsible for explaining policies to clients and helping them obtain appropriate coverage for specific situations.

Employment Outlook
- Slower than average growth is anticipated.
- As insurance is a basic societal requirement, there will be a steady need for agents.
- Agents who utilize both Internet efficiencies and automated claims processing should be able to expand their client base.

Job Titles
- Career Agent
- Financial Services Agent
- Licensed Sales Professional
- Agency Specialist
- Property & Casualty Underwriter
- Strategy Director, Protection Business

Needed Education/Skills
- As insurance policies are complex, a Bachelor's degree with a business or mathematics focus is often required.
- A state license is required to sell insurance.
- Professional certification is available to demonstrate competency in specialized areas.
- Continuing education is often mandatory.

What's it like to work in Insurance? Narelle, an independent insurance agent, is comparing automotive insurance policies from a variety of policy providers for her new client—a young driver. As an independent agent, Narelle matches the needs of her clients to the policies that provide the best combination of rates and coverage. Narelle knows that by providing her young client with economical, effective coverage as well as courteous service, she can probably secure him as a new long-term client.

After lunch, Narelle finishes the handouts she is preparing for tomorrow's lunch seminar at a local Small Business Administration meeting. She is planning to discuss the appropriate types of coverage for each stage of business development. Narelle has learned that participation in professional meetings often results in valuable sales leads. As an independent agent, finding new clients is essential to her ongoing success.

What about you? Would you like to help individuals and businesses identify their risks and help them obtain the appropriate insurance coverage to protect their assets?

Lincoln is a national award-winning city that takes great pride in its landscaping. Beautiful Spaces is a landscaping company owned by one of the Lincoln city council members (Chris). Beautiful Spaces has contracted with Lincoln for the past several years to plant, mow, water, and maintain the medians. The company has a $400,000 annual contract for its landscaping services.

Lincoln residents have not been happy with the work performed by Beautiful Spaces. The medians are not maintained, and many projects are incomplete. Beautiful Spaces has blamed its delays on bad weather, a low supply of water, and a shortage of flowering plants.

You are the city manager for Lincoln. You must meet with Chris to let him know that the city will not honor the contract with Beautiful Spaces because the company has not fulfilled its commitment. You must also work out an acceptable financial agreement that takes into account the inadequate and incomplete work. Based on the schedule outlined in the contract, Beautiful Spaces should have completed the project 60 days ago. The contract states that a $100 fine will be charged for each day of incompletion. Beautiful Spaces has been paid $150,000 for completion of one-fourth of the total project. You will meet with Chris to discuss an acceptable agreement for ending the contract and paying the city fines for incomplete work. You have ten minutes to determine your plan of action and ten minutes to explain your plan to the owner of Beautiful Spaces. Chris (the judge) can ask questions about your plan of action following your presentation.

Performance Indicators

- Describe legal issues affecting businesses
- Describe the nature of legally binding contracts
- Demonstrate responsible behavior
- Demonstrate honesty and integrity
- Explain business ethics in product/service management

Go to the DECA website for more detailed information.

THINK CRITICALLY

1. What is the conflict of interest in this case?
2. Why should Beautiful Spaces pay the city of Lincoln?
3. What compromise could the city propose to reduce the fines?
4. How can the city avoid this situation in the future?

www.deca.org

©Stephen Coburn/Shutterstock.com

CHAPTER 13

Management for the Future

13.1 Growth Strategies

13.2 Ethical and Social Issues

13.3 Global Trends and Opportunities

www.cengage.com/school/entrepreneurship/ideas

376

Reaching for the Stars

Shayna Turk has always had a deep love for musical theater. From the age of five, she spent her summers singing and dancing at drama camp. When her younger sister, Talia, was old enough to join camp, Shayna knew that Talia was more talented than most of the older campers. Unfortunately, Talia was not getting the scenes she deserved because it was a camper's age that determined who would get what part. This drove Shayna to start a drama camp of her own where everyone would receive a part.

Shayna Turk, Director and Founder of Shayna Turk's Academy of Rising Stars (STARS)

Shayna's grandparents converted their garage into an open space with a small stage. Although the space did not have the bright lights and big sound system of the drama camp, it was the perfect place to start her pursuit, Shayna Turk's Academy of Rising Stars (STARS). Then 11-year-old Shayna recruited her sister and 12 of her friends to star in her directorial debut of "You Are a Good Man, Charlie Brown." Shayna thought the lines would be easy for her young campers to learn, and the royalties were inexpensive. She charged each camper $25 for the four-week camp and held a production of the show for family and friends on the final day. "I thought it was going to be a one-time thing, but after seeing the parents fall in love with the production, I knew I had to do it again!" Shayna said.

Twelve productions later, STARS has become a thriving business. She now charges campers $400 per session, giving her enough money to hire a small staff, and puts on four performances of each play. She also believes it is her social responsibility to give back to the community by raising money for her favorite charity, Music for the Heart Foundation. The parents of one of her campers had another child with congenital heart disease, so they started the charity to help other children around the world afford proper surgeries. Shayna and her camp have raised enough money to save the lives of six children.

Because of Shayna's dedication to STARS and the Music for the Heart Foundation, she was named NFIB/VISA's "Young Entrepreneur of the Year." Even though Shayna will soon be starting college at the University of Southern California, she hopes to continue with the business and even expand by adding an additional camp. Although STARS now has multiple stages and a great sound system and lighting, Shayna never wants the business to get too big and lose its personal touch.

Photo courtesy of Shayna Turk

what do you know?

1. Why did Shayna want to start a drama camp of her own?
2. How has Shayna's business, STARS, expanded from the first production?
3. Why is it important for a business to be socially responsible and ethical?

GROWTH STRATEGIES

Goals

- Determine when a business is ready to expand.
- Explain the importance of planning for growth.
- Identify and describe three growth strategies.
- List and describe product life cycle stages and steps involved in product development.

Vocabulary

- market penetration
- market development
- product life cycle
- prototype

focus on small business

Know when to grow.

Mary Ardapple, owner of Apple's Bakery in Peoria, Illinois, has moved her business three times since she opened it in 1989. Her menu has expanded and now has three times its original offerings. She even makes her baked goods available to those outside the Peoria area through an online store. Mary is not content to conduct business as usual and is always looking for new opportunities. Currently, she is planning to add a low-fat line of baked goods to her offerings. Throughout all the moves and expansions, Mary and her team have not forgotten the company's original motto, "Where smiles are made from scratch!"

Business expansion should be carefully planned.

©Denise Kappa/Shutterstock.com

Work as a Team How do you think Mary knew when her business was ready to expand each time? Do you think it is important for Mary and her team to always remember their original motto?

Determine When to Expand

Sooner or later, you will consider expanding your business. Some businesses have difficulty growing. Others expand too quickly. To expand successfully, you will need to determine both when and how to expand. You will also need to control your growth.

Before deciding to grow your business, be sure that all of your operations are functioning well. Unresolved operational issues will only get bigger and cause more problems when the business gets larger. You also need to be sure that you take care of your current customers when you begin growing your business. Remember, they helped you get where you are. You want them to feel comfortable with the changes, knowing that their needs will continue to be met.

Determining when to expand depends on two main factors: the condition of your business and the economic conditions in the market in which your business competes.

Consider the Condition of Your Business

How do you determine when it is time to expand your business? Some of the signs you should look for include the following:

- Your business is recognized by your community and industry.
- Your sales are rising.
- You have a customer base that regularly buys from you.
- You are hiring more employees and now have managers.
- You need more space.

Assess Economic Conditions

If the condition of your business shows that you should expand, you should next analyze the economic climate that controls the business. You should ask the following questions:

- How is the national economy doing? Are people worried about spending money, or are they spending freely?
- What are the economic conditions in your industry or region?
- Have the demographics of your market changed?
- Is demand for your product or service expected to remain strong?
- Does your business face new competition?

 CHECKPOINT

What factors should you consider before deciding to expand your business?

Control Your Growth

Growing rapidly may sound like a great thing for a business, but uncontrolled growth may be just as bad as no growth at all. Businesses that grow too quickly often find that they don't have the resources to support their growth. They can lack money, employees, supplies, and more. As a result, they often overextend themselves. Sometimes they are even forced to go out of business.

To make sure that your business expands successfully, you will have to control its growth. This means you will need to come up with a plan for expansion that includes strategies for the following:

- attaining measurable objectives and goals (examples are reaching sales goals, increasing your customer base, and opening another store)
- hiring managers and supervisors
- financing expansion
- obtaining resources for expansion (capital, equipment, inventory, materials, and supplies)

Choose a Growth Strategy

You can expand your business in various ways. You can get more people to buy your products or services. You can expand into other geographic areas. You can also find new products and services to sell.

Penetrate the Market

Market penetration involves increasing the market share for a product or service within a given market in a given area. You can increase sales by increasing the number of people in your target market who buy from you. If total sales for your target market are $500,000 and your business attracts 5 percent of that market, your sales will be $25,000. If you raise your market share to 15 percent, your sales will be $75,000.

You can increase your market share by doing the following:

- Increase your advertising
- Offer customers special deals, such as frequent-buyer cards, incentives to purchase, and discounts
- Offer superior customer service

Taking these actions will cost you money. You may spend more on advertising or incur the cost of giveaway items. But spending money now will pay off with larger profits in the future if you obtain a larger market share.

Expand Geographically

Geographic expansion occurs when you decide to market your service or product in another town, city, county, state, or country. Sheila Velez owns a business that builds sunrooms in the northern part of her state. To increase sales, Sheila recently began advertising throughout the entire state. She has already received calls from consumers 100 miles away who are interested in her product.

Diversify with New Products or Services

Market development is a strategy for expanding the target market of a business. A business expands its target market by diversifying, which means selling new products or services in addition to what it already offers.

Sue Ann Rader owns a musical instrument store. Three years ago, she added a sheet music department. She reduced the inventory of instruments to make room for the inventory for the new department. Sheet music now contributes 25 percent of her annual profits.

Businesses can fail if they diversify into the wrong areas. Use the following guidelines to make sure that your business diversifies successfully.

- Do not go into areas that you know nothing about.
- Choose a product or service that complements what you already sell.
- Avoid allocating too much capital to new areas before you know if they will be profitable.
- Don't neglect your original product or service line.

Sue Ann would like to open a cafe in her musical instrument store. She would have to make room in her store to do so. Although Sue Ann likes the idea of a cafe, she knows nothing about running one. Her lack of experience and her concern about the effect on her main business convince her not to open the cafe.

CHECKPOINT

What are some ways you can expand your business?

what went *wrong?*

MAKEUP TEST

Sarah-Jane Stevens founded Charisma Cosmetics. Her company targeted professional cosmetics dealers serving makeup artists in the film, TV, and theater industries. Charisma Cosmetics had an excellent reputation as a high-quality manufacturer, a loyal customer base, and a major share of the market. However, competitors were slowly chipping away at Charisma's customer base. To remain competitive, Sarah-Jane rolled out a new brand, Picture-Perfect by Charisma. This brand was specifically designed to be sold in department stores.

The new strategy angered the professional cosmetics dealers who were the core customers of Charisma Cosmetics. Their competitive advantage had been to provide better products that were not available elsewhere. With Charisma's Picture-Perfect brand on the market, they no longer had the same competitive edge.

"We were determined to grow, and we strayed from our root value of 'don't be bigger, be better,'" Sarah-Jane said. Just eight months after getting into the department store market, Sarah-Jane got out. The company ended up losing hundreds of thousands of dollars in developing and marketing the Picture-Perfect brand.

Consider the risks when growing your business.

KULISH VIKTORIIA/Shutterstock.com

THINK CRITICALLY

1. What problems were created by the "Picture-Perfect by Charisma" brand?
2. How might Sarah-Jane have expanded without angering her dealers?

Product Life Cycle and Development

A business must constantly monitor the sales of products and develop new products. Consumer interest in most products will decline over time. A business must keep developing new products in order to maintain a presence in the market.

Stages of a Product Life Cycle

The stages a product goes through from the time it is introduced to when it is no longer sold is called its **product life cycle**. A product goes through four stages in its life cycle: introduction, growth, maturity, and decline. The stage of the life cycle can be determined by the type of competition the product is facing.

INTRODUCTION   The first stage of the product life cycle is the introduction of a new product into the market. At this stage, the product is quite different from existing products, so customers are not aware of it or how it can satisfy their needs. The price may be high during this stage as the company tries to cover development expenses. The competition, if any, for the product at this stage consists of older, established products.

GROWTH   If a product is successful in the introductory phase, it will enter the growth stage as sales begin to increase. The product will be distributed more widely as more consumers start to buy it. Competitors will see the opportunity for sales and introduce their own product. Each competitor's product needs to have different features and options in order to position it in the market as a better product. There will be a wider range of prices for the product during this stage due to competition.

MATURITY   During the maturity stage of the life cycle, sales peak and profits begin to decline. The product is in high demand and many companies offer it, so competition is very intense. Pricing becomes an important factor at this stage since customers view products on the market as being similar. Businesses will offer discounts or sale prices to encourage customers to buy their brand. Companies will make sure their product is easy for customers to find. During the maturity stage, a great deal of money will be spent on promotion because companies want to keep their brand of the product in the minds of customers.

DECLINE   The decline stage occurs when consumers decide that a product is no longer meeting their needs or when they discover new and better products. Sales will begin to drop rapidly, and profits will drop. During this stage, there is little opportunity for product improvement. Since the product is not contributing a profit, no more money will be invested in it. Distribution is cut to only areas where the product is still profitable. Many times the price is cut during the decline stage. Promotion is decreased and targeted specifically to loyal customers in an effort to keep them as long as possible.

New Product Development

In order to stay competitive in the market, a business must develop new products or services to offer to customers. The business wants to find out early in the development process whether the product is likely to be successful before investing too much money in it. It is also important for the business to determine that the product meets an important market need, can be produced efficiently and at a reasonable cost, and will be competitive with other products in the market.

Soft drink companies introduced more new products during 2000–2002 than were introduced during the entire decade of the 1990s. However, during the economic slowdown that began in 2008, the introduction of new products slowed. As the economy recovers, soft drink manufacturers will begin to look at new markets for existing products.

SOFT DRINKS INTRODUCED SINCE 2000			
Drink	Company	Drink	Company
Introduced in 2009		**Introduced in 2002**	
Pepsi Throwback	PepsiCo	Vanilla Coke	Coca-Cola
Mountain Dew Throwback	PepsiCo	Diet Vanilla Coke	Coca-Cola
		Dr Pepper Red Fusion	Dr Pepper/Seven UP
Introduced in 2007		dnL	Dr Pepper/Seven UP
Diet Pepsi Max	PepsiCo	Pepsi Blue	PepsiCo
		Diet Mountain Dew Code Red	PepsiCo
Introduced in 2006		Sobe Mr. Green	PepsiCo
Coca-Cola BlaK	Coca-Cola		
		Introduced in 2001	
Introduced in 2005		Diet Coke with Lemon	Coca-Cola
Coca-Cola Zero	Coca-Cola	Fanta (reintroduced in U.S.)	Coca-Cola
Coca-Cola with Lime	Coca-Cola	Diet Sierra Mist	PepsiCo
Mountain Dew MDX	PepsiCo	Mountain Dew Code Red	PepsiCo
Pepsi Lime	PepsiCo	Mountain Dew AMP	PepsiCo
Introduced in 2004		**Introduced in 2000**	
Diet Coke with Lime	Coca-Cola	Pepsi Twist	PepsiCo
Coca-Cola C2	Coca-Cola	Diet Pepsi Twist	PepsiCo
		Sierra Mist	PepsiCo
Introduced in 2003		Red Flash	Coca-Cola
Mountain Dew Livewire	PepsiCo		

Product development involves the following steps: (1) idea development, (2) idea screening, (3) strategy development, (4) financial analysis, (5) product development and testing, and (6) product marketing.

IDEA DEVELOPMENT   The first, and often the most difficult, step in product development is finding ideas for new products. Employees or customers can generate ideas. Many times salespeople will hear wishes and complaints from customers about what they would like to see and not see in products. If the salesperson shares this information with the development department, it can lead to ideas for new products.

IDEA SCREENING   Once ideas have been developed, they are screened to select the ones that have the greatest chance of being successful. Questions to be answered during the screening process include the following:

- Has a market been identified for the product?
- Is the competition in the market reasonable?
- Are resources available to produce the product?
- Is the product legal and safe?
- Can a quality product be produced at a reasonable cost?

STRATEGY DEVELOPMENT   Once an idea has been determined to be reasonable, the business will create and test a sample marketing strategy. The business performs research to identify the appropriate target market and to be sure that there are customers with adequate income who are looking to satisfy a need that the product meets. Questions asked during this stage include the following:

- What is the likely demand for the product?
- How would the introduction of the product affect existing products? Would the new product take away market share from existing products the company produces?
- Would current customers benefit from the product?
- Would the product enhance the image of the company's overall product mix?

FINANCIAL ANALYSIS   If a new product idea is determined to meet a market need and can be developed, the company will perform a financial analysis. Spreadsheet programs are often used in this step. Costs of production and marketing, sales projections for the target market, and resulting profits are calculated. Questions to be answered at this stage include the following:

- What impact could the new product have on total sales, profits, market share, and return on investment?
- Would the new product affect current employees in any way? For example, would it require people with different skills, the hiring of more people, or a reduction in the size of the workforce?
- What new facilities, if any, would be needed?
- How might competitors respond?
- What is the risk of failure? Is the company willing to take the risk?

PRODUCT DEVELOPMENT AND TESTING   When a manufacturer sees a market opportunity and decides to develop a new product, it makes a **prototype**, which is a full-scale model of a new product. After testing the prototype in the laboratory and making final adjustments,

Why is it necessary to perform a financial analysis when developing a new product?

©StockLite/Shutterstock.com

the company designs the production process, obtains needed equipment and materials, and trains production personnel. The product is then test-marketed in selected areas. If it receives a positive response, the manufacturer places the product into full production. If not, the manufacturer drops it.

PRODUCT MARKETING   Introduction of the product into the target market is the last step in the product development cycle and the first step of the product's life cycle. Before this takes place, many other things must be done. The marketing mix elements must be planned, and there must be an adequate supply of the product on hand to meet the target market's needs.

Once the product has been introduced into the market, the company will have to monitor its life cycle. Many new products fail even though the product development steps have been followed carefully. Products may not match the needs of customers, or customers may not see what differentiates the product from other products on the market. The product may be priced too high or too low, poorly distributed, or improperly promoted.

✔CHECKPOINT

Why must a business be concerned with the life cycle of a product and with new product development?

13.1 ASSESSMENT

THINK ABOUT IT

1. What are the negative consequences, if any, of not allowing your business to grow?

2. What are some ways you can control the growth of your business?

3. List the stages of the product life cycle and provide an example of a product in each stage.

MAKE ACADEMIC CONNECTIONS

4. **MATH**   Tony Balducci owns a deli and sandwich shop. Total sales for his target market are $1.75 million per year. If he attracts 12 percent of the market, what will his sales be? What will sales be if he increases market share to 18 percent?

5. **PROBLEM SOLVING**   You own a successful hair salon and want to expand the business. Outline a growth strategy for your business.

Teamwork

Form teams. List examples of business growth that you have seen. Classify the examples as market penetration, geographic expansion, or market development.

Goals

- Define ethics.
- Recognize the need for ethical practices in business.
- Discuss an entrepreneur's social responsibilities.
- List ways to meet a business's environmental responsibilities.

Vocabulary

- ethics
- code of ethics
- business ethics

Make a difference.

Perhaps you own a "Life is Good" shirt or some other item with Jake's smiley-face stick figure on it. Bert and John Jacobs, founders of the casual clothing company Life is Good, have found the slogan to be true and want to share that feeling with others. As they started the business and it began to succeed, they had to make decisions about how to grow their company while staying true to their belief in the simple pleasures of life.

When it came time to decide about an advertising campaign for the company, Bert and John decided to forego the traditional advertising route and instead invest the money to help those in need. Today the company works with a number of charitable organizations and holds a series of festivals each year in the New England area. Although it started out as a different way to spend marketing dollars, charitable work now has become a major focus for the company.

Businesses have a social responsibility.

Work as a Team What do you think about Bert and John's decision to spend their advertising dollars doing good for the community? Do you think this decision has helped their company grow more than it would have with a conventional advertising campaign?

What Is Ethics?

Ethics is the study of moral choices and values. It involves choosing between right and wrong. Behaving ethically means behaving in an honest and fair manner. As the owner of a business, you will have to make ethical decisions about the way you want to run your business. Thinking about ethical issues in advance will help you handle conflicts when they arise.

Culture and Ethics

Different cultures define ethical behavior differently. In some countries, it is considered unethical to take bribes. In other countries, paying bribes may be an accepted business practice. In some countries, employers may treat employees badly. In other countries, employees have established rights that employers are expected to respect.

Codes of Ethics

Even within the same culture, individuals develop different standards, or codes, of ethics. A **code of ethics** is a set of standards or rules that outlines the ethical behavior demanded by an individual, a business, or a culture. Some individuals have a very high code of ethics and do what is right in every situation. Other individuals do not develop a code of ethics at all. They act without thinking whether their actions are right or wrong.

Jan Sommers has a high personal code of ethics. Last week, she received a duplicate refund check from one of her suppliers. Jan knew that the check had been sent to her by mistake. She immediately called the supplier to report the error.

 CHECKPOINT

What does it mean to have a high code of ethics?

Ethics and Business

Ethical questions arise in every type of business. Large corporations, small companies, and home-based businesses all deal with ethical dilemmas at one time or another. **Business ethics** is the application of the principles of right and wrong to issues that come up in the workplace.

Digital Vision/Getty Images

Why is it important for a business owner to be aware of culture and ethics when conducting business internationally?

Would you be more likely to buy products that are less harmful to the environment? Why or why not?

Set High Standards

Business and ethics used to be considered unrelated to each other. Over the past hundred years, this view has changed dramatically. Businesses today recognize that they must behave in an ethical manner.

MYTHS ABOUT BUSINESS AND ETHICS

Some people believe that entrepreneurs need not concern themselves with ethical issues. They believe that their only goal should be increasing profits. They may treat someone or another business unfairly and use the excuse that "it is just business." They might think that acting ethically can hurt their profits. But in fact, using ethics in business can help you avoid disasters. It can also make customers and suppliers more willing to do business with you.

CONSUMER AWARENESS   Consumers and business owners are both sensitive to business ethics. Because consumers are so aware of ethical issues, businesses find ways to show customers that they practice ethics in their daily operations. Manufacturers of some shampoos and cosmetics print on their packaging that they do not test their products on animals. Consumers who have strong opinions about animal rights may be more willing to purchase such products.

Establish an Ethical Workplace

As the owner of your business, you are responsible for inspiring your employees to behave ethically. You will want to establish an ethical workplace for several reasons.

1. You want to do the right thing.
2. You want to serve as a role model to others.
3. You want to be proud of the way you conduct yourself, and you want others to be proud of you.
4. Ethical behavior is good for business because it gains the trust of customers.
5. Employees are more likely to act ethically if they see the business owner acting in an ethical manner.
6. Acting ethically reduces the possibility of being sued.

ENSURE CONFIDENTIALITY   Confidentiality is defined by the International Organization for Standardization (ISO) as "ensuring that information is accessible only to those authorized to have access" and is an important part of information security. As an entrepreneur, you will be responsible for protecting confidential information obtained from employees, clients, and customers and ensuring that it does not fall into the wrong hands. Laws govern the type of information that you can collect from customers and keep, as well as the type of information you can request from your employees.

How does a business benefit from doing business ethically?

CREATE A WRITTEN CODE OF ETHICS   One way that you can communicate your ethical beliefs to the people who work for you is by creating a written code of ethics. Such guidelines will help you and your employees make ethical decisions.

You should create a code of ethics as soon as you begin your business, even if you are your business's only employee. You should also establish company policies and procedures that specify how you and your employees should behave in certain situations.

To create an ethical code for your business, think about ethical dilemmas that may arise and come up with solutions for dealing with them. Talk to other business owners to see what kinds of ethical problems they have encountered.

Jackie Rand owns a large discount store. Every month, salespeople from various manufacturing companies come to his company to sell their services or products. They meet with the head of the purchasing department, Ellen Chao. Last month, a manufacturing representative offered Ellen a free vacation. Not sure whether she should accept the gift, Ellen checked the code of ethics outlined in the company handbook. It clearly stated that gifts worth more than $100 should never be accepted from manufacturing representatives. Accepting large gifts from a vendor may make an employee feel obligated to purchase from that vendor when it may not be the best choice to meet the business's needs. The guidelines helped Ellen solve an ethical dilemma.

 CHECKPOINT

Why is it important for entrepreneurs to establish and write a code of ethics?

Social Responsibilities

As an individual, you have personal responsibilities to yourself, to your family, and to your friends. Entrepreneurs also have personal responsibilities to the people they work and deal with, to the government, to the communities in which they are located, and even to the environment. What are these responsibilities, and how can you meet them?

Responsibilities to Government

Federal, state, and local legislatures all create administrative agencies to carry out laws. The federal Social Security Administration, your state's department of motor vehicles, and your county's zoning commission are all administrative agencies. These administrative agencies are sometimes authorized to create administrative laws, also called rules and regulations. As an entrepreneur, you will need to comply with all federal, state, local, and administrative laws that affect your business.

Responsibilities to Customers

Your customers are your most important asset. You will need to treat them properly, or they will no longer use your services or buy your products. When dealing with customers, you should do the following:

1. **Treat all customers with respect.** No one likes to be treated badly.
2. **Be honest.** Never take unfair advantage of customers who do not know everything about the product or service they want to buy. Help your customers make good purchasing decisions.
3. **Avoid exaggerating the merits of your products or services.** Customers who are not happy with what they purchase will not do business with you again.
4. **Inform customers of possible dangers of the products you sell.** Remember that this is also a legal requirement.
5. **Handle all disputes fairly.** Try to see the customer's side of an issue when there is a disagreement.

Target Corporation is an example of a company that places a high value on meeting its social responsibilities. Access www.cengage.com/school/entrepreneurship/ideas and click on the link for Chapter 13. Browse through Target's website and answer the following: What does Target do to give back to the community? Identify two environmentally friendly measures Target has taken.

www.cengage.com/school/entrepreneurship/ideas

Responsibilities to Suppliers

You depend on your suppliers for the goods you need to manufacture or sell your products. To maintain good relationships with them, you will need to do the following:

1. **Treat all suppliers with respect.** If you respect them, they will respect you.
2. **Avoid spreading rumors or incorrect information about suppliers.** Do not discuss nonfactual information with others. Rumors can damage a business's reputation.
3. **Give suppliers time to fill your order.** Try not to wait until the last minute to ask for merchandise.

Why does a business have a responsibility to its suppliers?

4. **Handle all disputes fairly.** Try to see both sides of the issue and work out a solution that is fair to both of you.
5. **If you change suppliers, let your current supplier know the reason.** This is a courtesy to the supplier and a good business practice. The supplier will appreciate the feedback to use in developing future competitive strategies.

Responsibilities to Creditors and Investors

Creditors and investors have shown faith in your ability to succeed. To repay them for their confidence in you, you should run your business as effectively as possible. You should also let creditors and investors know when things are not going well. Never conceal risks you are facing.

Responsibilities to Your Community

Business owners have a special responsibility to contribute to their communities. They can do so in various ways, including donating money, products, and services. They can also get involved in community issues or activities.

CONTRIBUTE MONEY Business owners should donate money to charities, cultural institutions, and causes in which they believe. It is their responsibility to give something back to the community. Not all business owners can make large contributions, but any donation is welcomed.

DONATE PRODUCTS OR SERVICES Some businesses donate the products or services their business sells. Used clothing stores donate unsold clothes to charities. Computer companies sometimes send technicians to community agencies to help the staffs learn about computers. Restaurants may donate leftover food to the local soup kitchen.

GET INVOLVED You can contribute to your community in other ways as well. Some entrepreneurs get involved in issues affecting their local governments, such as changes in zoning laws and the establishment of local parks. Others get involved by sponsoring local events or organizations, such as a school sports team.

CHECKPOINT

What are some responsibilities entrepreneurs have to suppliers, customers, and the community?

Respect the Environment

Damage to the environment comes from many different sources. The burning of coal and oil for energy pollutes the air. Release of toxic chemicals pollutes the ground, air, and water. Disposal of billions of tons of garbage every year also creates environmental problems.

In 1970, the federal government created the Environmental Protection Agency (EPA) to enforce the laws governing the environment. Environmental law is designed to regulate the interaction of humans and the natural environment. Its purpose is to reduce the impacts of human activity, both on the natural environment and on human beings. Environmental law covers two major areas: (1) pollution control and correction of problem and (2) resource conservation and management. If your business handles hazardous materials, you will need to become familiar with these laws.

Businesses have a major impact on the environment. As an entrepreneur, you will have an obligation to do as little harm as possible to your surroundings. To meet your environmental responsibilities, you should do the following:

1. **Protect the environment from pollutants.** Don't knowingly dump hazardous material on the ground or in lakes and rivers.
2. **Conserve nonrenewable resources, such as coal and oil, by using them efficiently.** Nonrenewable resources are not easily replaced once they are gone. It takes hundreds of years to regenerate a nonrenewable resource. Use alternative resources when available.
3. **Reduce waste and dispose of waste responsibly.** Recycle materials such as paper, plastic, aluminum, glass, and steel. Package products using recyclable or biodegradable materials.
4. **Use environmentally safe and sustainable energy sources to meet your business needs.** Electricity is a good example. It can be replaced quickly and is not a major source of pollution.
5. **Sell products that cause as little damage to the environment as possible.** For example, don't sell a car-wash solution that harms plant life.

CHECKPOINT

As a business owner, what are some things you can do to protect the environment?

13.2 ASSESSMENT

THINK ABOUT IT

1. All employees should practice ethical behavior. Think of some ethical dilemmas that a convenience store clerk might encounter. Then describe how the clerk could handle these situations.

2. Is it important for entrepreneurs to always act in an ethical manner? Why or why not?

3. Explain the concept of personal responsibility.

4. At what point do you think a business owner should tell creditors and investors of a new risk the business is facing? Why?

MAKE ACADEMIC CONNECTIONS

5. **COMMUNICATION**   Access www.cengage.com/school/entrepreneurship/ideas. Click on *Activities* and open the file *Business Ethics*. Print the case studies and work with a partner to decide the best way to handle each situation.

6. **RESEARCH**   Confidentiality of information is important to your employees and customers. Research laws governing the type of information that you can keep on file about your customers and the type of information that you can request from employees and job applicants. Prepare a PowerPoint presentation based on your findings.

7. **MATH**   Jade Yorida will donate 12 percent of her company's net income to the community if she makes her profit projections of a 5 percent increase over the previous year's net income of $235,000. Assuming Jade meets her projections, how much will she donate?

8. **RESEARCH**   There have been many cases in recent years of businesses and individuals who have not practiced ethical behavior. Research a business or individual who has been caught practicing unethical behavior and prepare a report on your findings.

9. **BUSINESS LAW**   Conduct online research to learn about recent EPA legislation. Prepare a one-page report describing how this legislation has or will affect businesses. Explain what businesses will need to do to comply with the new law.

Teamwork

Working with teammates, brainstorm five ethical dilemmas that entrepreneurs might face. Then determine what decisions you would make if you were faced with these problems. Share your thoughts with the class.

GLOBAL TRENDS AND OPPORTUNITIES

Goals

- Discuss the reasons and methods for participating in the global economy.
- Determine whether international business is right for you.
- Identify trade regulations that affect international business.

Vocabulary

- exports
- imports
- trade barriers
- quota
- tariff
- qualitative restriction

focus on small business

Explore international markets.

Monika had worked and grown her candy business for three years. She sold chocolate and mint candies that were very popular in her store and with her Internet customers. She recently visited friends in Vienna, Austria, and took them some of her candy as a gift. They loved her candy, as did their friends. Monika began to wonder if there would be a market for her candy in other countries. She went to her friend Lazlo for advice because he had experience selling antiques in the United States and other countries.

Selling globally can be a way to grow your business.

©Madien/Shutterstock.com

Work as a Team What advice do you think Lazlo might give Monika? What things should Monika research before deciding to sell her candy outside of the United States?

Exports and Imports

The global marketplace has dramatically changed the way businesses operate. It has made business more competitive, and it has opened new opportunities for companies, including small entrepreneurial businesses. As the global marketplace continues to expand, entrepreneurs can take advantage of even more opportunities.

International trade is one way you can become part of the global marketplace. This means you would export or import the products or services you sell or use in your business.

Exporting

Products and services that are produced in one country and sent to another country to be sold are **exports**. The United States exports agricultural products, automobiles, machinery, computers, and more. These products are shipped to countries all over the world.

DIRECT EXPORTING You can find buyers or distributors in foreign markets and ship your products to them. This is called *direct exporting*. For direct exporting, you may need to hire salespeople who live in or travel to the foreign countries.

Tiffany Wilson owns a mid-sized printing company. Last year, Tiffany decided to expand her business internationally. She hired a Dutch sales representative, Mieta Van Praag, to market her business in Europe. Mieta calls on customers in the Netherlands and France.

Why might direct exporting be more difficult than indirect exporting?

INDIRECT EXPORTING It can be difficult to make contacts with buyers in other countries. Some businesses use *commissioned agents* who act as brokers to find foreign buyers for products and services. Exporting through commissioned agents is *indirect exporting*.

SELLING WORLDWIDE THROUGH THE WEB Another way to get involved in exporting is through the Internet. Businesses translate and modify their websites to appeal to foreign customers. They fill individual orders and ship them directly to the foreign customer's address.

Shahid Mahmoud's business manufactures puzzles. He recently began promoting his products abroad over the Internet because research showed that Japanese buyers like puzzles. To target that market, he created an e-commerce website written in Japanese.

Importing

Products and services that are brought from another country to be sold are **imports**. The United States imports many products, such as automobiles from Europe, Japan, and Korea and oil from the Middle East.

Entrepreneurs may decide to import products to sell or to use in the production of their product. Price and quality are usually factors in their decision to import. Consumers like low prices and demand high quality.

James Sutton owns a business that makes African-style clothing. He imports all of his fabrics from West Africa because of their unique colors, designs, and textures. James's customers appreciate his attention to detail in creating authentic African clothing.

CHECKPOINT

Why do entrepreneurs participate in exporting and importing?

Is International Business Right for You?

Not every business can succeed internationally. You need to consider the pros and cons of competing globally. Then you must determine whether there is a market for your business in other countries and write an international business plan.

Reasons for Competing Globally

As discussed in Chapter 12, there are many risks associated with competing in the global marketplace. There are also many benefits that international business can provide, including increased profits. There are at least three good reasons to expand into other countries:

1. **Increased sales** You will attract new buyers and broaden your customer base. You may also import unique products that local customers can buy.
2. **Reduced costs** Manufacturers in other countries can produce goods less expensively because of low labor costs or availability of raw materials. This can mean a savings for you in the form of a lower price.
3. **Decreased dependence on current markets and suppliers** If economic conditions in the United States suddenly worsen, foreign markets and suppliers might help keep your profits high. Selling products and services abroad can also help you stabilize seasonal market fluctuations.

Analyze the Market

Analyzing whether there is an international market for your product will be very similar to how you analyzed your current target market and target customers. In addition to the kind of analysis you learned about in Chapter 4, you will need to consider other factors, including political, economic, social, and cultural issues. Additional taxes and regulations are also things to research and consider.

Various resources are available that can help you learn about doing business abroad.

- Trade fairs and seminars sponsored by the U.S. Department of Commerce
- Dun & Bradstreet's *Exporter's Encyclopedia*
- Trade statistics from the Bureau of the Census and the Small Business Administration
- Federal or state government market studies on your industry's potential abroad

Mark Milowski owns a business that processes payroll records. He recently met with several Hong Kong business owners who wanted Mark's company to handle their payrolls. Mark liked the idea of expanding globally, but he had many questions. He contacted the Department of Commerce to get information on doing

BE YOUR OWN BOSS

You manufacture toys for small children. You have found a manufacturer overseas who will make your toys for less than half of what you pay to have them manufactured in the United States. You are considering using the overseas manufacturer, but you want to be sure it uses quality materials, provides safe working conditions, and does not use child labor. Use the six-step problem-solving model to determine if you will use the overseas manufacturer.

Why should business owners analyze the foreign markets in which they want to do business?

business in Hong Kong. In addition, he referenced the *Exporter's Encyclopedia* to learn about the regulations he would face.

Write an International Business Plan

An international business plan is an extension of your business plan. It sets forth your goals for international expansion and defines the strategies for achieving those goals. Your plan should indicate the following:

- Why you want to expand your business into the global marketplace
- Which foreign markets you plan to enter and why
- What revenues your venture is expected to earn
- How you plan to finance your global expansion
- What costs (travel, shipping, marketing) you expect to have
- How you plan to market and sell your products or services abroad
- How you plan to deliver your products or services to foreign markets
- What legal requirements you will need to meet to sell your products or services abroad

CHECKPOINT

What are some sources of information that can help you learn about doing business abroad?

Government Regulation of International Trade

Some governments establish **trade barriers**, which are methods for keeping foreign businesses from competing with domestic producers. Quotas, tariffs, and qualitative restrictions are trade barriers. You will need to research the existing trade barriers that may affect your global expansion.

Quotas

A <u>quota</u> is a limit on the amount of a product that can be imported into a country over a particular period of time. Japan places quotas on the number of foreign automobiles that can be imported. These quotas protect Japanese car makers from losing business to foreign competitors.

Tariffs

A <u>tariff</u> is a tax on imports. Governments use tariffs to protect domestic manufacturers of products that compete with imports. The United States places a tariff on imported sugar. Foreign companies that sell their sugar in the United States must pay a tax. This makes their product more expensive and less competitive with sugar produced in the United States.

Qualitative Restrictions

A <u>qualitative restriction</u> is a standard of quality that an imported product must meet before it can be sold. A qualitative restriction can keep foreign businesses from competing with domestic producers. It is also used to protect consumers. For example, the United States requires that all meat sold in this country meet certain sanitary regulations and that imported toys meet U.S. safety requirements.

The North American Free Trade Agreement

Implementation of the North American Free Trade Agreement (NAFTA) began January 1, 1994. This agreement removed most barriers to trade and investment among the United States, Mexico, and Canada. This means that U.S. businesses can sell their products and services in Canada and Mexico just as they would in the United States. It also means that the United States imposes no quotas or tariffs on imports from Canada and Mexico. NAFTA makes it much easier to export and import products and services within North America.

©GQ/Shutterstock.com

What problems might occur if imported products did not have to meet qualitative restrictions?

Government Assistance to Companies Operating Abroad

Dozens of different government agencies are available to answer your questions about doing business overseas. They include the following:

- **The Office of International Trade of the Small Business Administration** The mission of this agency is to enhance the ability of small businesses to compete in the global marketplace. It works to facilitate access to capital to support international trade and to ensure that the interests of small businesses are considered and reflected in trade negotiations.
- **The International Trade Administration** This bureau of the U.S. Department of Commerce promotes trading and investing, strengthens industry competitiveness, and ensures fair trade.

famous entrepreneur

JOHNNY PAG The Johnny Pag Company is manufacturing a motorcycle line in China that is affordable for the average American. Johnny Pag has designed and built custom motorcycles for the past 30 years in Corona, California. He is well respected among his peers and has a keen eye for quality and style. He was commissioned by his son JR, the owner of Johnny Pag, to head up the design and building of the complete JohnnyPag.com line of motorcycles. He went overseas, taking his own designs, molds, and tools. He then guided Chinese welders and assemblers on how to build the Spyder bike line on their equipment and machines in Wenzhou, China. The Chinese have built top-quality motorcycles for the European market for the past 25 years. By manufacturing the bikes in China, the retail cost is one-third the cost of motorcycles manufactured in the United States due to labor rates and regulations.

In 2006, Johnny Pag entered into a joint partnership with his Chinese contacts. State-of-the-art equipment was installed in the new Chinese production facility. Quality standards were established to create a bike that gives the customer personal pride as well as safety assurance. In 2010, the Johnny Pag

Courtesy of Johnny Pag Motorcycles

How did the Johnny Pag Company grow its business?

Company expanded its line of motorcycles by introducing a new 80 horsepower V-twin chopper priced under $9,988. Still aiming for the "affordable" market, the company will welcome and consider financing first-time buyers, poor-credit-history buyers, and zero-credit-history buyers. Purchasing and financing a new motorcycle can be handled online! With the Johnny Pag name on each motorcycle, the company stands by its product and places an emphasis on customer service.

THINK CRITICALLY

Manufacturing costs are lower in Asian countries than in the United States. Some people view this as taking jobs away from Americans. Others see it as a way of making a better product that is more affordable for Americans. What do you think about outsourcing manufacturing overseas?

- **Bureau of Industry and Security** The Bureau of Industry and Security is another bureau of the U.S. Department of Commerce. Its mission is to advance U.S. national security, foreign policy, and economic objectives. It works to ensure an effective export control and treaty compliance system and promotes continued U.S. strategic technology leadership.

In addition to these agencies, the federal government offers many programs that help U.S. businesses operate in foreign markets. The programs include export counseling, export financing, and technical assistance.

 CHECKPOINT

Describe how governments can regulate international trade.

13.3 ASSESSMENT

THINK ABOUT IT

1. As an entrepreneur, what do you think are the pros of competing globally? What do you think are the cons of competing globally?

2. Do you think it is in our country's best interest to have U.S. companies engage in international trade? Why or why not?

3. What do you think would happen to the U.S. economy if there were no quotas on imported goods?

MAKE ACADEMIC CONNECTIONS

4. **MATH** A government in an Asian country applies a 20 percent tariff to all electronic goods imported to the country. If it collects $24 million in tariffs for these goods, what was their total value?

5. **HISTORY** Research the North American Free Trade Agreement (NAFTA) and write a one-page report on what you learn. State your opinion on whether or not NAFTA is beneficial to the United States.

Teamwork

You own a clothing boutique and have recently expanded into catalog sales to sell your products abroad. Select a country in which you want to sell. Working with team members, determine what method of exporting you will use. Discuss some of the government regulations that will affect your business. Think about how you might obtain further information about these regulations. Share your team's ideas with the rest of the class.

Time Management

You have learned that an entrepreneur has many responsibilities. You are probably wondering how you can fit everything into one day! Good time-management skills are essential to the success of your business.

In learning to manage your time, the first thing you should do is establish a plan. A plan forces you to think ahead, which helps you manage your time more effectively. A plan should list all of the routine tasks of your business as well as those tasks related to growing your business.

After creating a plan, you should prepare a "to do" list containing all of the tasks outlined in your plan. Prioritize the tasks from high priority to low priority. Assign due dates to each task. Review your list at the beginning of each day and again at the end of the day. Cross off tasks that have been completed, add new tasks that have come up, and reprioritize your list of tasks as necessary. Do not be afraid to ask for help as you grow your business. You may get to the point where you will not be able to do it all. There may also be tasks that you do not have the expertise to complete. To make effective use of your time, look for others who you can contract with or hire to perform these tasks. For example, you may contract with an accountant to do your financial recordkeeping and reporting.

Remember to allow for personal time. Take breaks occasionally. If you are working too much and overly stressed, you will not be an effective leader. Take time out for physical and leisure activities.

Try It Out

Before you can schedule your time, you need to understand how you use your time. Access www.cengage.com/school/entrepreneurship/ideas. Click on *Activities* and open the file *Time Log*. Print a copy and complete the activity log by keeping track of daily activities over a certain period of time.

©biker.derlondon/Shutterstock.com

SUMMARY

13.1 Growth Strategies

1. Determining when to expand your business depends on two main factors: the condition of your business and the economic conditions in the market in which your business competes.

2. Businesses that experience uncontrolled growth may find themselves overextended with inadequate resources to support the new level of business. You will want to create a plan for growth.

3. Growth strategies include market penetration, geographic expansion, and market development.

4. The stages of the product life cycle include introduction, growth, maturity, and decline. Steps in new product development include idea development, idea screening, strategy development, financial analysis, product development and testing, and product marketing.

13.2 Ethical and Social Issues

5. Ethics is the study of moral choices and values.

6. Entrepreneurs should create a code of ethics to establish appropriate behavior in the workplace.

7. An entrepreneur has social responsibilities involving the government, customers, suppliers, creditors and investors, and the community.

8. The purpose of environmental law is to reduce the impacts of human activity on the natural environment and on human beings. It covers (1) pollution control and correction and (2) resource conservation and management.

13.3 Global Trends and Opportunities

9. Entrepreneurs participate in the global marketplace through direct and indirect exporting, importing, and selling through the Web.

10. To determine if international business is right for you, consider the pros and cons of competing globally and write an international business plan.

11. Trade regulations that will affect your international business include quotas, tariffs, and qualitative restrictions established by the countries in which you will be doing business.

what do you **know now?**

Read *Ideas in Action* on page 377 again. Then answer the questions a second time. Have your responses changed? If so, how have they changed?

VOCABULARY BUILDER

Match each statement with the term that best defines it. Some terms may not be used.

1. The application of the principles of right and wrong to issues that come up in the workplace
2. A strategy for expanding the target market of a business
3. A limit on the amount of a product that can be imported into a country over a particular period of time
4. Products and services that are brought from another country to be sold
5. The study of moral choices and values
6. Increasing the market share for a product or service within a given market in a given area
7. Products and services that are produced in one country and sent to another country to be sold
8. A set of standards or rules that outlines the ethical behavior demanded by an individual, a business, or a culture
9. Methods for keeping foreign businesses from competing with domestic producers
10. The stages a product goes through from the time it is introduced to when it is no longer sold
11. A tax on imports
12. A standard of quality an imported product must meet before it can be sold

a. business ethics
b. code of ethics
c. ethics
d. exports
e. imports
f. market development
g. market penetration
h. product life cycle
i. prototype
j. qualitative restriction
k. quota
l. tariff
m. trade barriers

REVIEW YOUR KNOWLEDGE

13. **True or False**   The condition of your business and the economic conditions of the market in which you compete help determine when you should expand your business.
14. Which of the following is *not* a factor to consider when analyzing the economic climate that controls your business?
    a. condition of national economy
    b. new competition
    c. demographic changes
    d. prices you charge
15. A prototype of a product is created during which stage of new product development?
    a. idea screening
    b. strategy development
    c. product development and testing
    d. product marketing
16. **True or False**   During the introduction stage of a product's life cycle, people are familiar with the product and what it can do for them.
17. Deciding to increase your advertising and improve your customer service are examples of growing your business through
    a. market penetration
    b. geographic expansion
    c. market development
    d. none of the above
18. **True or False**   Culture has no effect on the ethics of an individual.
19. **True or False**   Ethical behavior is good for business because it gains the trust of customers.
20. **True or False**   For a business to diversify successfully, it needs to develop products that are unrelated to the products it already sells.

21. The North American Free Trade Agreement (NAFTA) removed most barriers to trade and investment among the United States and
    a. China and Japan
    b. Mexico and Cuba
    c. Mexico and Canada
    d. Canada and Korea
22. Which of the following is *not* an example of fulfilling environmental responsibilities?
    a. using solar energy to power your heating and cooling systems
    b. disposing of paper used by your business in the dumpster
    c. selling a laundry detergent with stain-removing enzymes that do not harm water ecosystems
    d. following federal guidelines for disposing of hazardous waste
23. **True or False**   Global competition has had no impact on the way businesses operate.
24. Selling in foreign markets through commissioned agents is known as __?__.
25. As an entrepreneur, you have a personal responsibility to all of the following *except*
    a. your community
    b. your customers
    c. your creditors and investors
    d. your competitors

APPLY WHAT YOU LEARNED

26. You publish a cooking magazine that is circulated in your local metro area. How can you expand your business? What growth strategy will you employ? Write a plan for growth that includes setting and achieving measurable objectives, hiring managers, financing the expansion, and obtaining resources for expansion.
27. You have opened a delicatessen in your town. What are some of the responsibilities you have to your customers? In what ways can your business benefit the community? How do you think fulfilling these responsibilities will help your business?

MAKE ACADEMIC CONNECTIONS

28. **COMMUNICATION**   Use the Internet, newspapers, and magazines to find examples of two companies that are environmentally responsible and one company that has violated environmental laws. Give a presentation to the class that details the companies' actions and their impact on society.
29. **MATH**   You have a business selling concrete to contractors. One of your suppliers in South America has quoted a price of $4.00 per 50-pound bag. Your U.S. supplier is charging $4.50 per 50-pound bag. Both suppliers have agreed to cover shipping costs, but the foreign company must pay a 12.5 percent tariff on each bag shipped and will pass that cost on to you. Which supplier will you buy from and why?
30. **RESEARCH**   Choose a business that has recently introduced a new product to the market. Research the company and find out what other products it had on the market before the introduction of the new product. Was the new product introduced to replace an existing product or to capture a new market?

What Would YOU Do?

You are an independent contractor hired by the state to inspect paving work done on a highway. The paving company had to complete the job on time or pay a fine to the state. In order to meet the deadline, the paving company did not follow all of the specifications in the contract. The president of the company has asked you to approve the job in exchange for a large sum of money. What are the ethical issues you face? What do you think would be the best way to resolve the issue? Who will be affected by your decisions?

build your
BUSINESS PLAN PROJECT

This activity will help you think about growing your business, conducting business ethically, and expanding your business globally. You will also finalize the business plan that you have been working on throughout the book.

1. What will indicate that you are ready to expand your business? Give specific examples, such as your sales growing by 20 percent or your business outgrowing its current location.

2. What effect can the present economy have on your business? Write a growth plan that includes strategies for attaining measurable objectives, hiring managers, financing expansion, and obtaining resources for expansion.

3. Write a code of ethics for your business that includes company policies and procedures for dealing with particular situations. What are some situations that are specific to your type of business that may pose an ethical dilemma?

4. Write an environmental policy for your business. Consider how EPA rulings might affect your business. What are some of the actions your business will take to protect the environment? Are these actions required by law? If not, why will you incorporate them into your policy?

5. What global opportunities exist for your business? Choose two global markets into which you could expand. Compare and contrast the two markets and decide which would be the best market for you to enter. Describe the strategy you would use to enter the market. List the specific benefits and risks of global expansion for your business.

6. Put it all together! Now that you have researched the different aspects of starting your own business, you are ready to use the information you have gathered in the *Build Your Business Plan Project* to compile your business plan. Access www.cengage.com/school/entrepreneurship/ideas. Click on *Activities* and open the file *Business Plan Template* to help you complete your final business plan.

Planning a Career in
TRANSPORTATION

Transportation, Distribution & Logistics

"My mom's husband has a job that requires travel to a lot of big cities. He often arranges to have a limousine pick him up at the airport and take him to his destination. It saves him a great deal of time to have the limo driver waiting for him when he arrives. At his level in the organization, it makes sense financially to pay a bit more for his transportation and get him to his meetings as quickly as possible."

How do people traveling to various cities get from the airport to their destination easily? How do people who have a physical disability that prohibits them from driving get to their appointments?

Chauffeurs are individuals who provide transportation to clients on a prearranged basis. Chauffeurs may be employed by an individual, family, or business. Some chauffeurs may have multiple duties for an employer. Additional duties might include personal security, household help, or administrative assistance.

EMPLOYMENT OUTLOOK
- Faster than average growth is anticipated.
- About a quarter of chauffeurs are self-employed.
- Large, thriving cities will offer the best opportunities.

JOB TITLES
- Luxury Vehicle Chauffeur
- Driver/Chauffeur
- Chauffeur/Houseman
- Chauffeur/Professional Driver
- Chauffeur/Executive Protection
- Personal Chauffeur

NEEDED EDUCATION/SKILLS
- A high school diploma is preferred.
- A good driving record is necessary.
- In addition to a regular driver's license, a chauffeur's license is required. Licensing requirements vary by state.
- Good interpersonal skills to handle a variety of customer personalities are important.
- Familiarity with the local terrain and good map-reading skills are helpful.
- The minimum age requirement is often 21.

What's it like to work in Transportation? Pedro has been leasing his limousine for two years. Paying a monthly fee to the limousine company entitles Pedro to full use of the vehicle, even when he isn't working. His monthly payment also covers routine vehicle maintenance and insurance fees. Pedro is saving money for a down payment on his own limousine.

Tonight Pedro is scheduled to drive a bride and groom from their wedding ceremony to their reception. After the reception, he will drive them to their hotel.

For the first three days of next week, Pedro is scheduled to provide transportation for a repeat client. The client, an executive who visits Pedro's city each month, often books Pedro's time for a series of days. When Pedro isn't driving the client to a destination, he often runs errands for the client. At the end of next week, Pedro is scheduled to drive a visually impaired client on a variety of errands.

What about you? Would you enjoy driving an array of clients on a variety of trips throughout your city?

Small Business Management Team Event

The Small Business Management Team Event requires participants to use strategic planning and problem-solving skills to provide advice to a startup business.

Three early-retiree teachers want to start their own business, Head of the Class, which will provide training to new teachers. They have noticed that the number of teacher education programs has declined, and many new teachers are not fully equipped to handle classroom management successfully. The business will work directly with school districts and universities that have reduced teacher-training programs. The three retired teachers have set up an appointment to meet with the Small Business Forum to seek assistance and financing in opening this business operation. The three entrepreneurs have $10,000 each in savings that they plan to use for their startup business.

Your team of two to four members will serve as consultants to the three entrepreneurs. You will provide them with information that they need for their presentation to the Small Business Forum. You must be aware of the location, competition, and budget needed to operate this business successfully. You will help the entrepreneurs determine what makes their business unique and give them ideas to convince the Small Business Forum to provide financial assistance. You also must suggest ideas for growing their business.

Prepare an oral presentation that addresses the questions that follow. You will have ten minutes to make your presentation and an additional ten minutes to answer the judge's questions.

PERFORMANCE INDICATORS

- Evaluate and delegate responsibilities needed to perform required tasks
- Demonstrate teamwork skills needed to function in a business setting
- Demonstrate self-esteem, self- and team-management, and integrity
- Demonstrate a working knowledge of business management concepts
- Demonstrate critical-thinking skills to make decisions and solve problems
- Demonstrate a working knowledge of entrepreneurial concepts

Go to the BPA website for more detailed information.

THINK CRITICALLY

1. How can the proposed business save school districts money?
2. What statistics can be used to prove the need for this business?
3. What is the potential growth for this business?
4. Why should school districts invest money in the services offered by this business?

www.bpa.org

Glossary

A

Account an accounting record that provides financial detail for a particular business item, such as for cash, sales, rent, and utilities

Accrual method an accounting method in which transactions are recorded when the order is placed, the item is delivered, or the service is provided, regardless of when the money is actually received or paid

Advertising a paid form of communication sent out by a business about a product or service; it keeps a product or service in the public's eye by creating a sense of awareness and helps convey a positive image

Advertising fees fees paid to a franchise company to support television, magazine, or other advertising of the franchise as a whole

Aptitude the ability to learn a particular kind of job

Authoritative management management style in which the manager is directive and controlling

B

Balance sheet a financial statement that lists what a business owns, what it owes, and how much it is worth at a particular point in time

Benefits rewards other than cash given to employees, including paid leave, insurance, and a retirement plan

Board of directors group of people who meet several times a year to make important decisions affecting the company

Bonus financial reward made in addition to a regular wage or salary that usually hinges on reaching an established goal

Bounced check check that is returned to the payee (person or business to whom the check is made payable) by the bank because the check writer's checking account has insufficient funds to cover the amount

Brainstorming a creative problem-solving technique that involves generating a large number of fresh ideas

Brand the name, symbol, or design used to identify a product

Business ethics application of the principles of right and wrong to issues that come up in the workplace

Business plan a written document that describes all the steps necessary for opening and operating a successful business

C

Capitalism the private ownership of resources by individuals rather than by the government

Cash budget a financial report that shows the projections of cash coming in and going out of a business

Cash flow statement an accounting report that describes the way cash flows into and out of a business over a period of time

Cash method an accounting method in which revenue is not recorded until cash (or a check) is actually received and expenses are not recorded until they are actually paid

Chain of command the working relationships within a business—who reports to whom—often shown in an organizational chart

Channels of distribution routes that products and services take from the time they are produced to the time they are consumed

Check register booklet in which an account holder records the dates and amounts of the checks as well as the names of people or businesses to whom he or she has written the checks

Code of ethics a set of standards or rules that outline the ethical behavior demanded by an individual, a business, or a culture

Collateral property that a borrower forfeits to the bank providing the loan if he or she defaults on the loan

Commission a percentage of a sale paid to a salesperson

Competition-based pricing pricing that is determined by considering what competitors charge for the same good or service

Competitive analysis identifying and examining the characteristics of a competing firm

Consumer credit offered when a retail business allows its customers to buy merchandise now and pay for it later

Contract legally binding agreement between two or more persons or parties

Controllable risk risk that can be reduced or possibly even avoided by taking action

Copyright form of intellectual property law that protects original works of authorship, including literary, dramatic, musical, and artistic works

Corporation business that has the legal rights of a person but is independent of its owners

Cost-based pricing pricing determined by using the wholesale cost of an item as the basis for the price charged

Cover letter a letter that introduces and explains an accompanying document or set of documents

Customer profile description of the characteristics of the person or company that is likely to purchase a product or service

Customer relationship management (CRM) the goal of a new marketing trend that focuses on understanding customers as individuals instead of as part of a group

D

Debt capital money loaned to a business with the understanding that the money will be repaid, usually with interest

Debt-to-equity ratio the relation between the dollars borrowed (debt) and the dollars invested in a business (equity)

Delegate to allow other people to share workloads and responsibilities

Demand the quantity of a good or service that consumers are willing to buy at a given price

Demand-based pricing pricing that is determined by how much customers are willing to pay for a product or service

Democratic management management style in which employees are involved in decision making and the manager provides less direction

Demographics data that describe a group of people in terms of their age, marital status, family size, ethnicity, gender, profession, education, and income

Direct channel a distribution channel that moves the product directly from the manufacturer to the consumer

Direct competition a business that makes most of its money selling the same or similar products or services to the same market as other businesses

Discount pricing offers customers a reduced price, encouraging them to buy

Distribution an important component of supply chain management that involves the locations and methods used to make products and services available to customers

Dividends distributions of corporate profits to the shareholders

E

E-commerce electronic commerce consisting of buying and selling products or services over the Internet

Economic decision making the process of choosing which needs and wants, among several, will be satisfied using the resources on hand

Economic resources means through which goods and services are produced

Economies of scale the cost advantages obtained due to expansion

Emotional buying decisions based on the desire to have a specific product or service; feelings, beliefs, and attitudes influence a consumer's buying decisions

Employees people who work for someone else

Enterprise zones areas that suffer from lack of employment opportunities

Entrepreneurs people who own, operate, and take the risk of a business venture

Entrepreneurship process of running a business of one's own

Equilibrium price and quantity point at which the supply and demand curves meet

Equity capital money invested in a business in return for a share in the profits of the business

Ethics the study of moral choices and values; involves choosing between right and wrong

Exchange rate the amount of one country's currency that can be traded for one unit of currency in another country

Executive summary a short restatement of the report portion of a business plan

Exports products and services that are produced in one country and sent to another country to be sold

F

Features product characteristics that will satisfy customer needs

Federal Employees' Compensation Act (FECA) law that provides benefits to employees who have suffered work-related injuries or occupational diseases

Fixed costs costs that must be paid regardless of how much of a good or service is produced

Focus group in-depth interview with a group of target customers who provide valuable ideas on products or services

Franchise legal agreement that gives an individual the right to market a company's products or services in a particular area

Franchise Disclosure Document (FDD) a regulatory document describing a franchise opportunity that prospective franchisees must receive before they sign a contract

Freelancers people who provide specialty services to businesses on an hourly basis or by the job

G

Geographic data data that help a business determine where its potential customers live and how far they will travel to visit the business

Gross lease a contract stating that the tenant pays rent each month for the space occupied and the landlord covers all property expenses for that space

Gross sales the dollar amount of all sales

H

Harvest strategy an exit strategy, or the way an entrepreneur intends to extract, or harvest, his or her money from a business after it is operating successfully

I

Ideas thoughts or concepts that come from creative thinking

Imports products and services that are brought from one country into another country to be sold

Income statement a financial statement that shows the business's revenues and expenses incurred over a period of time and the resulting profit or loss

Indirect channel a distribution channel that uses intermediaries, such as agents and wholesalers, to move products between the manufacturer and the consumer

Indirect competition a business that makes only a small amount of money selling the same or similar products and services to the same market as other businesses

Industrial park section of land that is zoned for industrial businesses only; usually located where space is less expensive, away from housing developments and downtown areas

Initial franchise fee amount the local franchise owner pays in return for the right to run the franchise

Insurable risk a pure risk that is faced by a large number of people and for which the amount of the loss can be predicted

Intellectual property the original, creative work of an artist or inventor, including such things as songs, novels, artistic designs, and inventions

Interns students who will work for little or no pay in order to gain experience in a particular field

Inventory the products and the materials needed to make the products that a business sells to its customers

J

Job analysis process of determining the tasks and sequence of tasks necessary to perform a job

Job description written statement listing the tasks and responsibilities of a position; also covers to whom the position reports, educational and professional experience required, and salary range

Journals accounting records of the transactions you make; there are five different journals that businesses use to record their transactions: sales, cash payments, cash receipts, purchases, and general journals

L

Landlord person who owns and rents out buildings or space

M

Management process of achieving goals by establishing operating procedures that make effective use of people and other resources

Manager person responsible for planning, organizing, staffing, implementing, and controlling the operations of a business

Marginal benefit measures the advantages of producing one additional unit of a good or service

Marginal cost measures the disadvantages of producing one additional unit of a good or service

Market development strategy for expanding the target market of a business

Market penetration strategy for increasing the market share for a product or service within a given market in a given area

Market research system for collecting, recording, and analyzing information about customers, competitors, products, and services

Market segments groups of customers within a large market who share common characteristics

Market share business's percentage of the total sales generated by all companies in the same market

Marketing all of the processes—planning, pricing, promoting, distributing, and selling—used to determine and satisfy the needs of customers and the company

Marketing concept uses the needs of customers as the primary focus during the planning, production, distribution, and promotion of a product or service

Marketing mix blending of the product, price, distribution, and promotion used to reach a target market

Marketing plan defines the market, identifies customers and competitors, outlines a strategy for attracting and keeping customers, and identifies and anticipates change

Marketing strategy plan that identifies how marketing goals will be achieved

N

Needs those things that a person must have in order to survive

Net lease a contract stating that the landlord pays building insurance and the tenant pays rent, taxes, and any other expenses

Net sales the dollar amount of all sales with any returns subtracted

Net worth difference between what is owned, called *assets*, and what is owed, called *liabilities*

O

Operations manual contains all of the rules, policies, and procedures that a business should follow in order to function effectively

Opportunities possibilities that arise from existing conditions

Opportunity cost value of the next-best alternative

Organizational structure plan that shows how the various jobs in a company relate to one another; often represented in a chart indicating the working relationships within the business

P

Partnership business owned by two or more people

Patent the grant of a property right to an inventor to exclude others from making, using, or selling his or her invention

Payroll list of people who receive salary or wage payments from a business

Percentage lease a contract stating that the tenant pays a base rent each month and the landlord receives a percentage of the tenant's revenue each month

Performance evaluation management control tool that helps determine whether the objectives for a particular job are being met

Periodic inventory method involves taking a physical count of a business's merchandise at regular intervals, such as weekly or monthly

Perpetual inventory method keeps track of inventory levels on a daily basis

Personal selling direct communication between a prospective buyer and a sales representative in which the sales representative attempts to influence the prospective buyer in a purchase situation

Physical distribution includes transportation, storage, handling, and packaging of products within a channel of distribution

Point-of-sale (POS) software system cash registers used with a software system that updates inventory records as each sale happens; bar-code scanners and credit card authorization systems can be integrated into the POS system

Positioning creating an image for a product in the customer's mind

Premium payment that is made to an insurance company to cover the cost of insurance; price paid to cover a specified risk for a specific period of time

Press release written statement meant to inform the media of an event or product

Primary data information collected for the very first time to fit a specific purpose

Pro forma financial statement a financial statement based on projected revenues and expenses

Problem-solving model A formal process used to help solve problems in a logical manner

Product life cycle stages a product goes through from the time it is introduced to when it is no longer sold; a product goes through four stages in its life cycle: introduction, growth, maturity, and decline

Product mix different products and services a business sells

Profit difference between the revenues earned by a business and the costs of operating the business

Profit sharing compensation arrangement in which employees are paid a portion of the company's profits

Prototype full-scale model of a new product

Psychographics data that describe a group of people in terms of their tastes, opinions, personality traits, and lifestyle habits

Psychological pricing pricing strategy based on the belief that certain prices have an impact on how customers perceive a product

Public relations act of establishing a favorable relationship with customers and the general public

Publicity nonpaid form of communication that calls attention to a business through media coverage

Pure risk risk that presents the chance of loss but no opportunity for gain

Q

Qualitative restriction standard of quality an imported product must meet before it can be sold

Quota limit on the amount of a product that can be imported into a country over a particular period of time

Quote an estimate for how much a business will pay for merchandise or service

R

Rational buying decisions based on the logical reasoning of customers

Rebate refund offered to people who purchase a product

Recruit to look for people to hire and attract them to the business

Reorder point predetermined level of inventory that signals when new stock should be ordered

Return on investment (ROI) amount earned as a result of the investment, usually expressed as a percentage

Risk possibility of some kind of loss; categorized as human risk, natural risk, and economic risk

Risk assessment involves looking at all aspects of a business and determining the risks it faces

Risk management involves taking action to prevent or reduce the possibility of loss to a business

Royalty fees weekly or monthly payments made by the local owner to the franchise company; these payments usually are a percentage of a franchise's income

S

Salary amount paid for a job position stated on an annual basis

Sales promotion incentive offered to customers in order to increase sales; examples include contests, free samples, rebates, coupons, special events, gift certificates, and frequent-buyer reward programs

Scarcity occurs when people's needs and wants are unlimited and the resources to produce the goods and services to meet those needs and wants are limited

Secondary data data found in already-published sources

Self-assessment evaluation of your strengths and weaknesses

Service Corps of Retired Executives (SCORE) group made up of retired executives who volunteer their time to provide entrepreneurs with real-world advice and know-how

Share of stock unit of ownership in a corporation

Shoplifting act of knowingly taking items from a business without paying

Small Business Administration (SBA) independent agency of the federal government that was created to help Americans start, build, and grow businesses

Small Business Development Centers (SBDC) centers that provide management assistance to current and prospective small business owners

Sole proprietorship business that is owned exclusively by one person; enables one person to be in control of all aspects of the business

Speculative risk risk that offers the chance to gain as well as lose from an event or activity

Staffing involves determining the number of employees a company needs and defining a process for hiring them

Startup costs costs associated with beginning a business, including the costs of renting a facility, equipping the outlet, and purchasing inventory

Statement of purpose brief explanation of why the writer of a business plan is asking for a loan and an explanation of what he or she plans to do with the money

Stock card paper inventory record for a single item

Stock turnover rate rate at which the inventory of a product is sold and replaced with new inventory

Supply the quantity of a good or service a producer is willing to produce at different prices

Supply chain management the coordination of manufacturers, suppliers, and retailers working together to meet a customer need for a product or service

Survey list of questions to ask customers to find out demographic and psychographic information; can be conducted by mail, over the phone, on the Internet, or in person

T

Target market the individuals or companies that are interested in a particular product or service and are willing and able to pay for it

Tariff tax on imports that governments use to protect domestic manufacturers of products that compete with imports

Telemarketing using the phone to market a product or service

Tenant person who pays rent to occupy space owned by someone else

Trade area area from which a business expects to attract customers

Trade associations organizations made up of professionals in a specific industry

Trade barriers methods for keeping foreign businesses from competing with domestic producers

Trade credit offered when one business allows another business to buy now and pay later

Trade shows special meetings where companies of the same or related industry display their products

Trademark name, symbol, or special mark used to identify a business or brand of product

Transaction any business activity that changes assets, liabilities, or net worth

U

Uncontrollable risk risk on which actions have no effect, such as the weather

Use-based data data that help a business determine how often potential customers use a particular service

V

Variable costs costs that go up and down depending on the quantity of the good or service produced

Vendors companies that sell products and services to businesses

Venture capitalists individuals or companies that make a profit investing in startup companies

Visual marketing the use of visual media to promote, sell, and distribute a product or service to a targeted audience

Visual merchandising the process of combining products, environments, and spaces into an appealing display to encourage the sale of products or services

W

Wages payments for labor or services that are made on an hourly, daily, or per-unit basis

Wants those things that a person thinks he or she must have in order to be satisfied

Index

R

Radio advertising, 163
  about
  disadvantages of, 164
Rational buying decisions, 173
Ray, Rachael, 231
Rebate, 174
Reconcile, bank account, 268, 271
Recordkeeping for businesses, 263–270
  accrual method, 264
  business records, 267–270. *See also* Business
    records
  cash method, 263–264
  choosing, 264
  recording transactions, 264–266
Recovery plan, 348
Recruiting, 315–316
  classified advertisements, 316
  college placement centers, 316
  employment agencies, 315–316
  in-store advertising, 316
  online career/employment sites, 315
  referrals, 316
Referrals, 316
Regional shopping centers, 222
Regulations
  competition and, 203–205
  employee protection, 363. *See also* Regulations to
    protect employees
  international trade and, 397–398
Regulations to protect employees, 326–328, 363
  Age Discrimination in Employment
    Act of 1967, 327
  Americans with Disabilities Act (ADA) of 1990,
    327–328
  Civil Rights Act of 1964, 327
  Fair Labor Standards Act (FLSA) of 1938, 326
  Family and Medical Leave Act of 1993, 328
  Immigration Reform and Control Act of 1986, 327
  National Labor Relations Act (NLRA) of 1935,
    326
  Occupational Safety and Health Act (OSH) of
    1970, 327
Renter's insurance, 356
Rent per customer, 229
Reorder point, 237
Repetitive stress injuries, 362–363
Research
  for business plan, 81–82
  your ideas, 23

Research connections, 43, 90, 121, 136,
  180, 195, 210, 214, 233, 238, 242,
  318, 328, 368, 393, 404
Research resources
  financial institutions, 83
  online, 83–84
  print, 83
  professional consultants, 83
  Service Corps of Retired Executives
    (SCORE), 82
  Small Business Administration (SBA), 82
  Small Business Development Centers
    (SBDC), 82
  trade associations, 83
Resources
  cost of doing business and, 53
  economic, 40–41
  limited, 41
  research, 82–83
Responsibility, delegate, 332–333
Results, evaluate, in market research, 107
Resume, prepare a, 86–87
Retail business, layout of, 231–232
Retail business, locating a
  community shopping centers, 221–222
  distribution and, 156
  locating a, 220–223
  regional shopping centers, 222
  stand-alone stores, 222–223
  super-regional shopping centers, 222
  warehouses, 223
Retailers, large, as competition, 112
Retailing businesses, as entrepreneurial, 6
Retirement plan, 325
Return on assets (ROA), 300–301
Return on equity (ROE), 301–302
Return on investment (ROI), 74, 138
Revenue, 260
Revere, Paul, 46
Review Your Knowledge, 31–32, 59–60, 89–90,
  119–120, 147–148, 179–180, 213–214, 241–
  242, 273–274, 305–306, 339–340, 371–372,
  403–404
Risk
  identification of, 74
  pure risk, 352–353
  speculative, 353
Risk assessment, 347
Risk management
  business risks, 346–351. *See also* Business risks
  buy insurance, 356–358